Freedom in the World

Freedom in the World

Political Rights and Civil Liberties
1988–1989

Raymond D. Gastil

With contributions by

Stephen Earl Bennett
Richard Jensen
Paul Kleppner

FREEDOM HOUSE

The Library of Congress has cataloged this serial title as follows:

Freedom in the world / Raymond D. Gastil.—1978–   —
New York : Freedom House, 1978–
v. : map ; 25 cm.–(Freedom House Book)
Annual.
Includes bibliographical references and index.
ISSN 0732–6610=Freedom in the world.
1. Civil rights—Periodicals. I. Gastil, Raymond D. II. Series.
JC571.F66   323.4'05–dc 19   82–642048
AACR 2   MARC–S
Library of Congress   [8410]
ISBN 0–932088–32–5 (pbk.: alk. paper)
ISBN 0–932088–33–3 (alk. paper)

Distributed by arrangement with

University Press of America, Inc.
4720 Boston Way
Lanham, MD 20706

3 Henrietta Street
London WC2E 8LU England

CONTENTS

Contents

TABLES

PREFACE

The Comparative Survey of Freedom was created in 1972 to provide an additional perspective on world events. It was felt that interpretations of international events in terms of the critical geopolitical struggle between "East" and "West" too often obscured those finer distinctions between societies that lay along the continuum between absolute repression and full freedom, regardless of the power blocs to which these societies might belong. Unavoidably, the Survey has recently come to be seen as a monitor of the movement toward more democratic systems evident in so much of the world.

This yearbook marks the seventeenth year of the Comparative Survey and the eleventh edition in this series of annual publications. Previous yearbooks, in addition to focusing on the Comparative Survey, have emphasized different aspects of freedom and human rights. The first yearbook, the 1978 edition, examined basic theoretical issues of freedom and democracy and assessed the record of the Year of Human Rights. The second yearbook reported extensively on a conference devoted to the possibilities of expanding freedom in the Soviet Union. The 1980 yearbook considered international issues in press freedom, aspects of trade union freedom, the struggle for democracy in Iran, elections in Zimbabwe, and the relationship between human rights policy and morality. The 1981 yearbook contained essays and discussions from a Freedom House conference on the prospects for freedom in Muslim Central Asia.

The 1982 yearbook emphasized a variety of approaches to economic freedom and its relation to political and civil freedom. The 1983-84 yearbook addressed the problems of corporatism, and the health of democracy in the third world. It also incorporated the papers and discussions of a conference held at Freedom House on supporting democracy in mainland China and Taiwan. We returned in the 1984-85 yearbook to the themes of the definition of freedom and the conditions for the development of freedom that were first addressed in the 1978 yearbook. It also looked at the particular problem of developing democracy in Central America. The 1985-86 yearbook considered America's role in the worldwide struggle for democracy, and reported the results of a conference on supporting liberalization in Eastern Europe. The 1986-87 yearbook offered a number of essays on the nature and value of liberal democracy, as well as comparative discussions of democracy in several countries. These discussions should be seen as a supplement to the theoretical essays in the 1978 yearbook. Last year we brought to our readers' attention something of the variety and scope of work of researchers outside Freedom House that is closely related to the Survey or its themes. These included other surveys of political and civil rights, attempts to find the relationship between development and Survey ratings, and a discussion of factors in democratic development.

A major change this year in the Comparative Survey is the dropping of the "free, partly free, not free" status of freedom ratings, replacing these with a simple summation of the political and civil rights ratings, labeled the "freedom rating". The director of the survey felt that too much emphasis had come to be placed on whether a country fell on one or the other side of the rather artificial lines between these three over-general statuses. The new system should allow readers or analysts to more flexibly group countries for different purposes.

This year the ratings and tables produced by the Survey are augmented by an additional table of social comparisons, one emphasizing the relative position of women. The discussion of criteria and definitions at the beginning of the 1988-89 yearbook now includes the checklists for political rights and civil liberties separately. The reader should also note some revamping of Table 6, the historical record of the Survey.

This year, for the first time, the Survey focuses on an aspect of political rights in the United States. The 1988-89 yearbook reports in full a small discussion held at Freedom House during the year on the continuing and deepening problem of political participation in the United States. Held just before the November 1988 elections, this material should provide useful background, and we hope a basis for action, for all those concerned about the low participation rates of the American voter that were once again emphasized in that election.

We acknowledge, more than ever, the contribution made by the advisory panel for the Comparative Survey. The panel consists of: Robert J. Alexander, Richard W. Cottam, Herbert J. Ellison, Seymour Martin Lipset, Lucian W. Pye, Robert Scalapino, and Paul Seabury. We also express our appreciation to those foundations whose grants have made the Survey and the publication of this year-book possible. Substantial support has again been given by the Pew Charitable Trust; their continuing confidence has been a key factor in achieving the Survey's goal of raising the level of understanding of freedom in the world. All Freedom House activities are also assisted by the generous support of individual members of the organization as well as trade unions, corporations, and public foundations that contribute to our general budget. No financial support from any government—now or in the past—has been either solicited or accepted.

We gratefully acknowledge the research and editorial assistance of Jeannette C. Gastil in producing this yearbook.

PART I

The Survey in 1988

FREEDOM IN THE COMPARATIVE SURVEY:

DEFINITIONS AND CRITERIA

Understanding freedom is not a simple task. To attempt to understand its many meanings would carry us far beyond the discussion of
political systems with which the Comparative Survey of Freedom
has been principally concerned. Yet in common parlance the meanings of freedom infect one another, so that a "free society" may be
taken to be a society with no rules at all, or a free man may be
taken to be an individual with no obligations to society, or even
another individual. This global sense of individual freedom leads
many Americans to scoff at the idea that theirs is a free society.
Not primarily concerned with politics, most Americans apply the
word "free" to their personal relationships, sensing correctly, but for
our purposes irrelevantly, the necessity to work at a job, or to drive
at a certain speed on the highway. To these individuals, "freedom"
sounds like a wonderful goal, but hardly a goal that their society has
achieved. Yet freedom, when addressed in a narrow political sense,
is the basic value, goal, and, to a remarkable degree, attainment of
successful democratic regimes.

Freedom as independence is important to the Survey, but this
too is not a primary basis of judgment. When the primary issue for
so many countries in the colonial era was to become free from a
colonial or occupying power, "freedom" meant that a country had
emerged from control by another state, much as the United States
had achieved freedom in the 1780s. This sense of freedom was
applied to the term "the free world" after World War II because the
Soviet Union forced satellization on so many countries of Eastern
Europe. By contrast those beyond this sphere were said to be free.
In this sense Spain was part of the free world, but at the time only in
its relative independence. Still, for a people to accept rule by
leaders of their own nationality rather than by foreign leaders is an
aspect of political freedom—self-determination is a democratic
right. But the fact, for example, that the dictators of Haiti have

been Haitians has done little for the freedom or democratic rights of their people.

Since democratic freedoms and human rights are often considered together, it is frequently assumed that the Survey of Freedom is equivalent to a survey of human rights. However, in spite of the considerable overlap of the two, concern for democracy and concern for human rights are distinct. A free people can deny human rights to some of their number, and they can certainly deny human rights to others. Thus, the Japanese tendency to exclude foreigners may be judged unfortunate but does little to affect its democracy. If people are beaten cruelly in the jails of Arkansas, this too is a violation of human rights, but the ill-treatment may be passively approved by the people of the state and not restrict free speech and nonviolent pluralism.

One concern that many have felt with the human rights movement has been its tendency to proliferate as "rights" an ever-lengthening list of desiderata, a list that mixes general principles of natural rights with the particular concerns of modern intellectuals. This weakens the proposition that there are basic natural rights that all peoples in all places and times should feel incumbent upon themselves and their societies. It also leads to an increasing opposition between expanding democratic freedoms (that is, the ability of a people to decide its own fate) and expanding human rights.

In the Survey, freedom or democracy is taken to mean "liberal democracy." It is surprising how many well-informed persons believe that since the "German Democratic Republic" also uses the term democracy in its label, we must include regimes of this type within our definition. It would be like saying that since the German fascists called their party "National Socialist," discussions of socialism must use definitions that would include the Nazis. Words can be appropriated to many uses, and no one can stop the appropriation, but when an extension of meaning adds little but confusion, and begins to call black white, it should be rejected.

In rejecting the Marxist-Leninist or extreme leftist usage of the word democracy, as in "people's democracy," we do not mean to imply that there is not a range of acceptable meanings of "democracy" that must be taken into account in any survey of democratic freedoms. We have explicitly addressed in previous volumes of the Survey the question of how "economic freedom" might be defined.[1] Our conclusion was that a system was free primarily to the extent that the people were actually given a choice in determining the nature of the economic system. Therefore, a system that produces economic equality, if imposed, is much less democratic than a more unequal system, if freely chosen. Of course, questions must always be asked about the extent to which a system is freely chosen by any people. Economic measures such as land reform in a poor peasant economy may play a significant fact in improving the ability of people to take part in the political process fairly, and thereby choose the economic strategies that they desire.

The Comparative Survey was begun in the early 1970s as an attempt to give a more standardized and relativized picture of the situation of freedom in the world than could be provided by essays of individuals from different backgrounds that had formed, and in part still form, Freedom House's annual review of the condition of freedom in the world. My own experience had been that the world media and, therefore, informed opinion often misevaluated the level of freedom in countries with which Westerners had become particularly involved. In many countries oppressions were condemned as more severe than they were in comparative terms. On the other hand, the achievements of the postwar period in expanding freedom were often overlooked. Many small countries had quietly achieved and enjoyed democracy with relatively little media attention. The most oppressive states were those about which there was the least news in the media. Although these imbalances are still present, it is possible that some improvement in the presentation of the state of freedom in the world has resulted from the development of these Surveys.

The Comparative Survey of Freedom was hardly the first survey. There had been a number of other surveys. Bryce had listed the number of democracies in the world in about 1920.[2] An extensive cross-comparison of societies on social and cultural variables was published in the early sixties by Banks and Textor.[3] Based on an analysis of qualitative and quantitative data for all nations in the period 1960-62, the authors ranked and categorized polities on a wide variety of indices. These included economic development, literacy, and degree of urbanization, as well as political and civil rights. Since the authors' purpose was ultimately to discover correlations among the variables, their indices were more specific than those used in the Comparative Survey. They were interested primarily in presenting detailed information on items such as the nature of the party system, the presence or absence of military intervention, the freedom of opposition groups to enter politics, or the freedom of the press.

The next major effort, by Robert Dahl and colleagues at Yale, was much closer in intent to the Comparative Survey.[4] In updating Banks and Textor's work they placed all significant states along a variety of scales relating to democracy. The resulting scales were then aggregated into scales representing the two fundamental dimensions of "polyarchy" according to Dahl: opportunities for political opposition and degree of popular participation in national elections. Dahl's lists of polyarchies and near-polyarchies were very similar to our lists of free states. A similar rating of democratic systems was developed about the same time by Dankwart Rustow.[5] In both cases, and especially that of Rustow, there seemed to be an overemphasis on the formal characteristics of participation in elections and too little regard for the civil liberties that must complement elections if they are to be meaningful. Nevertheless, the resulting lists were very similar to those produced a few years later in the first Comparative Survey of Freedom, as are the lists of higher ranking states in analyses of human rights conditions.[6]

The essential difference between the Comparative Survey and the other attempts of the last generation has been its annual presentation of the evidence and ratings, as opposed to what are essentially one-shot presentations. The latter often represent much more detailed study, but they suffer from the lack of experience with repeated judgments and changes over a period of years that has served to improve the Comparative Survey.

In many ways more comparable to the Survey are the annual reports on human rights to Congress of the State Department's Bureau of Human Rights and Humanitarian Affairs.[7] Presenting detailed information on the state of human rights in every country, the reports consider political and civil liberties as well as other issues. They are, of course, influenced by America's foreign policy concerns, but for the vast majority of countries they are remarkably informative. Improving in coverage and comparability are also the annual reports of Amnesty International.[8] Amnesty's concerns in the area are much narrower, but information on Amnesty's issues—execution, political imprisonment, and torture—often has a wider significance. Both of these efforts have now become basic sources of information for the Comparative Survey.

The purpose of the Comparative Survey, then, is to give a general picture of the state of political and civil freedoms in the world. By taking a consistent approach to the definition of freedom, distinctions and issues that are often overlooked are brought out. In particular, its comparative approach brings to the reader's attention the fact that the most publicized denials of political and civil liberties are seldom in the most oppressive states. These states, such as Albania and North Korea, simply do not allow relevant information to reach the world media. There may or may not be hundreds of thousands in jail for their beliefs in North Korea: few care because no one knows.

Besides giving a reference point for considering the performance of independent countries, by its existence the Survey stands for the importance of democracy and freedom in an often cynical world. Too often, Westerners believe that democracy is impossible outside a few Western countries, and consign the rest of the world to perpetual despotism. The story of the struggle for democratic freedoms is a much more complicated one, and needs to be told. In a sketchy manner the Survey records the advances and retreats of democracy, and alerts the world to trends that should be resisted and those that should be supported.

The Categories of the Survey

The two dimensions of the Survey are political rights and civil liberties. **Political rights** are rights to participate meaningfully in the political process. In a democracy this means the right of all adults to vote and compete for public office, and for elected representatives to have a decisive vote on public policies. **Civil liberties** are rights to free expression, to organize or demonstrate, as well as rights to a degree of autonomy such as is provided by freedom of religion, education, travel, and other personal rights.

Political rights and civil liberties are rated on seven-point scales, with (7) the least free or least democratic and (1) the most free. With no exact definition for any point on these scales, they are constructed comparatively: countries are rated in relation to other countries rather than against absolute standards. The purpose of the rating system is to give an idea of how the freedoms of one state compare with those of others. Different persons with different information, or even with the same information, might compare countries differently. But unless the results of such comparisons are wildly different, there should be no concern. For example, if the Survey rates a country a (3) on political rights, and another person, accepting the criteria of the Survey, rates it a (4), this is an acceptable discrepancy. If judgments of two persons should turn out to be more than one point off, however, then either the Survey's methods are faulty, or the information of one of the judges is faulty.

The Checklist for Political Rights

The criteria may for convenience be considered as checklists. The checklist for political rights asks the investigator to determine the presence or absence of aspects of the political process common to democratic states, and then checks for the status of other aspects of the system that may impinge on, or provide alternatives to, the normal democratic process. The following discussion of some checklist items is keyed to the accompanying tabular presentation of the political rights checklist.

(1-2) The alternatives listed after (1) and (2) reflect variations in the extent to which political systems offer citizens or subjects a chance to participate through electoral choice, as these variations have been discovered in the course of Survey monitoring. At the antidemocratic extreme are those systems with no popular process, such as inherited monarchies or purely appointive communist systems. Little different in practice are those societies that hold elections for the legislature or president, but give the voter no alternative other than affirmation. In such elections there is neither the choice nor possibility—in practice or even sometimes in theory—of rejecting the single candidate that the government proposes for chief executive or representative. In elections at this level the candidate is usually chosen by a secretive process involving only the top elite. More democratic are those systems, such as Zambia's, that allow the voter no choice, but suggest that it is possible to reject a suggested candidate. In this case the results may show ten or twenty percent of the voters actually voting against a suggested executive, or, rarely, rejecting an individual legislative candidate on a single list. In some societies there is a relatively more open party process for selecting candidates. However the list of preselected

TABLE 1

CHECKLIST FOR POLITICAL RIGHTS

1. Chief authority recently elected by a meaningful process

2. Legislature recently elected by a meaningful process

   Alternatives for (1) and (2):

   a. no choice and possibility of rejection
   b. no choice but some possibility of rejection
   c. government or single-party selected candidates
   d. choice possible only among government-approved candidates
   e. relatively open choices possible only in local elections
   f. open choice possible within a restricted range
   g. relatively open choices possible in all elections

3. Fair election laws, campaigning opportunity, polling and tabulation

4. Fair reflection of voter preference in distribution of power
   — parliament, for example, has effective power

5. Multiple political parties
   — only dominant party allowed effective opportunity
   — open to rise and fall of competing parties

6. Recent shifts in power through elections

7. Significant opposition vote

8. Free of military or foreign control

9. Major group or groups denied reasonable self-determination

10. Decentralized political power

11. Informal consensus; de facto opposition power

candidates is prepared, there is seldom any provision for serious campaigning against the single list.

The political system is more democratic if multiple candidates are offered for each position, even when all candidates are government or party selected. Popular voting for alternatives may exist only at the party level——which in some countries is a large proportion of the population——or the choice may be at the general election. Rarely do such systems extend voter options to include choice of the chief authority in the state. Usually that position, like the domination by a single party, is not open to question. But many legislators, even members of the cabinet, may be rejected by the voters in such a system, although choices are restricted to what the party approves. Campaigning occurs at this level of democracy, but the campaigning is restricted to questions of personality, honesty, or ability; for example, in Tanzania campaigning may not involve questions of policy. A further increment of democratic validity is effected if choice is possible among government-approved rather than government-selected candidates. In this case the government's objective is to keep the most undesirable elements (from its viewpoint) out of the election. With government-selected candidates there is reliance on the party faithful, but self-selection allows persons of local reputation to achieve office. More generally, controlled electoral systems may allow open, self-selection of candidates for some local elections, but not for elections on the national scale. It is also possible for a system, such as that of Iran, to allow an open choice of candidates in elections, but to draw narrow ideological limits around what is an acceptable candidacy.

Beyond this, there is the world of free elections as we know them, in which candidates are both selected by parties and self-selected. It could be argued that parliamentary systems, such as are common outside of the United States, reduce local choice by imposing party choices on voters. However, independents can and do win in most systems, and new parties, such as the "Greens" in West Germany and elsewhere, test the extent to which the party system in particular countries is responsive to the desires of citizens.

(3) In most of the traditional western democracies there are fair election laws, at least on the surface. This is not true in many aspiring democracies. The government of Senegal, for example, has tried to prevent opposition parties from forming a coalition. Since effec-

tive oppositions often emerge from coalitions, this regulation is a useful device for preventing fragmented opposition groups from mounting a successful challenge. At least until recently, election laws in Egypt and South Korea have been devised so that the size of the majority of the governing party is artificially inflated after its victory.[9] This is a useful device where there is a danger of excessive fragmentation leading to majorities too weak to govern, but it seems in these cases to have been intended to reduce the size of the opposition.

Political scientists dispute whether it is fairer to allow people to contribute to candidates as they like, or whether the government should disburse all campaign funds. Obviously, if the former system is allowed there will be advantages for the more wealthy. However, if the latter is allowed there will be advantages for those who already have power, since governmental disbursement systems must allow funds to be spent in accordance with past patterns (and impoverished campaigns favor incumbents who initially are better known). If outcomes of elections were determined simply by the amounts spent, then depending on government financing would support a quite unchanging vote distribution. One example of this tendency on a restricted scale is the use of the public media for electioneering, usually by giving the parties, or candidates, or at least the major parties and candidates, specified and equal time on television or radio.

Perhaps the most common accusation against the fairness of elections is the extent to which the government takes advantage of the resources of office to defeat its opponents. Incumbents and government officials can often issue statements and make appearances related to the campaign that are not strictly described as campaigning. "News," whatever its origin, is likely to favor incumbents simply because as long as they are incumbents their actions are more newsworthy. Other practices that continue in the less-advanced democracies, but were common in all democracies until recently, are various forms of "vote buying," whether this be by actually distributing money, the promise of large projects, or the promise of future positions to well-placed influentials in critical districts. The use of government equipment such as jeeps and helicopters has often been alleged in campaigns in the third world, such as those of Congress (I) in India or of Barletta in Panama in 1984.

Comparative Survey

Few democracies are now seriously plagued by direct manipulation of votes, except occasionally on the local level. However, new democracies and semidemocracies are plagued both by such manipulations and equally by accusations that they have occurred. Elections recently in Bangladesh, Guyana, and Mexico have been marred by such accusations, and with justification. One test of a democracy is the extent to which it has effective machinery in place to prevent flagrant cheating. Such methods generally include genuinely neutral election commissions and poll watchers from all major parties to observe the voting and tabulation of results—a requirement Senegal, for example, refuses to accept.

Given the advantages of the incumbents, and thereby generally the government and its party, any campaigning rules that restrict the campaign are likely to affect opposition candidates or parties most severely. The very short campaigns prescribed by many democratic systems might seem unfair to Americans—yet many countries have a fully competitive system with such limited campaigns (probably because their strong parties are, in effect, continuously campaigning). More serious are restrictions placed on campaigning or party organization, such as Indonesia's rule that opposition parties may not organize outside the cities.

(4) Even though a country has a fair electoral process, fair campaigning, and meaningful elections, it will not be a functioning democracy unless those elected have the major power in the state. The most common denial of such power has come through the continued domination of the political system by a monarch or a self-selected leader, as in Morocco or Pakistan. Another common denial of real parliamentary power is occasioned by the continued direct or indirect power of the military—or military and king as in Thailand. In Latin America it is common even in otherwise functioning democracies for the military services not to be effectively under the control of the civilian and elected government. By tradition, ministers of defense in most Latin American countries are appointed from the military services rather than being civilians as is the practice in more mature democracies. In countries such as Guatemala and El Salvador, the problem has gone beyond that of the military not being under civilian control. In such cases, at least until recently, an economic elite has been unwilling to let elected governments rule. Such an elite may directly and indirectly struggle against its oppo-

12

nents through violent internal warfare outside the control of the system—although elements of the system may be used to implement the desires of these shadowy rulers.

(5) In theory it should be quite possible for democracy to be perfected without political parties. Certainly the founding fathers of the American Republic did not think parties were necessary. The leaders of many countries that have moved from liberal democratic models to single parties argue for the necessity to reduce the adversarial spirit of parties; they claim to be able to preserve democracy by bringing the political struggle within the confines of one party. However, in practice policy is set in single parties by a small clique at the top; those in disfavor with the government are not allowed to compete for office by legal means—indeed, they are often ejected from the single party all together, as in Kenya.

The conclusion of the Survey is that while parties may not be necessary for democracy in very small countries such as Tuvalu, for most modern states they are necessary to allow alternatives to a ruling group or policy to gain sufficient votes to make a change. Therefore, the existence of multiple parties is important evidence for the existence of democracy, but is not absolutely conclusive. We are waiting for demonstrations of the ability of one-party or nonparty systems to achieve democracy. (Nepal's experiment with a nonparty system is worth watching in this connection.)

"Dominant party" structures such as those of Malaysia or Singapore allow oppositions to mobilize to the extent that they can publicize alternative positions and effectively criticize government performance, but not to the extent that they represent a realistic threat to the group in power. Controls over campaigning, expression of opinion, patronage, and vote manipulation, as well as "punishment" of areas that vote against the government are methods used in such systems to make sure that the governing party remains in power.

(6-7) An empirical test of democracy is the extent to which there has been a recent shift in power occasioned through the operation of the electoral process. While it is true that the people of a country may remain relatively satisfied with the performance of one party for a long period of time, it is also true that a party in power may be able over time to entrench itself in multiple ways to such a degree that it is next to impossible to dislodge it by legitimate means. For a time in the first years of the Survey there was the suspicion that the social democratic party of Sweden had accomplished this. However, in 1976 social democratic domination was ended after forty-four years. The extent of democratic rights can also be empirically suggested by the size of an opposition vote. While on rare occasions a governing party or individual may receive overwhelming support at the polls, any group or leader that regularly receives seventy percent or more of the vote indicates a weak opposition, and the probable existence of undemocratic barriers in the way of its further success. When a government or leader receives over ninety percent of the vote this indicates highly restrictive freedom for those opposing the system: over ninety-eight percent indicates that elections are little more than symbolic.

(8) A free, democratic society is one that governs itself through its own official processes. The two most blatant means of denying the control of a society by its elected leaders are military or foreign control. Since control of violent force is a basic requirement of all governments, when those who directly have this power begin to affect the political process, this aspect of government is turned on its head. The traditional democracies have long since been able to remove the military from power; at the opposite extreme are purely military regimes, as in much of Africa. A few countries remain under a degree of foreign control or influence. For example, in Europe, Finland, and to a lesser extent Austria, must remain neutral because of pressure from the Soviet Union. Mongolia and Afghanistan (until 1989) have been under direct Soviet occupation.

There are many vague accusations that one or another country is under military or foreign control. In this spirit the United States is said to be "ruled" by a military-industrial complex or Mexico is said to be under American control. But there is simply too much evidence that these "controllers" are frequently ignored or slighted for such accusations to be taken seriously. To a degree every country in the world is influenced by many others—large and small. (While smaller countries generally have less power of self-determination than larger countries, for most issues the power of the individual voter in the smaller states to control his life through the ballot is likely to be greater than that of people in larger countries.) The Survey's position in regard to both of these kinds of "outside" control is to record only the most conspicuous cases, and to not enter the area of more complex interpretations.

(9) A democratic polity is one in which the people as a whole feel that the process is open to them, and that on important issues all individuals can be part of a meaningful majority. If this is not true, then the democratic polity must either divide, or devise methods for those who feel they are not part of the system to have reserved areas, geographical or otherwise, in which they can expect their interests to be uppermost. In other words, the system must provide for either external or internal self-determination. Most democracies are relatively homogeneous. But even here, without some forms of elected local or regional government, people in some areas will feel crushed under a national majority that is unable to understand their particular problems or accept their values. Federal democracies, such as India or the United States, have devised elaborate methods for separate divisions of the country to be in important degrees self-governing. The problems of over-centralization in Europe have recently been addressed by countries such as France, Spain, and the United Kingdom, but in the case of Ulster current subdivisions or political boundaries continue to make a section of the people feel like foreigners in their own land.

(10) The question of self-determination is closely related to the extent to which political power has been decentralized. Since it would be possible for a country to have an elaborate degree of decentralization and still hand down all the important decisions from above, we must test empirically the extent to which persons or parties not under control of the center actually succeed politically. The fact, for example, that Japanese-Americans are able to play a leading role in Hawaiian politics, or that the Scots nationalists are able to achieve a significant vote in Scotland suggest an authentic devolution of political power.

(11) Finally, the Survey wants evidence for the extent to which the political-decision process depends not only on the support of majorities at the polls, but also on a less adversarial process involving search for consensus among all groups on issues of major public interest. A democracy should be more than simply a society of winners and losers. The most common way for this to be demonstrat-

ed is for the opposition to be taken into account in major decisions and appointments, even when it does not have to be consulted in terms of the formal requirements of the system. Sri Lanka and Lebanon are current examples of the breakdown of democratic systems when one or more groups are no longer willing to accommodate the interests of others, and accept the electoral process as an arbiter. Colombia's "la violencia" was another example, an example with analogies that continue to threaten several countries in Latin America. Obviously, the distribution of informal power is particularly important in judging the degree of success of one-party "democracies" that base their claim to legitimacy on their willingness to achieve national consensuses.

The Checklist for Civil Liberties

In considering the civil liberties checklist, we are entering on a field made familiar by many special or annual reports on human rights violations. It is important to mention one of the chief differences between such reporting and the Survey approach. The Survey is looking for patterns in activities and balances in activities, rather than numbers of failures to observe particular human rights standards. The quantitative human rights violations approach has at least three difficulties that we should strive to avoid. The first and most obvious is that countries differ dramatically in size. One case of government interference with the media in Barbados is of much greater importance to our judgment of its freedom than tens of such interferences in a country such as India. It is not just that there are infinitely more media channels in India, but also that there are so many channels that the repression of individual channels is unlikely to be effective. The significance of cases of repression is greater in Barbados. The second is that counting numbers of violations is often an inadequate measure of the presence or absence of the behavior at issue. Although the number of journalists imprisoned in North Korea in the 1970s might have been low, journalism was totally controlled. In South Korea journalists were much more likely to get in trouble with the law, but journalism was much freer. Finally, and most important, there is the question of the balance of positive and negative activities. For example, a very large number of civil liberties violations are reported every year in South Africa; yet every year we also find reports of a remarkable number of free and open dem-

TABLE 2

CHECKLIST FOR CIVIL LIBERTIES

12. Media/literature free of political censorship
    a. Press independent of government
    b. Broadcasting independent of government

13. Open public discussion

14. Freedom of assembly and demonstration

15. Freedom of political or quasi-political organization

16. Nondiscriminatory rule of law in politically relevant cases
    a. independent judiciary
    b. security forces respect individuals

17. Free from unjustified political terror or imprisonment
    a. free from imprisonment or exile for reasons of conscience
    b. free from torture
    c. free from terror by groups not opposed to the system
    d. free from government-organized terror

18. Free trade unions, peasant organizations, or equivalents

19. Free businesses or cooperatives

20. Free professional or other private organizations

21. Free religious institutions

22. Personal social rights: including those to property, internal and external travel, choice of residence, marriage and family

23. Socioeconomic rights: including freedom from dependency on landlords, bosses, union leaders, or bureaucrats

24. Freedom from gross socioeconomic inequality

25. Freedom from gross government indifference or corruption

onstrations, new organizations, critical publications and reports, and so on. If we are to use quantitative measures we must develop a means of measuring both demonstrations that occur and demonstrations suppressed; public criticisms not suppressed along with public criticisms suppressed.

(12)   At the top of the list are questions of freedom for the communications media. The analyst asks whether the press and broadcasting facilities of the country are independent of government control, and serve the range of opinion that is present in the country. Clearly, if a population does not receive information about alternatives to present leaders and policies, then its ability to use any political process is impaired. In most traditional democracies there is no longer any question of censoring the press: no longer are people imprisoned for expressing their rational views on any matter—although secrecy and libel laws do have a slight affect in some democracies. As one moves from this open situation, from ratings of (1) to ratings of (7), a steady decline in freedom to publish is noticed: the tendency increases for people to be punished for criticizing the government, or papers to be closed, or censorship to be imposed, or for the newspapers and journals to be directly owned and supervised by the government.

The methods used by governments to control the print media are highly varied. While pre-publication censorship is often what Westerners think of because of their wartime experience, direct government ownership and control of the media and post-publication censorship through warnings, confiscations, or suspensions are more common. Government licensing of publications and journalists and controls over the distribution of newsprint are other common means of keeping control over what is printed. Even in countries with a degree of democracy, such as Malaysia, press controls of these sorts may be quite extensive, often based on an ostensible legal requirement for "responsible journalism." Control of the press may be further extended by requiring papers to use a government news agency as their source of information, and by restricting the flow of foreign publications.[10]

Broadcasting—radio or television—are much more frequently owned by the government than the print media, and such ownership may or may not be reflected in government control over what is communicated. It is possible, as in the British case, for a government-owned broadcasting corporation to be so effectively protected from government control that its programs demonstrate genuine impartiality. However, in many well-known democracies, such as France or Greece, changes in the political composition of government affects the nature of what is broadcast to the advantage of incumbents. The government-owned broadcasting services of India make little effort to go beyond presenting the views of their government.

In most countries, misuse of the news media to serve government interests is even more flagrant. At this level, we need to distinguish between those societies that require their media, particularly their broadcasting services, to avoid criticism of the political system or its leaders, and those that use them to "mobilize" their peoples in direct support for government policies. In the first case the societies allow or expect their media, particularly their broadcasting services, to present a more or less favorable picture; in the second, the media are used to motivate their peoples to actively support government policies and to condemn or destroy those who oppose the governing system. In the first, the government's control is largely passive; in the second it is directly determinative of content.[11]

The comparison of active and passive control by government brings us to the most difficult issue in the question of media freedom—self-censorship. It is fairly easy to know if a government censors or suspends publications for content, or punishes journalists and reporters by discharge, imprisonment, or worse; judging the day-to-day influence of subtle pressures on the papers or broadcasting services of a country is much more difficult. Perhaps the most prevalent form of government control of the communications media is achieved through patterns of mutual assistance of government and media that ensure that, at worst, reports are presented in a bland, non-controversial manner—a common practice in Mexico and Pakistan.

Some critics believe that most communications media in the West, and especially in the United States, practice this kind of censorship, either because of government support, or because this is in the interest of the private owners of the media. However, in the United States it is noteworthy that National Public Radio, financed largely by the state, is generally much more critical of the government in its commentaries than are the commercial services. The critics would explain this difference by the greater ability of commercial stations to "police" their broadcasts and broadcasters. The primary explanation, however, lies in the gap between the subculture of broadcasters and audience for public radio and the subculture of broadcasters and especially audience for commercial stations.[12] The highly critical and elitist commentary on public radio serves and is produced by a narrow, emotionally disaffected segment of American society: its lack of commercial appeal suggests that it would be neither acceptable nor interesting to a broader public.

(13) Open public discussion is at least as important a civil liberty as free communications media. The ultimate test of a democracy is the degree to which an atmosphere for discussion in public and private exists free of fear of reprisal by either the government or opposition groups. Even in the relatively free communist society of Yugoslavia, at least until recently people have been imprisoned for the expression of critical opinions in private.[13] Certainly Iranians have had to be careful in recent years not to express too openly opinions that go against the prevailing ideology.

(14-15) Open discussion expressed through political organization, public demonstration, and assemblies is often threatening to political incumbents. There are occasions in which such assemblies may be dangerous to public order and should be closely controlled or forbidden. But in many societies this hypothetical danger is used as a pretense to deny opposition groups the ability to mobilize in support of alternative policies or leaders. In Malaysia, for example, the government's denial of public assembly to the opposition has been one of the main ways to restrict the ability of the opposition to effectively challenge the rule of the government.[14] Obviously, denial of the right to organize freely for political action is the most generalized form of the attempt to prevent effective mobilization of opposition to government policies. Control over political organization is a distinguishing characteristic of one-party states, but many multiparty states place limits on the kinds or numbers of political parties that may be organized. Controls over extremist parties that deny the legitimacy of democratic institutions, such as many fascist or communist parties, are understandable---still, they represent limits on freedom. Political and civil freedoms overlap closely on the right to political organization. The distinction is between denying the right to participate in elections and denying the right to organize to present alternative policies or arguments for and against change in other ways.

(16) A democratic system is not secured unless there is a legal system that can be relied on for a fair degree of impartiality. The electoral process, for example, needs to be supervised by electoral commissions or other administrative systems that ultimately can be checked or overruled by the judicial system. People accused of actions against the state need to have some hope that their cases will be tried before the courts of the society and that the process will be fair. One of the tests that the author often applies to a country is whether it is possible to win against the government in a political case, and under what conditions. A reliable judicial system requires a guarantee of the permanence of judicial tenure, particularly at the highest levels, as well as traditions of executive noninterference developed over a period of years. Although in no society are all trials fair or all judges impartial, in this respect fundamental differences exist between democracies and nondemocracies.

A significant, but less striking, difference exists between the ways in which security services treat the public in democracies and nondemocracies. Since the people of a democracy are the sponsors of the system,[15] in theory the security services are their hired employees, and these employees should treat them with the utmost respect. However, because of the nature of the task of police and army, and their monopoly over force, in larger democracies, at least, this relationship is often forgotten. For example, in France and certain parts of the United States security forces have the reputation of treating people with carelessness and even brutality. To the degree that security forces are the employees, even in theory, of a smaller group than the people as a whole, then their behavior will be even less "democratic." Security forces that serve "a party" or a particular leadership faction are particularly likely to disregard citizens' rights.

(17) Certainly democracy requires that people be free from fear of the government, especially in regard to their politically related activities. To this extent, the emphasis of organizations such as Amnesty International on the extent of imprisonment, execution, or torture for reasons of conscience is closely related to any measure-

ment of democracy. Oppressive countries imprison their opponents, or worse, both to silence the particular individuals, and to warn others of the dangers of opposing the system. Recently, exile and disappearances have been used as a further deterrent. "Disappearance" is generally a form of extra-judicial execution, often carried out in support of the ruling system. Such terrorism may or may not be directly under the orders of government leaders. These practices underscore the fact that a great deal of such internal state terrorism does not involve the normal legal process; frequently opponents are incarcerated through "detentions" that may last for years. In the Soviet Union and some other communist countries, the practice of using psychiatric institutions to incarcerate opponents has been developed on the theory that opposition to a people's state is itself a form of mental illness.

It is important in this regard to distinguish between the broader category of "political imprisonment" and the narrower "imprisonment for reasons of conscience." The former includes all cases that informed opinion would assume are related to political issues, or issues that can be defined politically in some states (such as religious belief in many Islamic societies). It includes those who have written articles that the regime finds offensive as well as those who have thrown bombs or plotted executions, or even caused riots, to dramatize their cause. Since clearly the latter actions cannot be accepted by any government, all states, at whatever level of freedom, may have some "political prisoners." But if we take the category of political prisoners and separate out those who appear to have not committed or planned, or been involved in supporting acts of violence, then we have the smaller category of "prisoners of conscience." Their existence must be counted against the democratic rating of any country. This is not to say that the existence of prisoners of conscience who have been involved in violence cannot also be taken in many countries as an indication that a system may not be sufficiently responsive to demands expressed nonviolently—too often there may be no effective means to express opposition without violence. The distinction between prisoners by reason of conscience and political prisoners is in practice often blurred by the outsider's difficulty in deciding whether particular incarcerated individuals have or have not committed or planned acts of violence. Nevertheless, by looking at the pattern of a regime's behavior over a period of years it is possible to estimate the degree to which a regime does or does not have prisoners of conscience.

Anti-dissident terror undertaken by groups that support the general system of a country but are not, or may not be, under government control is often difficult to evaluate in determining a country's rating. In the case where the terrorism is carried out by the security services, or their hired hands, we can either assume that these services are no longer controlled by the civilian administration, and to this extent the system cannot be called free, or that the civilian administration actually approves of the actions.

(18-20) Democracies require freedom of organization that goes far beyond the right to organize political parties. The right of individuals to organize trade unions, cooperatives, or business enterprises is a basic right that may be limited only with great care in a free society. The right of union or peasant organization has been particularly significant because it allows large groups of ordinary people in many societies to balance, through numbers, the ability of the wealthy to concentrate power. However, in some societies, such as those of western Africa, the ability of medical, bar, and academic associations to mobilize or maintain alternatives to ruling groups has been of equal importance. Democracies require freedom of organization because they require organized, countervailing power centers ---which is one definition of pluralism---in order to maintain free institutions against the natural tendency of governments to aggregate power.

(21) It is for this reason that religious freedom, in belief and in organization, has been particularly important for the defense of freedom in a more general sense. Religious institutions have been able to maintain opposition strength in societies as different as those of Poland and Chile. A strong religious institution can build a wall around the individual dissident that a government will be loathe to breach for the sake of imposing its order. In countries such as Argentina or Philippines the organized church and organized unions have gone a long way toward insuring a society able to resist the encroachments of government. The question is not whether a particular established organization, such as the church, is itself favorable toward democracy. It is rather whether organizational structures are able to exist independently of governmental direction.

Without such countervailing organizational power, it is unlikely that significant civil liberties can be maintained against government pressure.

(22) Civil liberties also include personal and individual social rights, particularly those that are likely to most directly affect the ability of people to withstand the pressures of the state. Especially important are those to property, travel (including emigration), and to an independent family life. The right to property does not necessarily mean the right to productive property, but it does mean the right to property that can provide a cushion against government pressures such as dismissal from a position, that will make possible private publications, or other activity that cannot be financed unless people have more than subsistence incomes. The ability of an individual to travel, particularly to leave the country, is of great importance to dissidents or potential dissidents. It allows them additional sources of support and an additional refuge should the effort to improve conditions in their own country fail. An independent family offers another type of emotional haven that makes possible independent thinking and action. Opposition to Mao during the 1960s in China became almost impossible when individuals could no longer trust even their spouses and children not to inform on their activities. The complete isolation of the individual, even in the midst of a crowded life, is the ultimate goal of oppressors.

(23-24) Civil liberty requires, then, that most people are relatively independent in both their lives and thoughts. It implies socioeconomic rights that include freedom from dependency on landlords, on bosses, on union leaders, or on bureaucrats. The kind of dependencies that the socioeconomic system imposes on individuals will vary from society to society, but widespread dependencies of these kinds are incompatible with democratic freedoms. This implies that there should be freedom from gross socioeconomic inequality. It should be noted that we are not saying that democracy requires that incomes or living standards be equalized. But we are saying that if inequalities are too great, if a small group of very wealthy lives in the midst of a large number of very poor individuals, it is likely that relations of dependency will develop that will make impossible the unfettered expression of opinion or a free and uncoerced vote.

24

(25) Finally, there would seem to be an indirect requirement that the civil liberties of a democracy include freedom from the extremes of government indifference and corruption. These conditions make it impossible for the people affected to feel that they are in any important sense the sponsors of their political system. Such indifference and corruption also implies that the mechanisms of democracy in the state are simply not working. If there is a continued record of disregard for the interests of the people, and yet the representatives of the people are not replaced by the electoral or judicial process, the system is not working. Such indirect tests are necessary for a rating system that is based in large part on regular monitoring of press reports from around the world.

Freedom Ratings

A three way division of countries into "free", "partly free", and "not free", the "status of freedom", was formerly used by the Survey. (For a fuller discussion of the status of freedom in earlier surveys see **Freedom in the World: 1987-88.**) In any event, the seven-point scales have always been the heart of the Survey, with the three-point generalized status of freedom little more than a heuristic devise for printing maps or adding up doubtful totals for free or unfree peoples. (The careful student may have noted that the author has avoided making such calculations——they are certainly not in recent yearbooks or the texts of the annual Survey articles appearing in the January editions of **Freedom at Issue.** Such calculations implicitly make a claim for Survey precision that it will not carry. To say that one percent more or less of the world's people live in tyranny this year than last rings hollow. After all, the dividing lines between the categories of the Survey are purely arbitrary points at which to cut into continua. However, I have found it useful to consider the 58 or so "free" countries to be a rough list of democracies.)

In this Comparative Survey, the status of freedom will be replaced by a **Freedom Rating** that simply adds together ratings for political rights and civil liberties. This rating, ranging from 2 for most free to 14 for least free, will allow for the division of countries into a variety of subgroupings, depending on the purpose. One division will be into high (1-5), medium (6-10), and low (11-14). Countries rated "high" in this accounting approximate a list of democracies as before. Obviously, maps may be drawn using many breakdowns.

The Survey is based on library research, updated by a more or less continuous flow of publications across the author's desk. Once the basic nature of the political system and its respect for civil liberties is established, following the flow of information has two primary objectives: 1) to confirm or disconfirm the level of freedom expected by the prior analysis, and 2) to bring to the Survey's attention changes in this level that might have occurred in successive years. It also has had the effect since the beginning of the Survey in 1972 of refining the author's sensitivity to those conditions and indicators that go with different levels of democratic rights.

The use of general descriptions and a flow of information is particularly useful because the Survey is based on evidence of democratic or nondemocratic behavior by the governments of countries in regard to their own peoples. Because interest in human rights and democracy is often centered in the legal community, many students or analysts in this area concentrate their attention on changes in laws or legal structures. Even Amnesty International takes the position that the numbers imprisoned or executed in a country is a less important indicator of change than change in the law in regard to these practices.[16]

The criticism is often made that the Survey ignores many "human rights," such as the right to adequate nutrition. This criticism can be addressed on several levels. Most appropriate is the remark that the Survey is of political and civil freedoms and not of human rights. (In philosophical terms neither freedom nor democracy are properly understood as including all "goods" and only "goods".) The Survey is seriously concerned with those social and economic rights, such as the right to the freedom of workers or businessmen to organize, that fall under its understanding of basic civil liberties. It is our feeling that some other proposed rights, including some of those implied by the Universal Declaration of Human Rights, would predetermine social priorities or social issues that societies have a right to decide for themselves through the political process. To get too out ahead of the attitudes and capabilities of the world's peoples is to threaten the growing respect given to the concepts of rights and freedom. In order to give people maximum freedom to develop their societies in terms of their needs and desires as they understand them, it is important that the list of rights be kept to a minimum so as not to diminish unduly the sphere of popular political determination.

The objection that the Survey should take more seriously "economic rights" in the narrower sense of economic freedom has been addressed in the 1982 and 1983–84 Freedom in the World volumes. As was mentioned in the beginning of this Chapter, the conclusion was that the basic economic right of all democracies was for the people to have an authentic and repeated opportunity to choose the economic system they desired. Their choice might range from libertarian to any one of a number of forms of socialist. To this we added that to be effective this economic freedom of choice must be based on some relative equalities in power; the absence of dependency that is included in the checklist above as a requisite civil liberty in a democracy must be generally present for economic freedom to be meaningful.

We have, of course, always been concerned with the relationships that might exist between needs variables, such as medical care, nutrition, or education, and the political and civil liberties with which we are concerned. It is important to see if there are any necessary relationships between freedom and standards in these areas, or whether the existence of civil and political liberties enhances the meeting of such needs by a society. Table 11 below offers the reader a chance to look empirically at some of the relations that exist. These relationships were addressed in **Freedom in the World: 1987–88**, Part IV.

If more resources were available for assistance and on-site investigations, the Surveys could be greatly improved. They began, and have continued to be, a generalized attempt to improve the informed public's picture of the world. In spite of their limitations, some political scientists, economists, and sociologists have used the yearly Surveys as a source of data for correlation analyses of related variables. They are useful because they represent the only annual attempt to compare the level of democratic rights in all the countries in the world. (For further discussion of the Survey see **Freedom in the World: 1986–87,** pages 79–96.)

NOTES

1. See R. D. Gastil, **Freedom in the World: 1982** (Westport: Greenwood Press, 1982), especially the article by Lindsay Wright, and **Freedom in the World: 1983-84.** For further discussions of the definitions of freedom and democracy from the viewpoint of the Survey see the relevant discussions in **Freedom in the World** 1978, 1984-85, and 1986-87.

2. James Bryce, Viscount, **Modern Democracies** 2 vols. (Macmillan, 1924).

3. Arthur Banks and Robert Textor, **A Cross-Polity Survey** (Cambridge: MIT Press, 1963).

4. Robert Dahl, **Polyarchy: Participation and Opposition** (New Haven: Yale University Press, 1971), pages 231-49.

5. Dankwart A. Rustow, **A World of Nations** (Washington: Brookings Institution, 1967).

6. For example, Charles Humana, **World Human Rights Guide** (New York: Facts on File, 1986). For some other surveys comparable to the Comparative Survey, see also **Freedom in the World: 1987-1988,** pages 89-125.

7. For example, United States Department of State, **Country Reports on Human Rights Practices for 1986,** Department of State (Washington, 1987).

8. **Amnesty International Report, 1983** (London: Amnesty International, 1983).

9. On Senegal see **Africa Research Bulletin,** December 1983, page 7050; on Egypt, **Middle East,** July 1984, page 22.

10. **Keesing's Contemporary Archives,** 1984, pages 32782-85; **Far Eastern Economic Review,** September 20, 1984, pages 40ff.

11. William Rugh, **The Arab Press: News Media and Political Process in the Arab World** (Syracuse: Syracuse University Press, 1979).

12. For an attempt to suggest the relatively greater importance of subcultural as opposed to class or other interests in determining the opinions of people in our society see R. D. Gastil, "'Selling Out' and the Sociology of Knowledge," **Policy Sciences,** 1971, 2, pages 271-277.

13. **Amnesty Action,** January 1985.

14. See, for example, **Far Eastern Economic Review,** August 23, 1984.

15. Alfred Kuhn, **The Logic of Social Systems** (San Francisco: Jossey-Bass, 1975), pages 330-61.

16. **Amnesty Action** January 1, 1985, page 7. Here it is suggested that improvement in human rights is seen less in changes in the numbers imprisoned or killed in a country than in changes in its laws, such as laws against torture or imprisonment without trial.

SURVEY RATINGS AND TABLES FOR 1988

Progress toward freedom and democracy in 1987 was strengthened and reinforced by the events of 1988. South Korea continued its march, begun at the end of 1987, to a more liberal, democratic state: by the time of the Olympics a working democracy had been established, and the process continues. Pakistan made a decisive move toward democracy near the end of 1988, placing it in the same position South Korea had found itself in a year earlier, or the Philippines about a year before that. In 1988 liberalization in the Soviet Union continued and accelerated. With all the caveats that must be made, including regional variations in the rate of change, the Soviet Union is a much freer country today than at any time since the 1920s.

The Tabulated Ratings

The accompanying Table 3 (Independent States) and Table 4 (Related Territories) rate each state or territory on seven-point scales for political and civil freedoms, and then provide an overall "freedom rating". For each scale, a rating of (1) is freest and (7) least free. Instead of using absolute standards, standards are comparative. The goal is to have ratings such that, for example, most observers would be likely to judge states rated (1) as freer than those rated (2). No state, of course, is absolutely free or unfree, but the degree of freedom makes a difference in the quality of life.[1]

In political rights, states rated (1) have a fully competitive electoral process, and those elected clearly rule. Most West European democracies belong here. Relatively free states may receive a (2) because, although the electoral process works and the elected rule, there are factors that cause us to lower our rating of the effective equality of the process. These factors may include extreme economic inequality, illiteracy, or intimidating violence. They also include the weakening of effective competition implied by

TABLE 3

INDEPENDENT STATES: COMPARATIVE FREEDOMS

	Political Rights[1]	Civil Liberties[1]	Freedom Rating[2]
Afghanistan	6 ○ ↑	6 ○ ↑	12
Albania	7	7	14
Algeria	5 ↑	6	11
Angola	7	7	14
Antigua & Barbuda	2	3	5
Argentina	2	1	3
Australia	1	1	2
Austria	1	1	2
Bahamas	2	3	5
Bahrain	5	5	10
Bangladesh	4	5	9
Barbados	1	1	2
Belgium	1	1	2
Belize	1	2 ○ ↓	3
Benin	7	7	14
Bhutan	5	5	10
Bolivia	2	3	5
Botswana	2	3	5
Brazil	2	3 ○	5
Brunei	6	6 ↓	12
Bulgaria	7	7	14
Burkina Faso[3]	7	6	13
Burma	7	6 ↑	13
Burundi	7	6	13
Cambodia[4]	7	7	14
Cameroon	6	6	12
Canada	1	1	2
Cape Verde Islands	5	6	11

	Political Rights[1]	Civil Liberties[1]	Freedom Rating[2]
Cen. African Rep.	6	6	12
Chad	6	7	13
Chile	5 ↑	4 ↑	9
China (Mainland)	6	6	12
China (Taiwan)	5	3 ↑	8
Colombia	2	3	5
Comoros	6	6	12
Congo	7	6	13
Costa Rica	1	1	2
Cote d'Ivoire [5]	6	6 ∘	12
Cuba	7 ∘	6	13
Cyprus (G)	1	2	3
Cyprus (T)	2	3	5
Czechoslovakia	7	6	13
Denmark	1	1	2
Djibouti	6	6	12
Dominica	2	2	4
Dominican Rep.	1	3	4
Ecuador	2	2 ↑	4
Egypt	5	4	9
El Salvador	3	3 ↑	6
Equatorial Guinea	7	7	14
Ethiopia	6	7	13
European Community	2	1	3
Fiji	5 ↑	4 ↑	9
Finland	1	2	3
France	1	2	3
Gabon	6	6	12
Gambia	3	3	6
Germany (E)	7	6	13
Germany (W)	1	2	3

Comparative Survey

	Political Rights[1]	Civil Liberties[1]	Freedom Rating[2]
Ghana	6 ∘ ↑	6	12
Greece	2	2	4
Grenada	2	1	3
Guatemala	3	3	6
Guinea	7	6	13
Guinea–Bissau	6	7	13
Guyana	5	5	10
Haiti	7 ↓	5	12
Honduras	2	3	5
Hungary	5	4	9
Iceland	1	1	2
India	2	3	5
Indonesia	5	5 ∘	10
Iran	5	6	11
Iraq	7	7	14
Ireland	1	1	2
Israel	2	2	4
Italy	1	1	2
Jamaica	2	2	4
Japan	1	1	2
Jordan	6 ↓	5	11
Kenya	6	6	12
Kiribati	1	2	3
Korea (N)	7	7	14
Korea (S)	2 ↑	3 ↑	5
Kuwait	6	5	11
Laos	6 ∘ ↑	6 ∘ ↑	12
Lebanon	6	5	11
Lesotho	6 ∘ ↓	6	12
Liberia	5	5	10
Libya	6	6	12

	Political Rights[1]	Civil Liberties[1]	Freedom Rating[2]
Luxembourg	1	1	2
Madagascar	5	5	10
Malawi	6	7	13
Malaysia	4 ↓	5	9
Maldives	5	6	11
Mali	6 ↑	6	12
Malta	1	2	3
Mauritania	6	6	12
Mauritius	2	2	4
Mexico	3 ↑	4	7
Mongolia	7	7	14
Morocco	4	5	9
Mozambique	6	7	13
Nauru	2	2	4
Nepal	3	4	7
Netherlands	1	1	2
New Zealand	1	1	2
Nicaragua	5	4 ∘	9
Niger	6 ∘ ↑	6	12
Nigeria	5 ↑	5	10
Norway	1	1	2
Oman	6	6	12
Pakistan	3 ↑	3 ↑	6
Panama	6 ↓	5	11
Papua New Guinea	2	3 ∘	5
Paraguay	6 ∘	6	12
Peru	2	3	5
Philippines	2	3 ∘	5
Poland	5	5	10
Portugal	1	2	3

Comparative Survey

	Political Rights[1]	Civil Liberties[1]	Freedom Rating[2]
Qatar	5	5	10
Romania	7	7	14
Rwanda	6	6	12
St. Kitts-Nevis	1	2	3
St. Lucia	1	2	3
St. Vincent	1	2	3
Sao Tome & Principe	6 ○ ↑	7	13
Saudi Arabia	6	7	13
Senegal	3	4	7
Seychelles	6	6	12
Sierra Leone	5	5	10
Singapore	4	5	9
Solomon Islands	2	2	4
Somalia	7	7	14
South Africa	5	6	11
Spain	1	2	3
Sri Lanka	3	4	7
Sudan	4	5	9
Suriname	3 ↑	2 ↑	5
Swaziland	5	6	11
Sweden	1	1	2
Switzerland	1	1	2
Syria	6	7	13
Tanzania	6	6	12
Thailand	3	3	6
Togo	6	6	12
Tonga	5	3	8
Transkei	7 ↓	6	13
Trinidad & Tobago	1	1	2
Tunisia	6	4 ↑	10

	Political Rights[1]	Civil Liberties[1]	Freedom Rating[2]
Turkey	2	4	6
Tuvalu	1	1	2
Uganda	5	5 ∘	10
USSR	6 ↑	5 ↑	11
Un. Arab Emirates	5	5	10
United Kingdom	1	1	2
United States	1	1	2
Uruguay	2	2	4
Vanuatu	2	4	6
Venezuela	1	2	3
Vietnam	6	7	13
Western Samoa	4	3	7
Yemen (N)	5	5	10
Yemen (S)	7 ∘	7	14
Yugoslavia	5 ∘ ↑	5	10
Zaire	6	7	13
Zambia	6 ∘ ↓	5	11
Zimbabwe	6 ↓	5 ∘	11

Notes to the Table

1. The scales use the numbers 1–7, with 1 comparatively offering the highest level of political or civil rights and 7 the lowest. An up arrow ↑, or a down arrow ↓ following a rating indicates an improvement or decline since the last yearbook. A rating marked with the diacritical sign ∘ has been reevaluated by the author in this time; there may have been little change in the country.
2. The Freedom Rating sums the first two scales.
3. Formerly Upper Volta.
4. Often written Kampuchea.
5. Formerly Ivory Coast.

the absence of periodic shifts in rule from one group or party to another.

Below this level, political ratings of (3) through (5) represent successively less effective implementation of democratic processes. Mexico, for example, has periodic elections and limited opposition, but for many years its governments have been selected outside the public view by the leaders of factions within the one dominant Mexican party. Governments of states rated (5) sometimes have no effective voting processes at all, but strive for consensus among a variety of groups in society in a way weakly analogous to those of the democracies. States at (6) do not allow competitive electoral processes that would give the people a chance to voice their desire for a new ruling party or for a change in policy. The rulers of states at this level assume that one person or a small group has the right to decide what is best for the nation, and that no one should be allowed to challenge that right. Such rulers do respond, however, to popular desire in some areas, or respect (and therefore are constrained by) belief systems that are the property of the society as a whole. At (7) the political despots at the top appear by their actions to feel little constraint from either public opinion or popular tradition.

Turning to the scale for civil liberties, in countries rated (1) publications are not closed because of the expression of rational political opinion, especially when the intent of the expression is to affect the legitimate political process. No major media are simply conduits for government propaganda. The courts protect the individual; persons are not imprisoned for their opinions; private rights and desires in education, occupation, religion, and residence are generally respected; and law-abiding persons do not fear for their lives because of their rational political activities. States at this level include most traditional democracies. There are, of course, flaws in the liberties of all of these states, and these flaws are significant when measured against the standards these states set themselves.

Movement down from (2) to (7) represents a steady loss of the civil freedoms we have detailed. Compared to (1), the police and courts of states at (2) have more authoritarian traditions. In some cases they may simply have a less institutionalized or secure set of liberties, such as in Portugal or Greece. Those rated (3) or below may have political prisoners and generally varying forms of censorship. Too often their security services practice torture. States rated (6) almost always have political prisoners; usually the legitimate media are completely under government supervision; there is no right of assembly; and, often, travel, residence, and occupation are narrowly restricted. However, at (6) there still may be relative freedom in private conversation, especially in the home; illegal demonstrations do take place; and underground literature is published. At (7) there is pervading fear, little independent expression takes place even in private, almost no public expressions of opposition emerge in the police-state environment, and imprisonment or execution is often swift and sure.

Political terror is an attempt by a government or private group to get its way through the use of murder, torture, exile, prevention of departure, police controls, or threats against the family. These weapons are usually directed against the expression of civil liberties. To this extent they surely are a part of the civil liberty "score." Unfortunately, because of their dramatic and newsworthy nature, such denials of civil liberties often become identified in the minds of informed persons with the whole of civil liberties.

Political terror is a tool of revolutionary repression of the right or left. When that repression is no longer necessary to achieve the suppression of civil liberties, political terror is replaced by implacable and well-organized but often less general and newsworthy controls. Of course, there is a certain unfathomable terror in the sealed totalitarian state, yet life can be lived with a normality in these states that is impossible in the more dramatically terrorized. It would be a mistake to dismiss this apparent anomaly as an expression of a Survey bias. For there is, with all the blood, a much wider range of organized and personal expression of political opinion and judgment in states such as India, or even Guatemala, than in more peaceful states such as Czechoslovakia.

In making the distinction between political terror and civil liberties as a whole we do not imply that the United States should not be urgently concerned with all violations of human rights and perhaps most urgently with those of political terror. Again it must be emphasized that the Survey is not a rating of the relative desirability of societies——but of certain explicit freedoms.

The Freedom Rating simply sums the political and civil liberties ratings, providing a thirteen-point scale from 2 to 14. States rating 5 or better have conventionally been considered to be "democracies" from the Survey's perspective, but the standard for democracy could be set at any level as desired.

The reporting period covered by this Survey (November 1987 to November 1988) does not correspond with the calendar of short-term events in the countries rated. For this reason the yearly Survey may mask or play down events that occur at the end of the year.

The Survey is aware that many of its judgments of what is or is not an independent country are questioned. The principle that we have used is a pragmatic one that combines several criteria. A country exists independently to the extent that persons from a central core of people identified with that country more than any other country rule in the name of their country through control of its territory, or at least what they define as the central area of that territory. It helps if a country, in the modern world, has some historical and geographical continuity. But historical existence in the past, such as that of Lithuania or Georgia in the USSR, or Tibet in China, is not enough to make the Survey's list. Whether a country's leaders are actually in control, or "rule" is also defined loosely. Many doubt, for example, the existence of a separate country of Transkei—and for good reason. However, the Survey believes that the independence or separateness of Transkei is comparable to that of Swaziland, Lesotho, Mongolia, Laos, or, in a different sense, Afghanistan or Lebanon. The separateness of the other homeland states is less clear, if only marginally.

Significant Declines in Freedom in 1988

Declines in freedom in 1988 were scattered, and none was substantial. Most important was the continuation of the erosion of freedom in **Malaysia.** In several of its states the use of certain words is now restricted to an Islamic context, and it is a crime to try to change a Muslim's religion. The imprisonment of opposition leaders has been supplemented by further interference with the already limited independence of the judiciary. The prime minister forced the ouster of the head of the supreme court as well as other judges that disagreed with him. Appeals to the court against security detentions were made impossible. The use of suspensions and other measures further emasculated the media. The suspension of parliament reduced political rights in **Jordan. Brunei's** nascent opposition party

TABLE 4

RELATED TERRITORIES: COMPARATIVE FREEDOMS

	Political Rights[1]	Civil Liberties[1]	Freedom Rating[2]
Australia			
Christmas Island	4	2	6
Cocos Island	4	2	6
Norfolk Island	4	2	6
Chile			
Easter Island	5	4 ↑	9
Denmark			
Faroe Islands	1	1	2
Greenland	1	1	2
France			
French Guiana	3	2	5
French Polynesia	3	2	5
Guadeloupe	3	2	5
Mahore (Mayotte)	2	2	4
Martinique	3	2	5
Monaco [4]	4	2	6
New Caledonia	2	2	4
Reunion	3	2	5
St. Pierre & Miquelon	2	2	4
Wallis & Fortuna	4	3	7
Israel			
Occupied Terrs.	5	5	10
Italy			
San Marino [3]	1	1	2
Vatican City [3]	6	4	10

Comparative Survey

	Political Rights[1]	Civil Liberties[1]	Freedom Rating[2]
Netherlands			
Aruba	1	1	2
Neth. Antilles	1	1	2
New Zealand			
Cook Islands	2	2	4
Niue	2	2	4
Tokelau Islands	4	2	6
Portugal			
Azores	2	2	4
Macao	3	4	7
Madeira	2	2	4
South Africa			
Bophuthatswana [4]	6	5	11
Ciskei [4]	6	6	12
SW Afr. (Namibia)	6	5	11
Venda [4]	6	6	12
Spain			
Canary Islands	1	2	3
Ceuta	2	3	5
Melilla	2	3	5
Switzerland			
Liechtenstein	3	1	4
United Kingdom			
Anguilla	2	2	4
Bermuda	2	1	3
B. Virgin Islands	2	1	3
Cayman Islands	2	2	4
Channel Islands	2	2	4
Falkland Islands	2	2	4
Gibraltar	1	2	3

	Political Rights[1]	Civil Liberties[1]	Freedom Rating[2]
United Kingdom (cont.)			
Hong Kong	4	3 ↓	7
Isle of Man	1	1	2
Montserrat	2	2	4
St. Helena	2	2	4
Turks and Caicos	2	2	4
United States			
American Samoa	2	2	4
Belau	2	2	4
Guam	2	2	4
Marshall Isls.	2	2	4
Micronesia (F.S.)	2	2	4
No. Marianas	1	2	3
Puerto Rico	2	1	3
Virgin Islands	2	2	4
France-Spain Condominium			
Andorra [3]	3	2 ∘	5

Notes to the Table

1. See Notes, Table 3.

2. See Notes, Table 3.

3. These states are not listed as independent because all have explicit legal forms of dependence on a particular country (or countries in the case of Andorra) in such areas as foreign affairs, defense, customs, or services.

4. The geography and history of these newly independent "homelands" cause us to consider them dependencies.

was disbanded and its leaders jailed. The attempt to create a democratic regime in **Haiti,** already failing in 1987, collapsed in 1988, turning the country over to arbitrary military rule. Nonviolent opposition was again dangerous. **Panama's** strongman, General Noriega, tore off the veils and took all but direct charge of the country. The remaining independence in the media was crushed and demonstrators regularly detained. **Transkei's** elected government was set aside in favor of a military regime, a pattern too common in Africa. (For **Zimbabwe** see "Other Changes and Trends" below.)

Significant Advances in Freedom

Major advances in freedom were recorded from nearly every part of the world.

Nigeria continued its slow movement toward another attempt at democracy. Local elections have been held and an indirectly elected constituent assembly has set to work, although political parties have still not taken part. The normally strong media are in the process of reestablishing their traditions. After the destruction of its fully democratic system, the new rulers in **Fiji** have moved toward a new constitutional system enshrining special rights for the Fiji natives. It is an advance over arbitrary rule, but still a long way from the democracy that existed before. **Mali** has introduced an electoral system that at least allows minimal choice. **China (Taiwan)** has ever-freer media. Opposition political activity is now fully accepted both in the streets and the legislature. In **Tunisia** many political prisoners have been released, exiles have returned, direct press censorship has been lifted.

In Latin America, **Chile** held a referendum on the continued rule of General Pinochet. Despite many doubts as to the legitimacy of the process, and the advantages offered by the repressive system of the state, the people voted against the system. By their vote they opted for a democratic election in 1989; the process and its results weakened the oppressive apparatus of the state in most spheres. In **Ecuador** a successful general election and runoff brought a moderate to power, thereby bringing to an end a particularly bitter conflict between the branches of government that had threatened the continuance of its democracy. At last successful, competitive elections without military interruptions are beginning to be part of Ecuador's

TABLE 5

COUNTRIES BY FREEDOM RATINGS

Most Free

2	4	7	11	13
Australia	Dominica	Mexico	Algeria	Burkina Faso
Austria	Dominican Rep.	Nepal	Cape	Burma
Barbados	Ecuador	Senegal	Verde Isls.	Burundi
Belgium	Greece	Sri Lanka	Iran	Chad
Canada	Israel	Western Samoa	Jordan	Congo
Costa Rica	Jamaica		Kuwait	Cuba
Denmark	Mauritius	**8**	Lebanon	Czechoslovakia
Iceland	Nauru		Maldives	Ethiopia
Ireland	Solomon Isls.	China (T)	Panama	Germany (E)
Italy	Uruguay	Tonga	South Africa	Guinea
Japan			Swaziland	Guinea-Bissau
Luxembourg	**5**	**9**	USSR	Malawi
Netherlands			Zambia	Mozambique
New Zealand	Antigua &	Bangladesh	Zimbabwe	Sao Tome &
Norway	Barbuda	Chile		Principe
Sweden	Bahamas	Egypt	**12**	Saudi Arabia
Switzerland	Bolivia	Fiji		Syria
Trinidad & Tob.	Botswana	Hungary	Afghanistan	Transkei
Tuvalu	Brazil	Malaysia	Brunei	Vietnam
United Kingdom	Colombia	Morocco	Cameroon	Zaire
United States	Cyprus (T)	Nicaragua	Cen. Afr. Rep.	
	Honduras	Singapore	China (M)	**14**
3	India	Sudan	Comoros	
	Korea (S)		Cote d'Ivoire	Albania
Argentina	Papua	**10**	Djibouti	Angola
Belize	New Guinea		Gabon	Benin
Cyprus (G)	Peru	Bahrain	Ghana	Bulgaria
European Com.	Philippines	Bhutan	Haiti	Cambodia
Finland	Suriname	Guyana	Kenya	Equatorial
France		Indonesia	Laos	Guinea
Germany (W)	**6**	Liberia	Lesotho	Iraq
Grenada		Madagascar	Libya	Korea (N)
Kiribati	El Salvador	Nigeria	Mali	Mongolia
Malta	Gambia	Poland	Mauritania	Romania
Portugal	Guatemala	Qatar	Niger	Somalia
St.Kitts-Nevis	Pakistan	Sierra Leone	Oman	Yemen (S)
St.Lucia	Thailand	Tunisia	Paraguay	
St.Vincent	Turkey	Uganda	Rwanda	
Spain	Vanuatu	United Arab	Seychelles	**Least Free**
Venezuela		Emirates	Tanzania	
		Yemen (N)	Togo	
		Yugoslavia		

tradition. In **El Salvador** new and more independent television programming, radio interviews, and new small publications have gotten around the stranglehold of the very conservative major print media. In addition, civilian leaders identified with the guerrilla movements, if not identical with them, have been able to return and speak openly for their cause. **Suriname's** elected civilian leaders have been able to reestablish the democratic system of the country's first years, both in the political and civil realms. The country still faces a small guerrilla movement among a disaffected people, and the problem of attaining complete control over its military.

The most dramatic move toward greater freedom in Latin America centered around the drama of **Mexico's** general election. In the past, Mexican elections have featured an overwhelming majority vote for the official presidential candidate of the dominant PRI party (picked secretly by a small elite group within the party) and PRI victory in all or nearly all legislative contests. A dedicated conservative party regularly attained fifteen or twenty percent of the vote from the middle class, especially in the north. Leftists received so few votes outside the PRI that most leftists campaigned on a factional basis within it. The PRI's electoral dominance was maintained by a combination of coercion, near-monopoly of the media, and presumed electoral fraud both in voting and tabulation. In spite of appearances, most voters either went through the motions of voting or did not vote. In 1988 a major leftist figure in the PRI quit the party, united the left behind him, and managed a major nationwide campaign. The same methods were used by the government as before, but the sheer size of the opposition effort, and its ability to break off parts of the PRI structure allowed the opposition to win nearly fifty percent of the reported vote. Conservatives and leftists won for the first time a significant number of legislative seats by election (by formula they had received seats before, but this new achievement transformed the legislature into a more effective body). The opposition claimed that the election was stolen through massive fraud. Certainly there was some fraud, it had become traditional, but how much of the government's eventual victory was due to fraud is impossible to determine without a major, and improbable, investigation.

At the beginning of 1988 **South Korea** had just gone through a traumatic presidential election in which the government's candidate had won with a narrow plurality. Although ideologically the three candidates running in opposition were not far apart, personality differences and regional loyalties could not be overcome in time to achieve victory. In addition, many South Koreans must have felt safer with a government candidate that retained the confidence of the military that had ruled in one form or another through most of the postwar period. The subsequent legislative elections in the spring allowed the opposition to achieve victory, and thus face a new president with an uncontrolled legislature for the first time. In this situation the country has steadily liberalized: many political prisoners have been released, and the corruption and abuse of power by past leaders have been brought increasingly into the spotlight by the courts and ever more aggressive media.

Pakistan's political system has oscillated between regimes based directly on the military and "transitional" civilian regimes with more or less military support. In 1988 Pakistan's military president continued to move hesitantly toward sharing power with an elected civilian government on the Westminster model. To maintain support for his position the president had instituted Islamic regulations that reduced civil liberties (for example, by reducing the equality of women before the law) and entrenched military officers throughout the society. In this situation it was unclear whether a truly open election with full party participation would take place in November. However, with the sudden death of President Zia the situation completely changed. The parties were allowed to campaign fully, and support for Zia's conservative allies plummeted. In a few weeks the opposition had come to power, the press was freer than ever, and women were being let out of jail as a symbolic reestablishment of their rights. In this period of euphoria, it is well to remember that the military and the president retain great, if somewhat vague, powers, and that Pakistan's civilian leaders have in the past also disappointed those who hoped for a permanent democracy.

Yugoslavia's continuing crisis of government has steadily eroded the power of central party and governmental authorities, thereby increasingly devolving power on regional officials. The process has seen an increasing involvement of the general public as people begin to take sides in the public quarrels of high officials or take to the streets in favor of popular (generally ethnic) causes.

On a worldwide scale the liberalization in the **USSR** is perhaps the most significant gain for freedom. In political rights this has meant a partial opening up of the decision-making process within the

47

communist party, and more effective and lively legislative bodies at all levels of the formal government. Yet most of the decision-making process at higher levels remains shrouded in mystery. The demands of the peoples of the Soviet Union for greater self-determination, demands expressed through popular action as well as regional governments, have been heard in forms and with a persistence unimaginable a few years ago. The reaction of Moscow to such demands has been mixed: some have been rejected, some have met with temporization, some seem to have been tacitly accepted. The main achievement, however, has been the mass organization of people, including communist leaders, in the Baltic republics, Armenia, and elsewhere, to openly press for policies not previously approved by Moscow. In civil liberties, change has meant the development of a much more open official press. Mass circulation publications now regularly and critically consider government policies and performance, and their alternatives, in many formerly forbidden areas. Movies long censored or suppressed are shown. Political prisoners continue to be released. Religious and economic freedoms are beginning to be countenanced. In the present climate, even when persons are detained, it seems to be for short periods. With all this, it is still true that the repressive apparatus, together with the lack of political choice, that has characterized the USSR remains in place. Theoretically, the gains of the last few years could be swept away overnight. But one suspects it would not be that easy. Too much hope has been aroused in too many millions; we are no longer speaking of the fortunes of a heroic but tiny group of hard core dissidents shuttling between Moscow and the camps.

Other Changes and Trends

Although there has been no decisive gain for freedom, by the end of 1988 it was time to recognize that the situation in **Afghanistan** has been steadily changing. With the government controlling little more than the major cities and the routes in between and the Soviets slowly withdrawing, political control is falling increasingly into the hands of a patchwork of resistance groups, or even local "neutralists". In Kabul and its environs, private discussion has been somewhat freed by the feeling of transition, with increasing numbers daring to say publicly they are neither for the guerrillas nor the communists. In many respects, Afghanistan is now in a state of anarchy comparable to that of Lebanon, and such anarchy gives a measure of freedom to those who survive.

The people of **Burma** made a major effort to overthrow their oppressive system in 1988. In the end they were defeated, and the military instituted a new, more explicitly military system. The ability of some leaders to continue to speak of alternatives in the aftermath of revolt suggested that there was some gain, but the brutality of the reimposition of tyranny offered little hope for permanent gain.

Following the general tendency in the communist world, the government of **Laos** has slowly eased its oppression in recent years. Buddhists are again more active; the government has allowed some opening of the flow of information from Thailand. Limited elections have been held.

Thailand is itself poised on the threshold of full democracy. Another successful election in 1988 was followed by the selection of the prime minister by a more regular process than in the past. However, the continued special powers surrounding the throne, and the insistence of military leaders that they play a direct role in politics makes us still hesitate to see the transition as having been achieved.

Zimbabwe took the final step and inaugurated one-party rule—and further strengthened discipline within that party. However, the continuing degree of open discussion in the society makes it impossible to reduce its overall rating, when compared to neighboring states.

In Latin America it should be noted that several democracies, notably **Brazil** and **Peru** are facing massive economic problems and a severe loss of confidence in the new, democratic political system. The hemisphere will be lucky to see such states through 1989 with their recent gains in freedom intact. If they do not make it through, much recent progress in the region could unravel.

Even though it does not directly affect the ratings, we cannot ignore the continuing civil strife, struggle, and starvation in the Sudan and Ethiopia, the racial and ethnic conflict that continues in countries such as South Africa or Burundi, or the heightened conflict in Israel's occupied territories (Palestine). Only when such conflicts are overcome will there be a chance for substantial progress toward greater freedom in these areas.

Comparative Survey

TABLE 6

COUNTRY RATINGS SINCE 1972

Country	72	74	76	78	80	81	82	83	84	85	86	87	88
Afghan-	4	7	7	7	7	7	7	7	7	7	7	7	6
istan	5	6	7	7	7	7	7	7	7	7	7	7	6
	PF	NF	NF	NF	NF	NF	NF	NF	NF	NF	NF	NF	12
Albania	7	7	7	7	7	7	7	7	7	7	7	7	7
	7	7	7	7	7	7	7	7	7	7	7	7	7
	NF	NF	NF	NF	NF	NF	NF	NF	NF	NF	NF	NF	14
Algeria	6	6	6	6	6	6	6	6	6	6	6	6	5
	6	6	6	6	6	6	6	6	6	6	6	6	6
	NF	NF	NF	NF	NF	NF	NF	NF	NF	NF	NF	NF	11
Angola1	7	6	6	7	7	7	7	7	7	7	7	7	7
	6	4	6	7	7	7	7	7	7	7	7	7	7
	NF	PF	NF	NF	NF	NF	NF	NF	NF	NF	NF	NF	14
Antigua &	2	2	2	2	2	2	2	2	2	2	2	2	2
Barbuda1	3	3	3	2	2	2	3	3	3	3	3	3	3
	F	F	F	F	F	F	F	F	F	F	F	F	5
Argentina	6	2	6	6	6	6	6	3	2	2	2	2	2
	3	4	5	5	5	5	5	3	2	2	1	1	1
	PF	PF	NF	NF	NF	NF	PF	PF	F	F	F	F	3
Australia	1	1	1	1	1	1	1	1	1	1	1	1	1
	1	1	1	1	1	1	1	1	1	1	1	1	1
	F	F	F	F	F	F	F	F	F	F	F	F	2
Austria	1	1	1	1	1	1	1	1	1	1	1	1	1
	1	1	1	1	1	1	1	1	1	1	1	1	1
	F	F	F	F	F	F	F	F	F	F	F	F	2

Notes to the Table

Ratings are from the Jan/Feb issues of the subsequent year in Freedom at Issue (eg. Jan/Feb 1973 rates 1972) through 1982. Ratings for 1983 and subsequently are based on this yearbook series (1983 from the 1983-84 edition, etc.). Previous editions of this table identified ratings from Freedom at Issue with the year of publication, instead of the previous year to which they applied. Because of this confusion the changeover to use of the book caused the ratings for 1982 to be omitted from the table. These ratings from the Jan/Feb 1983 FAI are included in this table for the first time. For reasons of space, ratings for 1973, 1975, and 1977 are omitted from this table, but may be obtained by consulting the 1985-86 annual (remembering they were listed there as 1974, 1976, and 1978, respectively).

Until 1988 the three lines are political rights, civil liberties, and status of freedom. Beginning with 1988 status of freedom is replaced by a summed "freedom rating", ranging from 2 to 14.

*. Indicates year of independence.

1. Until 1974 Angola, Mozambique, and Guinea-Bissau (formerly Portuguese Guinea) were evaluated together as Portugal Colonies (A), while Sao Tome and Cape Verde were Portugal (B). Until 1977 Antigua, Dominica, and St. Lucia were considered together as the West Indies Associ- ated States (and Grenada until 1974). Until 1974 Comoros and Djibouti (Territory of the Afars and Issas) were under "France: Overseas Territories", while Kiribati and Tuvalu were considered together as the Gilbert and Ellice Islands. Cyprus was regarded as a unit until 1980.

2. 1972 ratings for South Africa were white: 2,3,F and black: 5,6,NF.

3. Ratings for North Vietnam for 1972-1975 were 7,7,NF; those for South Vietnam were 4,5,PF for 1972-74, 7,7,NF for 1975.

Table 6 (continued)

Country	72	74	76	78	80	81	82	83	84	85	86	87	88
Bahamas	2 2 F	1 2 F	1 2 F	1 2 F	1 2 F	1 2 F	2 2 F	2 2 F	2 2 F	2 2 F	2 2 F	2 3 F	2 3 5
Bahrain	6 5 NF	4 4 PF	6 4 PF	6 4 PF	5 4 PF	5 5 PF	5 5 PF	5 5 PF	5 5 PF	5 5 PF	5 5 PF	5 5 PF	5 5 10
Bangla- desh	2 4 PF	4 4 PF	7 4 PF	4 4 PF	3 4 PF	3 4 PF	5 5 PF	6 5 PF	6 5 PF	5 5 PF	4 5 PF	4 5 PF	4 5 9
Barbados	1 1 F	1 1 F	1 1 F	1 1 F	1 1 F	1 1 F	1 1 F	1 1 F	1 2 F	1 2 F	1 1 F	1 1 F	1 1 2
Belgium	1 1 F	1 1 F	1 1 F	1 1 F	1 1 F	1 1 F	1 1 F	1 1 F	1 1 F	1 1 F	1 1 F	1 1 F	1 1 2
Belize	2 2 F	1 2 F	1 2 F	1 2 F	1 2 F	1 2 F	1 2 F	1 2 F	2 1 F	1 1 F	1 1 F	1 1 F	1 2 3
Benin (Dahomey)	7 5 NF	7 6 NF	7 7 NF	7 7 NF	7 6 NF	7 6 NF	7 6 NF	7 6 NF	7 7 NF	7 7 NF	7 7 NF	7 7 NF	7 7 14
Bhutan	4 4 PF	4 4 PF	4 4 PF	4 4 PF	5 5 PF	5 5 PF	5 5 PF	5 5 PF	5 5 PF	5 5 PF	5 5 PF	5 5 PF	5 5 10
Bolivia	5 4 PF	6 5 NF	6 4 PF	5 3 PF	7 5 NF	7 5 NF	2 3 F	2 3 F	2 3 F	2 3 F	2 3 F	2 3 F	2 3 5
Botswana	3 4 PF	2 3 F	2 3 F	2 3 F	2 3 F	2 3 F	2 3 F	2 3 F	2 3 F	2 3 F	2 3 F	2 3 F	2 3 5
Brazil	5 5 PF	4 4 PF	4 5 PF	4 4 PF	4 3 PF	4 3 PF	3 3 PF	3 3 PF	3 3 PF	3 2 F	2 2 F	2 2 F	2 3 5
Brunei	6 5 NF	6 5 NF	6 5 NF	6 5 NF	6 5 NF	6 5 NF	6 5 NF	6 5 NF	6 6 NF	6 5 PF	6 5 PF	6 5 PF	6 6 12
Bulgaria	7 7 NF	7 7 NF	7 7 NF	7 7 NF	7 7 NF	7 7 NF	7 7 NF	7 7 NF	7 7 NF	7 7 NF	7 7 NF	7 7 NF	7 7 14
Burkina Faso	3 4 PF	6 4 PF	5 5 PF	2 3 F	6 5 PF	6 5 PF	6 5 NF	6 5 PF	7 5 NF	7 6 NF	7 6 NF	7 6 NF	7 6 13
Burma	7 5 NF	7 5 NF	6 6 NF	7 6 NF	7 6 NF	7 6 NF	7 6 NF	7 7 NF	7 7 NF	7 7 NF	7 7 NF	7 7 NF	7 6 13

51

Comparative Survey

Table 6 (continued)

Country	72	74	76	78	80	81	82	83	84	85	86	87	88
Burundi	7	7	7	7	7	7	6	6	7	7	7	7	7
	7	7	6	6	6	6	6	6	6	6	6	6	6
	NF	NF	NF	NF	NF	NF	NF	NF	NF	NF	NF	NF	13
Cambodia	6	6	7	7	7	7	7	7	7	7	7	7	7
	5	6	7	7	7	7	7	7	7	7	7	7	7
	NF	NF	NF	NF	NF	NF	NF	NF	NF	NF	NF	NF	14
Cameroon	6	6	7	6	6	6	6	6	6	6	6	6	6
	4	4	5	5	6	6	6	6	7	7	6	6	6
	PF	PF	NF	NF	NF	NF	NF	NF	NF	NF	NF	NF	12
Canada	1	1	1	1	1	1	1	1	1	1	1	1	1
	1	1	1	1	1	1	1	1	1	1	1	1	1
	F	F	F	F	F	F	F	F	F	F	F	F	2
Cape Verde Isls.[1]	5	5	6	6	6	6	6	6	6	6	6	5	5
	6	5	6	6	6	6	6	6	7	7	6	6	6
	NF	PF	NF	NF	NF	NF	NF	NF	NF	NF	NF	PF	11
Central Afr. Rp.	7	7	7	7	7	7	7	7	7	7	7	6	6
	7	7	7	7	6	5	5	5	6	6	6	6	6
	NF	NF	NF	NF	NF	NF	NF	NF	NF	NF	NF	NF	12
Chad	6	6	7	6	6	7	6	7	7	7	7	6	6
	7	7	6	6	6	6	7	6	7	7	7	7	7
	NF	NF	NF	NF	NF	NF	NF	NF	NF	NF	NF	NF	13
Chile	1	7	7	6	6	6	6	6	6	6	6	6	5
	2	5	5	5	5	5	5	5	5	5	5	5	4
	F	NF	NF	NF	PF	PF	NF	PF	PF	PF	PF	PF	9
China (M)	7	7	7	6	6	6	6	6	6	6	6	6	6
	7	7	7	6	6	6	6	6	6	6	6	6	6
	NF	NF	NF	NF	NF	NF	NF	NF	NF	NF	NF	NF	12
China (T)	6	6	5	5	5	5	5	5	5	5	5	5	5
	5	5	5	4	6	5	5	5	5	5	5	4	3
	NF	NF	PF	PF	PF	PF	PF	PF	PF	PF	PF	PF	8
Colombia	2	2	2	2	2	2	2	2	2	2	2	2	2
	2	2	3	3	3	3	3	3	3	3	3	3	3
	F	F	F	F	F	F	F	F	F	F	F	F	5
Comoros[1]	4	2	5	5	4	4	4	4	5	6	6	6	6
	4	2	3	4	5	5	5	4	5	6	6	6	6
	PF	F	PF	PF	PF	PF	PF	PF	PF	NF	NF	NF	12
Congo	7	5	5	7	7	7	7	7	7	7	7	7	7
	7	6	6	6	7	6	6	6	6	6	6	6	6
	NF	PF	PF	NF	NF	NF	NF	NF	NF	NF	NF	NF	13
Costa Rica	1	1	1	1	1	1	1	1	1	1	1	1	1
	1	1	1	1	1	1	1	1	1	1	1	1	1
	F	F	F	F	F	F	F	F	F	F	F	F	2
Cote d'Ivoire	6	6	6	6	6	5	5	5	6	6	6	6	6
	6	6	5	5	5	5	5	5	5	5	5	5	6
	NF	NF	NF	NF	PF	PF	PF	PF	PF	PF	PF	PF	12

Table 6 (continued)

Country	72	74	76	78	80	81	82	83	84	85	86	87	88
Cuba	7	7	7	6	6	6	6	6	6	6	6	6	7
	7	7	6	6	6	6	6	6	6	6	6	6	6
	NF	NF	NF	NF	NF	NF	NF	NF	NF	NF	NF	NF	13
Cyprus(G)2	2	4	3	3	3	1	1	1	1	1	1	1	1
	3	4	4	4	3	2	2	2	2	2	2	2	2
	F	PF	PF	PF	PF	F	F	F	F	F	F	F	3
Cyprus(T)2						4	4	4	4	3	2	2	2
						3	3	3	3	3	3	3	3
						PF	PF	PF	PF	PF	F	F	5
Czecho-slovakia	7	7	7	7	7	7	7	7	7	7	7	7	7
	7	7	6	6	6	6	6	6	6	6	6	6	6
	NF	NF	NF	NF	NF	NF	NF	NF	NF	NF	NF	NF	13
Denmark	1	1	1	1	1	1	1	1	1	1	1	1	1
	1	1	1	1	1	1	1	1	1	1	1	1	1
	F	F	F	F	F	F	F	F	F	F	F	F	2
Djibouti1	4	4	3	2	3	3	5	5	5	6	6	6	6
	4	3	3	3	4	5	6	6	6	6	6	6	6
	PF	PF	PF	F*	PF	PF	NF	NF	PF	NF	NF	NF	12
Dominica1	2	2	2	2	2	2	2	2	2	2	2	2	2
	3	3	3	3	2	2	2	2	2	2	2	2	2
	F	F	F	F*	F	F	F	F	F	F	F	F	4
Dominican Republic	3	4	4	2	2	2	1	1	1	1	1	1	1
	2	2	3	2	3	3	2	2	3	3	3	3	3
	F	PF	PF	F	F	F	F	F	F	F	F	F	4
Ecuador	7	7	6	5	2	2	2	2	2	2	2	2	2
	3	5	5	3	2	2	2	2	2	3	3	3	2
	PF	NF	PF	PF	F	F	F	F	F	F	F	F	4
Egypt	6	6	5	5	5	5	5	5	4	4	5	5	5
	6	4	4	5	5	6	5	5	4	4	4	4	4
	NF	PF	PF	PF	PF	PF	PF	PF	PF	PF	PF	PF	9
El Salvador	2	2	3	4	6	5	4	4	3	2	3	3	3
	3	3	3	4	4	5	5	5	5	4	4	4	3
	F	F	PF	PF	PF	PF	PF	PF	PF	PF	PF	PF	6
Eq. Guinea	6	6	6	7	7	7	6	7	7	7	7	7	7
	6	6	7	7	6	6	6	6	6	7	7	7	7
	NF	NF	NF	NF	NF	NF	NF	NF	NF	NF	NF	NF	14
Ethiopia	5	6	7	7	7	7	7	7	7	7	7	6	6
	6	5	6	7	7	7	7	7	7	7	7	7	7
	NF	NF	NF	NF	NF	NF	NF	NF	NF	NF	NF	NF	13
Fiji	2	2	2	2	2	2	2	2	2	2	2	6	5
	2	2	2	2	2	2	2	2	2	2	2	5	4
	F	F	F	F	F	F	F	F	F	F	F	PF	9
Finland	2	2	2	2	2	2	2	2	2	2	2	1	1
	2	2	2	2	2	2	2	2	2	2	2	2	2
	F	F	F	F	F	F	F	F	F	F	F	F	3

53

Comparative Survey

Table 6 (continued)

Country	72	74	76	78	80	81	82	83	84	85	86	87	88
France	1	1	1	1	1	1	1	1	1	1	1	1	1
	2	2	1	2	2	2	2	2	2	2	2	2	2
	F	F	F	F	F	F	F	F	F	F	F	F	3
Gabon	6	6	6	6	6	6	6	6	6	6	6	6	6
	6	6	6	6	6	6	6	6	6	6	6	6	6
	NF	NF	NF	NF	NF	NF	NF	NF	NF	NF	NF	NF	12
Gambia	2	2	2	2	2	3	3	3	3	3	3	3	3
	2	2	2	2	2	4	3	4	4	4	4	3	3
	F	F	F	F	F	PF	PF	PF	PF	PF	PF	PF	6
Germany (East)	7	7	7	7	7	7	7	7	7	7	7	7	7
	7	7	7	6	6	7	7	7	6	6	6	6	6
	NF	NF	NF	NF	NF	NF	NF	NF	NF	NF	NF	NF	13
Germany (West)	1	1	1	1	1	1	1	1	1	1	1	1	1
	1	1	1	2	2	2	2	2	2	2	2	2	2
	F	F	F	F	F	F	F	F	F	F	F	F	3
Ghana	6	7	7	6	2	2	6	6	7	7	7	7	6
	6	5	5	4	3	3	5	5	6	6	6	6	6
	NF	NF	NF	PF	F	F	NF	NF	NF	NF	NF	NF	12
Greece	6	2	2	2	2	1	1	1	1	2	2	2	2
	6	2	2	2	2	2	2	2	2	2	2	2	2
	NF	F	F	F	F	F	F	F	F	F	F	F	4
Grenada	2	2	2	2	5	6	6	7	5	2	2	2	2
	3	4	4	3	5	5	5	6	3	3	2	1	1
	F	PF*	PF	F	PF	NF	NF	NF	PF	F	F	F	3
Guatemala	2	4	4	3	5	6	6	6	5	4	3	3	3
	3	3	3	4	6	6	6	6	6	4	3	3	3
	F	PF	PF	PF	PF	NF	NF	NF	PF	PF	PF	PF	6
Guinea	7	7	7	7	7	7	7	7	7	7	7	7	7
	7	7	7	7	7	7	7	7	5	5	5	6	6
	NF	NF	NF	NF	NF	NF	NF	NF	NF	NF	NF	NF	13
Guinea-Bissau	7	6	6	6	6	6	6	7	6	6	6	6	6
	6	6	6	6	6	6	6	6	6	6	7	7	7
	NF	NF*	NF	NF	NF	NF	NF	NF	NF	NF	NF	NF	13
Guyana	2	4	3	4	4	5	5	5	5	5	5	5	5
	2	3	3	3	4	4	4	5	5	5	5	5	5
	F	PF	PF	PF	PF	PF	PF	PF	PF	PF	PF	PF	10
Haiti	7	6	6	7	6	7	7	7	7	7	5	6	7
	6	6	6	6	6	6	6	6	6	6	4	5	5
	NF	NF	NF	NF	NF	NF	NF	NF	NF	NF	PF	PF	12
Honduras	7	6	6	6	4	3	2	3	2	2	2	2	2
	3	3	3	3	3	3	3	3	3	3	3	3	3
	PF	PF	PF	PF	PF	PF	F	PF	F	F	F	F	5
Hungary	6	6	6	6	6	6	6	6	6	5	5	5	5
	6	6	6	5	5	5	5	5	5	5	5	4	4
	NF	NF	NF	NF	NF	NF	NF	NF	PF	PF	PF	PF	9

54

Table 6 (continued)

Country	72	74	76	78	80	81	82	83	84	85	86	87	88
Iceland	1	1	1	1	1	1	1	1	1	1	1	1	1
	1	1	1	1	1	1	1	1	1	1	1	1	1
	F	F	F	F	F	F	F	F	F	F	F	F	2
India	2	2	2	2	2	2	2	2	2	2	2	2	2
	3	3	5	2	3	3	3	3	3	3	3	3	3
	F	F	PF	F	F	F	F	F	F	F	F	F	5
Indonesia	5	5	5	5	5	5	5	5	5	5	5	5	5
	5	5	5	5	5	5	5	5	6	6	6	6	5
	PF	PF	PF	PF	PF	PF	PF	PF	PF	PF	PF	PF	10
Iran	5	5	6	6	5	6	6	6	5	5	5	5	5
	6	6	6	5	6	6	6	6	6	6	6	6	6
	NF	NF	NF	PF	PF	NF	NF	NF	PF	PF	PF	PF	11
Iraq	7	7	7	7	6	6	6	6	7	7	7	7	7
	7	7	7	6	7	7	7	7	7	7	7	7	7
	NF	NF	NF	NF	NF	NF	NF	NF	NF	NF	NF	NF	14
Ireland	1	1	1	1	1	1	1	1	1	1	1	1	1
	2	2	1	1	1	1	1	1	1	1	1	1	1
	F	F	F	F	F	F	F	F	F	F	F	F	2
Israel	2	2	2	2	2	2	2	2	2	2	2	2	2
	3	3	3	2	2	2	2	2	2	2	2	2	2
	F	F	F	F	F	F	F	F	F	F	F	F	4
Italy	1	1	2	2	1	1	1	1	1	1	1	1	1
	2	2	1	2	2	2	2	2	1	1	1	1	1
	F	F	F	F	F	F	F	F	F	F	F	F	2
Jamaica	1	1	1	2	2	2	2	2	2	2	2	2	2
	2	2	3	3	3	3	3	3	3	3	3	2	2
	F	F	F	F	F	F	F	F	F	F	F	F	4
Japan	2	2	2	2	1	1	1	1	1	1	1	1	1
	1	1	1	1	1	1	1	1	1	1	1	1	1
	F	F	F	F	F	F	F	F	F	F	F	F	2
Jordan	6	6	6	6	6	6	6	6	5	5	5	5	6
	6	6	6	6	6	6	6	6	5	5	5	5	5
	NF	NF	NF	NF	NF	NF	NF	NF	PF	PF	PF	PF	11
Kenya	5	5	5	5	5	5	5	5	6	6	6	6	6
	4	4	5	4	4	4	5	5	5	5	5	6	6
	PF	PF	PF	PF	PF	PF	PF	PF	PF	PF	PF	NF	12
Kiribati	2	2	2	2	2	2	2	1	1	1	1	1	1
	2	2	2	2	2	2	2	2	2	2	2	2	2
	F	F	F	F*	F	F	F	F	F	F	F	F	3
Korea (N)	7	7	7	7	7	7	7	7	7	7	7	7	7
	7	7	7	7	7	7	7	7	7	7	7	7	7
	NF	NF	NF	NF	NF	NF	NF	NF	NF	NF	NF	NF	14
Korea (S)	5	5	5	5	5	5	5	5	5	4	4	4	2
	6	6	6	5	6	6	6	6	5	5	5	4	3
	NF	PF	NF	PF	PF	PF	PF	PF	PF	PF	PF	PF	5

Comparative Survey

Table 6 (continued)

Country	72	74	76	78	80	81	82	83	84	85	86	87	88
Kuwait	4	4	6	6	6	4	4	4	4	4	6	6	6
	4	3	5	3	4	4	4	4	4	4	5	5	5
	PF	PF	NF	PF	PF	PF	PF	PF	PF	PF	PF	PF	11
Laos	5	5	7	7	7	7	7	7	7	7	7	7	6
	5	5	7	7	7	7	7	7	7	7	7	7	6
	PF	PF	NF	NF	NF	NF	NF	NF	NF	NF	NF	NF	12
Lebanon	2	2	4	4	4	4	4	5	5	5	5	6	6
	2	2	4	4	4	4	4	4	4	4	4	5	5
	F	F	PF	PF	PF	PF	PF	PF	PF	PF	PF	PF	11
Lesotho	7	5	5	5	5	5	5	5	5	5	5	5	6
	4	4	4	4	5	5	5	5	5	5	5	6	6
	NF	PF	PF	PF	PF	PF	PF	PF	PF	PF	PF	PF	12
Liberia	6	6	6	6	6	6	6	5	6	5	5	5	5
	6	3	4	4	6	6	6	5	5	5	5	5	5
	NF	PF	PF	PF	NF	NF	NF	PF	PF	PF	PF	PF	10
Libya	7	7	7	6	6	6	6	6	6	6	6	6	6
	6	7	6	6	6	7	6	6	6	6	6	6	6
	NF	NF	NF	NF	NF	NF	NF	NF	NF	NF	NF	NF	12
Luxem-bourg	2	2	2	1	1	1	1	1	1	1	1	1	1
	1	1	1	1	1	1	1	1	1	1	1	1	1
	F	F	F	F	F	F	F	F	F	F	F	F	2
Madagascar (Malagasy Rep.)	5	5	6	5	6	6	5	5	5	5	5	5	5
	3	4	5	5	6	6	5	6	6	6	5	5	5
	PF	PF	NF	PF	NF	NF	PF	PF	PF	PF	PF	PF	10
Malawi	7	7	7	6	6	6	6	6	6	6	6	6	6
	6	6	6	6	7	7	7	7	7	7	7	7	7
	NF	NF	NF	NF	NF	NF	NF	NF	NF	NF	NF	NF	13
Malaysia	2	3	3	3	3	3	3	3	3	3	3	3	4
	3	3	4	3	4	4	4	4	5	5	5	5	5
	F	PF	PF	PF	PF	PF	PF	PF	PF	PF	PF	PF	9
Maldives	3	3	4	5	5	5	5	5	5	5	5	5	5
	2	2	4	5	5	5	5	5	5	5	6	6	6
	PF	PF	PF	PF	PF	PF	PF	PF	PF	PF	PF	PF	11
Mali	7	7	7	7	7	7	7	7	7	7	7	7	6
	6	6	7	7	6	6	6	6	6	6	6	6	6
	NF	NF	NF	NF	NF	NF	NF	NF	NF	NF	NF	NF	12
Malta	1	1	1	2	2	2	2	2	2	2	2	1	1
	2	1	2	2	3	3	3	4	4	4	4	2	2
	F	F	F	F	F	F	F	PF	PF	PF	PF	F	3
Mauri-tania	6	5	6	6	7	7	7	7	7	7	7	6	6
	6	6	6	6	6	6	6	6	6	6	6	6	6
	NF	NF	NF	NF	NF	NF	NF	NF	NF	NF	NF	NF	12
Mauritius	3	3	2	2	2	2	2	2	2	2	2	2	2
	2	2	2	4	4	3	2	2	2	2	2	2	2
	F	F	F	PF	PF	F	F	F	F	F	F	F	4

Table 6 (continued)

Country	72	74	76	78	80	81	82	83	84	85	86	87	88
Mexico	5	4	4	4	3	3	3	3	3	4	4	4	3
	3	3	4	4	4	4	4	4	4	4	4	4	4
	PF	PF	PF	PF	PF	PF	PF	PF	PF	PF	PF	PF	7
Mongolia	7	7	7	7	7	7	7	7	7	7	7	7	7
	7	7	7	7	7	7	7	7	7	7	7	7	7
	NF	NF	NF	NF	NF	NF	NF	NF	NF	NF	NF	NF	14
Morocco	5	5	5	3	4	4	4	4	4	4	4	4	4
	4	5	5	4	4	5	5	5	5	5	5	5	5
	PF	PF	PF	PF	PF	PF	PF	PF	PF	PF	PF	PF	9
Mozam-bique[1]	7	6	7	7	7	7	7	7	6	6	6	6	6
	6	6	7	7	7	7	7	6	7	7	7	7	7
	NF	NF	NF	NF	NF	NF	NF	NF	NF	NF	NF	NF	13
Nauru	2	2	2	2	2	2	2	2	2	2	2	2	2
	2	2	2	2	2	2	2	2	2	2	2	2	2
	F	F	F	F	F	F	F	F	F	F	F	F	4
Nepal	6	6	6	6	3	3	3	3	3	3	3	3	3
	5	5	5	5	4	4	4	4	4	4	4	4	4
	NF	NF	NF	NF	PF	PF	PF	PF	PF	PF	PF	PF	7
Nether-lands	1	1	1	1	1	1	1	1	1	1	1	1	1
	1	1	1	1	1	1	1	1	1	1	1	1	1
	F	F	F	F	F	F	F	F	F	F	F	F	2
New Zealand	1	1	1	1	1	1	1	1	1	1	1	1	1
	1	1	1	1	1	1	1	1	1	1	1	1	1
	F	F	F	F	F	F	F	F	F	F	F	F	2
Nicaragua	4	5	5	5	5	6	6	6	5	5	5	5	5
	3	4	5	5	5	5	5	5	5	5	6	5	4
	PF	PF	PF	PF	PF	PF	PF	PF	PF	PF	PF	PF	9
Niger	6	7	7	7	7	7	7	7	7	7	7	7	6
	6	6	6	6	6	6	6	6	6	6	6	6	6
	NF	NF	NF	NF	NF	NF	NF	NF	NF	NF	NF	NF	12
Nigeria	6	6	6	5	2	2	2	2	7	7	7	6	5
	4	4	4	3	3	3	3	3	5	5	5	5	5
	PF	PF	PF	PF	F	F	F	F	NF	NF	NF	PF	10
Norway	1	1	1	1	1	1	1	1	1	1	1	1	1
	1	1	1	1	1	1	1	1	1	1	1	1	1
	F	F	F	F	F	F	F	F	F	F	F	F	2
Oman	7	7	6	6	6	6	6	6	6	6	6	6	6
	6	6	6	6	6	6	6	6	6	6	6	6	6
	NF	NF	NF	NF	NF	NF	NF	NF	NF	NF	NF	NF	12
Pakistan	3	3	4	6	7	7	7	7	7	4	4	4	3
	5	5	5	5	5	5	5	5	5	5	5	5	3
	PF	PF	PF	PF	NF	NF	NF	NF	NF	PF	PF	PF	6
Panama	7	7	7	5	4	4	5	5	4	6	6	5	6
	6	6	6	5	4	4	5	4	3	3	3	5	5
	NF	NF	NF	PF	PF	PF	PF	PF	PF	PF	PF	PF	11

Table 6 (continued)

Country	72	74	76	78	80	81	82	83	84	85	86	87	88
Papua New Guinea	4	3	2	2	2	2	2	2	2	2	2	2	2
	2	2	2	2	2	2	2	2	2	2	2	2	3
	PF	PF	F	F	F	F	F	F	F	F	F	F	5
Paraguay	4	5	5	5	5	5	5	5	5	5	5	5	6
	6	5	6	5	5	5	5	5	5	5	5	5	6
	PF	PF	NF	PF	PF	PF	PF	PF	PF	PF	PF	PF	12
Peru	7	6	6	5	2	2	2	2	2	2	2	2	2
	5	6	4	4	3	3	3	3	3	3	3	3	3
	NF	NF	PF	PF	F	F	F	F	F	F	F	F	5
Philip-pines	4	5	5	5	5	5	4	5	4	4	4	2	3
	6	5	5	5	5	5	4	5	4	3	2	2	3
	PF	PF	PF	PF	PF	PF	PF	PF	PF	PF	PF	F	5
Poland	6	6	6	6	6	5	6	6	6	6	6	5	5
	6	6	6	5	4	4	5	5	5	5	5	5	5
	NF	NF	NF	PF	PF	PF	NF	PF	PF	PF	PF	PF	10
Portugal	5	5	2	2	2	2	1	1	1	1	1	1	1
	6	3	2	2	2	2	2	2	2	2	2	2	2
	NF	PF	F	F	F	F	F	F	F	F	F	F	3
Qatar	6	6	5	5	5	5	5	5	5	5	5	5	5
	5	5	5	5	5	5	5	5	5	5	5	5	5
	NF	NF	PF	PF	PF	PF	PF	PF	PF	PF	PF	PF	10
Romania	7	7	7	7	7	7	7	7	7	7	7	7	7
	6	6	6	6	6	6	6	6	7	7	7	7	7
	NF	NF	NF	NF	NF	NF	NF	NF	NF	NF	NF	NF	14
Rwanda	7	7	7	6	6	6	6	6	6	6	6	6	6
	6	5	5	6	6	6	6	6	6	6	6	6	6
	NF	NF	NF	NF	NF	NF	NF	NF	NF	NF	NF	NF	12
St.Kitts-Nevis[1]	2	2	2	2	2	2	2	2	1	1	1	1	1
	3	3	3	3	3	3	3	2	1	1	1	2	2
	F	F	F	F	F	F	F	F*	F	F	F	F	3
St.Lucia[1]	2	2	2	2	2	2	2	2	1	1	1	1	1
	3	3	3	3	3	2	2	2	2	2	2	2	2
	F	F	F	F	F	F	F	F	F	F	F	F	3
St.Vincent	2	2	2	2	2	2	2	2	2	2	2	1	1
	2	2	2	2	2	2	2	2	2	2	2	2	2
	F	F	F	F	F	F	F	F	F	F	F	F	3
Sao Tome & Principe[1]	5	5	5	6	6	6	6	7	7	7	7	7	6
	6	5	5	5	6	6	6	7	7	7	7	7	7
	NF	PF	PF	NF	NF	NF	NF	NF	NF	NF	NF	NF	13
Saudi Arabia	6	6	6	6	6	6	6	6	6	6	6	6	6
	6	6	6	6	6	6	6	7	7	7	7	7	7
	NF	NF	NF	NF	NF	NF	NF	NF	NF	NF	NF	NF	13
Senegal	6	6	6	4	4	4	4	4	3	3	3	3	3
	6	5	4	3	4	4	4	4	4	4	4	4	4
	NF	NF	PF	PF	PF	PF	PF	PF	PF	PF	PF	PF	7

Table 6 (continued)

Country	72	74	76	78	80	81	82	83	84	85	86	87	88
Sey-chelles[1]	3 2 PF	2 2 F	1 2 F*	6 4 PF	6 6 NF	6 6 NF	6 6 NF	6 6 NF	6 6 NF	6 6 NF	6 6 NF	6 6 NF	6 6 12
Sierra Leone	4 5 PF	6 5 PF	6 5 PF	6 5 PF	5 5 PF	5 5 PF	5 5 PF	5 5 PF	4 5 PF	5 5 PF	5 5 PF	5 5 PF	5 5 10
Singapore	5 5 PF	5 5 PF	5 5 PF	5 5 PF	5 5 PF	4 5 PF	4 5 PF	4 5 PF	4 5 PF	4 5 PF	4 5 PF	4 5 PF	4 5 9
Solomons	4 2 PF	4 2 PF	2 2 F	2 2 F*	2 2 F	2 2 F	2 2 F	2 2 F	2 3 F	2 3 F	2 2 F	2 2 F	2 2 4
Somalia	7 6 NF	7 6 NF	7 7 NF	7 7 NF	7 7 NF	7 7 NF	7 7 NF	7 7 NF	7 7 NF	7 7 NF	7 7 NF	7 7 NF	7 7 14
South Africa[2]		4 5 PF	4 5 PF	5 6 PF	5 6 PF	5 6 NF	5 6 NF	5 6 PF	5 6 PF	5 6 PF	5 6 PF	5 6 PF	5 6 PF
Spain	5 6 NF	5 5 PF	5 3 PF	2 3 F	2 3 F	2 3 F	1 2 F	1 2 F	1 2 F	1 2 F	1 2 F	1 2 F	1 2 3
Sri Lanka	2 3 F	2 3 F	2 3 F	2 3 F	2 3 F	2 3 F	2 3 F	3 4 PF	3 4 PF	3 4 PF	3 4 PF	3 4 PF	3 4 7
Sudan	6 6 NF	6 6 NF	6 6 NF	5 5 PF	5 5 PF	5 6 PF	5 5 PF	5 5 PF	6 6 NF	6 6 NF	4 5 PF	4 5 PF	4 5 9
Suriname	2 2 F	2 2 F	2 2 F	2 2 F	7 5 NF	7 5 NF	7 6 NF	7 6 NF	7 6 NF	6 6 NF	6 6 NF	4 4 PF	3 2 5
Swaziland	4 2 PF	6 4 PF	6 4 PF	6 5 PF	5 5 PF	5 5 PF	5 5 PF	5 5 PF	5 6 PF	5 6 PF	5 6 PF	5 6 PF	5 6 11
Sweden	1 1 F	1 1 F	1 1 F	1 1 F	1 1 F	1 1 F	1 1 F	1 1 F	1 1 F	1 1 F	1 1 F	1 1 F	1 1 2
Switzer-land	1 1 F	1 1 F	1 1 F	1 1 F	1 1 F	1 1 F	1 1 F	1 1 F	1 1 F	1 1 F	1 1 F	1 1 F	1 1 2
Syria	7 7 NF	6 7 NF	6 6 NF	5 6 PF	5 6 NF	5 6 NF	5 7 NF	6 7 NF	6 7 NF	6 7 NF	6 7 NF	6 7 NF	6 7 13
Tanzania	6 6 NF	6 6 NF	6 6 NF	6 6 NF	6 6 NF	6 6 NF	6 6 NF	6 6 NF	6 6 NF	6 6 NF	6 6 NF	6 6 NF	6 6 12

Comparative Survey

Table 6 (continued)

Country	72	74	76	78	80	81	82	83	84	85	86	87	88
Thailand	7	5	6	6	3	3	3	3	3	3	3	3	3
	5	3	6	4	4	4	4	4	4	4	3	3	3
	NF	PF	NF	PF	PF	PF	PF	PF	PF	PF	PF	PF	6
Togo	7	7	7	7	7	7	7	7	6	6	6	6	6
	5	6	6	6	6	6	6	6	6	6	6	6	6
	NF	NF	NF	NF	NF	NF	NF	NF	NF	NF	NF	NF	12
Tonga	4	5	5	5	5	5	5	5	5	5	5	5	5
	2	3	3	3	3	3	3	3	3	3	3	3	3
	PF	PF	PF	PF	PF	PF	PF	PF	PF	PF	PF	PF	8
Transkei			6	5	5	5	5	5	5	5	5	5	7
			5	5	6	6	6	6	6	6	6	6	6
			NF*	PF	PF	PF	PF	PF	PF	PF	PF	PF	13
Trinidad & Tobago	2	2	2	2	2	2	1	1	1	1	1	1	1
	3	2	2	2	2	2	2	2	2	2	2	1	1
	F	F	F	F	F	F	F	F	F	F	F	F	2
Tunisia	6	6	6	6	6	5	5	5	5	5	6	5	6
	5	5	5	5	5	5	5	5	5	5	5	6	4
	NF	NF	NF	NF	PF	PF	PF	PF	PF	PF	PF	PF	10
Turkey	3	2	2	2	5	5	4	4	3	3	3	2	2
	4	3	3	3	5	5	5	5	5	5	4	4	4
	PF	F	F	F	PF	PF	PF	PF	PF	PF	PF	PF	6
Tuvalu1	2	2	2	2	2	2	1	1	1	1	1	1	1
	2	2	2	2	2	2	2	2	2	2	1	1	2
	F	F	F	F*	F	F	F	F	F	F	F	F	2
Uganda	7	7	7	7	5	5	5	4	4	5	5	5	5
	7	7	7	7	5	5	5	5	5	4	4	4	5
	NF	NF	NF	NF	PF	PF	PF	PF	PF	PF	PF	PF	10
USSR	6	6	7	7	6	6	6	6	7	7	7	7	6
	6	6	6	6	7	7	7	7	7	7	7	6	5
	NF	NF	NF	NF	NF	NF	NF	NF	NF	NF	NF	NF	11
United Arab Emirates	7	6	5	5	5	5	5	5	5	5	5	5	5
	5	5	5	5	5	5	5	5	5	5	5	5	5
	NF	NF	PF	PF	PF	PF	PF	PF	PF	PF	PF	PF	10
United Kingdom	1	1	1	1	1	1	1	1	1	1	1	1	1
	1	1	1	1	1	1	1	1	1	1	1	1	1
	F	F	F	F	F	F	F	F	F	F	F	F	2
United States	1	1	1	1	1	1	1	1	1	1	1	1	1
	1	1	1	1	1	1	1	1	1	1	1	1	1
	F	F	F	F	F	F	F	F	F	F	F	F	2
Uruguay	3	5	6	6	5	5	5	5	5	2	2	2	2
	4	5	6	6	5	5	4	4	4	2	2	2	2
	PF	PF	NF	NF	PF	PF	PF	PF	PF	F	F	F	4
Vanuatu	4	4	3	3	2	2	2	2	2	2	2	2	2
	3	3	3	3	3	3	2	4	4	4	4	4	4
	PF	PF	PF	PF	F*	F	F	PF	PF	PF	PF	PF	6

Table 6 (continued)

Country	72	74	76	78	80	81	82	83	84	85	86	87	88
Venezuela	2	2	1	1	1	1	1	1	1	1	1	1	1
	2	2	2	2	2	2	2	2	2	2	2	2	2
	F	F	F	F	F	F	F	F	F	F	F	F	3
Vietnam[3]			7	7	7	7	7	7	7	7	7	6	6
			7	7	7	7	6	6	6	7	7	7	7
			NF	NF	NF	NF	NF	NF	NF	NF	NF	NF	13
Western Samoa	4	4	4	4	4	4	4	4	4	4	4	4	4
	2	2	2	2	3	3	3	3	3	3	3	3	3
	PF	PF	PF	PF	PF	PF	PF	PF	PF	PF	PF	PF	7
Yemen (N)	4	5	6	6	6	6	6	6	5	5	5	5	5
	4	4	5	5	5	5	5	5	5	5	5	5	5
	PF	PF	NF	NF	NF	NF	NF	NF	PF	PF	PF	PF	10
Yemen (S)	7	7	7	7	6	6	6	6	6	6	6	6	7
	7	7	7	7	7	7	7	7	7	7	7	7	7
	NF	NF	NF	NF	NF	NF	NF	NF	NF	NF	NF	NF	14
Yugoslavia	6	6	6	6	6	6	6	6	6	6	6	6	5
	6	6	6	5	5	5	5	5	5	5	5	5	5
	NF	NF	NF	NF	NF	NF	NF	PF	PF	PF	PF	PF	10
Zaire	7	7	7	7	6	6	6	6	6	7	7	6	6
	6	6	6	6	6	6	7	7	7	7	7	7	7
	NF	NF	NF	NF	NF	NF	NF	NF	NF	NF	NF	NF	13
Zambia	5	5	5	5	5	5	5	5	5	5	5	5	6
	5	4	5	5	6	6	6	6	5	5	5	5	5
	PF	PF	PF	PF	PF	PF	PF	PF	PF	PF	PF	PF	11
Zimbabwe	6	6	6	5	3	3	3	4	4	4	4	5	6
	5	5	5	5	4	5	5	5	5	6	6	6	5
	NF	NF	NF	PF	PF	PF	PF	PF	PF	PF	PF	PF	11

Comparative Survey

The Record of Gains and Losses: 1973-1988

Table 6 allows the reader to roughly trace the course of freedom since the Survey began. It should be noted that changes in information and judgment since 1973 make many ratings not strictly comparable from year to year. Nevertheless, the table reflects the direction of trends in each country. (The reader should also note a correction in this table when compared with previous editions of this annual: the correction is described in the Notes to the Table.)

Since the Survey began, the world has experienced a number of gains and losses of freedom, either immediate or prospective. Most generally, there has been an advance of Soviet communism in Southeast Asia after the fall of South Vietnam, and at least its partial institutionalization in South Yemen, Ethiopia, and the former Portuguese colonies of Africa. In the Americas an imminent danger of the spread of communism has arisen in Nicaragua, and an erstwhile danger in Grenada. Perhaps equally significant has been the modification of communism in many areas. While mainland China is still a repressive society, it has increased freedom through the support of private initiative, through more open discussion in some areas, and through the sending of thousands of students overseas. While limits on freedom are often galling, most East European countries are freer today than at the beginning of the 1970s. Recently, Soviet leaders have become leaders in this development.

In Western Europe gains for democracy in Spain, Portugal, and Greece were critical to its continual advancement everywhere. After the setback in Chile, gains have been achieved in many parts of Latin America. Argentina, Bolivia, Brazil, Dominican Republic, Ecuador, Honduras, Peru, and Uruguay reestablished democratic institutions. Several countries that the Survey listed as "free" (freedom ratings of 5 or less) at the beginning may now be more authentically free. Colombia is an example. (El Salvador and Guatemala probably should not have been listed as free in 1973. El Salvador is probably freer today than in 1973.)

African democracy has not fared well during these years. In many areas there has been a noticeable decline, especially in countries such as Ghana, Nigeria, Burkina Faso (Upper Volta), and Kenya in which great hopes were placed in the 1970s. In Sub-Saharan Africa only Senegal seems to have made progress, and this remains limited. While there has been a very modest resurgence of free institutions in Middle Eastern countries such as Jordan or Egypt, the destruction of Lebanon's democracy will be hard to make up. Further east, India has hung on tenaciously to its freedoms. The people of Sri Lanka have lost freedoms (although, amid violence, they may be regaining them); those of Thailand and Nepal have made some hopeful progress. In Southeast Asia, in the arc from Philippines to Korea, there has been a remarkable turn away from authoritarian institutions and toward democracy. We can only hope it continues.

During this period many new democratic states successfully emerged—in the South Pacific from Papua New Guinea to the east, and among the islands of the Caribbean. Yet 1987 saw the crown of this development in the Pacific—Fiji—succumb to an all too familiar military intervention in the name of ethnicity.

Elections and Referendums

Evidence for political freedom is primarily found in the occurrence and nature of elections or referendums. Therefore, as a supplement to our ratings we summarize in the accompanying Table 7 the national elections that we recorded for independent countries between November, 1987 and December, 1988. One or more elections from earlier in 1987 are included because they were overlooked in last year's annual. The reader should assume that the electoral process appeared comparatively open and competitive, unless our remarks suggest otherwise. For example, an extremely one-sided outcome implies an unacceptable electoral process. Its unacceptability may lie in the repressive context in which it is held, the exclusion of potential oppositionists from the process, or questionable electoral or tabulation procedures. To understand the context of elections in a particular country, consult the Country Summaries in Part III.

Although we do not include non-national elections in this table, they are occasionally more significant than national elections. Regional elections in the major democracies are certainly as important politically as minor elections in very small democracies. The reader's attention should also be drawn to the number of referendums that occurred during the year. In the course of the Survey work, we have seen a steady increase in the willingness of democracies to let their citizens more directly influence government policy through this means.

TABLE 7

NATIONAL ELECTIONS AND REFERENDUMS

Country Date	Type of Election	Results and Remarks
Afghanistan 4/5-14/88	legislative	geographically and politically restricted exercise; possibly some pluralism
Algeria 11/3/88	referendum	on constitutional changes; wins easily within a highly restricted system
Australia 9/3/88	referendum	people overwhelmingly defeat government's constitutional proposals
Bangladesh 3/3/88	legislative	most parties boycott, government wins; little independent supervision
Belgium 12/13/87	legislative	governing coalition wins narrowly
Botswana 9/26/87	referendum	80 percent approve change in electoral oversight
Cameroon 4/24/88	general	one party; choice among party-approved candidates; president receives 99 percent of votes
Canada 11/21/88	legislative	government wins bitter battle
Chile 10/5/88	referendum	people reject leader in very high turnout; demand change
Cyprus (G) 2/14,21/88	presidential	incumbent president comes in third; runoff shifts to left
Denmark 5/10/88	legislative	high turnout, mixed results

Ecuador
1/31/88	general	government loses badly; pres. runoff required
5//8/88	presidential (runoff)	moderate Borja wins

El Salvador
3/20/88	legislative	government loses to right, even in capital; winner disputes results low turnout as guerrillas oppose

Equatorial Guinea
7/3,10/88	legislative	99 percent approve single list

Finland
1/31,2/1/88	presidential	incumbent wins handily in first essentially direct election

France
4/24/88	presidential	incumbent far ahead (far right does well)
5/8/88	presidential (runoff)	incumbent wins
6/5/88	legislative	evenly balanced parties
6/12/88	legislative (runoff)	government narrowly misses majority
11/6/88	referendum	little interest in issue relating to New Caledonia

Haiti
1/17/88	general	major groups boycott; only serious contest at presidential level; army dominates

Iceland
6/25/88	presidential	incumbent wins handily; first time incumbent has been opposed

Iran
4/8/88	legislative	real contests; candidates must be approved by ruling group
5/13/88	legislative (runoff)	relatively low participation; lengthy checks of validity before and after

Israel

11/1/88	legislative	highly pluralistic, slight rightist gain

Kenya

3/21/88	legislative	controlled exercise; one-party nomination process criticized (President had been reelected by declaration 2/29)

Korea (S)

12/16/87	presidential	incumbent wins with third of vote; well contested, heavy turnout
4/26/88	legislative	divided opposition wins fair election

Maldives

9/26/88	presidential	incumbent wins with 96%; unopposed

Mali

6/26/88	legislative	some choice among one-party selected candidates

Mexico

7/6/88	general	first effectively contested election in generations; opposition makes important gains; accusations of widespread cheating plausible

Pakistan

11/16/88	legislative	opposition wins plurality; forms government

Paraguay

2/14/88	general	reported high turnout; incumbent 89%, little freedom in process

Senegal

2/28/88	general	contested; government wins handily; plausible accusations against process

Seychelles

12/5/87	legislative	single party, little contest

Singapore

9/3/88	legislative	well-contested within a repressive atmosphere

Sweden

9/18/88	legislative	government wins, "greens" gain

Switzerland 12/6/87	referendum	voters approve 2 (including one of the very few initiatives ever approved), reject one
Thailand 7/24/88	legislative	open pluralistic process; relatively fair
Turkey 9/25/88	referendum	government plan for local elections defeated
United States 11/8/88	general	governing party wins presidency easily; but opposition continues to control congress; only six incumbents in House defeated
Vanuatu 11/3/87	legislative	government wins with plurality; controls media
Western Samoa 2/26/88	legislative	incumbent party defeated; extremely close; outside judge brought in to decide
Yemen (N) 7/5/88	legislative	heavily contested; no formal parties
Zambia 10/26/88	general	government wins handily; little real opposition allowed

Comparative Survey

Political-Economic Systems and Freedom

The accompanying Table 8 (Political and Economic Systems) fills
two needs. It offers the reader additional information about the
countries we have rated. For example, readers with libertarian
views may wish to raise the relative ratings of capitalist countries,
while those who place more value on redistributive systems may
wish to raise the ratings of countries toward the socialist end of the
spectrum. The table also makes possible an analysis of the relation
between political and economic forms and the freedom ratings of
the Survey. Perusal of the table will show that freedom is directly
related to the existence of multiparty systems: the further a country is from such systems, the less freedom it is likely to have. This
could be considered a trivial result, since a publicly competitive
political system is one of the criteria of freedom, and political
parties are considered evidence for such competition. However, the
result is not simply determined by our definitions: we searched for
evidence of authentic public competition in countries without
competitive parties, and seldom found the search rewarded. Both
theoretical and empirical studies indicate the difficulty of effective
public political opposition in one-party systems.

The relation between economic systems and freedom is more
complicated and, because of our lack of emphasis on economic
systems in devising our ratings of freedom, is not predetermined by
our methods. Historically, the table suggests that there are three
types of societies competing for acceptance in the world. The first,
or traditional type, is marginal and in retreat, but its adherents have
borrowed political and economic bits and pieces from both the other
types. The second and third, the Euro-American and Sino-Soviet
types, are strongest near their points of origin, but have spread by
diffusion and active propagation all over the world. The Leninist-
socialist style of political organization was exported along with the
socialist concept of economic organization, just as constitutional
democracy was exported along with capitalist economic concepts.
In this interpretation, the relation of economic systems to freedom
found in the table may be an expression of historical chance rather
than necessary relationships. Clearly, capitalism does not cause
nations to be politically free, nor does socialism cause them to be
politically unfree.[2] Still, socialists must be concerned by the empir-

ical relationship between poor freedom ratings and socialism that is found in tables such as this.

The table shows economies roughly grouped in categories from "capitalist" to "socialist." Labeling economies as capitalist or socialist has a fairly clear significance in the developed world, but its usefulness may be doubted in labeling the mostly poor and largely agrarian societies of the third world in this manner. However, third world states with dual economies, that is, with a modern sector and a preindustrial sector, have economic policies or goals that can be placed along the continuum from socialist to capitalist. A socialist third world state usually has nationalized all of the modern sector—except possibly some foreign investment—and claims central government jurisdiction over the land and its products, with only temporary assignment of land to individuals or cooperatives. The capitalist third world state has a capitalist modern sector and a traditionalist agricultural sector, combined in some cases with new agricultural projects either on family farm or agribusiness models. Third world economies that fall between capitalist and socialist do not have the high taxes of their industrialized equivalents in the first world, but they have major nationalized industries (for example, oil) in the modern sector, and their agricultural world may include emphasis on cooperatives or large-scale land reform, as well as more traditional forms.

The terms inclusive and noninclusive distinguish between societies in which the economic activities of most people are organized by the labeled, nontraditional system and societies in which the economic activities of fifty percent or more of the population are still organized largely by the traditional economic system.

States with inclusive capitalist forms are generally developed states that rely on the operation of the market and private provision for industrial welfare. Taxes may be high, but they are not confiscatory, while government interference is generally limited to subsidy and regulation. States classified as noninclusive capitalist, such as Liberia or Thailand, have not over fifty percent of the population included in a capitalist modern economy, with the remainder of the population still living traditionally. In these the traditional economy may be individual, communal, or feudal, but the direction of change as development proceeds is capitalistic.

Capitalist countries grade over into capitalist-statist or mixed capitalist. The capitalist-statist category includes states, such as

TABLE 8

POLITICAL SYSTEM:	Multiparty			Dominant-Party
	centralized		decentralized	
ECONOMIC SYSTEM **Capitalist** inclusive	Antigua & Bar 5 Barbados 2 Belize 3 Colombia[4] 5 Costa Rica 2 Cyprus (G) 3 Cyprus (T) 5 Dominica 4 Dom. Rep.[4] 4 El Salvador[1,3] 6	Iceland 2 Ireland 2 Japan 2 Luxembourg 2 Mauritius 4 New Zealand 2 St. Lucia 3 St. Vincent[3] 3 Spain[3] 3 Suriname[1] 5	Australia 2 Belgium 2 Canada 2 Germany (W)[3] 3 Lebanon 11 St. Kitts-Nev. 3 Switzerland 2 United States 2	Malaysia 9
non- inclusive	Ecuador 4 Guatemala[1] 6 Honduras[1,4] 5	Thailand[1] 6 Western Samoa[2,4] 7	Botswana 5 Papua New Guinea 5 Solomons[2] 4	Gambia[4] 6 Liberia[1] 10
Capitalist-Statist inclusive	Argentina 3 Bahamas 5 Grenada 3 Italy 2 Jamaica[3] 4 Korea (S) 5	Panama[1] 11 South Africa 11 Sri Lanka 7 Turkey[1,4] 6 Venezuela 3	Brazil[3,4] 5 Trinidad & Tobago 2	China (Taiwan) 8 Mexico 7
non- inclusive	Bolivia 5 Morocco[3] 9 Pakistan[1,2] 6 Peru[4] 5	Philippines 5	India 5 Vanuatu 6	Bangladesh[1] Indonesia[1,4] 10 Iran[2,4] 11 Paraguay[1,3,4] 12
Mixed Capitalist inclusive	Austria 2 Denmark 2 Finland 3 France 3 Greece 4 Israel 4 Malta 3	Netherlands 2 Norway 2 Portugal 3 Sudan[6] 9 Sweden 2 U.K.[3] 2 Uruguay 4		Nicaragua 9 Senegal[3,4] 7 Singapore[5] 9 Tunisia[4] 10
Mixed Socialist inclusive				Egypt[1,3,4] 9 Guyana 10 Syria[1,4] 13
non- inclusive				Madagascar[1,2] 10
Socialist inclusive				
non- inclusive	**Notes to the Table** 1. Under heavy military influence or domination. 2. Party relationships anomalous. 3. Close decision along capitalist-to-socialist continuum. 4. Close decision on inclusive/noninclusive dimension. 5. Mixed Capitalist-Statist. 6. Noninclusive.			

POLITICAL-ECONOMIC SYSTEMS

One-Party			Non-Party	
socialist	communist	nationalist	military	nonmilitary
		Djibouti 12	Chile[3] 9	Jordan[2/3/4] 11
Sierra Leone[1] 10		Cameroon[3] 12 Comoros 12 Côte d' Ivoire[4] 12 Gabon 12 Kenya 12 Malawi 13	Chad 13 Fiji[4] 9 Haiti 12 Lesotho 12 Niger 12 Transkei 13 Yemen (N) 10	Bhutan[3] 10 Maldives 11 Nepal[3] 7 Swaziland 11 Tonga 8 Tuvalu 2
			Ghana 12 Nigeria[3/4] 10	Bahrain 10 Brunei 12 Qatar[5] 10 Saudi Arabia 13 United Arab Emirates 10
Zimbabwe 11		Central Afr. Rep.[3] 12 Zaire[1] 13	Eq. Guinea[3] 14 Mauritania 12 Uganda[3] 10	Kiribati 3 Oman 12
Burundi[1/6] 13			Guinea[6] 13	Kuwait[5] 11 Nauru[5] 4
Libya[1/2/3] 12 Seychelles[3] 12	China (M)[3] 12 Poland[1] 10 Yugoslavia[3] 10			
Burma[1] 13 Cape V.I.[3/4] 11 Congo[1/3] 13 Somalia[1/3] 14 Zambia[3] 11		Mali[1] 12 Rwanda[1/3] 12 Togo[1] 12	Burkina Faso 13	
Algeria[1] 11 Sao Tome & Principe[3/4] 13	Albania 14 Bulgaria 14 Cuba 13 Czecho-slovakia 13 Germany (E) 13	Hungary[3] 9 Korea (N) 14 Mongolia 14 Romania 14 USSR 11 Vietnam 13		
Angola 14 Benin[1/3] 14 Guinea-Bissau[1/3] 13 Iraq[3/4] 14 Mozambique 13 Tanzania 12 Yemen (S)[1] 14	Afghanistan 12 Cambodia 14 Ethiopia[1] 13 Laos 12			

Brazil, Turkey, or Saudi Arabia, that have very large government productive enterprises, either because of an elitist development philosophy or major dependence on a key resource such as oil. Government interferes in the economy in a major way in such states, but not primarily because of egalitarian motives. Mixed capitalist systems, such as those in Israel, the Netherlands, or Sweden, provide social services on a large scale through governmental or other nonprofit institutions, with the result that private control over property is sacrificed to egalitarian purposes. These nations still see capitalism as legitimate, but its legitimacy is accepted grudgingly by many in government. Mixed socialist states, such as Syria or Poland, proclaim themselves to be socialist but in fact allow rather large portions of the economy to remain in the private domain.

Socialist economies, on the other hand, strive programmatically to place an entire national economy under direct or indirect government control. States such as the USSR or Cuba may allow some modest private productive property, but this is only by exception, and rights to such property can be revoked at any time. The leaders of noninclusive socialist states have the same goals as the leaders of inclusive socialist states, but their relatively primitive economies or peoples have not yet been effectively included in the socialist system. Such states generally have a small socialized modern economy and a large preindustrial economy in which the organization of production and trade is still largely traditional. It should be understood that the characterizations in the table are impressionistic; the continuum between capitalist and socialist economies is necessarily cut arbitrarily into categories for this presentation.

Political systems range from democratic multiparty to absolutist one-party systems. Theoretically, the most democratic countries should be those with decentralized multiparty systems, for here important powers are held by the people at two or more levels of the political system, and dissent is legitimated and mobilized by opposition parties. More common are centralized multiparty systems, such as France or Japan, in which the central government organizes lower levels of government primarily for reasons of efficiency. Dominant-party systems allow the forms of democracy, but structure the political process so that opposition groups do not have a realistic chance of achieving power. They often face censorship, vote fraud, imprisonment, or other impediments.

The now classical form of one-party rule is that in states such as the USSR or Vietnam that proclaim themselves to be communist. The slightly larger group of socialist one-party states are ruled by elites that use Marxist-Leninist rhetoric, organize ruling parties very much along communist lines, but either do not have the disciplined organization of communist states or have explicitly rejected one or another aspect of communism. A final group of nationalist one-party states adopts the political form popularized by the communists (and the fascists in the last generation), but the leaders generally reject the revolutionary ideologies of socialist or communist states and fail to develop the totalitarian controls that characterize those states. There are several borderline states that might be switched between socialist and nationalist categories (for example, Libya). "Socialist" is used here to designate a political rather than economic system. A socialist "vanguard party" established along Marxist-Leninist lines will almost surely develop a socialist economy, but a state with a socialist economy need not be ruled by a vanguard party. It should be pointed out that the totalitarian-libertarian continuum is not directly reflected by the categorization in this table.

Nonparty systems can be democratic, as in the small island of Nauru, but generally they are not. Nepal's nonparty system is one of the most democratic of attempts to establish such systems. Other nonparty systems may be nonmilitary nonparty systems such as Tonga or Saudi Arabia, or military nonparty systems, such as that in Niger.

Social and Economic Comparisons

Table 9, social and economic comparisons, is intended to help the reader relate the discussion of political and civil liberties to the more standard measures by which countries are compared. The table offers three measures of social and economic health alongside the Survey rating. The measures are GNP/Capita, under five mortality, and literacy. In gathering the data for the first three, an attempt was made to derive from a wealth of conflicting data a reasonable figure for each country. In many cases the data are doubtful either because the figures have not actually been gathered, or because of political considerations. It seems most unlikely, for

TABLE 9

SOCIAL AND ECONOMIC COMPARISONS*

	GNP per Person	Under 5 Mortality per 1000	Adult Literacy per 100	Freedom Rating
Afghanistan[3/4]	200	330	24	12
Albania	950	52	75	14
Algeria	2500	117	50	11
Angola[2/3]	500	242	41	14
Antigua & Barb.	2500	32	89	5
Argentina	2100	40	96	3
Australia	10800	11	100	2
Austria	9100	13	100	2
Bahamas	7000	30	89	5
Bahrain	10500	35	72	10
Bangladesh	150	196	33	9
Barbados	4600	16	98	2
Belgium	9000	13	100	2
Belize	1100	23	91	3
Benin	270	193	26	14
Bhutan	150	206	18	10
Bolivia	500	184	74	5
Botswana	900	99	71	5
Brazil	1900	91	78	5
Brunei	20000	14	80	12
Bulgaria	5690	21	96	14
Burkina Faso	150	245	13	13
Burma	180	91	78	13
Burundi	230	200	34	13
Cambodia	75	216	75	14
Cameroon	800	162	56	12
Canada	13000	10	100	2
Cape Verde	400	95	50	11
Cen. Afr. Rep.	270	232	41	12
Chad	80	232	26	13
Chile	1800	26	97	9
China (M)	370	50	69	12
China (T)	2800	9	92	8
Colombia	1350	72	88	5
Comoros	300	135	48	12

Table 9 (continued)

	GNP per Person	Under 5 Mortality per 1000	Adult Literacy per 100	Freedom Rating
Congo	1000	122	63	13
Costa Rica	1250	25	94	2
Cote d'Ivoire	620	157	43	12
Cuba	1600	19	96	13
Cyprus (G)	3700	17	89	3
Cyprus (T)	na	na	na	5
Czechoslovakia	7000	17	100	13
Denmark	11000	10	100	2
Djibouti	480	257	12	12
Dominica	1100	30	80	4
Dominican Rep.	900	88	77	4
Ecuador	1150	92	82	4
Egypt	700	136	45	9
El Salvador[2]	710	91	72	6
Equa. Guinea	180	223	37	14
Ethiopia	130	257	11	13
Fiji	1800	34	86	9
Finland	10800	8	100	3
France	9800	11	99	3
Gabon	3500	178	62	12
Gambia	250	292	25	6
Germany (E)	8000	13	100	13
Germany (W)	10900	12	100	3
Ghana	380	153	53	12
Greece	3900	18	92	4
Grenada	900	20	50	3
Guatemala	1200	109	55	6
Guinea	330	259	28	13
Guinea-Bissau	180	232	31	13
Guyana	580	41	96	10
Haiti	340	180	38	12
Honduras	730	116	59	5
Hungary[3]	5000	21	99	9
Iceland	11000	7	100	2
India	250	158	44	5

Comparative Survey

Table 9 (continued)

	GNP per Person	Under 5 Mortality per 1000	Adult Literacy per 100	Freedom Rating
Indonesia	540	126	74	10
Iran[3]	3500	162	51	11
Iraq	1900	100	47	14
Ireland	4800	12	100	2
Israel	5000	16	95	4
Italy	6500	13	97	2
Jamaica	1000	25	92	4
Japan	11300	9	100	2
Jordan	1600	65	75	11
Kenya	300	121	59	12
Kiribati	460	100	100	3
Korea (N)	1000	35	90	14
Korea (S)	2100	35	92	5
Kuwait	16000	25	70	11
Laos	200	170	84	12
Lebanon	1600	56	77	11
Lesotho	500	144	74	12
Liberia	470	215	35	10
Libya	8000	130	66	12
Luxembourg	13000	11	100	2
Madagascar	250	97	68	10
Malawi	180	275	41	13
Malaysia	2000	38	73	9
Maldives	300	91	82	11
Mali	140	302	17	12
Malta	3400	14	81	3
Mauritania	425	223	17	12
Mauritius	1100	32	83	4
Mexico	2000	73	90	7
Mongolia	1000	64	90	14
Morocco[2]	650	130	33	9
Mozambique[2]	360	252	17	13
Nauru	19000	38	99	4
Nepal	160	206	26	7
Netherlands	9200	10	100	2

Table 9 (continued)

	GNP per Person	Under 5 Mortality per 1000	Adult Literacy per 100	Freedom Rating
New Zealand	7300	14	100	2
Nicaragua[2]	850	104	85	9
Niger	200	237	14	12
Nigeria	760	182	43	10
Norway	13900	10	100	2
Oman	7000	172	30	12
Pakistan	380	174	30	6
Panama	2000	35	88	11
Pap. New Guinea	720	94	45	5
Paraguay	1000	61	88	12
Peru	1000	133	85	5
Philippines	650	78	86	5
Poland[3]	4500	21	100	10
Portugal	2000	22	85	3
Qatar	18000	43	51	10
Romania[3]	3500	31	97	14
Rwanda	290	214	47	12
St. Kitts-Nevis	1500	36	92	3
St. Lucia	1200	22	60	3
St. Vincent	900	33	84	3
Sao Tome & P.	320	80	60	13
Saudi Arabia[2]	10000	101	30	13
Senegal	380	231	28	7
Seychelles[2]	2500	20	57	12
Sierra Leone	370	302	29	10
Singapore	7400	12	86	9
Solomon Isls.	600	50	50	4
Somalia[2]	270	257	12	14
South Africa[2/3]	2300	104	46	11
Spain	4500	12	95	3
Sri Lanka	350	48	87	7
Sudan[2]	350	187	25	9
Suriname	3000	41	90	5
Swaziland	800	182	68	11
Sweden	11800	8	100	2

Table 9 (continued)

	GNP per Person	Under 5 Mortality per 1000	Adult Literacy per 100	Freedom Rating
Switzerland	16000	9	100	2
Syria[2]	1600	71	60	13
Tanzania[2]	260	183	80	12
Thailand	825	55	91	6
Togo	250	160	41	12
Tonga[2]	1000	28	90	8
Transkei	na	na	na	13
Trinidad & Tob.	6500	26	96	2
Tunisia	1300	110	54	10
Turkey	1130	104	74	6
Tuvalu	700	40	95	2
Uganda[2]	300	178	57	10
USSR	7400	29	99	11
Un.Arab Emirs.	20000	43	71	10
United Kingdom	8500	12	100	2
United States[2]	16400	13	96	2
Uruguay	1700	32	94	4
Vanuatu[2/4]	800	100	10	6
Venezuela	3400	45	88	3
Vietnam	200	98	90	13
Western Samoa	700	50	98	7
Yemen (N)[2]	550	210	10	10
Yemen (S)[2]	550	210	40	14
Yugoslavia[2]	2200	31	90	10
Zaire[2]	170	170	61	13
Zambia	450	135	70	11
Zimbabwe	700	121	75	11

Notes to the Table

1. Aside from the Freedom Ratings (Table 3 above), the sources for the table data were UNICEF, **Statistics on Children in UNICEF Assisted Countries** (New York: 1987); UNICEF, **The State of the World's Children** (New York: 1987); Population Reference Bureau, **1987 World Population Data Sheet** (Washington: 1987); **1987 Britannica Book of the Year,** "World Data," pages 577ff. and 812ff.

2. This country's literacy figure is questionable or incomparable.
3. The GNP for this country is questionable or incomparable.
4. The mortality rates for this country are questionable.

TABLE 10

HUMAN SUFFERING, WOMEN'S EQUALITY, AND FREEDOM

	Human Suffering Index	Women's Status Index	Women's Advancement Rating	Freedom Rating
Afghanistan	88	74	7	12
Albania	47		6	14
Algeria	67	52.5	5	11
Angola	91		6	14
Antigua & Barb.			4	5
Argentina	38	32	3	3
Australia	16	20.5	3	2
Austria	9	24.5	3	2
Bahamas			4	5
Bahrain			5	10
Bangladesh	79	78.5	7	9
Barbados		26	3	2
Belgium	9	23	3	2
Belize			3	3
Benin	83		6	14
Bhutan	80		5	10
Bolivia	66	53	5	5
Botswana	60	47	4	5
Brazil	50	45.5	4	5
Brunei			6	12
Bulgaria	20	22	5	14
Burkina Faso	84		6	13
Burma	61		6	13
Burundi	77		6	13
Cambodia	80		6	14
Cameroon	78	60	5	12
Canada	9	19.5	2	2
Cape Verde			5	11
Cen. Afr. Rep.	84		6	12
Chad	88		6	13
Chile	46	40.5	4	9
China (M)	50	41.5	5	12
China (T)		33		8
Colombia	44	40	4	5
Comoros			6	12

Comparative Survey

Table 10 (continued)

	Human Suffering Index	Women's Status Index	Women's Advancement Rating	Freedom Rating
Congo	74		6	13
Costa Rica	40	30.5	3	2
Cote d'Ivoire	73		5	12
Cuba	31	31	4	13
Cyprus (G)			3	3
Cyprus (T)				5
Czechoslovakia	20	23	5	13
Denmark	9	20	3	2
Djibouti			6	12
Dominica			4	4
Dominican Rep.	53	43	4	4
Ecuador	54	39	4	4
Egypt	55	62	5	9
El Salvador	65	44.5	5	6
Equa. Guinea			6	14
Ethiopia	82		6	13
Fiji			4	9
Finland	16	15	2	3
France	14	24	3	3
Gabon			6	12
Gambia			5	6
Germany (E)	15	18	4	13
Germany (W)	5	24	3	3
Ghana	87		5	12
Greece	25	30	3	4
Grenada			4	3
Guatemala	64	54	5	6
Guinea	82		5	13
Guinea-Bissau			5	13
Guyana	42	40.5	5	10
Haiti	74	56.5	6	12
Honduras	62	48	4	5
Hungary	17	23	4	9
Iceland	16		2	2
India	61	56.5	5	5
Indonesia	62	53.5	5	10
Iran	65		7	11

Table 10 (continued)

	Human Suffering Index	Women's Status Index	Women's Advancement Rating	Freedom Rating
Iraq	64	53	6	14
Ireland	23	34	3	2
Israel	32	29	3	4
Italy	16	26	3	2
Jamaica	40	22.5	3	4
Japan	11	31.5	4	2
Jordan	53	50	5	11
Kenya	77	55	6	12
Kiribati			4	3
Korea (N)	40		5	14
Korea (S)	44	38	4	5
Kuwait	35	50.5	5	11
Laos			6	12
Lebanon	46		5	11
Lesotho	69	54.5	6	12
Liberia	71	66	6	10
Libya	53	63.5	6	12
Luxembourg	6		3	2
Madagascar	68		5	10
Malawi	83	68	6	13
Malaysia	48	42	5	9
Maldives			5	11
Mali	88	74	7	12
Malta			3	3
Mauritania	81		6	12
Mauritius	39		4	4
Mexico	47	38.5	4	7
Mongolia	47		6	14
Morocco	66	61	6	9
Mozambique	95	55.5	6	13
Nauru			4	4
Nepal	81	63	6	7
Netherlands	7	25	3	2
New Zealand	16	23.5	3	2
Nicaragua	67	45.5	5	9
Niger	85		6	12
Nigeria	80	71	6	10

Comparative Survey

Table 10 (continued)

	Human Suffering Index	Women's Status Index	Women's Advancement Rating	Freedom Rating
Norway	14	18.5	2	2
Oman	53		6	12
Pakistan	73	72	5	6
Panama	47	32.5	4	11
Papua N. Guinea	68		4	5
Paraguay	53	43	5	12
Peru	61	42.5	4	5
Philippines	55	36	4	5
Poland	25	24.5	5	10
Portugal	33	28.5	3	3
Qatar			7	10
Romania	25	32	5	14
Rwanda	80	61.5	6	12
St. Kitts-Nevis			3	3
St. Lucia			3	3
St. Vincent			3	3
Sao Tome & Pr.			6	13
Saudi Arabia	56	70.5	7	13
Senegal	71	67	6	7
Seychelles			5	12
Sierra Leone	76		5	10
Singapore	18	33.5	4	9
Solomon Isls.			4	4
Somalia	87		6	14
South Africa	52	47.5	5	11
Spain	25	30	3	3
Sri Lanka	58	40	4	7
Sudan	77	68.5	6	9
Suriname			6	5
Swaziland			6	11
Sweden	12	13	2	2
Switzerland	4	27	3	2
Syria	61	60	6	13
Tanzania	75	60.5	6	12
Thailand	47	42.5	5	6

Table 10 (continued)

	Human Suffering Index	Women's Status Index	Women's Advancement Rating	Freedom Rating
Togo	82		6	12
Tonga			4	8
Transkei				13
Trinidad & Tob.	21	32	3	2
Tunisia	56	51	5	10
Turkey	55	47.5	4	6
Tuvalu			4	2
Uganda	71		6	10
USSR	19	23	5	11
Un.Arab Emirs	40	57	6	10
United Kingdom	12	25.5	3	2
United States	8	17.5	2	2
Uruguay	37	30	4	4
Vanuatu			4	6
Venezuela	44	33	4	3
Vietnam	69		5	13
Western Samoa			4	7
Yemen (N)	78	73.5	7	10
Yemen (S)	74		5	14
Yugoslavia	32	28	5	10
Zaire	84		7	13
Zambia	74	58	6	11
Zimbabwe	69	53	5	11

Note to the Table

Lower scores are preferable. Where data was not available spaces have been left blank. The human suffering index is taken from the chart, "Human Suffering Index" produced by the Population Crisis Committee in Washington, D. C., 1987. The Women's Status Index is adapted from the the chart "Country Rankings of the Status of Women", Population Crisis Committee, 1988. The "total scores" given in the latter were subtracted from 100 to provide results comparable to those in the suffering index. The scores for women's advancement is based on Raymond Lloyd's publication, "Women and Men", September 3, 1988. Pakistan's rating was raised slightly to reflect recent events.

example, that the under five mortality rates for North and South Yemen are exactly the same, or those for North and South Korea. But variations among countries with different systems, and at different levels of development, are so extreme that precision is not necessary for understanding, or searching for, the major relationships.

The quantitative measures chosen are those that offer the best available evidence for the presence or absence of economic and social growth, on the one hand, and the extension of the results of this growth fairly over a population, on the other. If a country with a relatively high GNP/Capita does relatively poorly in providing health services and nutrition for its young (and the under five rate serves as an indicator for performance here), or allows its population to remain unlettered, then we can rightly question the desirability of its institutions. If it is a democracy, we can question whether the formal institutions of democracy are actually working as they should to give the majority of the people a means to pursue their interests.

Table 10 supplements Table 9 by offering ratings or indices focused on the extent of human suffering and the position of women in the world. The first set of figures is taken from the work of the Population Crisis Committee. Their "suffering index" incorporates data similar to those presented in Table 9 (including that from the Comparative Survey), but adds to this measures of inflation, growth in labor supply, urban growth, per capita calorie supply, access to clean drinking water, energy use, and personal freedom. One can quarrel with what has been included or excluded from the table, but by and large it is reasonable to suppose that people in countries toward the bottom of the list would wish to live in those toward the top more than the reverse. Better living offers certain kinds of "freedom" the Comparative Survey misses. It is also true that for those placing particularly high values on political and civil freedoms, on religious liberty, or on a locally- threatened belief system this table would not be a reliable guide. Terror in a general rather than politicized sense, might also have been included in the suffering index. For some, placing Lebanon in the middle of a ranking of countries by suffering may seem mistaken.

Since the position of women is another test of the growth of equality and liberty—where women are severely repressed modern democracy may be impossible—the table offers two series on the status of women. The first, again from the Population Crisis Committee, looks at health, marriage and children, education, employment, and social equality; this time considering these and other factors in relation to inequality in what is available to, or achieved by, males and females. The second rating scale for women's status is taken from work by an individual who has long studied women's issues and followed closely the development of the Comparative Survey and its categories. By using the same 1 to 7 scale that is employed for the Survey's political and civil rights scales, his results are quite easily related to those of the Survey. While it is impossible to make such ratings accurate, or "fair" in the face of legitimate arguments against ethnocentrism, one suspects that the accuracy of these ratings is in the same range as that of the Survey itself.

Conclusion

Freedom continues to expand. This expansion has in the past few years encompassed nearly all developed states outside the communist orbit. More recently democracy has become the dominant political form of organization in Latin America. Today, it is expanding in both East Asia and the communist world. Significantly, in the latter only the most backward states, such as Romania, Albania, or South Yemen remain outside the general movement. Sadly, the supporters of political and civil liberties have failed to achieve permanent success in either the Middle East or Africa.

In noting the recent advance of democracy, the reader should be cautioned that in much of the world new structures of freedom are very lightly built. Economic and social problems, the enmities aroused by nationalism and fanaticism, threaten many new or aspiring democracies. New elites, whether communist or capitalist, have in too many cases failed to make a firm commitment to share power—and thus income—with their fellow countrymen.

The movement toward freedom is more and more to be seen as an aspect of modernization and modern communication reaching out from the developed democracies to the rest of the world. While the rise of the fascist powers in relatively developed societies in the twenties and thirties demonstrated that there was no necessary relationship between development and democracy, in our era this relationship seems increasingly to be accepted. In spite of the excursions attempted by religious and ideological fanatics, as people develop their societies, as their desires are extended and modern-ized, both leaders and followers expect that there will be a growing regard for political and civil liberties, and human rights. It is our responsibility to see that we do nothing to divert the world from this course.

NOTES

1. For further details on the methods and criteria used in the Survey see the foregoing chapter on definitions and criteria.

2. See Lindsay M. Wright, "A Comparative Survey of Economic Freedoms," in R. D. Gastil, **Freedom in the World: Political Rights and Civil Liberties, 1982** (Westport, Connecticut: Greenwood Press, 1982), pages. 51-90.

PART II

Political Participation in America

INTRODUCTORY NOTE

As part of an attempt to understand changes in American political life that may effect the future of freedom in this country, a small discussion group was convened at Freedom House, August 26-27, 1988. The particular topic of discussion was political participation, as reflected in the first instance by the turnout in elections, and in the second, by willingness to go into government service. In addition to the director of the Comparative Survey, who produces this volume, the attendees were: Gabriel Almond, Professor of Political Science, Emeritus, Stanford University; Stephen Earl Bennett, Professor of Political Science, University of Cincinnati; Curtis Gans, Director, Committee for the Study of the American Electorate; Richard Jensen, Professor of History, University of Illinois, Chicago; Paul Kleppner, Director, Social Science Research Institute, Northern Illinois University; Charles Levine, Professor, School of Public Affairs, American University; Howard Penniman, American Enterprise Institute; J. Bingham Powell, Professor of Political Science, University of Rochester; Roberta Sigel, Professor of Political Science, Rutgers University; and Peter Zimmerman, Associate Dean, John F. Kennedy School of Government, Harvard University.

After opening remarks by the moderator, the section opens with the three invited papers by Professors Kleppner, Jensen, and Bennett and the recorded discussions subsequent to each. This is followed by more general discussions of the issues. The first day's discussion centered on the question of changes in the willingness of Americans to vote; the second day added to this the question of willingness to serve in the government or bureaucracy.

The reader may be interested to note that the decline in voter participation in the United States that concerned most participants in the discussion continued through the subsequent general election of November 8, 1988. According to Curtis Gans, 50.16 percent of potentially eligible voters participated. This represented a 2.9 percent decline since 1984. He also remarks that this was the lowest turnout in a presidential election since 1924, and outside the South, since 1824. Bush's mandate was given by 26.6 percent of potential voters, the smallest mandate in a two candidate election in this century. Numerically, fewer people voted in 1988 than 1984---only 1944, in the midst of war, recorded an equivalent numerical decline in successive presidential elections.

OPENING REMARKS

GASTIL: Before we turn to Professor Kleppner's paper, some opening remarks are needed to provide a context for the discussion. The broader question we are addressing is the nature and reality of the long-term progress of political institutions and political behavior, of political rights and civil liberties. Political development has led to increases in the size of political units, their complexity, and organizational efficiency; more qualitatively it has led to advances in political rights and civil liberty. This development started out in a few countries and then spread to many others. And within those original countries it has continually deepened and widened. In this process, in the last two centuries the United States has been a leader.

Very quickly this brings us to the question, "Where do we go from here?" We presume, looking at the past, that the future will show the evolution of a more and more developed and inclusive democracy. Of course, sitting where we are, with only the past to guide us, it is impossible to know in what ways the democracies of the future will appear advanced in relation to today. We can surmise that some rights will be extended, and new forms of participation developed. I hope that the age of voting will not continue to drop, to go on down from 18, to 16, to 12. There is no obviously rational stopping place. I believe they now vote in Massachusetts prisons. In any event, as time goes on we can expect more and more peoples to be involved with democratic institutions, democracy to diffuse to more and more countries, and, with that, increasing respect for human rights.

Perhaps we will eventually achieve a kind of universal democracy. I often irritate some of my friends by pointing out that the best argument the Soviet Union has against the United States, when we argue that they should freely allow emigration, is the rejoinder "You should freely allow anyone who wishes to come to America." Answering this demand will be a critical problem for democracy, as we go forward to a universalization of the concept.

The concern that brings us here is that in the process of this development, seeds of destruction may be growing within the oldest democracies. Since the United States is in many ways the oldest, we would expect to find this growth most evident within the United States.

All systems, as they develop, produce negative and positive feedback. Positive feedback has fueled democratic development—a little democracy leads to more—so that the system not only keeps operating, but starts expanding. You start with a few people voting, then more people voting, and then even more people, and eventually nearly everyone.

But any system also produces negative feedback. This provides stability based on an oscillating balance of forces. For the gains there are counterbalancing losses. In Kleppner's paper, his "middle period" is largely a discussion of negative feedback—as we were expanding the electorate with the right hand, we were contracting it with the left.

Negative feedback could also, of course, be much more than that. It could cause a permanent reversal of direction. This is one explanation of the history of the Weimar Republic: an explosion of democracy that eventually produced its opposite.

Another way to look at systems is to note that they all develop and adapt within specific contexts. This may be relevant to what we are doing here. When the context changes, the system may become maladaptive. Then it must change or collapse.

So we want to ask if democracy has produced changes that inhibit its functions. In terms of feedback, is democracy producing anti-democracy? And we want to ask if the environment of democracy has changed to where the system is no longer adaptive? Reasons for the problems American democracy faces may be found in increased mobility, increase and change in communications, in the sheer complexity of life, in the breakdown of a sense of community. With the incredible specialization of life today, there is a tendency of many people to collapse into their specialties, whether these be occupational or recreational or whatever, and to attenuate their identification with a larger, less specialized community.

Finally, if either of these tendencies are occurring—if democracy is feeding on itself, and destroying itself—or if the environment is changing in ways that make our old assumptions about democracy no longer adaptive, then are there ways to reduce or change these processes, or manipulate the environment, to get back on track? This is the policy aspect of our discussion.

Political Participation

To examine these questions we will look at the history and expansion of suffrage, and consider the role that political parties have played and may play in our political process. We will consider trends in political participation, particularly in voter participation, and examine arguments over the existence and meaning of these changes, including a comparative discussion of voter participation elsewhere. The day will conclude with a consideration of proposals to improve voter participation, asking whether these proposals are necessary or desirable, whether they will work or not.

Tomorrow we will go beyond voting to examine other problems of political participation, especially the willingness of competent people to participate in public service. We want to know whether the country is going to continue to have the quantity and quality of people that it needs to staff its political democracy.

Finally, we will try to put these questions together and ask whether there are general trends that may link together problems of voter participation and participation in the public service, and see if problems in both areas cannot be traced to similar causes. To the extent they can, we will consider whether there are common solutions or approaches to improving performance in these rather different forms of participation.

WHO HAS BEEN ELIGIBLE TO VOTE?

An Historical Review of Suffrage Requirements in the U.S.

Paul Kleppner

Popular control over government is the cardinal principle of the democratic formula in the United States. Citizens freely communicate their concerns to officials whom they have chosen, and these elected officeholders then make policy choices that reflect articulated popular preferences. Thus, by participating in the political process, citizens influence the public decisions that affect their lives.

Of course, it is only in textbooks that the process works so clearly and certainly. In the world of conflicting social groups and concrete political institutions, its operation is much more complicated. Which citizens communicate what concerns to public officials? When and how do they do the communicating? How do public officials pick and choose among diverse and even conflicting popular preferences? Questions such as these alert us to the gap between metaphor and reality and help us to recognize that participation in political life is a complex matter.

There are numerous political acts through which private citizens —whether as individuals or as members of groups—can attempt to influence governmental decisions. For example, they can make political contributions, attend political meetings, contact public officials, or work with others to address common problems. While all of these acts share a common aim, each differs from the others in what the citizen can get from the act, what the act gets the citizen into, and what is required of the citizen to engage in the act. It is plausible that when citizens choose to participate in political life they select whatever political act they think provides the best fit between their needs and their predispositions. If so, then we can fruitfully think of the democratic formula as describing a participation-response system that includes alternative, but not mutually exclusive, patterns of citizen-government relations.[1]

Political Participation

Of these patterned relations, voting is, and probably always has been, the most popular.[2]   This is mainly because it is the political act that requires the lowest resource investment from citizens. But it is also because it is the only mechanism that most citizens believe to be available to them for influencing what government does.[3]

This is not the place to assess the credibility of that belief. Nor can we here deal with whether, and if so how, voting influences public policy. For present purposes, it is enough to notice that voting is both a distinctive mode of political participation and a diffuse pressure that works to increase the effectiveness of other modes.[4] It is for this reason that the "who votes" question has come to occupy so central a place on the research agendas of those attempting to understand the dynamics of the larger participation-response system. The first part of the answer to the "who votes" question must take into account the legal context and the changes that have occurred at various points in the definition of voter eligibility. It is important to know what the rules of the electoral game were; how they changed from time to time; and what impact these changes had on identifiable groups within the society.

Framework for Discussion

The U.S. Constitution explicitly delegated to state legislatures the power to regulate the conduct of federal elections, including determining who would be eligible to vote. Article I, Section IV, one of the few clauses in the Constitution to delegate power to the states, stipulated that the legislature of each state should prescribe "the times, places, and manner" of holding elections for federal offices, while reserving to Congress the right to "make or alter such regulations." Section II of the same article left the question of voter eligibility to the states. Describing how the members of the only popularly elected body in the federal government were to be selected, this section simply provided that "electors [for the House of Representatives] in each State shall have the qualifications requisite for electors of the most numerous branch of the state legislature."[5]

Subsequent suffrage amendments to the Constitution have limited the prerogatives of state legislatures to determine voter eligibility. The Fifteenth, Nineteenth, Twenty-fourth, and Twenty-sixth Amendments have each provided that the right of citizens to vote "shall not be denied or abridged by the United States or by any State" because of membership in a particular categoric group. But even with these negative assertions of voting rights, the legal framework has always been a loose one, allowing considerable latitude to state legislatures. One of the prices of federalism, in other words, has been the absence of any uniform set of requirements determining voter eligibility.

With each state legislature free to establish its own standards, it has always been difficult to frame generalizations characterizing the regulations governing access to the ballot. To make some sense of this patchwork of rules, we need to impose order. And we can begin doing that by distinguishing between two basic types of rules governing the electoral game—substantive and procedural.[6]

Substantive rules are those which establish basic qualifications for voting. They define the shape of the eligible electorate and can be used directly to increase or reduce its size by designating particular categories of people as eligible to vote. On the other hand, procedural rules are those which make it easier or more difficult for members of the eligible electorate to cast their ballots on election day. Some of these involve procedures—like registering, paying poll taxes, taking literacy tests—that must be accomplished prior to election day. These types of requirements resemble substantive ones in the sense that they affect an individual's eligibility to vote; but they differ in not expressly singling out any categorically defined group of persons. But because they place another obstacle between the potential voter and the ballot box, they likely lead some persons to refrain from exercising their right to vote.[7] Other procedural rules—like the type and form of the ballot and the hours the polls are open—regulate the voting act itself. Because they affect whether the voting act is simple and easy to perform, or complex and difficult, they may also have an impact on the decision to participate.[8]

This distinction between the two basic types of election rules also appears in the historical trends that have characterized the adoption of suffrage legislation in this country. While periodizing schemes always involve using arbitrary dividing points, they assist us in ordering past events and allow us to detect patterns that otherwise might escape attention. In the case of the development of election rules, we can follow Jerrold Rusk and John Stucker in isolating three historical eras.[9]

Political Participation

The first ran from 1776 to 1860, the years between the American Revolution and the beginning of the Civil War. This was a period in which state legislatures concerned themselves mainly with substantive qualifications, especially those pertaining to citizenship and to property-owning and tax-paying requirements for voting. During these years, the separate states moved toward the principle of extending suffrage to adult white males who were citizens, although this development occurred more slowly and unevenly than has sometimes been described.

The second period ran from 1860 through 1920, the beginning of the Civil War through the general enfranchisement of women with the ratification of the Nineteenth Amendment. Mixed concerns marked this period. Federal action focused on substantive questions, extending the franchise across the boundaries of race and sex; while state legislatures adopted new procedural rules to restrict the exercise of the franchise.

The final period, from 1920 to the present, has been marked by a further expansion of suffrage rights. Congressional legislation, constitutional amendments, and Supreme Court decisions have combined to strike down a variety of substantive and procedural rules that either limited suffrage or restricted the exercise of voting rights. At the same time, state legislatures have acted generally to ease, or even to erase, earlier procedural barriers. As a consequence, there now remain only four requirements for voting: a person must be a citizen of the United States, at least 18 years of age, a resident of the locality for 30 to 60 days, and registered.

From Revolution to Civil War

Those who wrote the state constitutions of the 1780s and 1790s did not greatly depart from past practices when they defined voter eligibility. They generally accepted the substantive qualifications that prevailed before the colonies had declared their independence. In turn, these qualifications mainly reflected the colonists' adaptation of British practices to North American conditions. It is not surprising that these emigrants brought with them to the New World the theory of suffrage that shaped Britain's substantive election rules. That theory held that only freeholders—that is, owners of real property—should have the right to vote since it was only they who would have, "in a phrase as old as Aristotle, a common interest in and a permanent attachment to society and state." Consistent with this theory, since 1430 the right to vote for members of Parliament in Britain had been limited to those owning land worth 40 shillings a year in income or rental value.[10]

Britain's colonists in North America eventually accepted the same theory, although only after an uncertain start in which a vaguely defined franchise was nominally the right of a large number of inhabitants in the early colonies. But when they acted to implement the theory, the colonial assemblies developed their own formulas. By the end of the eighteenth century, only five of the original colonies—Connecticut, Massachusetts, New Hampshire, New York, and Rhode Island—required a freehold of some stipulated monetary value. The other eight colonies defined the freehold as an acreage requirement, most commonly limiting the franchise to inhabitants owning a minimum of 50 acres. As long as a large supply of free land was available, this sort of qualification did not limit the electorate as severely as it would have in Britain. For example, in South Carolina, where a 50-acre freehold was required to vote, the smallest land grant to freemen settlers was 70 acres, so that all freemen were assured of political rights.[11]

A few of the colonial assemblies introduced another important adaptation: they substituted the ownership of personal property for the real estate requirement. Yielding to the demands of the business and commercial interests in their cities and towns, Connecticut, Delaware, Maryland, Massachusetts, and Pennsylvania used a formula of this sort for at least some elections prior to the Revolution. While South Carolina went further, changing its requirement to allow persons to vote if they had paid a tax of 20 shillings during the year in which they wanted to vote, or in the previous year. And Rhode Island even extended the franchise to the oldest sons of freeholders.[12]

Despite such broadening adaptations, on the eve of the Revolution, property-owning requirements of one sort or another still operated to limit the size of the eligible electorate. Because the surviving evidence is very uneven both in its quality and its geographic coverage, it is difficult to estimate precisely how restrictive these qualifications were. However, the most thorough survey of that evidence revealed no locality in which as many as fifty percent of the adult white males were unqualified, while pointing to a good number in which seventy to eighty percent of them satisfied the prevailing economic requirement. To put these numbers into some meaningful context, one needs to remember that in the late eighteenth century probably less than twenty percent of the total adult male population of Britain qualified for the franchise.[13]

Some procedural innovations in colonial assemblies also worked to expand political democracy. The assemblies in Delaware, Massachusetts, North Carolina, and Pennsylvania introduced paper ballots to replace **viva voce** voting, a practice transplanted from Britain. In societies where deference to one's social and economic betters was expected, this action removed an important restraint on political expression. And Connecticut and Massachusetts also experimented with what amounted to primary elections as a means of nominating candidates for office.[14]

But some substantive innovations adopted by colonial assemblies were clearly restrictive. Free blacks were denied the right to vote in the Carolinas, Georgia, and Virginia. At one time or another, Catholics were expressly disfranchised in Maryland, New York, and New Jersey, while Jews were denied voting rights in Maryland, New York, Rhode Island, and South Carolina.[15]

Otherwise, colonial lawmakers were not very exact in stipulating voting qualifications. For example, only three colonies——Delaware, Pennsylvania, and South Carolina——expressly confined voting rights to males; and only six——Connecticut, New York, North Carolina, Pennsylvania, South Carolina, and Virginia——stated that the voter must be 21-years of age. And four colonies——Delaware, Massachusetts, New Hampshire, and Virginia——did not even specify that residence of any sort was a requirement. In actual practice, of course, in all colonies only males who were residents and at least 21 years old qualified to vote.

When the colonies declared their independence and became states, they had to define voter eligibility in their new constitutions. Only five states——Georgia, Maryland, New Hampshire, New Jersey, and Pennsylvania——used the opportunity to broaden their franchises. And of these only New Jersey and Pennsylvania acted boldly, abandoning the freehold requirement entirely and declaring taxpaying to be the only economic qualification for voting.[16]

However radical that action by New Jersey and Pennsylvania appeared to contemporary observers, it was only a limited step in the direction of eliminating economic qualifications for voting.

There were three phases involved in that long process. First, substituting personal property for the real estate requirement. Second, allowing the payment of a specified amount of taxes as an alternative or replacement for property owning. Third, abolishing all property owning and taxpaying prerequisites for voter eligibility, except for the requirement of paying minimal poll taxes.[17]

When the U.S. Constitution was ratified in 1789, only four states had moved into phase one, with two additional ones having pushed into phase two. The other seven still required real estate ownership, although they differed considerably in declaring what value of property or number of acres was required. The very diversity of rules governing this subject at the state level was no doubt the prime reason the framers of the Constitution chose to leave the matter to each state to determine for itself. After all, they were, above all else, realistic politicians and artful compromisers who would have perceived quickly the impossibility of arranging a broadly acceptable resolution of the issue.

After 1789 the first blows against economic tests were struck by states newly entering the Union. Vermont entered in 1791 with almost complete male suffrage, and Kentucky's constitution of 1792 provided for a franchise that was nearly as broad.[18] But the movement toward broader suffrage was neither confined to the new states nor led by them. And surely it was not especially a western phenomenon, as Frederick Jackson Turner claimed, since as late as 1812 only Kentucky among the western states had eliminated all property or taxpaying qualifications.[19]

In general, the movement to eliminate economic qualifications was slow and uneven, easily accomplished in some states and the outcome of strenuous battle in others. Voting qualifications became a focal point of controversy between contending political groupings in some localities, and these battles likely were important steps in the development of durable political alignments. But in other states where the suffrage was already rather broad, its further extension was not an issue that aroused great excitement.

Still, white manhood suffrage did not become universal as quickly as some commentators have assumed. As late as 1828, when Andrew Jackson was first elected to the presidency, fourteen states still had some form of property owning or taxpaying qualification for voting. It was only in the decade of the 1830s that suffrage expansion reached the South, although Louisiana retained its taxpaying qualification until 1845, Virginia did not abolish its property owning requirement until 1851, and South Carolina retained its economic test until Reconstruction. Among the northern states, Connecticut and New Jersey did not eliminate their taxpaying requirements until the 1840s, while Rhode Island's 1842 constitution allowed native born citizens to vote if they paid a $1 registry tax but required naturalized citizens to acquire a freehold valued at $134 or more to qualify for voting rights.[20]

Describing the process of change is further complicated by the fact that some states imposed distinct qualifications for voting for particular offices. For example, since 1777 North Carolina allowed taxpayers to vote for members of the lower house of its state legislature and, after 1835, for governor. Only 50-acre freeholders could vote for members of the upper house of the legislature until 1857. As a result, only about half of the electorate for the lower house could vote for state senators.[21]

By the outbreak of the Civil War, however, no states except Rhode Island and South Carolina required any economic test for voting. As they eliminated economic requirements, states tended to make some other substantive qualifications explicit. References to age, citizenship, residence, and sex had sometimes been omitted in the first state constitutions, perhaps because they were thought to be covered adequately by economic requirements. With the abolition of that test, however, it became necessary to define the other qualifications explicitly.

With a unanimity that has proven to be rare on matters of election rules, all states adopted twenty-one as the minimum age for voting. Second, each state imposed some sort of durational residency requirement, with varying rules both with respect to length and level of residency. Originally, most had specified their residency requirement—usually one year—at the county or township level. But the newer states, perhaps anticipating more mobility in their societies, tended only to require one year of residency in the state. Eventually, the older states adopted this more flexible standard, so that by 1860 only three states—Georgia, New Hampshire, and Tennessee—had no state level requirement.

While early state constitutions only rarely referred to "males" or to "white males," these words appeared in constitutions and election statutes much more frequently after 1800, effectively making legal what had already been accomplished in practice—the exclusion of women and free blacks from voting rights.

The movement to exclude free blacks from the suffrage was a new development, revealing the rise and diffusion of anti-black sentiments. Before the Revolution, only four southern colonies had explicitly excluded free blacks from voting; Delaware and Kentucky, border states in which slave owning was legal, did so in 1792 and 1800, respectively. After that, the contagion swept through northern and western states as well, so that by the beginning of the Civil War in 1861, only five states could lay claim to having successfully resisted this movement to deny voting rights to free blacks.[22]

During this same period states began to link citizenship with voting rights. The Constitution gave the central government the authority to regulate immigration and naturalization into United States citizenship, but it was not clear that this authority precluded state action. Moreover, most meaningful privileges were held to depend on state citizenship, and the states were largely free to establish their own qualifications.[23] The early state constitutions, had glossed over the question of citizenship, putting their emphasis on being an inhabitant, that is, satisfying a residency requirement, to secure the franchise. Among the original states, only Pennsylvania, in 1788, imposed a citizenship qualification; and through the first half of the nineteenth century, fully sixteen states at one time or another failed to mention citizenship as a requirement for voting.[24]

As antipathy toward "foreigners" developed, prompted in large part by international dealings and especially by the War of 1812, some nascent political groupings moved to capitalize on popular feeling by championing the exclusion of aliens from voting rights. New Hampshire enacted a citizenship requirement in 1814, and its example was followed by Connecticut and Virginia in 1818, by New Jersey in 1820, by Massachusetts and New York two years later, and by Delaware, North Carolina and Rhode Island within the following two decades. With the exceptions of Vermont, Tennessee, and Ohio, which did not adopt citizenship requirements until 1828, 1834, and 1852, respectively, all of the new states entered the Union with a citizenship requirement in their constitutions or election codes. Only Georgia and South Carolina had failed to link voting with citizenship prior to 1860.

Political Participation

While the effort to limit the franchise to citizens dominated during the 1820s and 1830s, especially in the states along the eastern seaboard, a counter movement of sorts emerged in the newly developing states of the Midwest. As large numbers of immigrants from Europe settled in the region, strong sentiments emerged over the question of enfranchising aliens who had declared their intention to become citizens. An alien-with-intent provision was adopted in Michigan in 1835, in Wisconsin in 1848, in Indiana in 1852, and in Minnesota in 1858; it was strenuously debated from 1838 through 1841 in election campaigns in Illinois and at Iowa's constitutional conventions in 1844 and 1846. In each of these cases, the issue pitted Democrats, who generally favored alien enfranchisement, against Whigs, whose commitment to cultural homogeneity impelled them to oppose the measure. Both sides realized that defining voter eligibility would determine, at least in the short run, which party controlled state government.[25]

While it is fitting to put emphasis on the changes in substantive rules that occurred during this antebellum period, we should also notice some significant procedural alterations. First, election replaced appointment as a means of filling a larger number of public offices. We now take the election of executive officers for granted, in early America mayors of cities were typically appointed officials —even the governorship of New Jersey became elective only in 1844. The persistence of appointive offices worked to blunt the relationship between popular participation and control over policy. To put it the other way, with more offices subject to electoral sanction, especially citywide and statewide offices, the stakes of the game were raised and inducement to encourage participation was correspondingly greater.

Second, during the 1830s, printed ballots (generally provided by the political parties) came into common use everywhere except Illinois and Virginia, where traditions of **viva voce** voting persisted.[26] Whatever the shortcomings of these party ballots, they represented an improvement over a practice that surely must have discouraged participation and constrained political expression.

Finally, the states acted in response to claims that "'true principles of Republicanism and genuine Liberty requires [sic] that elections should be brought as near to every Man's Door as possible so that the genuine voice of the People may be taken.'"[27] By making electoral units smaller, and polling places more accessible, they made voting an easier act to perform.

From Civil War to Female Suffrage

The second period of the development of suffrage legislation ran from about 1860 through the adoption of the Nineteenth Amendment in 1920. This period differed from the first in several important respects. There was significant action at the federal level to expand voting rights, while the states depended on both new substantive and procedural rules to narrow the franchise. On balance, and quite unlike the antebellum period, the overall tone of this era was distinctly restrictive.

The first major change during the period was a substantive one, the enfranchisement of blacks through the ratification of the Fifteenth Amendment in 1870. This action added over a million black males to the ranks of eligible voters; its impact was especially great in the southern parts of the country. Just under eighty percent of these newly enfranchised voters lived in the eleven states of the former Confederacy, and another 11 percent lived in the five border states of Delaware, Kentucky, Maryland, Missouri, and West Virginia. In some southern states, adult black males were a significant proportion of the total number of males of voting age. In South Carolina they made up 57 percent of the age-eligible electorate, and over 40 percent in Alabama, Florida, Georgia, Louisiana, and Mississippi, and 39 percent in Virginia. Overall, adult black males were 40.4 percent of the former Confederacy's adult males.[28]

The enfranchisement of blacks did not represent a victory for the principle of racial equality or for that of universal suffrage. The notion of political equality for blacks had never been popular with the country's voters. By 1865 only six northern states permitted blacks to vote, and efforts to extend voting rights to them in other states had usually been blocked either in state legislatures or by voters who refused to approve the required constitutional referenda. In all, 63 percent of the total ballots cast in twenty-two referenda between 1849 and 1869 were cast **against** black rights.[29]

Despite this popular opposition, the Fifteenth Amendment was introduced, passed by Congress, and ratified by the necessary number of states because Republicans made support for it a litmus test of party loyalty. To be sure, the motives of Republican leaders were diverse. Some saw support for it as a moral question, others were simply responding to the strident demands of their Yankee Protestant support groups. Perhaps other Republican officeholders were moved by nothing more complex than a vengeful antisouthernism, and some certainly were motivated by the hope of using the vote of the freedmen to make the South a bastion of Republicanism. Whatever the mixture of motives, in state legislatures throughout the North and Midwest, solid blocs of Republicans were arrayed against equally cohesive groups of Democrats on the issue.[30]

Certainly, Republican party leaders recognized the general unpopularity of their policy position on black suffrage. But they succeeded in channeling public opinion by portraying their action as an effort to secure "the fruits of the war" and by linking opposition to black suffrage with the treason-stained Democratic party and with that party's continuing efforts to "resuscitate the rebellion." It was this final linkage that was most critical. It provided the direct cue to behavior; and as it reverberated with the acts, speeches, and postures of Democratic officials, it transformed the issue into a test of party loyalty——not just among officials and activists, but among the mass electorate as well.

Another major expansion of the electorate occurred at the end of this period, and it also involved federal action. The ratification of the Nineteenth Amendment enfranchised approximately 26.7 million adult females, or about 49.1 percent of the total number of age-eligible voters in 1920.[31] This was by far the largest expansion of the electorate in U.S. history.

The battle for female suffrage was not easily or quickly won. The first organized opposition to the disfranchisement of women was a convention "to discuss the social, civil, and religious rights of women," held in the Wesleyan Chapel in Seneca Falls, New York, in 1848. That gathering produced a Declaration of Sentiments, listing first among other complaints that men did not permit women to exercise the "inalienable right to the elective franchise."[32]

Progress was slow after that, despite the strenuous efforts of activist women. In the two decades following the Civil War, about a dozen states granted limited voting rights to women, allowing them to cast ballots in school, tax, and bonding elections, and in municipal elections in Kansas. These were not really impressive gains: men were simply allowing women to vote in elections related to schools because they thought schooling involved an extension of the woman's role of rearing children. Permitting women to participate in these types of elections did not violate the long-standing norm that politics was essentially men's business. And the belief that women would bring a distinctly moral tone to politics underlay their grant of municipal voting rights in Kansas. Prohibition forces there sought to enlist the voting support of women to rid the cities of the baleful influence of demon rum.

Wyoming's entry into the Union in 1890 gave new momentum to the movement for female suffrage. Its constitution gave full suffrage rights to women, reaffirming the voting qualification it had adopted twenty-one years earlier as a territory. Within six years, Colorado, Idaho, and Utah granted women the right to vote for all elective offices. But progress stalled at that point; the next state to give full voting rights to women was Washington in 1910. Arizona, California, Kansas, and Oregon followed within three years, and by 1919 six other states had fully enfranchised women: Michigan, Montana, Nevada, New York, Oklahoma, and South Dakota.[33] Finally, on 4 June 1919, Congress transmitted the federal women's suffrage amendment to the states. On August 25, 1920, when Tennessee became the thirty-six state to ratify, it was proclaimed as the Nineteenth Amendment to the U.S. Constitution.

Unlike the Fifteenth Amendment, female suffrage was not seen by contemporaries as a partisan measure. Congressional voting showed divisions within both major parties, with only a marginally larger proportion of Republicans supporting voting rights for women than Democrats. Popular voting showed no consistent or significant patterns of partisan opposition on female suffrage referenda.[34]

But there was a clear relationship between female suffrage and prohibition. This was obvious at the interest-group level, of course, as the associations of brewers, liquor dealers, and wine producers had long led the battle against both proposed amendments to the Constitution. But it was equally true at the level of the mass electorate. Where referenda were held on both issues, eight out of ten supporters of female suffrage cast their ballots for prohibition.[35]

The Fifteenth and Nineteenth Amendments, both of which expanded the electorate, were federal initiatives, although state action was required for ratification. But left to their own devices, during this period the states implemented new substantive and procedural rules that restricted the sizes of their electorates.

What happened in the South was only the clearest example. Political elites there were simply more candid than their northern counterparts in declaring their intention to reverse the impact of the Fifteenth Amendment by disfranchising blacks.

The disfranchisement of southern blacks did not occur with one stroke. Some states acted before the mid-1890s, although there was slightly more activity after the 1896 election. The restrictive measures tended to come in two waves: the first (from 1888 to 1893) coincided with the threatened passage of the Lodge Fair Elections Bill, while the second (from 1898 to 1902) followed the extinction of Populist-Republican insurgency in the mid-1890s. The threats of external supervision of the conduct of elections and of serious challenge to continued control by the Democratic party made disfranchisement appear necessary; the failure of those threats made it possible.[36]

Southern disfranchisers did not depend on any single approach to achieve their aim. They blended new statutes with constitutional amendments, and substantive changes with procedural innovations, mixing longer residency and property requirements with poll taxes, registration laws, and literacy tests. Rigid voter registration laws, for example, often closed the process as much as a year prior to the election, and durational residency requirements were sometimes lengthened to as much as two years. While these and other types of restrictive practices played some roles, poll taxes and literacy tests were clearly the linchpins of the newly emerging "Southern System" of election laws.[37]

The poll tax laws usually required that a person pay some fixed sum of money, normally several months to a year prior to election day, and to retain the receipt and to present it at election time as proof of payment. Between 1889 and 1902, ten southern states imposed poll tax requirements, joining Georgia which had done so as early as 1871. While these laws were expressly aimed at blacks, whom the disfranchisers presumed lacked the money to pay the tax or would be unwilling to do so to vote, they also eliminated large numbers of poor whites. The impact on whites varied from state to state; overall perhaps as much as a quarter of the white electorate was effectively disfranchised by these requirements.[38]

In the event that the poll tax did not effectively deter blacks from voting, some southern states also imposed literacy qualifications. This procedure required a person to read a section of the state or federal constitution and give a reasonable interpretation of it. Because the legislation typically gave wide discretion to local election registrars, especially in judging what a "reasonable interpretation" was, they could easily use it to keep blacks from voting. Between 1890 and 1908, seven southern states adopted a requirement of this sort for voting eligibility.[39]

Whites faced with losing their political rights under one or another of these new restrictions could be expected to oppose them. To discourage low-income white Democrats from joining with Republicans or Populists to defeat these new rules, disfranchisers invented three types of escape clauses: the understanding clause, the grandfather clause, and the fighting grandfather clause. The understanding clause allowed an illiterate to register if he could understand a section of the state constitution that was read to him and explain it to the registrar's satisfaction. In some states, the registrar was also required to pass judgment on the illiterate applicant's "good character." Men could register under the grandfather clause if they had been eligible in 1867, which was before southern blacks were enfranchised, or if they were descendants of 1867 voters. The fighting grandfather clause allowed the registration of anyone who had fought for the Union or Confederacy, or had fought in any other U.S. war, and his descendants.[40]

These escape clauses were clearly designed for racial and partisan discrimination. When asked whether Christ could register under the good character clause, one of the participants in Alabama's constitutional convention admitted "that would depend entirely on which way he was going to vote." And a leader of Virginia's disfranchising convention proudly proclaimed its objective: "Discrimination! . . . [T]hat is precisely what we propose; that, exactly, is what this convention was elected for."[41]

And discrimination is exactly what Virginia's convention and the actions of the other southern states achieved. Black registration and turnout for elections dropped sharply in each state immediately following the imposition of its first piece of restrictive legislation. Black turnout in Alabama, for example, declined by 96 percent between 1900 and 1904, and in Louisiana by 93 percent between 1896 and 1900. In all eleven states combined, following the imposition of new restrictive rules, black turnout dropped by 62 percent. White turnout also declined, by 26 percent, reflecting the combined effects of disfranchisement of low income white voters and waning party competition. The demobilization of the region's electorate that occurred in the wake of the creation of this "Southern System" of election laws was the most severe and extensive that this nation has ever witnessed.[42]

The desire to reshape the electorate in particular ways was not confined to southerners. Northern leaders also moved around the turn of the century to purge their electorates of what they regarded as "undesirable" elements. Like their southern counterparts, northern restrictionists resorted to a mix of substantive and procedural innovations to achieve their aim.

Residency requirements were one of the substantive rules that northern registrationists altered. Between 1890 and 1920, eight states outside the South——Colorado, Delaware, Massachusetts, Michigan, Minnesota, Rhode Island, South Dakota, and Wisconsin——raised the length of their residency requirements for voting. Three of these states doubled the time required to qualify for voting: Colorado and South Dakota went from six to twelve months and Rhode Island from twelve to twenty-four months.

But the major substantive change outside the South involved the elimination of alien suffrage. By 1860 four midwestern states had extended the franchise to aliens who declared their intention to become citizens. In the years following the Civil War, the movement to enfranchise aliens spread to eight more states in the plains and western regions of the country——Colorado, Kansas, Missouri, Nebraska, North Dakota, Oregon, South Dakota, and Wyoming.[43] By the mid-1890s, however, the measure's popularity dimmed. Michigan and Wyoming acted in 1894 to restrict voting rights to citizens, and Minnesota and North Dakota followed their leads in 1896 and 1898, respectively. By the end of 1922, when Missouri acted, all eight other nonsouthern states had withdrawn voting rights from aliens.

The impact of disqualifying aliens who intended to become citizens was minimal nationally: qualified aliens in 1900 comprised only 1.1 percent of the nation's total electorate. But the repeal measure clearly had much greater impact in particular states. Nearly 8 percent of Wisconsin's electorate and perhaps as much as a third of North Dakota's was disqualified when these states disallowed alien suffrage. Taken collectively, repeal of alien suffrage provisions disfranchised slightly more than 289,000 aliens who had declared their intention to become citizens, or just about 4 percent of the total electorate of the involved states at the time each took action.[44]

In addition to these substantive changes, northern states also adopted procedural rules limiting access to the ballot or making the voting act more difficult. Between 1890 and 1920, Arizona, California, Delaware, Maine, New Hampshire, Oklahoma, Washington, and Wyoming passed laws that made proof of literacy a requirement for voting. Connecticut and Massachusetts had imposed literacy test requirements much earlier, in 1856 and 1858, respectively, thus bringing to ten the number of states outside the South that imposed this qualification. New York in 1922 and Oregon in 1926 joined the ranks of these states.

Even more commonly, northern restrictionists resorted to tightening voter registration requirements in their effort to reshape the electorates of their states. Requiring some sort of registration prior to election day was not a new idea: four states mandated preelection voter enrollment of one sort or another in the early nineteenth century, and seven more joined them by the opening of the Civil War. The experiences of the war and Reconstruction periods raised interest in these procedures, and fifteen more states imposed a voter-registration requirement by 1870. In some of these cases, the new law represented a transparent attempt by the dominant political party to consolidate and perpetuate its control of state government. In any case, by 1880, twenty-eight of the thirty-eight states in the Union had some sort of voter registration requirement in effect. Moreover, of the ten territories that became states in the 1890s and early 1900s, only South Dakota entered the Union without a voter-registration system.[45]

These early systems usually provided for nonpersonal registration systems. Designated election officers were responsible for "registering" voters by preparing lists of names of the eligible residents within their districts at some regular interval, typically two or four years. But there was no requirement that individuals personally appear before these officials to certify that they were qualified to vote. The registrars simply used whatever sources were available, including old registration and poll lists, to compile their enumeration. Clearly, systems of this sort were open to error and abuse. Some of the enrollment lists probably reflected nothing more than the registrar's imagination, since many statutes simply required election officials to enroll "the names of all those persons well known to them to be eligible to vote." Moreover, the registrars themselves were not professional civil servants; they were part-time "volunteers," usually nominated for their duties by local party officials. Thus, it may have been that in some places registration became a highly partisan affair, with the registrars setting down only the names of those persons well known to be dependable supporters of their party.

Beginning in the 1890s, states outside the South moved to remedy such defects by replacing these weak registration systems with more stringent ones. The central feature of this change involved imposing a personal registration requirement, a provision that shifted the burden for establishing eligibility from the state to the individual. By 1920, thirty-one nonsouthern states had put some type of personal registration requirement into effect, although the nature and coverage of these laws varied considerably. Some laws imposed a periodic registration requirement, making citizens renew their registration at established intervals, but most provided for "permanent" registration as long as the voter didn't fail to participate in consecutive elections. More importantly, in about thirteen states, including the most heavily populated ones, the laws provided for distinct types of registration in different categories of counties.[46] Personal registration was imposed on the urban counties, while nonpersonal or even no registration prevailed elsewhere. In time, as more counties satisfied the urban criterion, coverage by personal registration requirements became more extensive, so that some form of personal registration was in force in over half the counties outside the South by the end of the 1920s.[47]

The Australian ballot was another important procedural innovation adopted during this period. Unlike registration procedures, however, this one applied to election day activities. Since about the middle of the nineteenth century, political parties had prepared the ballots and dispensed them to voters on election day. Each party's ballot listed only its own candidates for office, so that a voter had to scratch out one name and write in another to split his ticket. Moreover, since each party printed its ticket on distinctively colored paper, and since party workers could observe voters depositing their ballots, there was little secrecy involved in the process.

Many of the same persons and groups pushing for the adoption of personal registration laws also argued for reform of the voting process. Within the short span of eight years, from 1888 through

1896, over 90 percent of the states adopted the Australian ballot.[48] Used initially in Australia in 1856, and common in Europe and Canada in the 1880s, this new ballot differed in important ways from the party ticket then widely in use. First, it was prepared and administered by the state, making it an official and uniform ballot and taking the role of making and distributing ballots away from political parties. Second, it was a consolidated ballot, listing the names of the candidates of all parties instead of only those of one party. Third, as a complement to its being a consolidated ballot, it brought secrecy to the process of voting. While utilizing these features, the states decided for themselves how to arrange the internal format of their ballots. Some states used the "office bloc" format that Australia used originally; others listed the offices under "party columns," usually adding a straight-ticket voting option and sometimes a party emblem at the top of each column.

This new ballot system offered the voter an impartial, multiple-choice instrument upon which he could deliberate in the privacy of the voting booth. The conditions it created reduced the influence of parties during the voting process itself and created greater opportunity for split-ticket voting than under the party ticket system.[49] At the same time, its multiple choice feature made the act of voting more difficult for many citizens, and it likely had an intimidating effect especially on those who were either illiterate or only marginally literate.

Their proponents extolled ballot and registration reform as a means to purify the electoral process. By using their access to the opinion magazines of the day, as well as to scholarly journals, they defined the context within which the battle over the adoption of these measures was fought. As they presented it, this was a struggle between "good government," on the one hand, and corruption and fraud, on the other. Given that choice, few opposed the forces and instruments of "good government."

We should not construe these contemporary claims literally. These self-declared proponents of "good government" were able to point to remarkably few cases of vote fraud or ballot-box stuffing. They gave the term a much broader meaning than we would now. To turn-of-the-century reformers, electoral politics was "corrupt" because too many persons "cast their vote not from principle" but from a narrow conception of their own (or their group's) self-interest. Indeed, one contemporary study of political corruption defined the term without referring to any of the typical illegal acts and instead emphasized "the intentional misperformance or neglect of a recognized duty, some advantage more or less directly personal."[50]

Above all, these reformers judged the electoral process to be "corrupt" because too many people of the wrong sort were allowed to participate. They regarded "universal suffrage [as] but another name for a licensed mobocracy." Since the right to vote "is applicable only to those peoples, if such there are, who by character and training are prepared for it, . . . the effects of flinging the suffrage to the mob are most disastrous." It kept "the best men" out of politics, while discouraging participation by the middle class, the store owners, bookkeepers, and physicians. They asked themselves, "'What is the use?' We shall be swamped by a gang of Poles, Hungarians, and Yawps that can't speak English, don't understand the system of government, and vote as they are told by the [political] bosses."[51]

Reformers often fused these antimajoritarian values with antiparty outlooks, arguing that "party spirit" was a prime source of political "corruption." As long as voters believe that they "must stand by [their] party, right or wrong, . . . we cannot hope to obtain that nonpartisan [sic] and public-spirited action" in politics that "is essential to honest and intelligent . . . government." Consequently, reformers viewed party voting as a danger to the cause of good government, while they praised independent voting as "the mark of the educated, intelligent class."[52]

In short, this multifaceted turn-of-the-century effort outside the South to restrict access to the ballot and to make the voting act more difficult cannot be understood as the product of some sort of generalized "good government" movement. Nor can it be explained as an attack on numerous and specific instances of vote fraud and corruption. Instead, it represented an attempt by society's self-designated "better element," its upper-class and upper-middle-class strata, to constrain the twin evils of "party spirit" and universal suffrage. However effective the resulting laws were in restricting the suffrage, changing party practices, and eroding party-vote linkages, these were precisely the consequences that reformers intended. And they proclaimed their purposive intentions as explicitly and unqualifiedly as southern disfranchisers.

From Female Suffrage to the Present

During the most recent era of the development of election rules in the United States, the changes have all moved in the direction of expanding access to the franchise. This has involved both an easing of the restrictions imposed by procedural requirements adopted around the turn of the century, as well as some substantive redefinition of the eligible electorate by lowering age and residency requirements. For the most part, these changes reflect greater federal involvement in suffrage questions during this period. This involvement has consisted of amendments to the U.S. Constitution, as in the previous period, and intervention by the federal judiciary and Congress in shaping the rules governing suffrage.

The most important development during this period was the effort to eliminate the "Southern System" of restricting access to the ballot. Two aspects of this system had already been struck down by the U.S. Supreme Court before the period began. In 1915 the court invalidated the grandfather clause of Oklahoma's state constitution, declaring that the standard of voting it established recreated and perpetuated "the very conditions which the [Fifteenth] Amendment was intended to destroy."[53] And in 1944, applying the protections of the same amendment to participation in primary elections, the court struck down a Texas law providing for an all-white primary.[54]

White primary laws originally had little impact on black voting participation. When they were put in place by state Democratic parties in the mid- to late 1870s, most blacks were Republicans and didn't seek to vote in Democratic primaries. At that point, too, there was still viable interparty competition and blacks were still active participants in general elections. As these conditions changed, especially as partisan competition was extinguished and suffrage restrictions limited the electorate, the Democratic party's practice of excluding blacks from participating in its primaries took on greater importance.[55]

While the Supreme Court early on recognized the exclusionary effect of this practice, it was slow to invoke the protections of the Fifteenth Amendment. In both 1927 and 1932, it struck down Texas statutes providing for white primaries, but on both occasions it relied on the equal protection clause of the Fourteenth Amendment. These narrow decisions left the central issue unresolved—whether in managing a primary, especially one whose winners invariably triumphed in the general election, a political party performed a public function, or whether it was, as the defendants claimed, simply a voluntary association, much like a business, church, or social club.[56] Unfortunately for the black plaintiffs, in 1935, after Texas had redesigned its statutes to meet the earlier objections, the court directly addressed this question. Speaking for a unanimous court, Justice Roberts held that the Democratic party was a private body and not subject to the strictures of the Fourteenth and Fifteenth Amendments. Furthermore, he argued that to accept the claim that a black could not legitimately be denied a ballot at a primary simply because its outcome determined the result of the general election was "to confuse privilege of membership in a party with the right to vote for one who is to hold public office."[57]

Six years later, however, in a Louisiana case dealing with vote fraud in a congressional primary, the court extended the protections of the Constitution to the right to vote "where the state law has made the primary an integral part of the procedure of choice, or where in fact the primary effectively controls the choice."[58] The decision remained silent on the status of its 1935 decision because the court had not considered whether an individual could be denied party membership on the basis of race, simply ruling that registered Democrats could not fraudulently be deprived of their vote in a congressional primary. But the court had clearly shifted the direction of its thinking, so that it came as no great surprise three years later when it ruled in Allwright that a party functioned as a state agency when it managed primary elections.

Grandfather clauses and white primaries were not the central features of the "Southern System," however, and so their elimination did not alter its operation that much. Neither did these successes give immediate impetus to attempts at removing other restrictions on blacks' access to the ballot. Indeed, no further legal progress occurred until the 1960s, when federal action eliminated both poll taxes and literacy tests.

Legislation to eliminate poll taxes, either by constitutional amendment or by statute, had been introduced in every Congress since 1939. None of these efforts had been successful, and five southern states still retained a poll tax as late as 1960. But in 1962 Congress passed a resolution calling for a constitutional amendment providing that persons should not be denied the right to vote in federal elections "by reason of failure to pay any poll tax or other tax." In February 1964, when the required number of states had ratified, the Twenty-fourth Amendment became part of the Constitution. In a 1965 test case, the Supreme Court held that for federal elections "the poll tax is abolished absolutely as a prerequisite to voting, and no milder substitute may be imposed." And when Virginia attempted to retain a poll tax requirement for state elections, a divided court invalidated it in 1966 as a violation of the equal protection clause.[59]

In several southern states, literacy test requirements operated as vital parts of restrictive registration systems. As early as 1898, the Supreme Court had given legal sanction to such tests, as long as they were drafted to apply to all applicants for the franchise and in the absence of any proof of discriminatory enforcement. And when the court first invalidated a literacy test requirement it did so on appropriately narrow grounds, holding in a 1949 case that a literacy amendment to Alabama's constitution violated the Fifteenth Amendment because its legislative history clearly indicated that it was intended to obviate the consequences of the Allwright decision.[60]

More than a decade later that the literacy test requirement came under broader attack. Then the assault was led by Congress, with the Supreme Court providing later support. The Civil Rights Act of 1964, which dealt mainly with public accommodations, employment, and education, initially tackled the issue by stipulating that completion of a sixth-grade education should serve as adequate proof of literacy. The Voting Rights Act of 1965 went considerably further. Its remedial provisions applied to any state or political subdivision found by the U.S. Attorney General to have maintained a "test or device" as a prerequisite to voting on 1 November 1964, and which the Director of the Census determined to have less than 50 percent of its voting age residents registered or voting in the November 1964 election. The remedies provided by the act included prompt suspension of such tests and devices and the appointment of federal registrars and poll watchers. The act also provided that the states thus identified had to obtain advance approval of the Attorney General or of the U.S. District Court for the District of Columbia for any "proposed change" in its laws adding such a "test or device." Subsequent challenges to these measures on constitutional grounds were rebuffed by the Supreme Court.[61]

Political Participation

In 1970 Congress amended the Voting Rights Act, banning until August 1975 the imposition of any literacy requirement not then in force in national, state, or local elections anywhere in the U.S.[62] Congress again renewed the Act in 1975, this time for seven years, and broadened its provisions to include language minorities.

When the Voting Rights Act again came up for extension in 1982, conditions had changed. The Reagan Administration favored eliminating preclearance requirements and it opposed inserting language to offset the limiting effect of a 1980 decision by the Supreme Court in a case involving the election system of the City of Mobile.

That case dealt with the question of whether at-large elections that dilute minority-group representation thereby violate the constitutional ban on racial discrimination. Lower courts had sided with the black plaintiffs, striking down the City of Mobile's at-large election of city commissioners and calling for single-member districts. The April 1980 decision by the Supreme Court reversed these rulings. Justice Stewart, speaking for the plurality in a sharply divided court, failed to find any violation of the Fifteenth Amendment since blacks had not been denied either the right to register or to vote. "The Fifteenth Amendment," he said, "does not entail the right to have Negro candidates elected." Furthermore, he dismissed plaintiffs' contention that the city's system of electing commissioners violated the Fourteenth Amendment's equal protection clause. Such a demonstration, he said, required proof of the intent to discriminate, not simply a showing of "disproportionate impact."[63]

Civil rights advocates in 1982 wanted to repair the damage caused by the Mobile decision by authorizing the judiciary to find vote dilution unconstitutional based on discriminatory impact as well as on intent. The Reagan Administration concentrated its opposition to the extension on this clause, arguing that it amounted to a type of reverse discrimination and raising the specter of a quota system for elected officials. Despite this opposition, however, the final version of the extension restored a result-oriented standard of proof, and it extended the preclearance feature of the act for twenty-five years.

With these actions against grandfather clauses and the white primary, and especially against poll taxes and literacy tests, and with the use of federal registrars, the peculiar "Southern System" of franchise restriction collapsed. Black registration in southern states increased sharply following passage of the Voting Rights Act, jumping from 35 percent of the region's adult black population in 1964, to 57 percent in 1967, and to 65 percent in 1969. Black turnout also went up dramatically, reaching a level in presidential elections that was 41 percentage points higher than it had been over the 1952-60 period.[64]

Dismantling suffrage restriction in the South largely entailed eliminating procedural rules adopted earlier in the century. But this period also saw two substantive changes in voter qualifications that affected all areas of the country.

The first substantive change lowered the minimum age for voting. The state constitutions adopted after the American Revolution had set the minimum age at twenty-one, and there was no serious effort to change that until the late 1910s. It was when the U.S. entered World War I that the expression "old enough to fight, old enough to vote" initially came into use. But the war ended quickly, and so did this first demand for giving 18 to 20 year olds the right to vote.[65]

With the outbreak of World War II, discussions about lowering the voting age resumed, and Georgia broke precedent and did so in 1943. But there was no further action until 1955, when Kentucky lowered its voting age requirement to 18. And in 1959 Alaska and Hawaii entered the Union with 19 and 20 year old voting requirements, respectively.

From World War I through the early 1960s, however, there was really very little pressure, especially from the young, for lowering the voting age. The demand for change became greater in the late 1960s. Once again, the country was involved in a war, and one which was especially unpopular with the nation's youth. The old claim that if young people must risk their lives fighting, they should have a right to participate in selecting those who make decisions about war and peace seemed to take on new importance. Congress responded positively, and the Voting Rights Act of 1970 lowered the minimum age requirement to 18 for state and federal elections.

But later that year, the Supreme Court, while accepting the 18-year-old provisions for federal elections, declared them to be "unconstitutional and unenforceable insofar as they pertain to state and local elections."[66] That left the states with the problem of establishing double registration and balloting systems to accommodate two different groups of eligible voters. The prospect of administrative chaos resulting from this situation undoubtedly accounts for the speed with which Congress and the states acted in 1971 to approve the Twenty-sixth Amendment, which allowed the new age to apply to all elections. With the ratification of this amendment, eleven million 18 to 20 year olds entered the eligible electorate.

The residence requirement was the second substantive voter qualification changed in this period. These were initially imposed by states in the first half of the nineteenth century, as they weakened their economic tests. They then usually required a comparatively long period of residence, typically a year; and some states around the turn of the century moved to make their requirement even more stringent.

By the mid-twentieth century, objections to these requirements had become commonplace. The society's increased rates of geographic mobility meant that more and more people found themselves disfranchised in their new states of residence. By the late 1960s, several states had shortened their required periods of residence, and Michigan and Oregon had even passed statutes allowing former residents to vote for president if they were disqualified from voting in their new states because of residence restrictions. In the 1970 Voting Rights Act, Congress put a limit of thirty days as the length of residence that states could require for voting in federal elections. Two years later, the Supreme Court struck down Tennessee's one-year requirement for state elections, indicating instead that a maximum period of thirty to sixty days was a reasonable requirement.[67]

In addition to these federal initiatives to alter substantive rules, the states have acted during this period to offset the effects of some of the procedural rules they adopted earlier in the century. They have particularly moved to make it easier for citizens to register to vote. For example, most states have extended the time period for registration, increased the number of registrars, and decentralized the places for registration, allowing deputy registrars to enroll people in libraries, high school classes, motor vehicle bureaus, and even in offices dispensing public aid and unemployment compensation. A few states have gone even further, allowing citizens to register by mail or on election day at the polling place.[68] And measures have been introduced in Congress to provide for nationwide standards for voter registration.[69]

Conclusions

Without doubt, the franchise is broader in 1988 than it was in 1789. Blacks, women, and 18 to 20 year olds are eligible to vote; there are no property owning or taxpaying qualifications; and residency requirements are considerably shorter. Moreover, later procedural rules that worked to limit access to the ballot or make the voting act more difficult have been eased or eliminated. Poll taxes and literacy tests have been effectively abolished and registration requirements and procedures generally have been made less onerous.

This movement toward a broadened suffrage has gone through distinct stages. During the first, action at the state level predominated, as individual states eliminated economic qualifications, increased the number of elective offices and sometimes the frequency of elections, adopted paper ballots to replace public voting, and reduced the size of election jurisdictions. Some of the new midwestern states even allowed aliens to vote upon declaring their intention to become citizens.

This initial period of franchise expansion was followed by one during which the signals and sources of action were mixed. Federal initiatives worked to expand the suffrage by admitting blacks and women to the electorate through the adoption of the Fifteenth and Nineteenth Amendments. But action at the state level moved in the opposite direction. The southern states relied on combinations of new procedures, especially on poll taxes and literacy tests, to disfranchise blacks and thus offset the effects of the Fifteenth Amendment. Other states targeted the foreign born and moved to eliminate alien enfranchisement provisions. Some states lengthened their residency requirements, all of them adopted some form of the Australian ballot, and most imposed a personal registration requirement, thus shifting the burden of establishing eligibility from the government to the individual.

The final period of election law development has again been expansionary. The franchise has been broadened by lowering age and residency requirements, the "Southern System" of legal restrictions has been dismantled, and elsewhere procedural rules have become less restrictive.

In addition to the fluctuation between expansionary and restrictive emphases, other aspects of these historical patterns are worth noticing. The first is the shift in policymaking from the state to the federal level. Prior to the Civil War, state action dominated, and the next period was marked by a combination of state and federal initiatives. During the final period, however, the balance clearly and decisively tilted toward the federal level. The Supreme Court and Congress, which for the first time assumed responsibility for regulating the conduct of elections in the Voting Rights Act of 1965, led the way during this period, with the states either challenging their actions or only slowly accepting them.

Second, the history of the franchise in the United States gives no evidence of widespread commitment to the principle of universal suffrage. To the contrary, the various exclusions and restrictions that have been written into the laws point in the opposite direction. Franchise expansion has occurred, nevertheless; but always in a piecemeal fashion and mainly motivated, at least until the most recent period, by calculations of partisan, or at least political, advantage.

Efforts eliminating economic tests for voting in the eastern states, as well as those enfranchising aliens in the Midwest, were closely connected with the development of party formations in those locales. The enfranchisement of blacks was at least partially motivated by calculations of benefits to the Republicans, while construction of the "Southern System" was explicitly and exclusively aimed at extinguishing organized opposition to the Democratic parties in the region. The Nineteenth Amendment cut across Democratic and Republican lines, because it was pushed by prohibitionists in both major parties. And outside the South, the drive for longer residence requirements, personal registration laws, and literacy tests, as well as other procedures complicating the voting act, was led by groups of upper and upper-middle class persons and aimed at eliminating working class, and especially immigrant, elements from the electorate.

Actions in the most recent period have not seemed to originate in partisan calculations, although they clearly have had such effects. Dismemberment of the "Southern System," for example, by opening the way to viable interparty competition, has mainly aided Republicans in the South. Yet Republican officeholders and spokespersons there and elsewhere denounced and resisted the court decisions and congressional actions that made it possible.[70] While shorter residence qualifications, easing some registration restrictions, and even lowering the minimum voting age had considerable bipartisan support.

Calculations of partisan gain haven't yet been entirely eliminated from this area of policymaking. The movement for some type of universal voter registration act has generally been viewed in those terms, with Democrats favoring and Republicans opposing it. All sides agree that easing the registration process, whether through election day registration, mail registration, or returning to nonpersonal registration would lead to higher rates of enrollment among low income and poorly educated citizens. Expanding the electorate along these economic and social dimensions has obvious appeal to Democratic partisans, while Republicans look upon it with disfavor for equally transparent reasons.

As long as this issue continues to elicit responses along party lines, under present conditions, the country is unlikely to adopt a uniform and more facilitative set of registration rules. But it is certainly even less likely to move in the other direction, reintroducing the more stringent substantive and procedural rules of earlier eras. Thus, whenever changes do occur in the future, they are likely to be in the direction of still easier access to the ballot.

NOTES

1. Sidney Verba and Norman H. Nie, **Participation in America: Political Democracy and Social Equality** (New York, 1972), pp. 44-55, outline this conceptual framework.

2. For example, actual turnout averaged 61.4 percent in the presidential elections between 1952 and 1976; while the closest rival, self-reported attempts to persuade others how to vote, averaged 31.7 percent; see Paul Kleppner, **Who Voted? The Dynamics of Electoral Turnout, 1870–1980** (New York, 1982), pp. 5 and 167.

3. Donald J. Devine, **The Political Culture of the United States: The Influence of Member Values on Regime Maintenance** (Boston, 1972), p. 42. My own analysis of the SRC/CPS National Election Studies from 1952 through 1984 provides confirmatory evidence. For example, in 1980, 60.2 percent of the sample saw voting as its only available opportunity to influence public decision making, and in 1984, 64.9 percent said that elections make the government pay a good deal or some attention to what the people think.

Political Participation

4. Verba and Nie, **Participation in America,** pp. 322-27 and 333.

5. The same formula was invoked when Article I, Section III was superseded by the Seventeenth Amendment (1913) providing for direct election of U.S. Senators.

6. This distinction and its discussion in the next paragraph follow Jerrold G. Rusk and John J. Stucker, "Legal-Institutional Factors in American Voting" (unpublished manuscript, 1975 revision), p. 3.

7. For empirical evidence on this point, see Paul Kleppner and Stephen C. Baker, "The Impact of Voter Registration Requirements on Electoral Turnout, 1900-16," **Journal of Political and Military Sociology** 8 (Fall 1980): 205-26; and Kleppner, **Who Voted?,** pp. 58-62 and 86-87. For evidence for more recent elections, see Raymond E. Wolfinger and Steven J. Rosenstone, **Who Votes?** (New Haven, 1980); and The Committee for the Study of the American Electorate, **Creating the Opportunity: How Voting Laws Affect Voter Turnout** (Washington, D.C., 1987)

8. For a more complete and reasoned statement of this argument, see Jerrold G. Rusk, "The Effect of Australian Ballot Reform on Split Ticket Voting," **American Political Science Review** 64 (December 1970): 1220-38; and Jerrold G. Rusk, "Comment: The American Electoral Universe: Speculation and Evidence," **American Political Science Review** 68 (September 1974): 1028-49.

9. Rusk and Stucker, "Legal-Institutional Factors in American Voting," pp. 4-5.

10. Chilton Williamson, **American Suffrage from Property to Democracy, 1760-1860** (Princeton, 1960), p. 5.

11. Albert J. McCulloch, **Suffrage and Its Problems** (Baltimore, Md., 1929), pp. 20-21; Charles Seymour and Donald Paige Frary, **How the World Votes: The Story of Democratic Development in Elections** (2 vols.; Springfield, Mass., 1918), 1:211-12.

12. Williamson, **American Suffrage,** pp. 14-15.

13. Williamson, **American Suffrage,** pp. 21-22 and 24-39. Also see, Robert E. Brown, **Middle-Class Democracy and the Revolution in Massachusetts, 1691-1780** (Ithaca, N.Y., 1955); and David S. Lovejoy, **Rhode Island Politics and the American Revolution, 1760-1776** (Providence, R.I., 1958).

14. Seymour and Frary, **How the World Votes,** 1:216-20.

15. Williamson, **American Suffrage,** pp. 15-16.

16. Three states—Massachusetts, New York, and North Carolina—adopted more restrictive economic qualifications, and there were no significant changes from late colonial practices in the other states. See Williamson, **American Suffrage**, pp. 92-116.

17. Discussions of this process often overlook the fact that some states retained poll tax requirements well beyond 1860. For example, Massachusetts kept its requirement in place until 1894 when the voters of the commonwealth adopted a constitutional amendment eliminating payment of the poll tax as a prerequisite for voting.

18. Williamson, **American Suffrage**, pp. 97-99 and 211-12.

19. Frederick Jackson Turner, **The Rise of the New West** (New York, 1906), p. 175; idem, **The Frontier in American History** (New York, 1920), p. 250. And see Williamson, **American Suffrage**, pp. 208-22, for a review of developments in the western states.

20. The final vestiges of Rhode Island's property-owning requirement were not eliminated until 1928. For that state's peculiar franchise history, see Chilton Williamson, "Rhode Island Suffrage since the Dorr War," **New England Quarterly** 28 (March 1955): 34-50; and for the other developments discussed in the paragraph, see William G. Shade, "Political Pluralism and Party Development: The Creation of a Modern Party System: 1815-1852," in **The Evolution of American Electoral Systems**, by Paul Kleppner et al. (Westport, Conn., 1981), p. 78.

21. Williamson, **American Suffrage**, pp. 110 and 235.

22. Rusk and Stucker, "Legal-Institutional Factors in American Voting," pp. 11-13. The five "resisting" states were: Maine, Massachusetts, New Hampshire, New York, and Vermont.

23. James H. Kettner, **The Development of American Citizenship, 1608-1870** (Chapel Hill, N.C., 1978), pp. 224, 264-65, and 340-41; and Rogers M. Smith, "The 'American Creed' and American Identity: The Limits of Liberal Citizenship in the United States," **Western Political Quarterly** 41 (June 1988): 225-52, for a review of the lack of fit between democratic ideology and the actual limits on political membership. Citizenship was not defined in federal law until the Fourteenth Amendment was adopted and the Civil Rights Act was passed in 1866; see Kirk H. Porter, **A History of Suffrage in the United States** (Chicago, 1918), pp. 40-41.

24. Rusk and Stucker, "Legal-Institutional Factors in American Voting," p. 13, claim that this description would apply to thirteen states, but a reading of the state-by-state information that they provide in Tables 5 and 6 indicates that the larger number is the correct one.

25. Ronald P. Formisano, "A Case Study of Party Formation: Michigan, 1835," **Mid-America** 50 (April 1968): 83-107, is the best study of the relationship between alien enfranchisement and party development in the Midwest.

26. Williamson, **American Suffrage,** p. 275.

27. New Jersey State Library, Item AM 1,976, quoted in Williamson, **American Suffrage,** pp. 179-80.

28. **A Compendium of the Ninth Census (1870)** (Washington, D.C., 1872), Table 56, p. 554. In the United States as a whole, adult black males were only 10.9 percent of the total population of adult males.

29. The basic data are in, Tom LeRoy McLaughlin, "Popular Reaction to the Idea of Negro Equality in Twelve Non-Slaveholding States, 1864-1869: A Quantitative Analysis" (Ph.D. dissertation, Washington State University, 1969), Table 1, p. 37.

30. For more detail and documentation of matters discussed in this and the following paragraph, see Paul Kleppner, **The Third Electoral System, 1853-1892: Parties, Voters, and Political Cultures** (Chapel Hill, N.C., 1979), pp. 88-95.

31. Department of Commerce, Bureau of the Census, **Fourteenth Census of the United States Taken in the Year 1920. Volume III. Population** (Washington, D.C., 1922), Table 5, p. 18.

32. Anne Firor Scott and Andrew MacKay Scott, **One Half the People: The Fight for Woman Suffrage** (Urbana, Ill., 1975), pp. 9 and 56-59.

33. Between 1912 and the ratification of the Nineteenth Amendment, twelve other states granted women the right to vote for president. For a detailed chronology, see Rusk and Stucker, "Legal-Institutional Factors in American Voting," pp. 21-23.

34. Anne Firor Scott and Andrew MacKay Scott, **One Half the People,** report the partisan division on Congressional roll calls on pp. 161-63; and for the behavior on referenda, see Eileen L. McDonagh and H. Douglas Price, "Woman Suffrage in the Progressive Era: Patterns of Opposition and Support in Referenda Voting, 1910-1918," **American Political Science Review** 79 (June 1985): 415-35, and Paul Kleppner, **Continuity and Change in Electoral Politics, 1893-1928** (Westport, Conn., 1987), Table 33, p. 174.

35. Kleppner, **Continuity and Change,** Table 32, p. 173.

36. J. Morgan Kousser, **The Shaping of Southern Politics: Suffrage Restriction and the Establishment of a One-Party South, 1880-1910** (New Haven, Conn., 1974), pp. 238-40.

37. Jerrold G. Rusk and John J. Stucker, "The Effect of the Southern System of Election Laws on Voting Participation: A Reply to V. O. Key, Jr.," in **The History of American Electoral Behavior**, eds. Joel H. Silbey, Allan G. Bogue, and William H. Flanigan (Princeton, N.J., 1978), pp. 198-250.

38. Kousser, **Shaping of Southern Politics**, pp. 71-72, and p. 239 for a convenient chronology of the passage of restrictive measures in the southern states.

39. Arkansas, Florida, Tennessee, and Texas were the four states of the former Confederacy that did not adopt literacy tests.

40. Kousser, **Shaping of Southern Politics**, p. 58.

41. Both quotations are from Kousser, **Shaping of Southern Politics**, p. 59.

42. Kousser, **Shaping of Southern Politics**, data in Table 9.2, p. 241; and also see, Kleppner, **Who Voted?**, pp. 65-66.

43. Seven southern states also enfranchised aliens during this period, probably as part of the larger effort to counter the effects of enfranchising blacks. But immigrants comprised only a trivial proportion of the adult populations of these states, so that such measures had quite limited impact. For example, by 1900 Texas had the largest number of qualified aliens among the alien suffrage states of the South, and they amounted to only 15,588 potential voters there, or 2.2 percent of the size of that state's total electorate. In all seven states combined, there were only 18,824 qualified aliens in 1900, or only 8.1 percent of the total number of qualified aliens in the country. For the data, see United States Census Office, **Abstract of the Twelfth Census of the United States 1900** (Washington, D.C., 1902), Table 60, p. 78.

44. Kleppner, **Continuity and Change**, Table 30, p. 166.

45. Maryland and Missouri are classic examples of states in which post-Civil War voter-registration laws were attempts by the temporarily dominant party to consolidate its power; see Kleppner, **Third Electoral System**, pp. 115-20. For the chronology and discussion of the adoption of voter-registration requirements, see Rusk and Stucker, "Legal-Institutional Factors in American Voting," pp. 23-26; and Richard J. Carlson, "The Effects of Voter Registration Systems on Presidential Election Turnout in Non-Southern States: 1912-1924" (Ph.D. dissertation, University of Illinois, 1976), pp. 52-126. And for

the arguments and analysis of a participant in the "reform" movement, see Joseph P. Harris, **Registration of Voters in the United States** (Washington, D.C., 1929); and **idem, Election Administration in the United States** (Washington, D.C., 1934).

46. Numerical generalizations are complicated by the fact that some states changed from a mixed to a single system, and a few even shifted from single to mixed registration systems.

47. Kleppner, **Continuity and Change,** Table 31, p. 168.

48. For the chronology, see Eldon C. Evans, **A History of the Australian Ballot System in the United States** (Chicago, 1917); and Arthur C. Ludington, **American Ballot Laws: 1888-1910** (Albany, N.Y., 1911).

49. Rusk and Stucker, "Legal-Institutional Factors in American Voting," p. 29; Jerrold G. Rusk, "The Effect of the Australian Ballot Reform on Split Ticket Voting: 1876-1908," **American Political Science Review** 64 (December 1970): 1220-1238.

50. Respectively, the quotations are from Jeremiah W. Jenks, "Money in Practical Politics," **Century Magazine** 44 (October 1892): 947; and R. C. Brooks, **Corruption in American Politics and Life** (New York, 1910), p. 46. For a more detailed discussion of this and related matters, see Kleppner, **Continuity and Change,** pp. 167-71.

51. William L. Scruggs, "Citizenship and Suffrage," **North American Review** 177 (December 1903): 845; Francis Parkman, "The Failure of Universal Suffrage," **North American Review** 127 (July-August 1878): 8, 10, 20; Charles Francis Adams, "Municipal Government: Lessons from the Experience of Quincy, Mass.," **Forum** 14 (November 1892): 291; and E. L. C. Morse, "The Debasement of the Suffrage," **Nation** 76 (25 June 1903): 515. It is ironic that reformers declaimed against "universal suffrage" at a time when females——about half the adult population——were disfranchised.

52. Jenks, "Money in Practical Politics," p. 948; Editorial, "The First Step Toward Municipal Reform," **Century Magazine** 44 (October 1892): 947.

53. Guinn & Beal v. U.S., 238 U.S. 347 (1915).

54. Smith v. Allwright, 321 U.S. 649 (1944); and see Steven F. Lawson, **Black Ballots: Voting Rights in the South, 1944-1969** (New York, 1976), for a comprehensive view of the actions involved in dismantling the "Southern System."

55. Kousser, **Shaping of Southern Politics,** pp. 72-82, for an insightful analysis of the origins and changing significance of white primary laws.

56. Nixon v. Herndon, 273 U.S. 536 (1927); Nixon v. Condon, 286 U.S. 73 (1932).

57. Grovey v. Townsend, 295 U.S. 45 (1935)

58. U.S. v. Classic, 313 U.S. 299 (1941).

59. Harman v. Forssensius, 380 U.S. 528 (1965); Harper v. Virginia Bd. of Elections, 383 U.S. 663 (1966).

60. Williams v. Miss., 170 U.S. 213 (1898); Davis v. Schnell, 81 F. Supp. 872 (1949), **affirmed,** 336 U.S. 933 (1949).

61. South Carolina v. Katzenbach, 383 U.S. 301 (1966); Katzenbach v. Morgan, 384 U.S. 641 (1966).

62. The Supreme Court unanimously upheld this provision in Oregon v. Mitchell, 400 U.S. 112 (1970).

63. City of Mobile v. Bolden, 446 U.S. 55 (1980). For the background on this case and discussion of the 1982 extension of the Voting Rights Act, see Steven L. Lawson, **In Pursuit of Power: Southern Blacks and Electoral Politics, 1965-1982** (New York, 1985), pp. 276-92.

64. Kleppner, **Who Voted?,** pp. 114-22, and the data are on pp. 116-17.

65. Rusk and Stucker, "Legal-Institutional Factors in American Voting," pp. 30-31.

66. Oregon v. Mitchell, 400 U.S. 112 (1970).

67. Dunn v. Blumstein, 405 U.S. 330 (1972). The court also upheld that provision of the Voting Rights Act of 1970 mandating a closing date of at most thirty days for registration for presidential elections.

68. G. Smolka, **Registering Voters by Mail: The Maryland and New Jersey Experience** (Washington, D.C., 1975); and idem, **Election Day Registration: The Minnesota and Wisconsin Experience in 1976** (Washington, D.C., 1977).

69. U.S. Congress, House, Committee on House Administration, **Hearings on H.R. 5400, to Establish a Universal Voter Registration Program, and for Other Purposes.** 95th Cong., 1st sess., 1977.

70. The sequence of developments was more complicated than this description suggests. Once the process was underway, public opposition to broader voting rights for blacks served to attract white resisters, repel blacks, and thus create one of the significant fault lines of the South's newly emerged two-party system.

DISCUSSION AFTER PROFESSOR KLEPPNER'S PAPER

GASTIL: One could make the argument that there is more continuity between your middle and last periods (1860-1920 and 1920-) than your paper allows. Your middle period enfranchised more people than any other, and yet it is a period of restrictive movement, as you stated. In the middle period women's voting started at the state level, and moved into the federal level. So it wasn't like what happened after the Civil War. After the Civil War, voting rights were imposed from the federal level down, and they didn't take, in effect. It was a long time before they "took." Whereas with the women's vote, it came up from below and then was federalized. It already had enough support to "take."

KLEPPNER: True, there was no turning back from women's suffrage. There were problems with it, but there was no turning back, as there was, for example, with the 15th Amendment and the enfranchisement of blacks. But one has to be wary of expressing it quite the way that you have. Whenever one is talking about a federal amendment to the Constitution, after all, you must remember that action also has to be taken at the state level. And ratification of the 15th Amendment was effected at the state level. There were no survey data, or public opinion polls in the 1870s, but there were, as I point out in the paper, a number of referenda, and only one or two of them, in Iowa (the third time around as I recall) and one in Minnesota (I think the second time around) gave majority support to the enfranchisement of blacks.

Typically, enfranchisement of blacks, when put to a vote, even in northern states where there were very few blacks, was voted down by very wide margins. Indeed, Illinois, during the 1850s, had voted in favor of a measure that excluded blacks from residing in the state, let alone from voting in the state.

The enfranchisement, the passage of the 15th Amendment, really succeeded because it had become a partisan issue. The Republicans, particularly national Republicans, consciously made it a partisan issue to secure its adoption.

GASTIL: Perhaps in a period of enthusiasm it was imposed on the country. But the country had not quite caught up to it. That is really the point you are making. The basis of the change had not been developed.

JENSEN: I wouldn't call it enthusiasm. It was felt necessary to win the war after Appomattox. The Republican war administration was terrified that the war they had won on the battlefield might be lost at the peace table. They saw the goals of the Civil War as twofold: to restore the Union, which meant to destroy everything Confederate, and to abolish slavery, which meant to abolish all forms and substitutes for slavery as well.

There was very grave doubt, in 1865 through 1867, that these war goals had been achieved. Remember that in 1865 the Confederate States surrendered in April and then held elections that September. A number of Confederate colonels and other Confederate personnel were elected. The Vice President of the Confederacy, Alexander Stevens, who was the number two man of the Confederacy in April, became a United States Senator in September. That was more than many Republicans were willing to swallow.

There was a strong sense that the war goal of destroying the Confederacy was in jeopardy. The quasi-Confederate southern states were reimposing a form of slavery through the so-called Black Codes that strongly restricted what the free blacks could do. So it wasn't at all clear that slavery had been abolished, either. Washington felt an urgent sense of crisis. This led to a series of pressures, most of which President Johnson resisted and avoided. He announced the war was ended immediately. He accepted the idea that by snipping off their Confederate uniform buttons, just the buttons, Confederate soldiers were good Yankees again. He thought the Black Codes were rather a good idea.

The result was severe tension between Congress and the Presidency. The leadership in Congress, the war leadership, the continuation of the Republican coalition controlling Congress, won a spectacular election in 1866—not on the basis of Negro suffrage, but on the basis of winning the war after Appomattox.

They then destroyed the quasi-Confederate governments in the South and put the southern states under the United States army. So comprehensive army occupation started for the first time two years after the war. The Republicans decided that there was only one loyal group in the South that could be trusted to destroy the Confederacy, the blacks. Therefore, the only way to save the Union, to win the war, was to enfranchise this thirty or forty percent of the southern population. These blacks, together with a small minority of whites who really were anti-Confederate, would do the trick.

That's why they pushed the 15th Amendment. It was a war measure. It was not the idea that freedom or democracy should be expanded. It was a desperate attempt to restructure the political system. It was rammed down southern white throats, but northern whites did not like it either. Northern Democrats almost unanimously opposed it. And so did a large fraction of northern Republicans, but in 1866-68 they accepted it because it was necessary.

By 1869, certainly by 1870 and most certainly by '72, many of these northern Republicans said that the Confederacy was dead. "It's been some years now, and there's no sign whatever, no guerrilla warfare, no resurgence of Confederate spirit and neo-slavery. The war is over." That was the basis of Horace Greeley's liberal Republican campaign in 1872. He charged Grant was using these war devices to continue a corrupt Republican Party. So by 1872, a large fraction of northern Republicans no longer felt emergency measures were necessary.

They were put into the Constitution as the 15th Amendment because Grant and his people quite reasonably figured out that was the only way to make them permanent. Legislation was not enough.

PENNIMAN; In any case, they could do it because they didn't have a vote in the South.

JENSEN: That's right. Black suffrage was imposed by Congressional vote in the Reconstruction Acts of 1867. But that was not a guarantee. They were very worried, for example, that the Supreme Court would throw it out, which the Supreme Court eventually did, in civil rights cases a few years later.

So the constitutional amendment had no support among whites in the South, and very little popular support in the North. The blacks were the only major group to support it. As a result, it did not have legitimacy. The formal disenfranchisement programs began around 1890 (there were some informal ones earlier). When the "Force Bill" was proposed as federal legislation to prevent the southern states from disenfranchisement, it received little support from anyone— not Congress, the Republican Party, or the courts. By 1896, the Supreme Court had clearly indicated that the new southern system was acceptable. By then it was locked in, in a variety of different forms.

It is interesting, though, that the northern states never disenfranchised the blacks. The border states didn't either. Blacks were allowed to vote in Kentucky, Maryland, and Missouri, and they were allowed to continue voting in all northern states. In fact, disenfranchisement was not quite universal in the deep South: blacks were allowed to vote in pockets, here and there.

GASTIL: In reading your paper, Paul, I wondered about the difference between the legal situation and actual behavior. For example, in the colonial period, there were property qualifications. But I understand that in some places, like New Hampshire, they simply ignored the property qualifications in some elections, and just let people vote.

KLEPPNER: Yes.

GASTIL: Now is it true that in some parts of the North, by custom, blacks could not vote?

JENSEN: They were not allowed to vote in most of the northern states before the Civil War. ·

GASTIL: No, I mean in recent years. In the 1950s, let's say.

KLEPPNER: No.

GASTIL: In the 1950s, you say, in all places except most of the South, blacks voted without any feeling that they were not supposed to vote? Is that true?

JENSEN: Yes, After 1870, at all times I would say, outside these deep southern states, the blacks have voted in an unrestricted fashion. And they voted.

PENNIMAN: It becomes useful politically. You are trying to get votes, and so there is a competition for their vote.

JENSEN: Lexington, Kentucky, is a good example of a southern city in which blacks voted at all times. They were well organized. And they continue to be.

GASTIL: Indians didn't vote in some places until quite recently?

KLEPPNER: Indians did not vote.

GASTIL: They do vote now, though. Most Places?

KLEPPNER: They are allowed to, but they don't.

GASTIL: Is this by custom? Or is it their choice?

KLEPPNER: Indians on reservations were not citizens until the 1920s.

LEVINE: What I read from this history is that changing the franchise system happens because a target group is perceived to give the dominant political party or an emerging political party some advantage. It becomes a political football. I was trying to think of two populations that something is going on with and speculate what changes one might guess at.

    The first is the depression era population, which is now aging and having a tougher time getting to the polls. It is very liberal on some social policy issues, particularly Social Security, Medicare, Veterans' Rights and preferences, and so on. I could see this group as a target in both directions. On one side, because of Alzheimer's disease or similar problems, new requirements for voting might be developed that would exclude some people. On the other side, provision might be made making it easier for these people to vote by telephone, by mail ballot, by absentee ballot.

Political Participation

(GASTIL: For telephone voting, you could have tapes that keep a record of who voted.)

LEVINE: The other target group is the blacks. And if the Democratic Party takes a few more shots at the national level, because of the perception that they have to swallow the Jackson Coalition pill, then it seems to me that somewhere along the line some genius is going to come up with the idea of changing the electoral system in such a way that in some places blacks will not be a factor, because a "three-party system" will make them less of a factor. Some genius will figure out some structural way to change the game. I'm wondering, as I read your history, if you have given that any thought.

KLEPPNER: A quick answer to that is no, I have not. I think you correctly surmise that most of the expansions or contractions that I talked about were related to partisan politics. I had not thought of the issue of facilitating access to the ballot on the part of the extremely elderly. What's the term that's used for that? The people over 85?

SIGEL: The old old.

KLEPPNER: I had not thought about that. I'm not quite sure I follow the logic of creating a three-party system, since we have had cases, particularly in the 19th century, where there were viable minor parties for quite some time, and they either won elections, or determined outcomes. There were many cases in the 1830s, 1840s, 1850s, particularly in local elections, where suddenly someone comes from virtually nowhere to win an election. There is no announced candidacy for this person: political writers in the 19th century frequently referred to the "still hunt", that is, a covert movement of people who ultimately organize and elect a candidate.

There were a number of cases in Boston (I have done some work on elections to the mayoralty of Boston in the 1830s) where the newspapers were talking about rivalry between A and B, and suddenly when the ballots are counted, C, who nobody thought was going to run, wins the election. His friends have organized for him, and turned out.

This possibility has been reduced, largely as a consequence of changes in the early part of the 20th century in the procedural laws

134

that regulate the activities of political parties. It is easier to put a minor party in the field when you have unofficial ballots and don't have to get it organized and on the ballot sixty or ninety days before. This becomes very difficult when filing must be done by a particular date.

ALMOND: Is it a general rule, Paul, that newly enfranchised groups, vote less frequently? In the net, after an enfranchisement, do you end up with a decline in voting?

KLEPPNER: That was the case when women were enfranchised, although there are some other factors going on in the 1920s.

ALMOND: How about blacks?

KLEPPNER: It is difficult to determine right after the Civil War, because statistics on voting in the South are questionable for that period. But it does not seem that there was a decline in turnout when blacks were enfranchised.

PENNIMAN: In South Carolina they got 101 percent.

KLEPPNER: They were very well organized. One may be suspicious of the precise figures, but one can argue that they are so well organized for the political reasons that Richard has detailed, that it is doubtful that there was a decline in turnout.

BENNETT: If you look at what happened after the Voting Rights Act of 1965, they moved in quickly.

GANS: Initially they voted less than whites, but the spiral was upward until 1988. Yet the absolute statistics look like there is no movement in black participation unless you factor in the 18 to 20 year-olds.

KLEPPNER: Yes, you should control for age, and also for differences in education and income.

SIGEL: One of the problems with your question, as with voting statistics generally, is that we don't very often take the compositional factor into consideration. For instance, you mentioned women. When the Women's Suffrage Amendment was adopted, many women that theoretically could have voted were of Eastern European immigrant stock, where the idea of a woman voting was very new. But we don't take that into consideration. Now with blacks, what you say is absolutely right. But with many new groups, we ask why their voting doesn't increase when it is legalized, and fail to get beyond the legality to ask who they are.

KLEPPNER: Yes, there are good cultural reasons, as you suggest, for many women not participating right off. It was not just Eastern European women. For example, German Lutherans: the Missouri Synod believed that women should not play this kind of role.

ALMOND: How about aliens?

KLEPPNER: As best one can tell, and I've looked at the figures for the 1830s and '40s, once a state or a territory actually begins to allow aliens to vote, there is no decline in turnout. They do participate. Again, it is a matter of being well organized. This became a divisive question, for example in the midwestern states or territories of the time. When they were talking about alien enfranchisement in the 1830s and '40s, aliens were organized by the political parties and they turned out to vote in very high numbers.

BENNETT: That's another thing we have to take into consideration. The changes in the party systems over the years.

KLEPPNER: Yes, local organization.

BENNETT: Those "army campaigns" that you talked about, we don't have those anymore.

KLEPPNER: Age also makes a difference. When we enfranchised the 18, 19, and 20 year olds, there was a decline. They turn out at a much lower rate.

GANS: This is just a minor point relating to your last segment on expanding the franchise. There is one small countervailing legal trend which has to do with purging. In an era of declining turnout and declining participation, purging registration lists for nonvoting (which is 50 percent in presidential elections and 63 percent in midterm elections) can create a barrier of reregistration for potential voters with low motivation.

GASTIL: Do we have any aliens voting now?

KLEPPNER: We shouldn't have. Do we have is another question.

GANS: There was some thought on the part of the California Democratic Party, when the Republican legislature was considering the Sebastiani initiative, that they would make use of liberalized absentee voting for the registration of a few aliens. But in theory we don't have any.

GASTIL: I ask because there's been a movement in Europe in several countries to enfranchise aliens. If we follow the model that has been suggested in our discussion, if it's in some party's interest to do it, they'll push for it. Obviously, it will be in some party's interest to have Hispanic aliens or other groups enfranchised.

KLEPPNER: Yes, we've done that without allowing it. The push has come not through enfranchising aliens but by making it easier to become citizens.

JENSEN: That's what the parties used to do. They elaborately organized the citizenship process. The alien dealt with his local precinct man to become a citizen. Some groups were prevented from citizenship in the United States, of which the Japanese and the Chinese are the most famous. And that completely disenfranchised those groups until the 1950s.

It's an inducement to become citizens. That's the reason we have the enfranchisement rules on aliens. We have a strong national policy, which European countries do not have, that immigrants should become citizens. That has been so since the 1790s. Indeed, when the frontier states that Paul mentioned were giving citizenship to aliens, that was an inducement to come to their state. They wanted people, Germans, for example, to move to Minnesota, or Michigan. Citizenship and voting were attractive, because these people couldn't vote back in Germany. "You come to America, you'll vote right away, you'll be welcomed." Symbolic of this, in debate over the Kansas-Nebraska Act of 1854, a major issue was whether or not German aliens would be allowed to vote in the Nebraska territory.

The policy issue in recent years has to do with illegal immigrants who do not become citizens. There are millions of people who are not eligible for citizenship, for all sorts of reasons. The question is should they be eligible to vote? This is very much an open question right now. The Supreme Court has ruled that you have to put the children of aliens in the public schools. Eventually we will come around to the question of what should be the voting rights of people who legally cannot be citizens.

GASTIL: We may have a continuing problem with "guest workers". But they are a different kind of problem, people who don't want to be citizens but are part of a community for a period of time.

POWELL: That has an interesting effect on the way we count. Everyone knows what the numerator is in voter turnout, but the denominator is not so obvious. One of the really not obvious parts of it is the illegal population.

GASTIL: Before we simply accept the interest view of enfranchisement, I would like to question the statement in your paper that there is "no evidence of widespread commitment to the principle of universal suffrage." I imagine we can see working through US history at least two moralistic principles. Daniel Elazar argued that a "moralistic" political culture was dominant in many states. This moralistic approach had a lot to do with pushing for the abolition of slavery in the middle of the 19th century, and, in spite of Richard's remarks, which I'm sure are correct, played some part in laying the basis for the constitutional amendment granting universal male suffrage. Later it had a great deal to do with the development of the women's and prohibition movements. This cultural tradition is also reflected in the legislation and the constitutional changes in the 1960s and 1970s. This reflected the same kind of group that was working for abolition in the middle of the 19th century, was working for the women's movement later, for progressive ideas of all sorts in the early 20th century. In spite of its restrictive tendencies, this movement also led to the "good government" movement, to registration, and many other electoral regulations; in the 1960s its descendants helped bring southern blacks back into the electoral process.

KLEPPNER: There is some continuity there, I would agree. The movement you are talking about in the nineteenth century does exist. Richard is generally correct in talking about the attitude towards the 15th Amendment or toward blacks among northern whites. The major exception, however, is the Yankees. Whenever you look at the referenda, you can pick out Yankee counties just by finding which counties voted for enfranchisement. The only states in the Union prior to 1860 that enfranchised blacks were the New England states. There they were explicitly enfranchised. And New Englanders, when they move to the Middle West, will vote in favor of enfranchising blacks, or against the various restrictive measures that come up. There is that kind of moralism there. There is no question about that.

This carries over in a broadly based kind of way after the Civil War into prohibition movements, or before the Civil War, in temperance movements. You're right. It gets hooked in with a variety of kinds of women's participation in civic activities, one dimension of which becomes the women's suffrage movement.

However, by the time you get to the turn of the century, while one can see some of this old-fashioned Yankee moralism in much of the preachings about good government reform, behind that there were very clear class dimensions. That was not the case in the 19th century with abolitionism. It was not the case in the 19th century with prohibition and the beginnings of the women's movement.

You begin to get still another layer of support for these kinds of good government movements in the early part of the 20th century, the technocrats, efficiency experts, city specialists, urban planners. These kinds of people became very interested in all kinds of good government movements, political and nonpolitical.

BENNETT: There's also another aspect to that moralism that crops up at times. Yankee or other moralism takes on different connotations and different manifestations, depending upon whether its proponents feel that history is on their side, which clearly it still was in the mid-1800s, when they were still a dominant demographic, economic, and cultural force. But by the 1890s they are seriously challenged, at least in the big cities, by rising immigrant groups.

The moralism is still present, but now it has taken a decidedly different tack. It's not as optimistic. They are less interested in inclusionary practices with a moralistic emphasis. They are beginning to say well, let's start keeping "them" from muddying up or dirtying up the process. I hate to put it down to something as crass as looking to one's self-interest, but when you get into politics, there's always an element of that.

ALMOND: In the discussions of the Reform Act of 1832 in Britain, the principle on the basis of which the suffrage was to be granted or withheld, was explicated. There always is some kind of a debate in relation to a suffrage extension. But the seeds for the next expansion of suffrage are laid in the preceding. So I agree, there is a kind of dialectical process here. There are often counterforces, but in the long run a democracy is not going to be able to resist the power of the generalization that men are equal, and educated women cannot be excluded.

BENNETT: One of the problems in talking about enfranchisement in the United States is that outside of the South the 1820s are the last time that people could stand up in public and articulate an antidemocratic point of view, the view that certain groups are not fit to participate.

KLEPPNER: But many people still talked that way in 1910 in the North, although they had to couch the objection somewhat differently.

BENNETT: You haven't been reading George Will lately.

PENNIMAN: By the time you get to 1900, 1912, 1916, an intellectual group is leading the movement to enfranchise people. The very people that we would normally have thought of as the ones who would be supporting it on the theory that working class people help working class people, did not support it. The working people saw immigrants as competitors. And so you get a blockage that is coming not from the wealthy, and not from the intellectuals, it's coming from the working class. This was contrary to what many people, especially socialists in this period, believed should happen.

GASTIL: Let me pin down this argument before we go further. It seems to me Steve is saying that a moralistic elite backed away from pushing for expansion of the electorate in the 1890s because a different kind of group was coming in that it didn't really want to participate in the electorate. Howard seems to be saying that in fact, it was the people just above the level of the immigrants, in class terms, who were the ones who wanted to block this group from voting. Is that what you are saying?

PENNIMAN: Yes.

SIGEL: I want to side with Paul, and be a little bit be more cynical than you were in this discussion. I think Paul's next book really would have to be interesting. Every time you have an enfranchisement, or whether you have aliens wanting to vote or anything, the question is not whether it's nice. American rhetoric and American practice are two different things. You have to look at what special interest would benefit from letting people in.

As much as I'd like to think that it was educated women that pushed for women's suffrage, history has documented well enough that there were very good political reasons why some groups decided to let the women in "so that we can win for a change." The history of the suffrage——the dropping of restrictions, or adding of restrictions——is always dependent on whose ox is being gored.

KLEPPNER: But on the question of women's suffrage, it was educated women who got the issue on the agenda.

SIGEL: Oh, sure.

KLEPPNER: It becomes enacted at the state level, state by state, and then finally at the federal level, for particularistic, highly particularistic, political reasons. And one of the critical ones there was its connection with prohibition.

BENNETT: Also, in the early going, for some social reasons. Some of the first states to enfranchise women wanted women, such as Wyoming in 1869.

SIGEL: The same thing as giving tax benefits to corporations.

Political Participation

LEVINE: I was just struck by some data in Professor Bennett's paper on nonvoting by noncollege whites. They are an unorganized, easily displaced population that would pay a heavy price for the inclusion of blacks in the electorate. I wonder if the obverse isn't always the case. In other words, where a fairly focused interest group meets a disorganized group the latter will always pay a price—a corollary to your central argument.

GANS: Many things have happened in our history because of some mixture of public good and interest. We ended segregation legally in 1964 and 1965. We did it partly because there was a civil rights movement, and broad public support. But we also did it because it was an embarrassment to the country, because the business climate in the South was adversely affected. Support was pragmatic, self-interested, and from a conception of general welfare. That's how change is made in this country, by and large, threads of self-interest and common interest working together.

BENNETT: It has been that way in many different countries. One of the greatest enfranchisers in German history was Bismarck, no woolly-headed liberal.

GASTIL: Let me add to my argument that Paul maligned his middle period. It was during this period that the direct election of senators and the initiative and referendum became very popular. To some extent, both of those things are an expansion of suffrage—if you can vote for more things, you have more suffrage.

BENNETT: Paul's latest book deals with the period from 1893 to 1928. There is so much going on in that period that is at cross-purposes. You also have, in the middle of that period, the war, which led to a sort of mini-McCarthyite period of witch-hunting. People were actually expelled from the country, if they had been suspected or had been caught engaging in radical activities. They were put on a boat and shipped back to where they had come from. So that period has so many different forces working at the same time.

JENSEN: We still do that, by the way. People who can be proven forty-some years later to have been Nazis are stripped of their citizenship and sent back somewhere. It doesn't happen to many people, but it's exactly the same legal structure as 1919.

GASTIL: I'm still concerned about the cynicism. In preparation for a follow-up conference on education, I've come to realize that the mid-19th century reformers, the people that pushed for abolition, were the same group of people who pushed for improvement in the schools. They had the idea that schools should be forced down people's throats, from the top down, an approach related to the development of restrictive registration and other voting require- ments. Their idea was that yes, it's true, as Jefferson says, that everybody should take a part in the process---but they should be educated. Even if they don't want to be well educated, we'll see to it that they, or their children, are. They opposed local control, because they wanted to improve education from the top down. They had a vision, if you will, that came right through from there, through the '90s, and I would say right up until today. It is an elitist vision that assumes that there are two aspects of participation, quality and quantity. They said let's raise the quality, and then increase the quantity. Other people said let's increase the quantity, and worry about the quality later. I think these are two different approaches to the same goal.

Of course, people will always push for their interests. That's a basic assumption for any study of human behavior. What is interest- ing about the development of democracy is that there have been other influences going on at the same time that have also played a part. That's all we need to say.

KLEPPNER: The moralistic strain that you are referring to I have elsewhere referred to as Yankee cultural imperialism. This leads to all kinds of problems once you get groups coming into the country like serious German Lutherans or Roman Catholics, who want their own school systems. You have enormous conflicts in values, because Yankees will say that parochial schools are not real schools. They will want to do away with them.

JENSEN: There are two ways of looking at this history. On the one hand, most historians, although only a narrow majority, identify a reform tradition in America, taking it back as far as you want ---Jefferson is a good place to start. They see progressivism and a democratic spirit as part of this reform tradition. Democratic Party historians have identified it as the tradition of Jefferson, Jackson, Franklin Roosevelt, and John Kennedy.

But there are many historians who disagree with that, who would say that this moralism we are talking about is basically a purification movement, and that the New England spirit reflects a deeply religious desire for purification, in the sense that there are impure elements in society that have to be purged, that compulsory schooling is a compulsory technique to purge people of their ignorance. Literacy tests are a device to purge the electoral rolls of people infected with ignorance, those who you haven't educated yet.

From this perspective, women's suffrage is not designed to enlarge the ballot. It's designed to purify the political process by bringing in millions of a much purer people who have a sense of female morality, who have been largely free of the influence of the saloon and party loyalty. The direct election of senators is a way of purifying the electoral process of the upper house, by getting it out of the state legislatures, which are impure and boss-ridden. That was my argument, basically, on the history of the 15th Amendment: it was pushed through by those who wanted to purify the Confederacy by, on one hand, disenfranchising most of the Confederates, then, by enfranchising a pure population that is loyal to American ideals and installing them.

The purification motif is very strong in New England. This is why the Puritans came in the first place. That's the "City on the Hill" they wanted to build, that everybody seems to be quoting these days. (Both Reagan and Dukakis were quoting that last month.) The Puritans wanted to get out of the impure English system. Many other groups—the German Lutherans are a good example of this— were terrified that the German religious system was unsatisfactory. They also wanted a pure land in which they could practice their religion.

This feeling is very strong today among southern evangelicals, southern Baptists, who are convinced that the Government is evil, and they have to purify the system—the Baptist ideology, if you will, for the Baptists are basically a Puritan group. The purification motif is not a democratic one at all. It does not think that the more the better. It is of the view the purer the better. If the new people are purer, they are willing to broaden it.

144

GASTIL: Richard, why are these interpretations necessarily in conflict? They could be two aspects of the same thing. Leaving aside the religious, let's look at the secular version (or secularism) that came by the middle of the 19th century.

JENSEN: Well, secularized. It has a religious origin. But it's secularized, yes.

GASTIL: Once you get a secularized version, then it could be a version of a democratic ideal. I don't see it necessarily being so much in conflict.

JENSEN: It is a different ideal. It is later used to purge the blacks in the South. The main reason the blacks were purged is that they were ruining the electoral system. The black vote in 1890 was a purchased vote. Usually the leading white politicians would go in and pay cash to the black ministers and get the vote of the entire congregation. They disfranchised blacks in a couple of states by purchasing the black vote to vote for their own disfranchisement. For example, in Arkansas the whites voted against the amendment, and the blacks voted for the disfranchising amendment. They were very clear on the purging motive. They didn't like blacks, either, but the reform ideal was foremost. In the progressive era, the registration laws were explicitly designed to purge the system of corrupt voters—the sponsors, the bosses, and the local party organizations.

So, if you are in a purification mode, by no means do you give everybody the vote. You try to remove the impure. In a sense that is antidemocratic, and restrictive.

GASTIL: In the short term. I'm sure many of these people thought in the long term it wasn't, although in the short term it obviously would have reduced the voting.

JENSEN: They had a long-term universalism, a missionary spirit that everybody's going to be uplifted. That's also very important. And the long-term techniques were things like education: compulsory education was essential. There is no sense in America that groups be permanently kept out. Even in the South, the whites said that the blacks were not ready to vote. That was their argument throughout the twentieth century, that eventually blacks will be uplifted, but not now. And they said it often enough that I think they meant it. Strom Thurmond is a good example.

SIGEL: I think you and Howard could join forces. Again, speaking cynically, what you have in the history is not antidemocratic feeling, but a real distaste for the great unwashed masses. We only have to look at the discussions in the early 1920s on installing the quota system for immigration, and the system for blacks. Or take reform of city government, getting the machines out. The interesting thing is what Howard mentioned, that the labor movement, because it thought its own self-interest was involved, joined the very people who they looked upon as their enemies. There is a strong tendency to believe we are fine the way we are now, and don't rock the boat. Who needs the great unwashed masses. The blacks won't do, the Poles won't do. The Germans, the British, and the Scandinavians, they are okay, because they're like us.

ALMOND: But there was always a group that wanted to "wash" the masses. To clean them up. For example, the German Jews did this with the Eastern European Jews.

SIGEL: It's the same thing. The tremendous philanthropic activity of the German Jewish community to bring education and other services to the Eastern immigrants was because they were an embarrassment to them. It doesn't sound nice, but it's true. We always think of ourselves as egalitarian, but this elitist strain is one of the real conflicts in the United States. It's not only quantity, it's quality, I agree with you. But it's equality versus elitism.

KLEPPNER: I think what you say is absolutely accurate. The restrictionists in the North were very explicit about their intentions and purposes. Whether you are talking about voter registration laws or other proposals, the objectives were very clear-cut. One prominent political scientist of the time suggested that votes should be counted and then weighted by the IQ of the voter. (Never mind how you would know who cast which vote. The practicality of the approach was not addressed.)

JENSEN: I would argue that in American political history we don't disfranchise people we compete against. The labor unions are a good example of this. They worked very hard for immigration restriction. They never worked hard at all for restrictions on voting rights. Between 1890 and the 1920s the American Federation of Labor worked very hard and successfully to restrict immigration. But they never worked, as I recall, to restrict the suffrage.

PENNIMAN: Not the leadership, but the rank and file doesn't go with them.

JENSEN: I don't think any of the union people were especially active in restricting the suffrage. To restrict the suffrage, you need a Puritan sensibility of purifying things. The unions wanted to keep competition out, and therefore, they wanted restrictions on a variety of things, and they got them, finally. Immigration collapsed in the United States after the early 1920s. Voting patterns offer evidence. There was an interesting poll in Michigan when they repealed by referendum the Alien Suffrage Law. The Bureau of Labor Statistics in Michigan interviewed several thousand people and asked them what they thought of alien voting. Most opposed alien voting, and the referendum passed overwhelmingly. Those opposed included people who were, themselves, immigrants. The immigrants in Michigan were already there. They didn't want any further immigration. And that actually comes up again in the 1980s—the Mexican community is in very much doubt—do they really want more Mexican immigrants in Los Angeles? Well, no, they don't actually. They are very ambiguous on that.

ALMOND: I just was wondering, would it then be correct to say that this evangelical moralism that we are speaking of could work both ways? That is, in agrarian populism, it might lead to the extension of the suffrage? In urban reformism, it might lead to restriction of suffrage?

GASTIL: This brings us to the second point I was going to bring up with Paul, the populist tendency in US history. Support for the initiative and referendum, or the direct election of senators, didn't have much to do with the moralism.

ALMOND: I'm asking that, too. My impression of populism is that it did have a moral, religious content.

Political Participation

BENNETT: Yes, maybe a different kind of religion. Methodist.

JENSEN: Populism as a political movement of the 1890s is not especially involved in restricting suffrage. It was not a major issue because its supporters were also victims of the restrictions. The southern populists were disfranchised by things like poll taxes. Voting suddenly requires a day's wages, or several days wages. That's a factor.

But basically, the evangelical religious spirit is still very strong. This is the moralism of Jesse Jackson. Jesse Jackson is an excellent example of the way most people talked a hundred years ago. Pat Robertson still talks that way, too, it's not restricted to blacks. But it is a dominant feature of the black political community today, to the extent that Martin Luther King and Jesse Jackson are the dominant figures. Pat Robertson is an outsider in the white community, but the old rhetoric is still there. For the blacks, the rhetoric is always inclusionary, because they are going to get excluded. They know that. But for whites, it's a much more subtle matter. I think most of the purification is a hostility to the people, to the unwashed, if you will, to unsanctified, evil people.

SIGEL: I see white fundamentalists, especially Southern Baptists, Texans, as in desperate fear of change. It is a class war, in a certain sense, because many of them aren't going to make it into the Yuppie world; in addition, they hate the new values. But I don't think this is really related to voting.

GASTIL: Roberta is right. We shouldn't confuse the evangelical and moralistic movements. As to the southern evangelical movement, the Pat Robertsons and others, in the first place, it's southern, and therefore it isn't the moralism of the Yankee. So the regional basis was somewhat different. Second, it is opposed to change, and as you say, it has to do with keeping the past. Whereas the moralism I was talking about was very change-oriented. These people from the middle of the 19th century on that I was talking about were always wanting to change. That's why they wanted universal education, more college education, and the education of women. The progressive movement in the early part of the century was very much a part of that.

BENNETT: Let me argue a minute from the point of view of some-one who would find Robertson believable. The people from my part of the country are southerners, one or two or three generations removed, but they still have a southern outlook. They would say they are advocating change——if you can get them to talk about politics at all, which is a doggondest difficult thing to do because of their view that politics is inherently dirty and corrupt. They see themselves as advocating tremendous changes. They think that about thirty or twenty-five years ago——some of them go all the way back to 1933——that the country went badly in the wrong direction. What they want to do is steer it back so that we can then get to the "City on the Hill."

KLEPPNER: Yes, but it is change whose aim is restoration. Unlike change that the Yankee evangelicals would have preached in the 1830s.

BENNETT: No, they see it as a chance to get to the City on the Hill, which would be a forward movement in their thinking. We have to put ourselves into their mental framework. When you listen to them, what they are saying is the country was on the right track, but then got off the track. What we want to do is put it back on that track and move forward.

JENSEN: Yes, they're high tech. Electronics is something they strongly approve of. They run fancy electronic churches and fancy electronic mailing operations to bring in a heck of a lot of little five-dollar and twenty-dollar contributions.

SIGEL: I agree with Paul. That City on the Hill is what they thought the good old days were. When kids respected parents. They may consider it moving forward, but with a difference.

BENNETT: There is a duality in their thinking; no question about that. Many of my wife's relatives are from the South, and they've never lost that pattern of thinking. Indeed, part of the paper I did, "Left Behind," (mimeographed) was based on watching these people, watching who they were and listening to them talk. Their response to this would be, "We're change oriented." They don't know who the heck Ignatius Donnelly was, or old Tom Watson when he was a young man, but that's what they want to go back to. And that's what they want to see done.

SIGEL: Change can go forward or backward. I think that's all Paul is saying, if I understand him correctly.

JENSEN: But the Yankees, I quite agree, had a future orientation. They thought that the City on the Hill—we're nowhere close to it, but we want to move and create a brand new world a hundred years from now. The southern mind, in that sense, is reactionary, that "we once had it." There was a golden age in the past. Where's your golden age? The southerners have it in the past; the Yankees always have it in the future. The Yankees never say that a hundred years or two hundred years ago was our good days. They say it's a hundred years from now. And to get a hundred years from now, we'll build a school now, and in a hundred years this will be something.

BENNETT: You have to differentiate. Well-educated southerners may think of Tara, but lower-class southerners remember Tara when they were the poor sharecroppers who never did get a piece of the pie. If you get down into that part of the southern mind that didn't write novels and didn't write history, they were the ones that were shut out in the movements in the 1890s. They don't see the old South in quite the same romantic way. When they say they want change, maybe they do mean backward change. But it's very difficult to convince them of that.

KLEPPNER: Before we end up blaming too much of what occurred, particularly in the early part of the twentieth century, the restrictionist legislation, on either evangelicals or elites, let me add one caveat to my own generalizations by drawing your attention to one group that does not satisfy either definition, yet played a role in enacting restrictionist legislation.

   Much restrictionist legislation, particularly in the northern areas, and particularly voter registration law, was promoted by political bosses, ward control bosses. You get beautiful cases of this, for example, in Massachusetts, when many of the ward bosses from Boston were sitting in the legislature. Martin Lomasney of Ward 8 is the key example here, but others are involved. They want to control their populations. They have their wards under control now. They are concerned about the influx of immigrants. They want to make it more difficult for these people to vote and participate; they want to slow change in their own neighborhoods.

SIGEL: Gerrymander is another example.

KLEPPNER: Yes, but that's much earlier.

ALMOND: Well, I was just in a vague kind of way recalling some of my biblical past. And you know, there is a kind of Deuteronomic aspect——a return to the original pastoral conception of the covenant——that enters into nineteenth century and even contemporary politics.

GASTIL: There is an interesting footnote to that. The points that have been made about the southern evangelical being interested in technology and the goodies of modern civilization. It is very much the thesis of V. S. Naipaul, if you are familiar with his work. It is remarkably true of Iran under the Ayatollah. The Ayatollah wants to create a past that never existed, and at the same time he is quite willing to accept all the technological goodies.

ALMOND: It is also true of the eighth century prophets. They were the ones who put their prophecy in writing.

JENSEN: One of the major advances in democracy in the United States, in the last twenty years has indeed been invented by these southern evangelicals. The mass mailings and the idea of being able to reach out to people in a very direct fashion, asking for money and what not through direct mail, were largely invented by these groups. This is a whole new mode of participation, and in many ways it's a dominant mode. These direct approaches control funding in many activities, although they probably peaked around 1980. It is a new democratic phenomenon, of being directly in two-way contact with people: money flows one way and letters the other. Other countries have not yet adopted this mode of participation. It will take them a while to figure out how to do it. But it has radically changed American politics. It has made direct mail probably more important than television commercials, which were dominant from the 1950s to 1970s.

GANS: I disagree in part. You are right about the peak of direct mail, which hit about 1980, and now it is receding in effectiveness. It is also receding in effectiveness as an election tool. It's receding simply because when you flood the mailboxes, it becomes less effective.

Television remains far and away a more important tool. When we get to Jensen's paper, that was one of the things I wanted to raise, because I think it is about eight years out of date in terms of where we are today.

PARTY SYSTEMS AND DEMOCRACY

The American Experience

Richard Jensen

Admirers of multiparty parliamentary systems have always puzzled over the two-party system in the United States. The rules of the game determine a number of structural characteristics. Because of the winner-take-all electoral system based on geographical districts, only two parties are viable. Because of the importance of federal policy and patronage, the same two parties emerged in each state. The dynamics favor a balanced equilibrium. A party that wins a big landslide (such as 1820, 1868, 1908, 1936, 1964 and 1972) soon runs into trouble. Thus we have two equally matched parties, with a wide-based electorate. How democratic is it? More precisely, are issues of interest to the people expressed through the parties?

The usual approach is dynamic. Changing conditions bring forth new issues, which are seized upon by the parties. Democracy is expressed in the inter-party competition over these issues. As some issues fade, new ones arise, generating a steady pace of change in the political system. The spirit of this approach is incrementalist. Government is the enactment of small changes in a system that, as Louis Hartz argued, reflects a broad liberal consensus.[1] Looking at democracy from the point of view of the parties more than the voters suggests a different interpretation––one that is static rather than dynamic. More exactly, it is one of punctuated equilibria. The normal status of politics is stability or equilibrium. Every so often that equilibrium is shattered and, after a brief turmoil, a new equilibrium is established.

The conceptual tool that can unravel the interactions among people, parties and democracy is the notion of a party system. The idea is that American political history is characterized by long stretches of stable or "normal" contests, punctuated by short, high tension upheavals. The upheaval (or "critical election") marks a realignment of the political agenda, the government's policies, the attitudes of the voters, the structure of party coalitions, and (often) the rules of the game. After the excitement subsides a new stable phase ensues, only to run out of momentum eventually when its logic becomes irrelevant to the new domestic and foreign problems faced by the nation.

Each party system is characterized by a dominant and a subordinate party, and by an agenda, or set of issues, controlled by the dominant party.[2] The minority party typically comprises two factions. One is thoroughly repelled by the majority agenda, and is determined to frustrate or sabotage it at all costs. Usually this faction is reactionary, in the sense that it is still clinging to the old agenda of the last party system. The other faction largely accepts the new agenda, promising improvements here, and better administration there. Both factions complain about the corruption of the incumbents. In 1988, with the Republicans dominant, the two Democratic factions are well represented by Jesse Jackson and Michael Dukakis.

Every so often it is possible that the opposition comes to power (usually because of a factional split in the majority). The unexpected victory seldom is satisfactory because the two minority factions rarely agree on what to do. Consider the troubles of the Whig party after their victories in 1840 and 1848; Grover Cleveland's second term; Woodrow Wilson's second term; and Jimmy Carter's only term. The majority party probably has factions, but all of them are generally committed to the core values, and so it can govern.

Table 11 identifies six party systems.[3] Before and between the periods when these systems were dominant, we find transitional periods of turmoil, confusion and false starts. (See Table 12.)

Power comes not merely from offices held, but even more from the ability to set the agenda: to define the salient issues and the acceptable solutions. Since Lincoln's era, the Democrats have been the party of the outsiders—the marginal and peripheral groups in society, jealous of the good fortune of the core Republican groups, and eager to be counted in. In a democracy their votes counted just as much, and by organizing pressure on the government they could get recognition, and, even power over the masters of capital. To give legitimacy to their claims, they pleaded for sympathy for the downtrodden, attacked the corruptions of the rich and powerful core groups, or couched their demands in terms of rights and entitle-

TABLE 11

THE SIX PARTY SYSTEMS

System	Dates	Dominant Party	Opposition Party
FIRST	1796-1812	Republican (Jefferson, Madison)	Federalist (Hamilton, Adams)
SECOND	1828-1854	Democratic (Jackson, Van Buren)	Whig (Clay)
THIRD	1854-1896	Republican (Lincoln, Grant)	Democratic (Cleveland)
FOURTH	1896-1932	Republican (McKinley)	Democratic (Bryan, Wilson)
FIFTH	1932-1966	Democratic Roosevelt)	Republican (Dewey, Taft)
SIXTH	1966-	Republican (Reagan)	Democratic (Mondale, T. Kennedy, J. Jackson)

****

TABLE 12

THE TIMES OF TROUBLE

Period	Causes	Key Problems
1790s	French Revolution	isolation; nature of republicanism
1820s	depression	national power; banks; corruption
1850-61	slavery	constitutional status of states & slavery; war
1890-96	depression	economic modernization vs redistribution
1929-37	depression	federal regulation; welfare state; labor unions
1963-74	social change	Vietnam; status of blacks, women; government regulation & taxation of business, private lives; Watergate

TABLE 13

THE DOMINANT PARTY'S ISSUES

FIRST	(Jeffersonian):	states' rights; limited federal government
SECOND	(Jacksonians):	Democracy; geographical expansion; anti-banks; antimoralism; white supremacy
THIRD	(GOP):	national power; universal legal & political rights (for blacks); anti-Confederacy; cultural universalism; pro-business; pietistic moralism
FOURTH	(GOP):	economic modernization; high tariff; gold standard; cultural pluralism; pro-business; pro-labor
FIFTH	(New Deal):	Welfare state; federal supervision of economy; regulation of business; pro-union; high taxes; anti-totalitarian foreign policy; Cold War
SIXTH	(Reagan):	pro-business; deregulation of economy; low taxes; religious moralism; anti-racism; universal legal and economic rights (for blacks & whites, men & women); rearmament; ending Cold War

****

ments. The Democrats did that in the New Deal System. The core of their economic liberalism involved commitment to government control of macroeconomics, regulation of business, fostering labor unions, high taxes, and extensive benefit programs for the "victims of capitalism. (See Table 13.)

FDR's emphasis on welfare dominated the nation's attention for a generation, until the 1960s. The turmoil then——ranging from assassinations and full-scale riots in hundreds of cities to bitter confrontations within private families——demonstrated that the New Deal system no longer spoke to the nation. Richard Nixon was

156

poised to make the breakthrough to a new party system——and indeed he restructured foreign policy. But he was too wedded to the past in domestic policy, and too deeply embroiled in suicidal battles with his old enemies, to show the way to a new politics. The transition was further prolonged by the inept and incompetent presidencies of Ford and Carter.

An old party system collapses when the issues structuring it are displaced by new burning issues among the citizenry. It is not merely that the old issues are irrelevant, for the momentum produced by partisan loyalty and active organizations can keep churning out the votes. There must be a new moral sensibility or a repudiation of an administration's economic failures. America is a religious land in the sense that political issues must be based in moral outlooks before they can dissolve old partisanship affiliations. The voters become convinced that the old ways will no longer work. The new issues divide the people differently, so that voter coalitions are realigned. Some groups move one way; others move in or out of the electoral universe; some stay pat, but with a new way of thinking and deciding about public affairs.[4]

Efforts to inject new moralistic issues are fiercely resisted by the parties. The abolitionists of the 1830s were roundly repudiated by every politician. Indeed, when the Republicans built an anti-slavery coalition they deliberately excluded the abolitionists, most of whom refused to vote for Lincoln. In the late nineteenth century the prohibitionists attempted to sway the GOP, but were repeatedly rebuffed by the party professionals. The drys solved their problem of access by creating a non-partisan pressure group, the Anti-Saloon League, which efficiently lobbied for dry laws one step at a time, without committing the parties to a new morality, or the politicians to any morality.[5] The wets finally figured out their solution: appeal to constitutional protections of liberty, and mobilize their own bipartisan lobby. On the other hand, the moralism on both sides of the abortion issue was a founding component of the Sixth Party System. The parties have not resisted but welcomed debate and support for their clear-cut positions, though they have turned the ultimate decision over to the Supreme Court.

The minority party has often shown ingenuity in locating a niche that allows local and state candidates to flourish, and occasionally assault the majority. During the New Deal heyday the Republicans discovered that they did best with candidates who largely accepted the liberal New Deal agenda, but who had reputations as crime fighters. Thus prosecutors Thomas Dewey and Earl Warren built their reputations. Historically, big city machines had collaborated with organized crime, but that also included Republican machines (such as the sponsors of Al Capone). By 1938 nearly all the Republican machines were gone, so the gangbuster theme took on a partisan and conservative aura. The fighting DAs could not stop Roosevelt in 1944, nor even Truman in 1948, but they did make crime a favorite Republican theme. In 1952 Eisenhower used it effectively; Democratic aspirants like Senators Kefauver and Kennedy quickly copied. Crime was not an "issue" like the tariff that divided people according to material interests or moral suasion. No one spoke out for crime. However, the issue went deeply into the nature of government: could the government and courts be trusted to deal fairly with the individual? Corruption, and subversion, likewise, have been handy issues for the opposition party. Corruption proved a winner in 1828 for Andrew Jackson, in 1860 for Abraham Lincoln, and in 1952 for Dwight Eisenhower. It backfired for Horace Greeley in 1872, John W. Davis in 1924, and Walter Mondale in 1984. The advantages of the corruption and subversion (or anti-communism) issues are that they can unite the minority party, and, seemingly, reach down to the moralistic level where fundamental issues are created.

The parties genuinely hold to the core principles. To be sure, there was some localized variation, some shifting of emphasis in different years, and some questioning at the fringes. It often happened that one faction of the one party largely agreed with the core of the other on some issues, so that cross-party coalitions were possible. The "Conservative Coalition" of Northern Republicans and Southern Democrats during the Fifth Party System is the most important example. It lingered on into the Sixth System in the persona of some old Southerners, but their replacements seem to have little taste for the coalition. The platforms, speeches and editorials harken to the same themes, assume the same fundamentals, and mostly come to the same conclusions. They reiterate what the voters want to hear——or, more exactly, what the voters are able to understand. Political affairs are so subtle and complex in America that it requires an elaborate matrix of shared assumptions and evaluations to be able to follow what is going on.

Clear evidence of the tenacity of the fundamental issues appears in the collapse of the party systems. Stephen Douglas, the successor to Andrew Jackson as the spokesman for democracy in American politics, set in motion the destruction of the Second Party System in the name of democracy. His Kansas-Nebraska Act of 1854 was posited on the belief that the right of the people to decide their own form of government was paramount both to the property rights and states rights claimed by the South, and the "higher law" of freedom. At a time when opposition was fragmented and leaderless, the Act shocked Yankee moralists to the core, leading immediately to the formation of a powerful new party.[6]

The end of the Third Party System (1890-94) clearly reveals the dynamics of parties and issues.[7] The Republicans had the first chance. In 1888 they took control of the presidency and Congress for the first time in decades, and were ready with a comprehensive program affirming and extending their core values. Speaker Thomas Reed's new rules gave the Republicans working control of Congress, and sparked the first wave of resistance against authoritarian rule. The GOP then appropriated money for a billion dollar national budget. (Reed's response to cries of extravagance was, "It's a billion dollar country".) A bill to protect black voting rights in the South failed, but not before memories of Reconstruction were revived. In the states, Republican legislatures were enforcing cultural homogeneity by legislation enforcing compulsory education and crippling Catholic and Lutheran schools, and by supporting prohibition laws. To top it off Congress passed a new, higher tariff. Congressman William McKinley's argument that it was the best way to promote rapid economic development and move the nation to a high wage economy was premature, and within weeks the tariff and the other evidences of Republican paternalism caused the worst defeat in Republican Party history. The explanation is that large blocs of formerly committed Republicans, especially Catholics and Lutherans, felt betrayed by the actions and the threatened future behavior of the GOP. They did not all join the Democrats, but they voted against the GOP in large enough numbers to ruin the party in every major state.

The Democrats under Grover Cleveland now had their chance, but the consensus that undergirded the Third Party System was fast dissolving, and Cleveland never knew what hit him. Cleveland tried to make his party the champions of gold money and low tariffs. The severe depression of 1893 made economic action urgent. The Treasury had to borrow from Wall Street, to a chorus of silverite outrage,

expressed most articulately by William Jennings Bryan. The Democratic control of Congress was an illusion, because new forces were
ripping the old Third Party System Democratic coalition apart.
Cleveland himself never changed a bit—one of his problems; he
never understood what was happening. The most admired man in the
party in 1888, he had become the most hated by many Democrats in
1894. The President used the army to break the Pullman strike,
alienating both the left wing of his party and the southerners who
could never tolerate federal interference in local affairs. The Wilson–Gorman tariff act of 1894 was a humiliation, raising the tariff
more than anything. Cleveland denounced it (and let it become law
without his signature), as the initiative on one of the signature issues
of the Fourth Party System passed to William McKinley. The tariff
itself may not have lost many votes, but the demonstration that the
party consensus had collapsed destroyed morale, opened the exit
gates for disgruntled workers, farmers and southerners, and convinced everyone that a new Republican realignment was at hand. In
1896, the man in the White House was repudiated by his party's
national convention, and in state after state his supporters were
purged. Most of them went into a third party (the Gold Democrats),
or went over to McKinley in a realignment that crippled the
Democracy for decades.[8]

The McKinley coalition, despite the temporary Progressive split
that elected Woodrow Wilson, held together until the Great Depression. When that downturn hit, the GOP relied instinctively on its
core issue: it raised the tariff. Most (but not all) historians agree
the Hawley-Smoot Tariff of 1930 worsened the depression; it certainly did not promote the prosperity that formed the raison d'etre
of the Republican Fourth Party System. Liberal historians have
often complained that Herbert Hoover was too inflexible, too bound
by the past in his response to the Depression. That criticism misses
the mark; Hoover was more innovative in his responses to crises than
any president before or since. The obstructionism came from the
Republicans and the Democrats in Congress who remained wedded to
their old Fourth Party System core principles, and blocked or sabo-
taged Hoover's efforts. (Even with a free hand, I think Hoover would
have failed because he did not realize until the end that the main
source of the damage lay in the Federal Reserve's policies.)[9]

The final example of how core issues control the agenda comes
from the last stages of the Fifth Party System. After years of

stalemate, Lyndon Johnson finally achieved mastery of Congress in 1964-65, and rammed through a neo-New Deal. The Great Society at home, and anti-totalitarian military action in Southeast Asia echoed Franklin Roosevelt and Harry Truman, but was rewarded with electoral disaster. Worse than that, the New Deal coalition broke up in flames and frenzy, opening the way to a new realignment. While the logic of party systems suggests that Barry Goldwater or Ronald Reagan should have been the 1968 nominee, in fact Richard Nixon defeated Reagan. Nixon realigned foreign policy issues successfully, but, too personally identified with the Fifth Party System, was unable to find a new synthesis on the domestic front. Change was inevitable, however, and the first wave of deregulation arrived in the Ford and Carter administrations. Tax reduction, however, had to percolate up from the state level before Washington finally took notice. The Reagan administration marks the full flowering of the Sixth Party System, in both domestic and foreign affairs. The Dukakis-Jackson dialogue clearly indicates that the mainstream of the Democratic party has accepted the new terms of debate.

The linkage between parties and voters in the 19th century differed from that of the 20th century. A century ago the parties aggressively sought out supporters. They combed the byways and backwoods for votes, because contests were close and victory depended on turnout. Typically 90 percent of the eligible men voted in presidential contests. (Occasionally the rates exceeded 100 percent. The parties were more thorough in tracking down potential voters than the census takers.) The parties worked with natural "communities"—that is, with groups of people who interacted constantly and shared a common outlook. At the micro level, this meant extended families, church congregations. or clusters of people beholden to a local notable. With both parties seeking support, the communities usually chose the one with the most congruent position on broad political and moral issues. After a few elections, a sense of party loyalty generated a momentum that carried the group for decades (as long as the original congruence of values existed). To heighten turnout, the parties forged ties of convenience that would produce good turnouts in dull times. The most important ties were patronage, in the sense of jobs and pork barrel, and recognition in terms of public offices.[10]

Political Participation

Each party system developed its own communications media to link voters with the politicians and the issues of the day. The party newspaper, which made its first appearance in the mid 1790s, came of age with the Second Party System in the 1830s. New technology (of printing presses, telegraphic communication, and low-cost mail or street distribution) coupled with general literacy, and adequate funding through printing patronage and choice offices awarded to editors, combined to create a network of party newspapers that saturated all urban areas, and most rural ones as well. The papers were designed primarily to coordinate an extremely elaborate inter-state network of coalitions; they increasingly emphasized an intellectual control of issues. Slogans for some; long intricate speeches and pamphlets for the most devoted. The result was the average voter then was much more aware of and articulate about complex issues than his counterpart today. The articulation between party and people, in terms of core issues, was excellent despite the weak educational credentials of the population.

Psychologically, nineteenth century voters were mostly traditionalistic, rooted in ethnic communities and inclined toward loyalty toward a patron. Parties adapted to this psychology by army-like organization. The party was a hierarchical structure, with party bosses as generals, functionaries in the middle, and voters as the rank and file. Loyalty to party was not only psychologically satisfying to voters, it was the way to win. Elections were contests over organizational prowess in the ability to turn out supporters. Few voters were "independent" and anyway their vote hardly mattered as much as the turnout of the loyal core. An army-party did not automatically assume the loyalty of its troops, and apart from extremely traditionalistic areas (in backwoods Arkansas, or lower Manhattan) did not attempt to buy support with cash. The party had to earn its votes by representing what its supporters wanted.

They were, however, only allowed to want certain positions on certain topics. Items not on the system agenda were considered irrelevant, nonpartisan, or "local." General Hancock, the Democratic presidential nominee in 1880, betrayed the superficiality of his briefings when he dodged a question about the tariff by saying it was a "local" issue. By the end of the century the realization that most local issues fit poorly into the national agenda led to reforms that installed nonpartisan local government in most smaller towns and cities; this gradually replaced a partisan bureaucracy with a professional civil service.

If nineteenth century parties were armies mobilizing their battalions for battle on election day, twentieth century parties are merchants hawking their wares to potential customers. Advertising is used heavily to convince the audience that the candidate of the moment understands the voter's needs and values. While the thirty-second political commercial is an art form not to be gainsaid, the most effective merchandising has been at a more personal level. In the Sixth Party System direct mail and phone bank operators pitching a personalized message have proven more effective than all-purpose television spots.[11]

In conclusion, the party system approach helps explain how democracy is a deep characteristic of our polity. The parties are not merely vehicles of convenience for the expression of transient opinions, like public opinion polls or referenda or letters to the editor. Rather they are expressions of firmly held value systems, rooted in the moral sensibilities of the people. The constellation of beliefs is embedded in the core of the party during each system, and everything it attempts flows from that standing commitment. That is why loyal partisans do trust their party, believe in it, and work hard for it. That is why confirmed partisans really do believe doom will befall the nation if the opposition is elected.

NOTES

1. Louis Hartz, **The Liberal Tradition in America** (New York, 1955); see J. David Greenstone, "Political Culture and American Political Development: Liberty, Union, and Liberal Bipolarity," **Studies in American Political Development** 1 (1986) 1-49.

2. The recent scholarship on antebellum politics is especially revealing of the interaction of ideology and party. John Ashworth, **'Agrarians' and 'Aristocrats': Party Political Ideology in the United States, 1837-1846** (New York, 1987); Jean H. Baker, **Affairs of Party: The Political Culture of Northern Democrats in the Mid-Nineteenth Century** (New York, 1987); Daniel Walker Howe, **The Political Culture of the American Whigs** (Chicago, 1980); Stephen E. Maizlish and John J. Kushma, eds., **Essays on American Antebellum Politics, 1840-1860** (College Station, 1982); Major L. Wilson, **Space, Time and Freedom: The Quest for Nationality and the Irrepressible Conflict, 1815-1861** (Westport, 1974).

3. Paul Kleppner et al, **The Evolution of American Electoral Systems** (Westport, 1983) is the standard guide; see also William Chambers and W. Dean Burnham, eds., **American Party Systems** (New York, 1968); and Bruce A. Campbell and Richard J. Trilling, **Realignment in American Politics: Toward a Theory** (Austin, 1980).

4. Samuel P. Huntington, **American Politics: The Promise of Disharmony** (Cambridge, 1981); Richard Jensen, "Religion, Morality, and American Politics," **The Journal of Libertarian Studies** 6 (1982), 321-32; A. James Reichley, **Religion in American Public Life** (Washington, 1985); Kenneth D. Wald, **Religion and Politics in the United States** (New York, 1987).

5. W. Austin Kerr, **Organized for Prohibition: A New History of the Anti-Saloon League** (New Haven, 1985); Peter H. Odegard, **Pressure Politics** (New York, 1928); David E. Kyvig, **Repealing National Prohibition** (Chicago, 1979).

6. Eric Foner, **Free Soil, Free Labor, Free Men: The Ideology of the Republican Party Before the Civil War** (New York, 1970); William E. Gienapp, **The Origins of the Republican Party, 1852-1856** (New York, 1987); Michael F. Holt, **The Political Crisis of the 1850s** (New York, 1977); Joel Silbey, **The Partisan Imperative: The Dynamics of American Politics before the Civil War** (New York, 1985).

7. Richard Jensen, **The Winning of the Midwest: Social and Political Conflict, 1888-1896** (Chicago, 1971); Morton Keller, **Affairs of State: Public Life in Late Nineteenth Century America** (Cambridge, 1977).

8. R. Hal Williams, **Years of Decision: American Politics in the 1890s** (New York, 1978).

9. Martin L. Fausold, **The Presidency of Herbert C. Hoover** (Lawrence, 1985).

10. Richard Jensen, **Grass Roots Politics: Parties, Issues Voters,** 1854-1983 (Westport, 1983); Michael E. McGerr, The **Decline of Popular Politics: The American North, 1865-1928** (New York, 1986); Keller, **Affairs of State.**

11. Robert Westbrook, "Politics as Consumption: Managing the Modern American Election," in Richard Wightman Fox and T. J. Jackson Lears, eds., **The Culture of Consumption** (New York, 1983), 143-73; McGerr, **The Decline of Popular Politics;** Richard Jensen, "Armies, Admen and Crusaders: Strategies to Win Elections," **Public Opinion** 3 (October 1980), 44-53.

DISCUSSION AFTER PROFESSOR JENSEN'S PAPER

ALMOND: I was intrigued by your preference for the market model. Wouldn't you say that is essentially Anthony Downs' **Economic Theory of Democracy**?

JENSEN: Yes.

ALMOND: That has been the dominant model in political science now for a couple of decades, but there seems to be a moving away from it. A critical literature is emerging that reaffirms the importance of issues and policy. Empirical research suggests voters and politicians are not what the Downs model requires. It may be that you are exaggerating, or perhaps both these models are necessary.

JENSEN: The Downsian model had a dynamic in it: there is a center of gravity, because the parties will move toward a center, a maximizing position. The original model comes out of Hotteling's work in economics in the 1930s, asking where you locate a retail store, or a gas station if customers are constrained.

I am saying that while a particular party system lasts, the parties are frozen in place. They cannot compete with the voters by changing issues; the dominant party does not change issues. It is in its place, and it goes out to find customers, in the twentieth century, that are willing to shop there. But it does not and cannot appeal to those who are uninterested—it can't change its geographic location in an "issue space." So that's where I differ with the Downs argument. Downs assumes parties in motion. He argues that if there's a bimodal, bell shaped distribution, they will move to the middle. One gets one side, and the other gets the other side.

ALMOND: He would also argue that as the shape of the curve changes, the issues change, and the party system changes.

JENSEN: I argue that the party system emerges out of a historic moment and freezes there. Even if the distribution of issues changes, the parties remain immobilized unless the change is so severe that it cracks and breaks the old system, in a crisis. These crises tend to come in depressions, like the 1890s or 1930s, in which the economic or social system appears to be collapsing.

I think there was a collapse of the old system in the 1960s. I quite agree that in the 1960s we had a revolution. It was not accompanied by depression, but all sorts of things happened in the mid-60s. This created a new party system, the one we are now in.

GANS: This raises the question of issues. There were two specific things that led to the dissolution of the democratic coalition. First was the issue of civil rights and the overt taking on of the black question, which they had avoided. The second was the issue of the war in Vietnam. There was actually a third, which was subliminal---the success of the combination of New Deal programs and World War II in overcoming the depression and making people comparatively affluent. All those things eroded the democratic coalition.

BENNETT: And the rise of cultural issues and environmentalism.

GANS: I agree that environmentalism is real, but it should have served to augment the Democratic Party rather than erode it. Support of environmentalism came largely from the Democratic Party.

ALMOND: Originally it was a Republican issue.

GANS: Yes, but as far as the numbers, they were Democratic numbers.

I will grant Jensen's history, but I believe we are in an interregnum rather than a period of change. The critical election would be 1968. I'm uncomfortable with speaking of the "Reagan revolution". I am uncomfortable because the articulated new majority perspective was probably Nixon's in the second inaugural, although he didn't get a chance to play it out. Because there are elements of extremism in Ronald Reagan that are not generally acceptable, the person who may be able to play it out could be George Bush—if Ronald Reagan's single-entry economics will allow Bush to survive.

GANS: The other thing that you have to call into question in terms of your categorization is that I don't think you can ascribe the end of the cold war to Reagan. It was Nixonian, and it's Gorbache-vian. Reagan got dragged in kicking and screaming. There was no conscious desire to end the cold war on the part of this administration.

SIGEL: But he's going to take the credit for it.

GANS: And I'll give it to him, if he does it.

JENSEN: I see Nixon as a transitional figure. In terms of foreign policy, it's Nixon's initiative.

GANS: Read that second inaugural.

JENSEN: Right. In terms of domestic policy, however, Nixon is very New Dealish. He supports the regulation of society that was violently reacted against in recent years. Deregulation is definitely a post-Nixon phenomena. It starts with President Ford. It gets strong under Carter, and is dominant now. The taxation issue was never a Nixon issue. Nixon expanded the welfare state in a number of important directions.

In foreign policy he makes a dramatic break, and in cultural issues. Those are brand new issues. He comes down, of course, on the right on issues like abortion. Nixon is a transition figure. Who do we name the era after? Well, we're still debating some of these eras. McKinley is coming up rapidly and replacing Teddy Roosevelt. We used to call it the Teddy Roosevelt Era, the era of progressivism. A lot of historians are now calling it the McKinley Era. It was a good fifty years, at least, before they started calling the 1820s the Jacksonian period. Is Reagan the dominant person in our time? Give him twenty years and we'll see.

GANS: That's all I was saying—I think it's a little early.

JENSEN: However, Reagan is much more dominant. He clearly is central to the new era while Nixon was still mixed.

BENNETT: As a counterperspective to Dick's paper, there is a growing body of literature in political science that calls for characterizing the contemporary period as one not of realignment, but de-alignment. This is a term that Everett Ladd and others have popularized. In this view, rather than having party systems, sun and moon, as a dominant motif, what we see in the modern era is Curt's "interregnum."

Parties in the United States must be seen in a multifaceted context. On the one hand, they are organizations. The 1970s reflected a major change in the organizational composition of the parties, with the rise, for the first time, of meaningful national entities. Before, where they were viable at all, parties were effectively organized only on county and state levels. There were little armies of precinct captains out there, but there was almost nothing at the national level.

You also need to look at parties as entities in government, that is, at individuals who hold elective office as representatives of the party, and decreasingly in our society, individuals who hold appointive office——patronage appointments.

When we start talking about parties at the grass roots level, there are several possible approaches. We can ask a question such as, "Do you identify with the Democrats, the Republicans, the Populists, or the Prohibitionists?" Then we can ask the respondent whether he is a strong one or a weak one. But we can also see whether people repeatedly vote for the candidates of a party, and do so up and down the line. That is, do they support, lockstep, the Republicans or Democrats for president, congress, senator, or governor?

If we look at these measuring instruments, at least since the 1960s the parties have not fared very well. There was a boomlet in the early 1980s, when it looked like there was a movement to replenish identification. (Historically I've used the national election studies as my primary data base. Now I am going away from that and I'm making much more use of those general social surveys that the National Opinion Research Center at Chicago has been doing almost every year since 1972. They ask that partisanship question almost every year.) Now——in '86 and '87——this has disappeared again. So maybe what we need to do is look at the current period in party history as one in which there are a variety of developments.

For instance, I argue some place in my paper that I don't think we have a competitive two-party system. My wife, who is an institutionalist, is saying we are increasingly verging on the modified one-party system that Austin used to talk about——and all that old literature from the 50s. You have a situation in which the Republicans have controlled the White House for sixteen of the last twenty-eight years, but have only been able to control the Senate for six of the last thirty-plus years, have never controlled the House, and two-thirds of state legislators are Democrats. You have to go a long way to find a Republican mayor of a big city. This suggests a number of different movements going on, none of which suggests a definitive party era.

JENSEN: I agree that the present era is not the same as other party eras. But I think there has been a significant qualitative change: the parties are different than they were before. The voting alignments are somewhat different. The issues are different. That's why I call it a different party system.

LEVINE: It is organizationally different. You started talking about organizational systems, and wound up talking about issues marketing.

I want to go back to organizations, because I think something really happened with parties, and largely fueled by money that went to the top, the Republican "eagles", and then the Democrats with their game. It is happening at the very time when the industrial organization is changing its form. The form you identified in the nineteenth century was the military form. It was common all over the United States and Europe, and across all kinds of organizations.

Now we are moving to a new form, with less hierarchy, organizations that are more participatory, with more lower-down leadership. This is the new industrial model, with goals all over the place, involving as many people as you possibly can. These organizations that we have in Washington are running in the opposite direction. I would say they are going to need more and more money to fuel less and less results in each election, until somebody invents a new organizational form for parties that synchs better with the kinds of expectations the citizenry has for the other services it buys.

GASTIL: You are saying that national parties don't fit the current organizational ethos?

LEVINE: Yes, they are way off the mark. They are in the old model.

JENSEN: Too hierarchical? Well, one experiment along these lines has been the use of caucuses versus presidential primaries. The results were highly unsatisfactory this year.

LEVINE: From whose point of view "unsatisfactory"?

JENSEN: The runaway caucuses, of people losing control of the system. The Michigan and Texas cases being the most dramatic this year (and Iowa). The caucuses were an effort to put in what you are asking for—decentralized, localized systems. I think that they will get rid of them. One of the reforms of the system will be that everybody goes to primaries.

LEVINE: I will bet you that if you can do the study of people who participated in primaries versus the people who participated in caucuses, the level of satisfaction of those who participated in the caucuses is a darn sight higher.

KLEPPNER: That's an argument for return to nineteenth century practices, where the caucuses were very common.

GANS: The only piece of support for your de-alignment argument is that as far as I know, both Republican and Democratic pollsters agree that there are now essentially six groups in which partisan loyalty is fixed: secular and religious right-wingers, very affluent and large-business people with the Republican Party; and, in diminishing order, blacks, Jews, Latinos, and union members in the Democratic Party. As far as the rest are concerned, it's all up for grabs.

SIGEL: Basically I find the argument intriguing. The only thing I have some problem with is when you said that it is really not the public but the party that sets the agenda. The causality there strikes me as a little bit too simple.

In some ways parties are like the mass media. It's true, until it gets on the agenda, it ain't going nowhere. But it doesn't get on the agenda with the parties unless it is safe or advantageous to get it there. FDR came in on balancing the budget, and then needs a New Deal, an agenda item. I am not saying parties are answering a ground swell of some new popular ideology, but situations change. If there is enough noise, the issue will be taken up, like the current appeal to the Hispanic vote. A much better example is Bush's adorable conversion to day care, because somebody said to him there is a gender gap. But I don't think this is put on the agenda unless it's safe to put it on and it pays off.

ALMOND: There's a potential coalition.

JENSEN: The agenda is set by the crisis period. The Civil War crisis, depression crises of the 1890s and again the 1930s, these set agendas for decades to come. In the 1960s we again had a crisis, and many issues went on the agenda. Feminism was one of the very important ones——suddenly it went on the agenda in 1966-1968. Other issues are quite minor. If they don't go onto the agenda in a crisis, they have to wait thirty more years.

In the year 2000 there may be another crisis---God knows what---and there will be a whole set of issues, some of which have been percolating and are already starting to emerge. Which ones will go on the agenda in the next crisis I have no way of guessing. But the historian will look back and say, "Oh, yes, feminism started in the late 50s. And suddenly burst out in the mid-60s." Civil rights, they will say, starts out here and then it suddenly bursts to the top of the agenda in 1964. And Vietnam, the crisis of America as an imperialistic nation, suddenly bursts onto the agenda within a matter of months in 1965-66.

GASTIL: Richard, that seems a little rigid to me. Let me just give one example. Herman Kahn put out a book at the Hudson Institute called The Year 2000, in 1966. It was an interesting discussion of the future. Unfortunately, there was nothing about environmentalism in the book. Environmentalism rapidly became an issue and then gradually percolated through. It's becoming more and more of an issue. I don't think it has to wait till the next revolution.

GANS: Earth Day was in 1970, which was the first time it really went on the agenda.

BENNETT: The Cincinnati **Enquirer** noted that Earth Day was April 22, 1970, which also happened to be Lenin's birthday. We had one of our right-wing commentators, Frank Weikel, ask what was this communist conspiracy to turn Lenin's birthday into Earth Day? He asked us to oppose environmentalism because it was a secret communist plot to make Lenin an attractive character.

GASTIL: Richard, let me ask you, and anybody else, to clear up one issue before we go further. You mentioned periods in the nineteenth century, peaking in the 1890s, in which there is 90 to 100 percent participation. It seems to me that we have another paper that casts doubt on that.

JENSEN: Of those eligible to vote.

GASTIL: Even then, is there reason to believe that we have gone down from a peak of something like 90 percent?

JENSEN: I'd say between 1840 and 1896 or 1900, in general the turnout is in the 80 to 90 percent range. In really exciting years, it goes well above 90 percent.

PENNIMAN: For the national vote in the presidential election, we got there only three times——1840, 1860, and one other.

KLEPPNER: Yes, nationwide, we have only on those occasions you've mentioned reached anything close to that. Richard is saying that there are many places in the North and Middle West, in the 1880s and 90s, with turnouts of 90 percent or more. I don't want to minimize what he is saying. It's not an isolated county here or there. It is a very large number of them.

For example, in Ohio, which ties in nicely with his description of the sort of army-style campaigning, a statewide office of some significance was contested every single year. So it was constantly in mobilization. You get very, very high turnouts throughout the state of Ohio.

BENNETT: I might add that a political scientist, the late Bernie Hennessy, came across some data from that period, from some of the rural counties in Ohio, in the period from 1876 to about 1890. He published a paper called, "The Supercitizens of the Victorian Era" (American Politics Quarterly, about 1983, 84), in which he had actual lists of people who had voted---recorded from poll books. He also had census data and tax-paying data to show that those turnouts were 80 to 85 percent routinely. They were super-citizens. Driven to the polls in those army-style campaigns, they participated.

The problem with looking at the nineteenth century is that from a distance the statistics look so hard. So much has been made of them---that battle between Burnham and Converse and Rusk. But when you come closer and start really doing research in the era, they seem squishy soft. For example, Shortridge said that the Census Bureau routinely undercounted the citizenry by ten to fifteen percent. When you start moving that denominator up or down ten to fifteen percent, we are talking about millions of people. And there is the problem of what went into the numerator as well.

GASTIL: On this issue, to get comparable figures to a statement that there were many communities in the North that were getting eighty to ninety percent returns---what's the dispersion today? In other words, are there any places in the United States that get these kind of figures now?

JENSEN: Statewide, I don't think you find rates much above seventy percent any more.

ALMOND: Some districts such as Palo Alto.

JENSEN: But in the nineteenth century we are talking about entire states, under difficult physical conditions.

KLEPPNER: I just happened to look at the frequency distribution the other day for voting in Illinois counties. In presidential voting from 1876 to 1896, 100 of 102 counties had a mean turnout of over eighty percent.

SIGEL: Can I ask, could not undercounting by the census be one of the explanations? You may actually in those days have undercounted the very people who, if you had counted them, would not have voted because they are the less advantaged and less rooted. This would have inflated the averages.

Secondly, it was quite customary in the 19th century to pay people to get them out to vote. Communities were also smaller, and it was more embarrassing not to vote. And people moved around less. Are we really talking about the same thing? I'm not saying there wasn't more participation then---there are other reasons for that, too. But are we maybe, because of the type of data we have collected, and the type of explanation, exaggerating the earlier enthusiasm for voting? Were people really such super-citizens?

KLEPPNER: Let me take your two points. First, there was some census undercount. Ray Shortridge (in Jerome Clubb et al, **Analyzing Electoral History**) points out that the most severe undercount is likely to occur precisely in those categories that are not going to be eligible to vote anyway, namely recent immigrants. In those states that would have allowed alien intent that would not have been an issue. My judgment is that the undercount is much less than his estimate of 15 percent at the high point, more like 5 percent overall.

Secondly, where people have been able to resurrect poll books---there are some in Ohio, in Illinois, and California---they find exactly what Hennessy found: the people are there, and they are voting.

On the question of the role of machines in the 19th century, there has been a tendency from the very old literature, the Lincoln Steffens kind of literature, to exaggerate the role of political machines, particularly in the cities. The political machines are really a 20th century phenomenon, not a 19th century phenomenon. While people like to talk about them in the 19th century, they couldn't do what political machines have to do, reward friends and punish enemies, because they were not very effectively organized beyond the ward level. City government was terribly decentralized in the

19th century. It's only in the progressive era that you make city government highly centralized, and it becomes worthwhile to develop a citywide machine.

When the mayor's office becomes something worth grabbing on to, then you develop a citywide machine. But as long as the mayor is an impotent chairman of the board, and the board is being run by a group of councilmen fifty strong, or a hundred strong, then the mayor's office isn't worth having, and you don't bother organizing a citywide machine to get it.

SIGEL: If you are right, if it is the wards that got out the vote—in a military fashion or whatever fashion—then I could imagine that it would be to my advantage if somebody comes and says to vote so that my son may become page boy at the state legislature, or at City Hall.

KLEPPNER: Yes, but you are assuming for good intuitive reasons that the ward boss wants to maximize his vote. He may on some occasions, but on other occasions he doesn't care to maximize his vote. As Martin Lomasney points out, he wants to win his ward, not necessarily the city, or the state. If he can win his ward with 500 eligible voters, 450 of whom are voting his way, that's fine. Why bother naturalizing and enrolling the other 600 voters, who might vote the other way?

JENSEN: To control your ward, the smaller the numbers, the better. You only have so many jobs. But you have to make sure that nobody else goes after those nonvoters in your ward.

GANS: In 1880, there were probably a million patronage appointments in the United States and ten million voters. There were a lot of patronage appointments, at all levels of government. So the stakes were substantial for your ward workers.

JENSEN: I'm convinced that the turnout figures for the 19th century are absolutely legitimate. Furthermore, there were many other forms of participation, parades and rallies and picnics and newspapers and pamphlets. We've got the audited budgets saying, "I spent $17,000 on pamphlets, at two cents each. And distributed them. Please send more."

KLEPPNER: Let me add one other thing to finish up the argument. Let's forget about the issue of what the denominator is and what the numerator—or particularly what the denominator is here. Just look at the absolute size of the vote in a county in off-year elections. In recent years there is a tremendous drop, but in the 19th century there was very little drop.

BENNETT: As Dick pointed out earlier, we have to remember that the 19th century citizen did not pick up the newspaper or turn on the television in the morning primarily for the purpose of finding out how the Tigers did. When it came to recreation the 19th century citizen had very little going for him. For many, politics became a form of entertainment and amusement. Even when I was growing up, as late as the late 1940s, a day at the county fair to hear the speechifying was a favorite recreation. I can recall being trucked as a very young child 20, 30, 40 miles to the county seat to spend a whole day, for no other purpose, allegedly, than to hear the congressman from our district. That was a very real way that politics had of grabbing people, and it carried over.

We also have to remember that politics was often rooted in ethno-religious and cultural identities. Appeals to such identities were common and riveting, like the slogan "Romanism and rebellion". We see this type of phenomenon in the black church today. We see it in some of the evangelical southern churches to some degree. This was a very common phenomenon in the 19th century, a very different world.

The historian Michael McGerr has published a fascinating book about the decline of popular politics; he shows how the media were in the 19th century. He has some fascinating quotes from local newspapers about campaigns. He tells how a reporter from the Democratic paper would go to a Republican affair and say it was flat and nobody was there, the speeches were dull, and everybody agreed they had a rotten time. The Republican paper would say the hall was packed and the speeches were wonderful.

The first book on Middletown by the Lynds, has a very poignant chapter. Their research was done in Muncie, Indiana, in the 1920s. People then in their forties and fifties were talking about how politics had been eviscerated in the 1920s compared to what it had been when they were in their late teens and early twenties. One particular individual can misremember, or even a few people can misremember, but when you get the same response from large numbers, it means something. One of the things the Lynds pointed out was that it was a technological development that did in the old army-style campaigns. It was called radio. With the advent of radio, people stopped going for entertainment to political campaigns and political rallies---they could stay in their house and be entertained.

GASTIL: It was also the automobile, I think.

KLEPPNER: Well, that's later, but first comes the wire service, which changes the way of reporting news.

JENSEN: The automobile makes it much easier to go to polls. But in fact immediately turnout falls. It goes in the wrong direction.

GASTIL: It's easier to get out of town.

ALMOND: There were other things you could do in the back seat of those automobiles.

JENSEN: In 1880, it is physically very hard to get to vote. It is a lot of trouble. You hitch up the wagon and you go through the mud and the rain, and it may take you hours to get there. If we had those physical conditions today, our turnout would be 20 percent if we were lucky.

SIGEL: Yes, but you see we have a highly urbanized population now, which, just as you said has a heck of a lot of other things to do that are fun. It has changed. When I lived in Detroit, it still had a county fair. And every year the attendance dwindled. I took my kids once thinking they'll have fun. Well, they said, "Come on, let's go home." Kids don't think this is fun any more. I know a little community in a place called Paradise, Michigan, on Lake Superior. It has high voting turnout, but I can understand why, because we were stranded there once for three days, and you know what the entertainment in the town is? I'm going to ask you to guess.

BENNETT: Bingo?

SIGEL: No, that's too sophisticated. No, going to the dump and watching the bears scrounge in the dump.

ALMOND: Would it help any to suggest that you could model politics in different ways? Maybe you have different combinations of models appropriate in different periods. Politics can be a game in which people play. It can be a market in which people buy and sell. It can be a church in which people pray. It can be a war in which people fight. Which would you say were the predominant models of the 19th century? And which are the predominant models today? I'm not going to give the answer, but just suggest it as a way to get into the problem analytically.

I have a second question. One of the most popular fads today is the return to the state. Its adherents are dissatisfied with the model in which issues and policies are initiated from below, from the society, as distinguished from the organized agencies of the state. They see this as a reductionist approach that does not explain how issues get formed and policy gets made. Its adherents argue that the impetus is predominantly from the top down in all countries. How do you brush that off?

JENSEN: I don't brush it off. The sociologist Theda Skocpol has been pushing this line of argument (on the importance of the state in determining issues). I think she's wrong for the United States, but her case looks much better for Germany. The question is does the bureaucracy, the civil service, create the issues? The debating points are issues like Social Security. It is true that the Social Security Administration, between 1937 and 1955, and even later, kept coming up with expansions of the program.

However, the basic crisis that puts it into effect, I will argue the decisive change, has to do with great national issues. The incrementalism that comes after is often bureaucracy generated, but the great crisis of putting it in and accepting it is a great national political issue. It's the central issue of the 1936 election, and it is still politically dynamite. Reagan every once in a while gets his hands burned fooling with it.

The bureaucracy is of incrementalist importance, but by far the most important events have been political. The crisis of

Social Security in the early 1980s was a great political crisis for Reagan. He was on the verge of destroying his coalition around 1982 on the Social Security issue. He solved his problem with the Greenspan Commission, and they resolved it. But that's not the bureaucracy. That is very high politics.

GANS: I just have a light comment on what Roberta said. There is a radio program that has a wide listenership in Vermont called, "Music to Go to the Dump By." The second thing, any sensible campaign manager in New England has literature and coffee at the town dump.

GASTIL: I wanted to ask Richard why the change from the army to the post-army model of how a party operates. I was wondering if the problem isn't that the army disappeared, and the party had to change. Isn't that what happened? Was it led from below or was it led from above?

JENSEN: An interesting chicken and egg question; it's not too clear. The armies don't quite disappear. In certain big city organizations, they survive. The famous case was the Chicago machine lasting much longer than any others. Black politics today uses the army style; you can see them line up and get enthused and excited in rallies and in churches in a remarkable way—no other group in the country behaves this way. So there are still army features. I would argue, however, that it was in the 1890s that the top politicians suddenly figured out that the army system wasn't going to work anymore, and they had to radically change overnight.

GASTIL: Why wouldn't it work?

JENSEN: Because of the systemic crisis of the 1890s. All of a sudden, within a matter of two, four years, there were large groups of voters who were alienated, who refused to fall in line. They could not be reached anymore. They absolutely refused. They felt betrayed. The largest group was the wets, who felt betrayed on the prohibition issue. There was a school issue, and a populist issue. Between the populists and the Germans and the Catholics and a few related groups, there was suddenly twenty-some percent of the electorate that was very upset. They refused to be soldiers anymore. Hence you had to regear. And both parties suddenly did that. And 1896 is the first of the new elections in which the emphasis shifted to going after disaffected voters.

GASTIL: I don't quite understand why this change didn't lead to just a reformation of battalions?

JENSEN: The alienated groups felt betrayed by both parties.

LEVINE: Don't forget the short ballot and the Pendleton Act (electoral and civil service reform). The short ballot started happening in the 1890s. The effects of the Pendleton Act started slowly, but they built up and some of the states went at it more than the federal government.

SIGEL: Then the argument is that there was less to be gotten out of voting?

JENSEN: Yes, that's true. At the same time as the disaffection spreads the sergeants and lieutenants disappear because you can't feed them anymore.

POWELL: I guess that's really it. It is the articulation between these local armies and national party organization that I keep losing in this discussion. What we are talking about right now is terribly important.

JENSEN: The change is quite rapid because of the changes at the presidential level. Every time your party is voted out, you freeze in all your appointments. And suddenly, 1884, '88, '92, and '96, consecutively, they freeze in most of the federal appointments. By 1896 most of the federal jobs that had been patronage jobs twelve years before are no longer. Overnight the lieutenants you count on to do the mobilizing and who you promise nice jobs have become permanent civil servants.

SIGEL: Now that I've heard the discussion, I feel a little different about what you said. What you have is fewer people who are interested in being foot soldiers for the machine because they have permanent jobs anyway. Meanwhile, in the public at large, fewer people think it makes a hell of a lot of difference which way they vote.

JENSEN: There are three levels. The top politicians, the sergeants and lieutenants (the precinct workers and party people), and then finally the foot soldiers. The foot soldiers are alienated and the sergeants and lieutenants have good jobs.

SIGEL: Why are they alienated, they have a steady job in the state capital?

JENSEN: It's the sergeants who have the steady job, not the foot soldiers. Only a very small percentage of the population get these jobs. Suddenly at the federal level three-fourths of the good patronage jobs disappear. At the state level, it's much more gradual. But by the early 20th century, most states are developing a more professional civil service, locking into place their sergeants.

SIGEL: Does the secret ballot make any difference? It must have been embarrassing to work for a shoe factory with thirty-two people in Lowell, Massachusetts, and openly vote against the boss. With the secret ballot, doesn't that also make a difference?

JENSEN: That's controversial.

BENNETT: We are watching so many changes take place in such short order that there is a very limited capacity to distinguish those factors that are fundamental from those that are incidental, especially when you are changing so many different elements of the environment, of the rules and procedures by which elections are conducted.

The generation that had fought the Civil War, or had been young enough to be affected by it, was passing by the 1890s. Paul Beck has argued that many of our realignments have centered on these generational transformations of the electorate, especially in the leadership.

To come back to Paul Kleppner's point on the Australian ballot. There is an old book by William Riordan called, Plunkett of Tammany Hall. In one story his hero hears that his opposite number had hired a group of repeaters——repeat voters——who would travel around the city and vote at the various precincts. Moreover, they were carrying three ballots per repeater, ballots provided by the party organization. So each repeater was stuffing the ballot box each time he voted, three at a pop. This worried Mr. Plunkett until his wife showed him that he could iron his party's ballots together so that his own repeaters could stuff at eleven a pop. He won in a walk.

We don't know how to generalize such stories. We don't even know if that happened. But the point is when you go to the Australian ballot, the parties are no longer in control of a very key mechanism of voting——what gets counted.

JENSEN: Look at it from Plunkett's point of view. If I were Plunkett, I would want the Australian ballot. The rules are very clear, and I don't have to worry about the other guy screwing us up. If I can get 850 votes, I can carry my district, and I don't have to worry about cheating.

POWELL: That probably explains why it happened. But when it happened, it also ended such practices.

LEVINE: Why, where you had bosses, did they go to extraordinary lengths to control the input into the ballot, right into the fifties?

GASTIL: Let me make another interjection here, because I think it is important for the whole discussion to have the figures right. In the 1890s there were a lot of changes, and after the 90s the participation rates decline. It would be an interesting exercise——maybe it's been done——for some political scientist to use some of the evidence that has been tossed out here almost anecdotally. For example, the statement that in the South lots of blacks were paid for their vote, and voted in blocks. It was mentioned that in Arkansas, they actually voted against voting, because of this practice. Or the Plunkett story about the number of ballots that were stuffed. Somebody should try to put this all together and come up with a figure for "legitimate voting" versus "statistical voting". In other words, to what extent are the figures we are looking at in the 19th century, in fact due to some of these deviations? Clearly, in some of the southern states it must have been important. Is there some way to think about correcting the figures?

GANS: Yes, there are aberrations, but I don't think there's any data to suggest that you are going to drop it by 20 percent or 30 percent down to the level of the post 1920s.

JENSEN: He's right.

PENNIMAN: The votes at the state level in 1896 were pretty solid in the South. By 1904 there are damn near no votes in the South coming out, because they didn't have to get out the vote anymore.

KLEPPNER: Well, you'd have to believe in corruption in the South on an unbelievable scale to say that it underlay those high figures.

GANS: Howard's point is that the South, in general, from 1904 on, even until the 1960s, has to be taken as an aberration, because of its special conditions.

PENNIMAN: And that's one of the many reasons for the huge drop in participation occurring at that time.

JENSEN: Paying for people's vote is very common in the 19th century, but it is not something to correct for. It was the way things were done. It does not mean that a person's vote was illegitimate or involuntary. Republicans were paid to vote Republican. Democrats were paid to vote Democratic. They demanded pay from their party people, "walking around money," as it was usually called, and they got the cash. It was quite rare in the 19th century for a person to be for sale to either party. That was unacceptable to the politicians, and considered immoral. It's one thing to be paid if you are a Republican, to vote Republican. But it was quite immoral for that person to vote Democratic because he was paid to do so.

GASTIL: But Richard, regardless of whether it was legitimate or illegitimate to pay voters from the 19th century point of view, this surely affected participation.

JENSEN: Probably not enough to make the difference. We have an excellent case in Adams County, not far from Cincinnati, a real backwoods area. During the Progressive era a judge cracked down and got most of the voters in the county to confess. He then disenfranchised them. Since this became a national scandal we have a lot of detail on Adams County. The way it worked was that the wealthier people in the county were expected to contribute lots of money; the poorer people expected to be paid. They would not vote unless they got their two dollars, or maybe five. The funny thing about Adams was that with turnout running 98 percent the percentages for each party remained the same. Whether the state of Ohio is moving Republican or Democratic, Adams is very level. It's about fifty-fifty. Neither party could afford a landslide. But nobody "bought an election".

SIGEL: But they bought participation.

ALMOND: I'm surprised that there is no reference to Merriam and Gosnell's study of nonvoting. I'm surprised it hasn't been referred to. It was the first laboratory experiment in American political science.

BENNETT: I used it extensively in some other work that I've done. It helps us understand the impact of the nineteenth amendment, at least on the local level. And it's a tremendous help because the issues they raised set the intellectual agenda for the study of voting participation. A number of political scientists are going back to it, not just an antiquarian like myself, but people like Greg Calder and Pat Patterson have rediscovered it.

Published in 1924, Merriam and Gosnell was an analysis of 6,000 nonvoters in the Chicago election of the previous year. It is the first social survey in political science that I'm aware of. Their question was: Why were people abstaining from participating in that election? They went about it in a surprisingly modern way, in the sense that they looked at the type of variables that have fascinated students of grass-roots turnout ever since. They looked at demographic factors, such as gender, age, and ethnicity. And they looked at some of the institutional aspects that went into the voting process, the time the polls were open and things of this nature. They also examined the attitudes that were involved in the decision to abstain from the elections.

In many ways the conclusions they arrived at stand the test of time, in very handsome fashion. They found that the biggest single predictor of nonvoting, the biggest single factor in leading people to abstain, was apathy, indifference. They didn't use the term in the way it has come to be refined, and certainly their measurements can be subjected to some question. Unfortunately, their work fell into disuse, and has only recently been rediscovered. It gives us a place to look for some comparative analyses to our own time.

THE WITHERED ROOTS

The Impact of Declining Turnout on Democracy in America

Stephen Earl Bennett

Introduction

"From the Athenian Assembly in Plato's time to our current presidential elections, democracy has always implied widespread participation among those recognized as citizens" (Pomper, 1988: 4). Definitions of democracy often make participation by ordinary people the concept's leitmotif. "Democracy involves popular participation by definition" (Pennock, 1979: 445), and "participation is the key notion in its definition" (Cohen, 1973: 7). Many assume that any true democracy must include the full participation of the citizenry among the criteria for its health. Therefore, "every variety of non-participation is a flaw in a democracy" (Cohen, 1973: 10).

It is now commonplace to equate modern democracy "with the electoral process, so that the quality of that process becomes a measure of the quality of democracy itself" (Pomper, 1988: xiii). Hence, voter participation is "an important indicator of the relative health of democracy in any political system based upon elections and the consent of the governed" (Burnham, 1987b: 131-132).

Unfortunately, "if the health of a democracy can be measured by the level of popular participation in its electoral system, ours is ailing" (Orren, 1987: 75). Not only has turnout in American national elections been lower in the twentieth century than every western democracy except Switzerland, it has been below what was normal during the 30 years after the Civil War.[1] Just between 1960 and 1980, voter participation fell from 62.8% of the voting age population to 52.6%.[2] Despite massive voter registration drives by both major political parties and their supporters, turnout only inched up to 53.1% in 1984. Turnout in the 1986 mid-term elections was 35.7%, the lowest since the wartime contests of 1942, and one of the lowest since the 1820s. Projections call for a low turnout in 1988 (Barnes, 1988), perhaps as low as 1948's 51.1%.

Lower turnouts have occurred despite efforts to make voting easier for all citizens and to guarantee access to those previously denied the franchise—especially southern blacks—and in spite of social changes that should have led to higher rates of voting, such as increased educational attainment and women's increasing entry into the work force.

Reaction to the turn-down in turnout has sounded basically two themes. One decries declining voter turnout as injurious to democracy. In this view, if voting continues to decline, "the erosion of the vital underpinnings of American democracy will continue and, perhaps, sadly accelerate" (Gans, 1978: 57; see also Burnham, 1987a, 1987b). A less apocalyptic reaction argues that "the unrelieved preoccupation with turnout figures as measures of the health of our national electoral process is too simplistic" (Miller, 1980: 9; also Ranney, 1983). In this view, although voting in national elections is fundamental, other forms of political action have a higher potential for leverage over elites, and increased rates of citizen involvement in them since 1960 more than compensate for any deleterious consequences of lower turnout. Hence, "while the sheer proportions of those voting may have declined, the overall quality of national political participation . . . has remained constant" since 1960 (Miller, 1980: 13).

The purpose of this paper is twofold. First, previous research on turnout decline will be reviewed, and the central propositions derived therefrom will be critiqued. Although previous studies have identified several putative causes for declining voter participation, they have not been judged particularly successful (Cassel and Luskin, forthcoming). In particular, scholars have not investigated the significance of declining political interest (Bennett, 1986), and they have not adequately explained why young, lesser educated and poorer whites have contributed disproportionately to the diminution in turnout. Second, an attempt will be made to plumb changes in the quality of ordinary people's involvement in public affairs. Quantity is important, of course, if for no other reason than "a situation which results in high participation by members of a group normally has higher potential for democracy . . . than is one where few people show interest or participate in the political process" (Lipset, 1981: 184). But, just as the potential for democracy lessens when rates of grassroots participation decline, the reality of democracy is threatened when high rates of citizen involvement are not accompanied by high levels of quality. Turnout in the 1930s Weimar elections that made the Nazis the largest bloc in the Reichstag were far higher than any in twentieth century America, but few democrats would include them among democracy's finest hours. As Gans (1978: 54) has put it, "the legitimacy of a democratic leadership and the health of the democratic process depend squarely on the informed and active participation of the electorate"[3] (emphasis added).

What Are the Consequences of Nonparticipation?

Before considering these issues, a brief aside is in order concerning whether nonparticipation has any deleterious consequences for democracy. Some argue that in the U. S. "there is no compelling reason to believe that a high level of nonvoting is, by itself, a symptom of a sickness in American society" (Ranney, 1983a: 17). Ranney points to studies showing that American voters and nonvoters do not differ significantly in their policy opinions, their presidential choices, or their cynicism of governmental honesty, competence, or responsiveness. He also argued that "there is no clear or strong relationship between high levels of voting turnout and high levels of civic virtue" (1983a: 17). Therefore, "we need not fear that our low voting turnouts are doing any serious harm to our politics or our country, or that they deprive us of the right to call ourselves a democracy" (Ranney, 1983a: 19).

Nonetheless, democratic theorists have constructed many arguments about the importance of participation (for example, Pateman, 1970; Thompson, 1970; Parry, 1972; Salisbury, 1975). Several will be briefly mentioned here.

One claims that legitimacy is an important result of participation in a democracy. In contemporary democracy "the legitimacy of government is now inseparable from universal suffrage" (Pomper, 1988: 4). Participation is said to be "a legitimizing act" (Salisbury, 1975: 326; see also Gans, 1978: 54). Therefore, participation is necessary for the system's legitimacy and stability, and nonparticipation is a symptom of systemic disorder or will allow antidemocratic forces to take over. By participating in the governmental process, citizens give their consent to elites' decisions and to the regime itself. Hence, it is often asserted that the greater the participation, the more legitimate a democracy, which is said to be a prerequisite for stability (Salisbury, 1975: 327). Throughout the 1980s, critics of the Reagan administration have assailed its legitimacy by pointing out that, due to low turnout, "the party of nonvoters" was more than twenty million larger than the number of votes cast for President Reagan (for example, Burnham, 1985: 214-217). Interestingly, by this criterion, with the exception of LBJ, the legitimacy of every president since Herbert Hoover would be called into question, as 1964 was the only time since 1928 when the size of the "nonvoter party" was not larger than the number of ballots cast for the victor. At that, in 1964, Johnson's vote only equaled the number of nonvoters (see Tarrance, 1978: 84).

A second argument for the value of participation contends that by participating ordinary people exercise control over political elites (Parry, 1972: 19-26). Since the people are the best judges of their own interests, they have a right to participate in politics to protect themselves against elites' depredations (Thompson, 1970). The focus of this "instrumental" perspective on participation is largely on public policy. Nonparticipation is said to skew policy in the direction of participants because "the blunt truth is that politicians and officials are under no compulsion to pay much heed to classes and groups of citizens that do not vote" (Key, 1949: 527). This is alleged to introduce class and racial biases into the process of policy formation and implementation (Burnham, 1987a, 1987b). Often this argument denies that nonparticipation is voluntary; it is seen as a conscious or nonconscious form of domination by the ruling class, caste, or gender. The heart of this argument is that increasing participation will result in a shift toward more egalitarian policies. To bring the claim full circle, increased participation may be alleged to make public policy more "democratic" (Piven and Cloward, 1988).

At the very least, it can be said that the presence of a substantial number of nonvoters has the potential to alter dramatically the balance of partisan power in American politics (Schattschneider, 1960: 98-111). Hadley (1978: 113) argued that large "numbers of refrainers [nonvoters] hang over the democratic process like a bomb, ready to explode and change the course of our history as they have twice in our past." Just before Jackson's election in 1828 and immediately before FDR's selection in 1932, nonvoters rose to about 45% of the voting age population. In each instance, when they entered the electorate, "sudden radical shifts of power . . . occurred" (Hadley, 1978: 113). Although scholars have disputed whether higher rates of turnout would significantly alter the partisan composition of the electorate (De Nardo, 1980, 1986; Tucker and Vedlitz, 1986), many assume they would necessarily redound to the Democrats' advantage (Burnham, 1987b; Piven and Cloward, 1988). As Burnham (1987b: 49) put it, "granted the demographics and the class composition of the 'party of nonvoters,' there seems little reason to doubt that these would be largely Democratic voters, had the Democratic party been interested in, or capable of, the mobilizing incentives to reach them . . . ." According to Petrocik (1987) surveys from 1984 and especially 1980 indicate that the entry of nonvoters into the electorate would have measurably altered the results. "The 1980 election may be the only one in recent American history in which the winning candidate depended on turnout for his victory" (Petrocik, 1987: 240).

Participation is also said to have important salubrious effects for the individual. This proposition is supported by some variety of the Aristotelian assumption: participation is a good that every normal human being desires (Barker, 1958: 6-7), and its corollary, that nonparticipation is a symptom of some psychological abnormality or sickness, often thought to be caused by the political system (that is, false consciousness). This view is often linked with the "developmental" perspective associated with John Stuart Mill (1958) and early twentieth century "citizenship" theorists (Thompson, 1970). These theorists believed that political activity is intrinsically valuable since it offers ordinary people the opportunity for self-improvement. Individuals are said to be capable of becoming more competent citizens through greater participation (Thompson, 1970: 13-22; Barber, 1984). By participating, people not only learn more about their own interests, but also develop a better understanding of other groups' needs (Parry, 1972: 26-31).

Empirical research on the developmental consequences of political participation offers mixed results (see, for example, Finkel, 1985, 1987). The clearest evidence that participation can have significant and lasting consequences for a variety of political dispositions and behaviors comes from Jennings' studies of those from the high school senior class of 1965 who had engaged in political protest during the late 1960s and early 1970s (Jennings and Niemi, 1981: chap. 11; Jennings, 1987). Although self-selection appears to have played a part, those who had protested were, as young adults, more politically aware, competent, and knowledgeable than nonprotesters, even when the two groups were matched according to the quantity and quality of education received after high school (Jennings and Niemi, 1981: 339-341). Protesters were a good deal more likely to engage in conventional political activity, to be more committed to the Democratic Party and to support egalitarian governmental programs (Jennings and Niemi, 1981: 344-350). Also, protest had left its participants far more mistrustful of government than were nonprotesters (Jennings and Niemi, 1981: 350-352). Most of the differences between protesters and nonprotesters observed in 1973 were still present in 1982 (Jennings, 1987).

In short, participation in a democracy is important for at least three reasons: (1) high turnout lends legitimacy to the polity and credibility to elected officials' policy proposals; (2) participation leads to citizen empowerment; and (3) participation results in individual self-development. With this in mind, the concern about low and declining rates of voter participation since the 1960s becomes understandable.

"Why Is Turnout Down?"[4]   A Review of the Literature

Before turning to explanations for the turnout decline, a brief review of voter participation since World War II is necessary to put recent scholarship into a proper context. Beginning with 1948, turnout in presidential elections can be divided into basically three eras: (1) a low turnout, 51.1% of the voting age population in 1948; which was followed by a substantial spurt to 61.6% in 1952 that initiated (2) a series of relatively high turnout (in twentieth century terms) elections, 59.3% in 1956, 62.8% in 1960, 61.9% in 1964, 60.9% in 1968; which were succeeded by a sudden decline to 55.4% in 1972, that commenced (3) a series of low turnouts, 54.4% in 1976, 52.6% in 1980, and 53.1% in 1984 (Johnson, 1980). Several of these postwar contests are noteworthy: 1948 because it was low even by comparison to the wartime contest of 1944, and lower than all of the New Deal elections from 1932 to 1940; (2) 1960, which saw turnout reach a twentieth century peak; (3) 1972, because it was the year in which the turnout decline, which we now know began in 1964, became noticeable, and because it was the first national election after passage of the 26th Amendment lowering the legal minimum voting age from 21 to 18; and (4) 1984, because turnout remained depressed despite massive efforts to register new voters and mobilize them on election day.

In retrospect, it is not surprising that little attention was paid to declining turnout between 1964 and 1972. A decline of 1% per quadrennial cycle after 1960 would have been well within the normal turnout oscillation in this century (Johnson, 1980), and 1968's figure would have still been on the high side for presidential contests since 1900.

When turnout dropped 5.5% between 1968 and 1972, the initial reaction was to ascribe it to legal changes in the electorate's composition. Incorporation of 11 million youths into the voting age population was bound to have a depressive effect on turnout, so it was believed, because the young were known to have abysmal rates of turnout (see Converse, with Niemi, 1971). After all, it was thought, the last major change in the electorate's composition by constitutional amendment, the 19th, was also accompanied by lower turnouts in 1920 and 1924 because it took women some time to shuck off their traditional socialization into passivity. (It has since been demonstrated that turnout had been declining before the 19th Amendment, and would have declined further even had the eligible electorate remained entirely male [Kleppner, 1982a].) Nor, despite the youth protests of the late 1960s and early 1970s, was young people's tendency to eschew voting thought a symptom of alienation. Rather, it was just the result of the "start-up" phenomenon: preoccupied with completion of schooling and the quests for a lifemate and suitable career, young people have little interest in public affairs and are often prevented by residential mobility from satisfying registration requirements as well (Converse, with Niemi, 1971).

It is not surprising, then, that the first sophisticated analysis of changes in turnout between 1952 and 1972 ascribed most of the decline to changes in the age and cohort composition of the electorate (Hout and Knoke, 1972; see also Shaffer, 1981; Kleppner, 1982b). It was expected that once the postwar "baby boomers", who were then entering the electorate as the largest birth cohort in history, aged, they would progressively take up the responsibilities of citizenship, and turnout would increase. Eventually, it would be concluded that extension of the franchise to 18-20 year-olds contributed to a small but significant proportion of the decline in voting after

1971 (Wolfinger and Rosenstone, 1980), and that, at most, changes in the electorate's age structure—resulting from the 26th Amendment and the baby boom's coming of age—contributed to 10% of the turnout decline after 1964 (Boyd, 1981). In other words, most of the reasons for lower voter participation had to be sought elsewhere.

By the late 1970s, sanguinity about declining turnout was no longer possible. Several factors beyond the gross turnout statistics made it impossible to ignore the trend. First, it had become apparent that nearly twenty million people who were once regular voters, had withdrawn from the electorate and showed little likelihood of returning. Second, scholars were also learning that the same years in which turnout turned down also revealed a waning attachment to the two major political parties (see Nie, Verba, and Petrocik, 1979) and, given the long-standing finding that stronger partisans were much more likely than independents and weak identifiers to vote (Milbrath and Goel, 1977), it was natural to wonder if the two developments were related. (They were.) More ominous, although the late 1950s and early 1960s revealed a citizenry with overwhelmingly positive views about the American political system and officials (Almond and Verba, 1963), the late 1960s saw a sea change as Americans became more and more cynical of politicians' motives and competence (Lipset and Schneider, 1987). Although some viewed these changes as a profound alienation (Miller, 1974a, 1974b; Caddell, 1979), others saw them as either merely fashionable cliches (Citrin, 1974) or, at worst, partisan disgruntlement (Miller, 1979). The presumption that growing cynicism and lower turnout stemmed from Vietnam, urban riots and campus disorders, or Watergate, gave way to the realization that the public grew more choleric long after the war ended, the cities and the campuses grew quiet, and the Unindicted Coconspirator resigned to private life. By decade's end, President Carter would muse on national TV about the "crisis of the national spirit," and "national malaise" became a hackneyed phrase. The obvious question arose, were growing public cynicism and declining turnout related? Initially, some thought so (Tarrance, 1978: 77). Eventually it was determined that cynicism was unrelated to turnout (Lipset and Schneider, 1987), but the public's declining belief that public officials were attentive to and responsive to public opinion was.

Since the late 1970s, the turnout decline has generated a large corpus trying to explain it. Despite applying different theoretical perspectives, relying on diverse data bases,[5] and utilizing disparate statistical techniques, some consensus has been reached. Scholars agree that turnout has increased among southern blacks, and that the traditional gender gap in voter participation has been closed, due more to declining turnout among men than to increased participation by women. It is also widely agreed that turnout would have fallen even further had it not been for a rise in educational attainment.

Beyond these few points, however, there is disagreement on the factors responsible for the turn-down in turnout. Some researchers have focused on institutional factors, such as the decoupling of state and local electoral calendars from the schedule of federal elections (Boyd, 1981, 1986). Others have looked at changes among demographic groups, noting that the drop in turnout has been concentrated among the lower classes, thereby producing a greater class skew to turnout (Reiter, 1979; Miller, 1980; Cavanagh, 1981; Burnham, 1982; Kleppner, 1982b). Several studies have concentrated on the public's weakened attachments to the major political parties (Brody, 1978; Cassel and Hill, 1981; Shaffer, 1981; Abramson and Aldrich, 1982; De Nardo, 1987; Teixeira, 1987), and on the growing belief that public officials are less responsive to ordinary folk (Brody, 1978; Reiter, 1979; Cassel and Hill, 1981; Abramson and Aldrich, 1982; Kleppner, 1982b; Teixeira, 1987). Still others have identified declining concern about which political party will win the election as a factor (Aldrich, 1976; Ferejohn and Fiorina, 1979; Rollenhagen, 1984). Patterns of public reliance on the mass media, and in media coverage of elections have been considered. For example, decreased reliance on newspapers for campaign information has been found to play a role in lower turnouts (Shaffer, 1981; Teixeira, 1987). The television networks' early election-night projections of the outcome are also alleged to have contributed to reduced voter participation, although this has been hotly debated (Wolfinger and Linquiti, 1981; Epstein and Strom, 1981; Jackson, 1983).

Careful reading of the research on turnout decline reinforces Brody's (1978) conclusion that the phenomenon is, at bottom, "a puzzle." As he (1978: 323) put it, "the picture of participation in America is confusing because we cannot arrive at any simple conclusions." Confoundment is added to confusion by Hadley's (1978) discovery that there are at least six types of "refrainers" (nonvoters); each type refrains for quite different reasons. Unfortunately, it cannot be determined whether the six types change in size over time.

Another Look at the Turnout Decline

Ultimately, research on the turn-down in turnout leaves a disquieting sense of incompleteness. A recent analysis admits that, even when sophisticated statistical techniques are employed, most of the reasons for the decline in voter participation are undetected (Teixeira, 1987). Although some researchers claim to have identified all or most of the factors responsible, a forthcoming critique charges most earlier studies with focusing on too few potential explanatory factors (Cassel and Luskin, forthcoming). As Cassel and Luskin note, studies that have cast a wider net for putative causes have resulted in statistical models with extremely limited explanatory capacity (for example, Ashenfelter and Kelley, 1975; Reiter, 1979; Cassel and Hill, 1981).

There are several reasons for anticipating that a complete explanation for the decline in turnout may elude us. First, it is well to remember that the data sets most often relied on to study the phenomenon **were not designed with this purpose in mind.** The series of National Election Studies conducted since 1952 by the University of Michigan's Survey Research Center/Center for Political Studies are a rich and unparalleled source of data on ordinary people's voting behavior. But their design has changed over the years, so that variables drop out or crop up from time to time, thereby frustrating those wishing to pursue change over time. Second, the instruments used to tap political behavior are known to contain measurement error, sometimes a goodly amount thereof, and the resulting "noise," which is then entered into high-powered statistical procedures that presume perfect measurement, undermines scholars' capacity to account for turnout decline. Third, we are learning that contextual factors, such as the level of party competition in a state or a congressional district and the resulting level of party effort to mobilize supporters in those areas can be powerful determinants of turnout (see Kim, Petrocik, and Enokson, 1975; Caldeira and Patterson, 1982a, 1982b; Tucker, 1986). Only recently have contextual variables become routinely available with CPS National Election Studies. Until these factors are brought to bear, a certain portion of the reasons for lower turnout since 1960 will be missed, and the phenomenon will remain a "puzzle."

In the meantime, there is one factor that can be shown to have had an important effect on lower voter participation since 1960 which has received short shrift in previous scholarship: interest in public affairs. Although Teixeira (1987: 89) mentioned "a generalized withdrawal from politics" as possibly responsible for falling turnout, he did not fully appreciate its significance. The relative inattention to political interest as a determinant of turnout decline is surprising for two reasons. First, the attention ordinary people pay to public affairs has long been known to be a prime determinant of actual participation (Campbell, et al., 1960; Milbrath and Goel, 1977). Second, a number of studies employing multivariate analysis procedures have found one facet or another of psychological involvement in politics—for example, reliance on the mass media—to be important predictors of turnout (Reiter, 1979; Cassel and Hill, 1981; Shaffer, 1981; Bennett, 1986; Teixeira, 1987).

One reason for scholars' inattention to political interest stems from the assumption that only those factors that have changed over the years can account for lower turnout (for example, Shaffer, 1981: 68). Several studies have remarked that since interest in campaigns has not changed markedly since 1960, it can be discounted as a culprit in lower turnout.

Here we encounter a methodological conundrum. Interest in campaigns is only one component of psychological involvement in public affairs, and one of the more error-prone facets at that (Bennett and Bennett, forthcoming). Properly to tap attentiveness to government and public affairs, one needs a richer and more reliable indicator. Fortunately, one is available, and provided proper precautions are taken, can be employed with SRC/CPS data from 1960 to 1986 (Bennett, 1986).

Almond and Verba (1963: 88) suggested that measures of general political interest and attentiveness to campaigns can be combined to tap what they call the "civic cognition," that is, "following governmental and political affairs and paying attention to politics. . . ." Theirs was a sound idea. The two items can be combined to create the Political Apathy Index, which has been shown to be a valid and reliable indicator of grassroots' psychological involvement in politics (Bennett, 1986: chapter 3).

For present purposes, the Political Apathy Index is useful for three reasons. First, it is known to be a significant predictor of self-reported and validated turnout, even when education, "the universal solvent" of political participation (Converse, 1972: 324), is controlled. Second, its relationship to validated turnout from 1964 to 1984 has increased (Bennett, 1986: 57). Third, the Apathy Index shows that, from the mid-1960s to the mid-1980s, Americans have become less attentive to government and public affairs. In 1964, for example, the Index shows that 22% of the adult public could be classified as "very interested" in public affairs, 19% were "slightly interested," 30% were classified as "neutral," 17% were "slightly apathetic," and 7% were "very apathetic." Twenty years later, 16% were very interested, 21% were slightly attentive, 37% were neutral, 16% were slightly apathetic, and 9% were totally indifferent to public affairs (see Bennett, 1986: 63). An excess of 17% more interest than apathy in 1964 had dwindled to 12% by 1984. The decline in political attentiveness transpired despite Americans' increased exposure to higher education.

To appreciate political interest's impact on turnout even when the effects of other factors known to shape the likelihood of voting are taken into account, multiple discriminant analysis runs were conducted for the 1964, 1976, 1980, and 1984 National Election Studies. Multiple discriminant analysis is a statistical technique that allows a researcher to assess the simultaneous effects of several independent variables, called predictors, on a dependent variable. At bottom, discriminant analysis provides the information to describe the differences between two or more groups within a population, in this case, voters and nonvoters (Klecka, 1980; Daniels and Darcy, 1983; Sigelman, 1984).[6] In each case, the dependent variable was a determination as to whether the person had voted or not as established by the SRC/CPS's vote validation studies. The aim was to cast as wide a net as possible in the quest for predictive power even at the risk of building some redundancy into the models. Twenty-one predictors were entered into the equations: gender, race, age, education, family income, respondent's occupation, home ownership, length of residence in the home, union membership, subjective social class, strength of partisanship, concern about which party will win the election, psychological involvement in public affairs, reliance on television for campaign information, usage of newspapers for campaign news, trust in government, perceptions of governmental attentiveness, belief that government is responsive to public opinion (external political efficacy), belief that government and politics are understandable (internal political efficacy), and for

1976, 1980, and 1984, sense of civic duty.[7]   Over the years, each has been found to have an important bearing on the probability that one would vote. To save space, and for ease of discussion, only the data from 1964 and 1984 are depicted in Table 14.   Save for relatively minor details, the 1976 and 1980 data mirror those depicted in the table.

Several types of information are included in the table: (1) those predictor variables determined by the discriminant models to be significant predictors of turnout; (2) Wilks' lambda, which is a multivariate measure of group differences over those predictor variables retained in the discriminant models; (3) the standardized canonical discriminant function coefficients, which are directly analogous to a standardized regression coefficient (beta weight); (4) since means and standard deviations differ from year to year, the unstandardized canonical discriminant function coefficients; (5) the percentage of "grouped" cases correctly classified by the discriminant analysis model; and (6) the number of cases upon which the models are based.

Although there are many interesting facets to these data, only a few will be touched on. First, note that the initial predictor entered into the models in each year is the Political Apathy Index, thus confirming the hypothesis that previous researchers had under-specified their models by leaving out this important predictor. Note also that the values of Wilks' lambda for the two years confirm that the Apathy Index was a stronger predictor of turnout in 1984 than it had been in 1964.[8]   In short, not only did the slight decline in political interest among the American public between 1964 and 1984 have a depressive impact on turnout, the amount of this effect was slightly larger than the absolute level of the change itself.

Second, although the data confirm previous research on the importance of waning partisanship, other factors frequently mentioned do not emerge as consistently strong predictors. For example, although among the top discriminators in 1964, education played only a minor role twenty years later. Also, age was only a minor factor in each year. In addition, while mass media usage does enter the models, it is slightly different from year to year. In 1964, the more one relied on TV for campaign information, the **less** likely he or she was to vote. In 1984, however, it was the amount of reliance on newspaper stories about the campaign that had an impact on increasing the probability of voting.

TABLE 14

Multiple Discriminant Analyses of Validated Vote, 1964 and 1984

Variable	Wilks' Lambda Function Coef.	Standardized Canonical Discriminant Function Coef.	Unstndrdized Canonical Discriminant
		1964	
Home Ownership	.91	.23	.51
Race	.90	.24	.84
Strength of Partisanship	.88	.29	.32
Education	.87	.33	.11
Length of Residence	.86	.22	.17
Care Who Wins	.85	.24	.52
TV Reliance	.85	-.22	-.23
Age Deviation Squared	.84	.18	.01
Subjective Social Class	.84	.17	.35
Age Deviation	.84	-.18	-.00
Internal Political Efficacy	.83	-.12	-.25

Constant   -5.23

Percentage of Grouped Cases Correctly Classified: 66.4 (N = 1316)

Variable	Wilks' Lambda Function Coef.	Standardized Canonical Discriminant Function Coef.	Unstndrdized Canonical Discriminant
		1984	
Political Apathy Index	.91	.28	.14
Length of Residence	.85	.35	.26
R's Occupation	.83	.15	.08
Strength of Partisanship	.81	.27	.29
Newspaper Reliance	.80	.27	.27
Civic Duty	.78	.22	.44
Home Ownership	.78	.18	.40
External Political Efficacy	.77	.20	.26
Gender	.76	-.20	-.39
Family Income	.76	.14	.01
Age Deviation Squared	.76	-.12	-.00
Education	.76	.14	.06
Gov'tal Attentiveness	.75	.10	.05

Constant   -4.74

Percentage of Grouped Cases Correctly Classified: 74.8 (N = 944)

Source: University of Michigan's Survey Research Center/Center for Political Studies' 1964 and 1984 National Election Studies.

There are some differences between the two models that are noteworthy. Although race was an important predictor in 1964, when many southern blacks were still denied the franchise, it had ceased to be significant by 1984. Also, although gender was not a factor in 1964, in 1984, it played a minor albeit interesting role; when all other factors were held constant, women were slightly **more** likely than men to vote.

The increased importance of residential mobility in 1984 is also worth considering, for it suggests that length of residence plays a bigger role in depressing turnout in the 1980s than in the 1960s. Since the mid-1960s, many states had changed voter registration statutes to lessen the burden of mobility on access to the ballot, and it would have been thought that one result would have been to reduce mobility's depressive impact on turnout. Instead, it has increased, suggesting that proposals to ease registration statutes even more, **insofar as they apply to turnout,** may not have the desired effect.

An obvious question is how successful the models were in accounting for variation in turnout. By the standards usually applied to survey research, they were reasonably successful. One means normally applied to judge the success of a discriminant analysis model is the percentage of grouped cases that can be correctly classified (Klecka, 1980: 49-51). In 1964, 66.4% of the grouped cases were correctly classified, and in 1984, 74.8% were. Lest the reader jump to the conclusion that the discriminant models were whopping successes, it should be noted that, with a dichotomous dependent variable (vote/did not vote), a 50% successful classification could be expected just by chance. So we see that the models were a slight improvement over random assignment into the voter/nonvoter categories, and that the rate of correct classification increased between 1964 and 1984, thereby indicating the latter was a more successful discriminant model.

But just how much better was 1984? Some researchers have suggested that the final value of Wilks' lambda can be subtracted from 100, and that value treated as analogous to the R^2 statistic in multiple regression (Sigelman, 1982). (In regression, the value of R^2 tells how much variation in the dependent variable is due to the combined effects of the independent variables.) By that test, 17% of the "variance" in turnout could be accounted for in 1964, and 25% could be "explained" in 1984. In short, the discriminant models can be judged reasonably successful. Equally important, the rate of success improves over time. Still, a very large percentage of "variance" in turnout is left unexplained, a point that will be dealt with in the conclusion.

It is also important to be aware of the growing importance of basic political dispositions as predictors of turnout. In 1964, the only one included in the model was internal political efficacy. By 1984, however, belief that government was responsive to public opinion and perceptions of governmental attentiveness to public opinion were included, though in relatively minor roles. This suggests there may be a small element of political discontent in nonvoting in the 1980s that was not present in 1964. We shall return to this point in the concluding section.

There is one final difference between the two models worthy of attention. Other than education, objective indicators of social class had no bearing on voter participation in the mid-1960s. By the mid-1980s, the respondent's occupation and family income played small but important roles, thereby lending support to those who have detected an increasing class skew to turnout (Reiter, 1979; Cavanagh, 1981; Miller, 1980; Burnham, 1982; Kleppner, 1982b). That growing class skew merits a brief analysis, for it provides the leverage needed to put some of the other changes in Americans' turnout in the proper light.

Left Behind: Increased Economic Marginality among Young Noncollege Whites

Scholars have noted that the decline in turnout has occurred disproportionately among lesser educated, poorer whites (Reiter, 1979: 304; Cavanagh, 1981: 59-60). SRC/CPS voter validation studies between 1964 and 1986 indicate that special attention needs to be focused on young whites whose formal education ended at or before the twelfth grade. In 1964, 59% of young whites (under 35) with twelve grades or less of schooling voted, compared to 71% of those with at least some college. Young, lesser educated whites' validated turnout averaged 41% in the last three presidential elections, as compared to 69% of their college-educated counterparts. What had been only a 12% gap in the turnout rates of college and noncollege young whites in 1964 has averaged 28% in presidential elections since 1976. In off-year elections since 1974, the validated turnout of young noncollege whites has averaged 20%, precisely half that of whites with college exposure. Voting has fallen among other age categories, but among noncollege whites over 35 it has not fallen to the depths recorded among the noncollege young.

At the outset, it is important to recall the "start-up" phenomenon. Although the start-up problem is common to young people in general, "it is among the poorly educated that the [turnout] differences by age become extreme" (Converse, with Niemi, 1971: 446). The college-educated young are only slightly less likely to vote than similarly schooled older persons (Converse, with Niemi, 1971: 446-452). Among the least educated, however, the young vote at much lower rates than those over 35. Although registration tends to be a particularly high hurdle for lesser schooled young persons, who are likely to be apprehensive about the bureaucratic routines involved, Converse and Niemi believed that lack of motivation was a much more potent cause of nonvoting among the poorly educated young (1971: 460). Indeed, nonvoting among the poorly educated young is just "one symptom of a broader insulation from the public affairs of the society" (Converse, with Niemi, 1971: 448).

Converse and Niemi relied on National Election Studies (NES) in 1952 and 1956, and when they referred to the poorly educated, they meant grade schoolers (1971: 447). The focus here is on young whites without college background, and particularly those who did not finish high school. As American society has come more and more to require completion of high school, and now college, as certification for economic advancement, low educational attainment has left the young increasingly disadvantaged, economically and politically. Let us consider economic factors first.

Data from the 1964 and 1984 National Election Studies depict increasing economic marginality among young, noncollege-educated whites (Bennett, 1988b). The problem is particularly serious among those without high school diplomas. In this sense, the data dovetail with studies indicating that changes in the American economy during the last three decades have left younger persons with limited education at a particular disadvantage (Youth and America's Future, 1988). While the women among noncollege young whites were much less likely to be nonworking housewives in the 1980s than in the 1960s, lower-educated whites in general were much more likely to be unemployed or toiling in low-level blue collar or service jobs, and less likely to be in upper-level, skilled blue collar occupations. Also, to the degree they still have white collar jobs, these are low-paying clerical and sales positions. By 1984, young noncollege whites had virtually disappeared from the ranks of managers or professionals. In short, they are increasingly among the "working poor" whose plight has recently stirred debate among federal policymakers (Kosterlitz and Rauch, 1988). Meanwhile, there was a slight upgrading in occupations among college-educated whites.

Questions about recent unemployment and job security reveal the economic insecurity of noncollege young whites. In 1984, almost two-fifths of them said they had been laid off or had to take wage cuts or reduced hours during the past six months, compared to slightly more than one-quarter of those with exposure to college. Noncollege young whites were also a good deal more likely to worry about losing their jobs.

If decreased occupational prestige and greater job insecurity hint at the straightened economic circumstances of noncollege young whites, their family incomes leave no doubt. Those who had not completed high school had suffered worse; although only one-ninth had had family incomes in the lowest quintile in 1964, by 1984, nearly one-half did. Moreover, only a trace element still had family incomes in the highest quintile. Those who had graduated from high school had not suffered as badly, but they were also a good deal less well-off in the 1980s. By contrast, although those with some college experience had experienced a slight downward trend, college graduates were doing slightly better in the mid-1980s than in the mid-1960s.

The essential point is that it has been young, lesser-educated whites who have suffered the biggest declines in family incomes since the mid-1960s. Their diminished economic fortunes are apparent in many ways. For example, while college-educated young whites were more likely to be homeowners in the 1980s than in 1960s, their noncollege-educated counterparts were less likely. In addition, noncollege young whites were less likely to think that their families' financial situation had improved recently and less likely to believe things would get better next year.

Increased economic marginality among young noncollege whites between the mid-1960s and mid-1980s was accompanied by important changes in their political outlooks. They were less likely to be interested in public affairs and to utilize the mass media, especially newspapers, for political information. They were substantially more cynical of public officials' competence, honesty, and responsiveness to the opinions of people like themselves. They were also a good deal less likely to identify strongly with a political party, especially the Democrat party. Although 24% of noncollege young whites had been strong Democrats in 1964, only 5% were in 1984. Most of the decline in strong attachment to the Democrats among this group seems to have been superseded by either refusal to identify with either party, or by tenuous affiliation with the Republicans. (Since the NES's are not panel surveys, it is impossible to discover where shifts in partisanship have occurred.)

Young lesser-educated whites were much less likely in the 1980s than in the 1960s to think of reasons for liking the Democrat party and less likely to feel favorably toward the party as well (Bennett, 1988b). As a result, the party had lost ground among those who once had been a critical element in FDR's New Deal coalition. It should also be pointed out that the GOP had not won the hearts and minds of young noncollege whites, although its relative standing vis-e-vis the Democrats had improved. The essential message is that the Democrats have lost the affections of a substantial portion of noncollege young whites. The alienation of affection for the Democrat party has been particularly severe among young whites who have not completed high school. Republican attempts to appeal to these people have fallen on particularly barren soil. The GOP has done only slightly better among high school graduates.

What seems to have happened is that the parties have failed as agencies of representative government in the minds of young whites in general, and among the noncollege young in particular. When asked in 1964 how much do parties help make the government pay attention to what the people want, 43% of the noncollege young said "a great deal," 48% said "some," and only 9% said "not much." In 1980, the last time the CPS (Michigan's Center for Political Studies) asked the question, only 12% of noncollege young whites thought the parties helped a great deal, 59% said they helped some, and 29% virtually dismissed them as agencies of representative government. The parties' reputations as representative agencies also fell among the college-educated young, but since many of them could still find reasons for liking one or both, this decline did not have the debilitating impact that it did among those without exposure to higher education.

Commenting on the decline in turnout among working class whites in general, Reiter (1987: 135) argued that "it is hard to imagine that this largely low-income group refrains from voting because they are satisfied with the [political] system." Multiple discriminant analyses from 1964 and 1984 establish that a combination of growing economic marginality, decreased partisanship, and growing indifference to public affairs account for the lion's share of the turnout decline among young noncollege whites (Bennett, 1988b). In short, at least among young noncollege whites, their abysmal rates of turnout in the 1980s stem not so much from political discontent as from indifference. Their indifference stems from their preoccupation with keeping body and soul together and a growing belief that neither political party offers much they find attractive.

Perhaps Reiter's contention that increased nonvoting among whites reflects political discontent is premature. Data from the 1964 and 1984 National Election Studies (NES) show that noncollege young whites have lost a good deal of faith that elections "make government pay attention to what the people want." In 1964, 74% said that elections made government pay "a good deal" of attention to public opinion, 21% thought they had some effect, and only 5% thought they did not make much difference. By 1984, only 33% still believed elections were very effective in making government pay heed to the people, while 45% said they were only somewhat effective, and 21% virtually dismissed them as institutions of representative government. In the face of such a loss of confidence in the electoral process, is it any wonder that young noncollege whites manifest such low rates of turnout? Moreover, when a core element of the American democratic creed (Dennis, 1970) comes into question among a significant group of Americans, can political discontent be far behind?

Quantity vs. Quality: Fewer but Better?

While the decline in turnout since the 1960s has worried many, some observers profess not to be unduly concerned, claiming that increased participation in other forms of political action, which may more effectively influence elites' policy decisions, amply offsets any deleterious results of lower turnout. For example, Miller (1980) argued that other forms of campaign activity, such as attempting to influence others' votes, and donating to candidates' and parties' coffers, rose during the period when voting declined. He also pointed out that the percentage of the public claiming to have written to a public official to express a political opinion increased from 17 in 1964 to 28 in 1976. In this view, declining numbers of voters were offset by enhancement of the quality of overall participation.

If it could be established that lower rates of turnout were somehow compensated for by increased participation in other forms of political activity, much of the lamentations about democracy's endangerment might be assuaged. However, the evidence indicates that, at best, the very low rates of participation in other forms of political action evidenced in the 1960s remain unchanged today. As part of its 1987 General Social Survey, the University of Chicago's National Opinion Research Center (NORC) replicated many of the questions about political activity that had been part of its 1967 Political Participation in America Study (see Verba and Nie, 1972). The data from the two NORC surveys are depicted in Table 15.

For present purposes, there are two messages in the table. First, for the most part, the data bespeak an essential continuity over the two decades. Americans are more likely to report contacting public officials, and slightly more likely to contribute money to political causes. They are slightly less likely to say they always vote in local elections. Other forms of participation show virtual constancy. In short, declining turnout in national elections has not been offset by increased involvement in other political activities. Second, political participation is largely the province of a minority, sometimes a tiny fragment of the public. Based on evidence from a survey taken nearly 40 years ago, Woodward and Roper (1950: 875) concluded that "in America the few act politically for the many," and that proposition still holds.

TABLE 15

Trends in Americans' Political Participation, 1967–1987

Activity	1967	1987
Has R Ever Worked With Others in This Community to Try to Solve Some Community Problems?	30 %	34 %
Has R Ever Taken Part in Forming a New Group or a New Organization to Try to Solve Some Community Problems?	14 %	17 %
During Elections Has R Ever Tried to Show People Why They Should Vote for One of the Parties or Candidates?		
Often	11 %	9 %
Sometimes	17	22
Rarely	12	14
Never	60	54
Has R Done Other Work for One of the Parties in Most Elections, Some Elections, Only a Few, or Has R Never Done Such Work?		
Most Elections	5 %	3 %
Some Elections	9	9
Only a Few	11	15
Never	75	73
In the Past Three or Four Years, Has R Attended Any Political Meetings or Rallies?	19 %	19 %
Has R Ever Personally Gone to See, or Spoken to, or Written to Some Member of Local Government or Some Other Person of Influence in the Local Community about Some Needs or Problems?	20 %	35 %

Has R Ever Contacted or Written to
Some Representative or Government
Officials Outside the Local Community
—on the County, State, or National
Level about Some Need or Problem?   18 %   30 %

Does R Always Vote in Local Elections,
Sometimes Miss, Rarely Vote, or Never Vote?

Always Vote	47 %	35 %
Sometimes Miss	29	33
Rarely Vote	8	12
Never Vote	16	19

In the Past Three or Four Years, Has R
Contributed Money to a Political Party
or a Candidate, or to Any Other Political
Cause?   13 %   23 %

Sources: University of Chicago's National Opinion Research Center's 1967 Political Participation in America Study and its 1987 General Social Survey

****

Is it possible, however, that declining turnout has been accompanied by increasing quality of another kind: citizens' information about and understanding of government and public affairs? If it could be shown that the electorate of the 1980s, albeit a smaller percentage of the voting age population, were more politically sophisticated than the 1960s electorate, there might yet be grounds for optimism about democracy's fate.

Admittedly, as soon as the topic of the "quality" of grassroots political thinking is raised, problems crop up. First, there is a reluctance in some circles to consider issues related to "quality"; to do so, it is said, smacks of "elitism." That is an odd response, considering that democratic theorists from Jefferson to the early twentieth century "citizenship" theorists regarded the quality of public decision making every bit as important as the quantity of citizen participation (see Thompson, 1970). Second, there are serious methodological problems associated with attempts to tap the quality of the public's political reasoning. Anyone familiar with the tenacious scholarly debate over changes in Americans' political belief systems since the 1960s will recognize that the most hotly contested issues center on methodology (for good reviews of this literature, see Converse, 1975; Kinder and Sears, 1985).

Despite some daunting methodological problems, most associated with the conception and measurement of key concepts, some meaningful points can be made. None gives much comfort to those who would argue that lower quantity of grassroots participation has been offset by higher quality of public deliberation. First, just as Campbell and his associates (1960) found during the allegedly issueless 1950s, the contemporary public's political belief systems can be characterized as devoid of the ideologies that shape politicians', pundits', and professors' political discourse (Kinder and Sears, 1985). Second, Americans' opinions about major public policies, many of which have been long a part of the public agenda, are inconsistent, malleable, and readily susceptible to manipulation by methodological artifact. Many people seem to change their opinions on even fundamental questions of public policy almost willy-nilly, as if they were inventing their opinions at the moment they are polled (Converse, 1964, 1970; Converse and Markus, 1979). Seemingly minor shifts in the wording of survey questionnaires can produce profound shifts in the distribution of opinions on even major questions of domestic public policy (Smith, 1987). Third, the public is woefully ignorant of public affairs. "Americans are . . . hazy about many of the principal [political] players, lackadaisical regarding debates on policies that preoccupy Washington, ignorant of facts that experts take for granted, and unsure about the policies advanced by candidates for the highest public offices" (Kinder and Sears, 1985: 664). Moreover, recent studies have shown no improvement in the public's information about and understanding of public affairs since the 1940s and 1950s (Neuman, 1986; Bennett, 1988a).

The public's continuing innocence of political affairs has occurred despite a massive upgrading of its exposure to formal schooling, and despite herculean efforts by the print and electronic media to make information about public affairs widely available and relatively cost-free. What accounts for the continuing political ignorance of a public that, if judged by its formal schooling, should put Pericles' Athenians to shame, and is daily exposed to a massive outpouring of information flowing through media channels? "Bombardment with political information and low levels of intake can co-occur only if there is, in a very substantial portion of the electorate, a steady and systematic 'tuning-out'" (Converse, 1975: 96). In short, apathy begets political ignorance, which is the theme of at least two recent studies of political ignorance among the American public (Neuman, 1986; Bennett, 1988a).

Of course, concern about continuing ignorance among the public as a whole would diminish if it could be established that, at least among voters---who decide who shall govern---the quality of deliberation, that is, the amount of political information, had increased since the 1960s. Unfortunately, no such finding can be made. In 1964 and 1984, it is possible to create a Political Information Index based on identical items: knowledge of which political party held the more seats in the U. S. House of Representatives, and which party won the more House seats in the recent election. Based on this measure of admittedly "stray facts" (Converse, 1975),[9] the active electorate of 1984 was less politically informed than that of 1964. In 1964, 69% of voters got both questions correct, 22% missed one, and 9% missed both. Twenty years later, only 54% knew the answers to both questions, 19% got one right, and 27% missed both. Granted, in each year voters were more knowledgeable than nonvoters, and the gap in political knowledge between voters and nonvoters was larger in 1984. But, and here's the rub, if the quality of the electorate's deliberations can be tapped by the amount of information it brings to bear on democracy's most fundamental act, **the last two decades have witnessed not an improvement, but a slight deterioration in the informational backlog the average voter takes into the voting booth.** In short, those who worry about the impact of declining turnout on democracy in America should be even more concerned. Fewer voters with less information about public affairs can hardly be an occasion for rejoicing.

Conclusion

Few can be pleased when the nation claiming to be the world's oldest and largest democracy has lower turnouts in national elections than it did a century ago and lower than virtually every other democracy in the world today. From scholars who worry about low turnouts' implications for democracy's well-being, to editors who scourge their fellow citizens' sloth, to politicians who worry that a sudden irruption of nonvoters into the polling booths might signify their electoral doom, many bemoan low turnout and seek to divine its meaning, causes, and cures.

When comparing today's low turnouts with those in other countries, and even with those in the U. S. a century ago, it is natural to point to an American anomaly: the U. S. is the only industrial democracy requiring individual initiative to register before election day (Rosenstone and Wolfinger, 1978; Crewe, 1981; Powell, 1986; Jackman, 1987; Piven and Cloward, 1988). It has been claimed that registration is the strongest factor influencing the probability that one will vote, thereby leading to the novel interpretation that many people vote simply to remain registered (Erikson, 1981). It has been argued that, if registration statutes were substantially relaxed, turnout in national elections would increase from 9 to 16% (Rosenstone and Wolfinger, 1978; Powell, 1986). If that were true, American turnouts would improve from the bottom to near the middle of voter participation in western democracies. The thrust of a recently published tome is that the revitalization of American democracy can occur only if voter registration statutes are fundamentally eased by getting government to assume the burden of registration (Piven and Cloward, 1988).

But will democracy flourish under such circumstances? Most likely not, for several reasons. First, while critics of current practices, such as Burnham and Piven and Cloward, justifiably contend that personal registration statutes place a greater burden on lesser educated, poorer citizens, they pass over in silence one key datum: **the decline in turnout since 1960 has occurred during a period when registration laws were substantially relaxed.** In short, at the very time the costs associated with clearing the hurdle of registration were significantly reduced, turnout declined. Hence, it is difficult to understand why easing registration requirements further would be the panacea its proponents claim (see also Katosh and Traugott, 1982). Changes in the perceived value of the vote must occur before many more people will come to the polls.

Second, it is well to recall the data in Table 14 showing that, unlike the case in the mid-1960s, there is little evidence that political discontent is responsible for voter abstention today. It would be mistaken to argue that large portions of nonvoters are profoundly alienated. The largest group among Hadley's (1978) abstainers were the "positive apathetics," that is, people whose lives were going so well that voting was not worth the time and effort. Hadley's group coming closest to being "alienated" was the "politically impotent" because they felt "helpless," not "hostile," when it came to politics. Hadley's data on nonvoters came from the 1976 election, in the midst of a period of declining public confidence and trust in governmental leadership. Part of the increasing "malaise" during these years was a substantial decline among the public as a whole in the belief that elections make government pay attention to public opinion. Sixty-five percent of the public thought that elections made government pay a great deal of attention to the people in 1964, 25% thought they were of some use, and only 6% said they did not have much effect. By 1980, only 51% still thought elections had a great deal of impact on what government did, 35% felt they had some impact, and 13% said they did not help very much. Scholars noted a slight decline in cynicism during the first four years of the Reagan era (Miller, 1983; Citrin and Green, 1986; Lipset and Schneider, 1987). One belief that did not improve, however, was about the efficacy of elections as institutions of representative government. In 1984, only 43% of the public opined that elections make government pay a great deal of attention to the people, 42% said they had some impact, and 14% felt they did not help very much. Until the public's faith in the utility of the electoral process is substantially rekindled, it is bootless to expect much improvement in turnout.

Those who hope for higher voter participation must come to grips with the fact that the biggest factor behind nonvoting is apathy (see also Teixeira, 1988). Declining reliance on newspapers and increased dependence on TV, which are said to conduce lower turnout (Shaffer, 1981; Ranney, 1983b; Teixeira, 1987), are but symptoms of indifference to public affairs. Many factors explain massive public indifference, of course, some of which are virtually impossible to overcome, for example, limited educational attainment (Bennett, 1986). One important factor that could be rectified, however, is the eviscerated state of America's major political parties. It is commonplace today to decry the dilapidated condition into which both parties have fallen (for example, Ladd, 1982). Perhaps because they find the parties increasingly irrelevant (Wattenberg, 1986), fewer and fewer Americans generally, and young persons particularly, strongly identify with the Democrats or the Republicans. One result is political indifference; another is nonvoting.

The "electoral demobilization" that occurred during "the System of 1896" was due more to declining party competitiveness than to the imposition of personal registration statutes (Kleppner and Baker, 1980; see also McGerr, 1986). During the 1920s, which were noted for very low turnouts, Walter Lippmann (1928) also identified the absence of meaningful party competition as the primary cause of public apathy.

A factor largely overlooked today is a similar absence of meaningful two-party competition in large parts of the United States. Although the Republicans have held the presidency for 16 of the last 28 years, the Democrats have controlled both houses of the U. S. Congress for all but 6 years, and they have held roughly two-thirds of state legislatures during most of the same period. The number of Republican mayors of big cities is minuscule, and city councils in the major metropolitan areas are mostly a Democratic preserve. It should also be pointed out that seats in the House of Representatives and in many state legislatures as well are increasingly "safe" (Mayhew, 1974). Added to decreasingly competitive legislative elections is the growing power of incumbency as a determinant of electoral outcomes. In the 1986 mid-term elections, 98.4% of House incumbents seeking reelection were successful. Although incumbents seeking reelection to the Senate do not do quite so well, they also benefit from their status.

One consequence of declining competitiveness of legislative seats at the state and federal levels is that parties put less and less effort into districts that have not changed parties in years. As parties make either only a token effort or, none at all, to unseat incumbents in safe districts, they are less and less likely to try mobilizing potential supporters to go to the polls. The result is lower turnout (Kim, Petrocik, and Enokson, 1975).

It costs time and energy to vote. Not much, perhaps, especially in comparison to more demanding political activities, but some. Until more people come to believe that the electoral process makes a difference to representative government, turnouts are not going to rise much above their current levels. Until voting increases, democracy's roots will continue to starve. Robert Maynard Hutchins wrote that "the death of democracy is not likely to be an assassination from ambush. It will be a slow extinction from apathy, indifference, and undernourishment" (1952: 80). The point is worth considering.

NOTES

1. Over the past 20 years controversies have swirled about virtually every aspect of electoral turnout in the late nineteenth century. Did it average 75-80% as some have claimed, or are the figures inflated by either Census Bureau undercounts of the population (Shortridge, 1981) and/or by corrupt practices on the part of political machines, urban and rural (Rusk, 1970; Converse, 1972; but also see Allen and Allen, 1981)? When it began to decline in the 1890s, did that signify an eviscerated democratic process due to enervated partisanship among ordinary people (Burnham, 1965, 1974), or just an incidental consequence of changes in the administration of electoral rules and regulations (Rusk, 1970, 1974; Converse, 1972, 1974)? The literature on these questions is vast, and largely beyond our scope. The best study remains Kleppner (1982b).

2. There are at least two ways that turnout can be measured: (1) the percentage of the voting age population (VAP); and (2) the percentage of registered voters (PRV) casting ballots. The first is usually the "official" count, but it is problematic when the goal is to compare American figures with other nations because the U. S. is alone in requiring personal initiative to become registered. The second is said to come closer to practices in other western democracies. Even when the PRV is used, the U. S. still falls in the middle of two dozen democracies' turnout rates (Glass, Squire, and Wolfinger, 1984: 52).

3. As implied in the quotation, "quality" refers to the level of relevant political information citizens bring to the political process. All other things being equal, an informed electorate has a higher level of "quality" than an ignorant one. Of course, "all other things" are not always equal, and quality is not an all-or-nothing thing. As was recently demonstrated, only a tiny fraction of the contemporary electorate is completely innocent of political knowledge (Bennett, 1988a).

4. I apologize to Howard L. Reiter, whose 1979 **Public Opinion Quarterly** article bore this title.

5. There are two main sources of data relied upon by scholars to study electoral participation in the U. S. The first, and longer running, is the series of National Election Studies conducted by the University of Michigan's Survey Research Center/Center for Political Studies (SRC/CPS) since 1952. These are a rich source of data about turnout, other campaign activities, and the demographic factors and political dispositions long alleged to influence participation. The second series was begun under congressional mandate in 1964 by the United States Bureau of the Census to include questions about registration and voting in national elections on its Current Population Survey conducted immediately after the election. The Census

Bureau data have one major advantage over most surveys: they include 85,000 to 95,000 cases. Therefore, they permit in depth exploration of subgroups who would include far too few cases in the usual social science survey. Several of the more important studies of voting have been based on these data (Rosenstone and Wolfinger, 1978; Wolfinger and Rosenstone, 1980; Cavanagh, 1981). The Current Population Surveys have two major weaknesses. First, they do not include questions about political dispositions that are the prime determinants of participation. Second, since they only ask about turnout, often about the turnout of someone in the family other than the interviewee, they are subject to over-report of turnout. Of course, the human tendency to shade the truth a bit when asked about socially approved activities such as voting also occurs with the SRC/CPS National Election Studies. Fortunately, beginning with 1964, the SRC conducted voter validation studies that permit researchers to determine with greater accuracy who did and who did not vote. The CPS has conducted vote validation studies in 1974, 1976, 1978, 1980, 1984, and 1986. A number of studies have appeared that provide useful information on the amount and location of "misreporting" of turnout by survey respondents (Clausen, 1968-1969; Traugott and Katosh, 1979; Katosh and Traugott, 1981; Sigelman, 1982; Hill and Hurley, 1984; Silver, Anderson, and Abramson, 1986). Although those who would study changes in turnout over time find changing administration of the voter validation study somewhat vexatious (see Anderson and Silver, 1986), and Sigelman (1982) indicates either may be used, it is generally recommended that validated vote rather than self-reported vote be used when available (Cassel and Hill, 1981).

6. Discriminant analysis is one of several multivariate statistical procedures used by social scientists to achieve one or both of two main goals: (1) to determine the relative impact on a dependent variable of two or more independent variables, even when the effects of the other independent variables have been taken into account; and (2) to assess how well all the independent variables can account for variation in the dependent variable (for a comparison of discriminant analysis to regression and probit analysis, see Aldrich and Cnudde, 1975). Although discriminant analysis can be extrapolated to handle a polychotomous dependent variable, its greater utility is to investigate relationships between a dichotomous dependent variable and a set of continuous (interval or ratio) independent variables (Daniels and Darcy, 1983: 360). One major restriction is that all relationships are linear. In the present case, the chief difficulty crops up with age, which is known to have a curvilinear relation to turnout. To deal with this problem, the Cohens (1975) recommend creating an age polynomial as follows: (1) each respondent's age is subtracted from the sample's mean age; (2) the product is squared, and (3) the individual deviation from the sample mean and its square are entered into the discriminant analysis model in tandem.

7. Discriminant analysis requires interval- or ratio-level measurement for all predictors, and that was attempted here. Where possible, .e.g., education, the exact year was coded. In other instances, e.g., gender, race, union membership, etc., dummies were used coded 0 and 1. Detailed descriptions of codes are not provided to save space. I will provide specific information upon written request.

8. Wilks' lambda is an "inverse" measure, so that smaller values indicate better predictive strength.

9. "Stray facts," yes, but this measure is closely related to more fundamental tests of the public's understanding of public affairs (see Bennett, 1988a).

REFERENCES

Abramson, Paul R., and John H. Aldrich. 1982. "The Decline of Electoral Participation in America." **American Political Science Review,** 76: 502-521.

Aldrich, John H. 1976. "Some Problems in Testing Two Rational Models of Participation." **American Journal of Political Science,** 20: 713-733.

_____, and Charles Cnudde. 1975. "Probing the Bounds of Conventional Wisdom: A Comparison of Regression, Probit, and Discriminant Analysis." **American Journal of Political Science,** 19: 571-608.

Allen, Howard W., and Karen W. Allen. 1981. "Vote Fraud and Data Validity." In Jerome M. Clubb, William H. Flanigan, and Nancy H. Zingale (eds.), **Analyzing Electoral History.** Beverly Hills, CA: Sage Publications, Inc.

Almond, Gabriel A., and Sidney Verba. 1963. **The Civic Culture: Political Attitudes and Democracy in Five Nations.** Princeton, NJ: Princeton University Press.

Anderson, Barbara A., and Brian D. Silver. 1986. "Measurement and Mismeasurement of the Validity of Self-Reported Vote." **American Journal of Political Science,** 30: 771-785.

Ashenfelter, Orley, and Stanley Kelley, Jr. 1975. "Determinants of Participation in Presidential Elections." **Journal of Law and Economics,** 18: 695-733.

Barber, Benjamin. 1984. **Strong Democracy: Participatory Politics for a New Age.** Berkeley, CA: University of California Press.

Barker, Ernest, ed. & trans. 1958. **The Politics of Aristotle.** New York: Oxford University Press.

Barnes, James A. 1988. "Tuned-Out Turnout." **National Journal,** 20: 1743-1747.

Bennett, Stephen Earl. 1986. **Apathy in America, 1960-1984.** Dobbs Ferry, NY: Transnational Publishers, Inc.

_____. 1988a. "'Know Nothings' Revisited: The Meaning of Political Ignorance Today." **Social Science Quarterly,** 69: 476-490.

_____. 1988b. "Left Behind: Economic and Political Causes of Turnout Decline among Young, Lower Educated Whites." Mimeographed.

_____, and Linda L. M. Bennett. 1986. "Political Participation," In Samuel Long (ed.), **The Annual Review of Political Science.** Norwood, NJ: Ablex Publishing Corp.

_____. Forthcoming. "Americans' Interest in Presidential Election Campaigns: Fragile or Robust? **Polity.**

Boyd, Richard. W. 1981. "Decline of U. S. Voter Turnout: Structural Explanations." **American Politics Quarterly,** 9: 133-159.

_____. 1986. "Election Calendars and Voter Turnout." **American Politics Quarterly,** 14: 89-103.

Brody, Richard. A. 1978. "The Puzzle of Political Participation in America." In Anthony King (ed.), **The New American Political System.** Washington, DC: American Enterprise Institute.

Burnham, Walter Dean. 1965. "The Changing Shape of the American Political Universe." **American Political Science Review,** 59: 7-28.

_____. 1974. "Theory and Voting Research." **American Political Science Review,** 68: 1002-1023.

_____. 1982. **The Current Crisis in American Politics.** New York: Oxford University Press.

_____. 1985. "The 1984 Election and the Future of American Politics." In Ellis Sandoz and Cecil V. Crabb, Jr. (eds.), **Election 84: Landslide Without a Mandate?** New York: New American Library.

_____. 1987a. "The Turnout Problem." In A. James Reichley (ed.), **Elections American Style.** Washington, DC: The Brookings Institution.

_____. 1987b. "Elections as Democratic Institutions." In Kay L. Schlozman (ed.), **Elections in America.** New York: Allen & Unwin.

Caddell, Patrick H. 1979. "Crisis of Confidence, I: Trapped in a Downward Spiral." **Public Opinion,** 2 (October/November): 2-8, 52-55, 58-60.

Caldeira, Gregory A., and Samuel C. Patterson. 1982a. "Bringing Home the Votes: Electoral Outcomes in State Legislative Races." **Political Behavior,** 4: 33-67.

_____. 1982b. "Contextual Influences on Participation in U. S. State Legislative Elections." **Legislative Studies Quarterly,** 7: 359-381.

Campbell, Angus., et al. 1960. **The American Voter.** New York: John W. Wiley & Sons.

Cassel, Carol A., and David B. Hill. 1981. "Explanations of Turnout Decline: A Multivariate Test." **American Politics Quarterly,** 9: 181-195.

Cassel, Carol A., and Robert C. Luskin. Forthcoming. "Now You See It, Now You Don't: Simple Explanations of Turnout Decline." **American Political Science Review,** 82.

Cavanagh, Thomas E. 1981. "Changes in American Voter Turnout, 1964-1976." **Political Science Quarterly,** 96: 53-65.

Citrin, Jack. 1974. "Comment: The Political Relevance of Trust in Government." **American Political Science Review,** 68: 973-988.

_____, and Philip Green. 1986. "Presidential Leadership and the Resurgence of Trust in Government." **British Journal of Political Science,** 16: 431-453.

Clausen, Aage. 1968-1969. "Response Validity: Vote Report." **Public Opinion Quarterly,** 32: 588-606.

Cohen, Carl. 1973. **Democracy.** New York: The Free Press.

Cohen, Jacob, and Patricia Cohen. 1975. **Applied Multiple Regression/Correlation Analysis for the Behavioral Sciences.** Hillsdale, NJ: Lawrence Erlbaum Associates, Publishers.

Converse, Philip E. 1964. "The Nature of Belief Systems in Mass Publics." In David E. Apter (ed.), **Ideology and Discontent**. New York: The Free Press.

_____. 1970. "Attitudes and Non-Attitudes: Continuation of a Dialogue." In Edward R. Tufte (ed.), **The Quantitative Analysis of Social Problems**. Reading, MA: Addison-Wesley Publishing Co.

_____. 1972. "Change and the American Electorate." In Angus Campbell and Philip E. Converse (eds.), **The Human Meaning of Social Change**. New York: Russell Sage Foundation.

_____. 1974. "Comment on Burnham's 'Theory and Voting Research.'" **American Political Science Review**, 68: 1024-1027.

_____. 1975. "Public Opinion and Voting Behavior." In Fred I. Greenstein and Nelson W. Polsby (eds.), **Handbook of Political Science**. Reading, MA: Addison-Wesley Publishing Co.

_____, and Gregory B. Markus. 1979. "Plus ca Change. . . : The New SPS Election Study Panel." **American Political Science Review**, 73: 32-49.

_____, with Richard G. Niemi. 1971. "Non-voting among Young Adults in the United States." In William J. Crotty, Donald M. Freeman, and Douglas S. Gatlin (eds.), **Political Parties and Political Behavior**. Boston: Allyn & Bacon.

Conway, M. Margaret. 1985. **Political Participation in the United States**. Washington, DC: Congressional Quarterly Press.

Crewe, Ivor. 1981. "Electoral Participation." In David Butler, Howard R. Penniman, and Austin Ranney (eds.), **Democracy at the Polls: A Comparative Study of Competitive National Elections**. Washington, DC: American Enterprise Institute.

Daniels, Mark R., and Robert Darcy. 1983. "Notes on the Use and Interpretation of Discriminant Analysis." **American Journal of Political Science**, 27: 359-383.

De Nardo, James. 1980. "Turnout and the Vote: The Joke's on the Democrats." **American Political Science Review**, 74: 406-420.

_____. 1986. "Controversy: Does Heavy Turnout Help Democrats in Presidential Elections?" **American Political Science Review**, 80: 1298-1304.

_____. 1987. "Declining Turnout in a Era of Waning Partisanship." **British Journal of Political Science**, 17: 435-456.

Dennis, Jack. 1970. "Support for the Institution of Elections in the United States." **American Political Science Review**, 64: 819-835.

Epstein, Laurily, and Gerald Strom. 1981. "Election Night Projections and West Coast Turnout." **American Politics Quarterly**, 9: 479-491.

Erikson, Robert S. 1981. "Why Do People Vote? Because They Are Registered." **American Politics Quarterly**, 9: 259-276.

Ferejohn, John A., and Morris P. Fiorina. 1979. "The Decline in Turnout in Presidential Elections." A paper prepared for delivery at the National Science Foundation Conference on Voter Turnout, San Diego, California.

Finkel, Steven E. 1985. "Reciprocal Effects of Participation and Political Efficacy: A Panel Analysis." **American Journal of Political Science**, 29: 891-913.

_____. 1987. "The Effects of Participation on Political Efficacy and Political Support: Evidence from a West German Panel." **Journal of Politics**, 49: 441-464.

Gans, Curtis B. 1978. "The Empty Ballot Box: Reflections on Nonvoters in America." **Public Opinion**, 1 (September/October): 54-57.

Glass, David P., Peverill Squire, and Raymond E. Wolfinger. 1984. "Voter Turnout: An International Comparison." **Public Opinion**, 6 (December/January): 49-55.

Hadley, Arthur T. 1978. **The Empty Polling Booth.** Englewood Cliffs, NJ: Prentice-Hall, Inc.

Hill, Kim Quaile, and Patricia A. Hurley. 1984. "Nonvoters in Voters' Clothing: The Impact of Voting Behavior Misreporting on Voting Behavior Research." **Social Science Quarterly**, 65: 199-206.

Hout, Michael, and David Knoke. 1975. "Change in Voting Turnout, 1952-1975." **Public Opinion Quarterly**, 39: 52-68.

Hutchins, Robert Maynard. 1952. **The Great Conversation: The Substance of a Liberal Education.** Chicago: Encyclopedia Britannica, Inc.

Jackman, Robert W. 1987. "Political Institutions and Voter Turnout in the Industrial Democracies." **American Political Science Review**, 81: 405-423.

Jackson, John E. 1983. "Election Night Reporting and Voter Turn-out." **American Journal of Political Science,** 27: 617-635.

Jennings, M. Kent. 1987. "Residues of a Movement: The Aging of the Protest Generation." **American Political Science Review,** 81: 367-382.

_____, and Richard G. Niemi. 1981. **Generations and Politics: A Panel Study of Young Adults and Their Parents.** Princeton, NJ: Princeton University Press.

Johnson, Charles E., Jr. 1980. **Nonvoting Americans.** Current Population Reports: Special Studies, P-23, no. 102. Washington, DC: U. S. Government Printing Office.

Katosh, John P., and Michael W. Traugott. 1981. "The Conse-quences of Validated and Self-reported Voting Measures." **Public Opinion Quarterly,** 45: 519-535.

_____. 1982. "Costs and Values in the Calculus of Voting." **American Journal of Political Science,** 26: 361-376.

Key, V. O., Jr. 1949. **Southern Politics in State and Nation.** New York: Alfred A. Knopf, Inc.

Kim, Jae-On, John R. Petrocik, and Stephen N. Enokson. 1975. "Voter Turnout Among the American States: Systemic and Individu-al Components." **American Political Science Review,** 69: 107-131.

Kinder, Donald R., and David O. Sears. 1985. "Public Opinion and Political Action." In Gardner Lindzey and Elliott Aronson (eds.), **The Handbook of Social Psychology.** Third edition. New York: Random House.

Klecka, William. R. 1980. **Discriminant Analysis.** Sage University Paper series on Quantitative Applications in the Social Sciences, 07-019. Beverly Hills, CA: Sage Publications, Inc.

Kleppner, Paul. 1982a. "Were Women to Blame? Female Suffrage and Voter Turnout". **Journal of Interdisciplinary History,** 12: 621-643.

_____. 1982b. **Who Voted? The Dynamics of Electoral Turn-out, 1870-1980.** New York: Praeger.

_____, and Stephen C. Baker. 1980. "The Impact of Voter Regis-tration Requirements on Electoral Turnout, 1900-1916." **Journal of Political and Military Sociology,** 8: 204-226.

Kosterlitz, Julie, and Jonathan Rauch. 1988. "Working, But Still Poor." **National Journal,** 20 (June 18): 1600-1604.

Ladd, Everett Carll. 1982. **Where Have All the Voters Gone?** The Fracturing of America's Political Parties. Second ed. New York: W. W. Norton & Co.

Lippmann, Walter. 1927. "The Causes of Political Indifference To-day." In Walter Lippmann, **Men of Destiny.** New York: The Macmillan Co.

Lipset, Seymour Martin. 1981. **Political Man: The Social Bases of Politics.** Revised ed. Baltimore, MD: The Johns Hopkins University Press.

_____, and William J. Schneider. 1987. **The Confidence Gap: Business, Labor, and Government in the Public Mind.** Revised ed. Baltimore, MD: The Johns Hopkins University Press.

Mayhew, David R. 1974. "Congressional Elections: The Case of the Vanishing Marginals." **Polity,** 295-317.

McGerr, Michael E. 1986. **The Decline of Popular Politics: The American North, 1865-1928.** New York: Oxford University Press.

Milbrath, Lester W., and M. L. Goel. 1977. **Political Participation.** Second ed. Chicago: Rand McNally.

Mill, John Stuart. 1958. **Considerations on Representative Government.** C. V. Shields, ed. Indianapolis, ID: Bobbs-Merrill Co., Inc.

Miller, Arthur H. 1974a. "Political Issues and Trust in Government: 1964-1970." **American Political Science Review,** 68: 951-972.

_____. 1974b. "Rejoinder to 'Comment' by Jack Citrin: Political Discontent or Ritualism?" **American Political Science Review,** 68: 989-1001.

_____. 1983. "Is Confidence Rebounding?" **Public Opinion,** 6 (August/September): 16-20.

Miller, Warren E. 1979. "Crisis of Confidence, II: Misreading the Public Pulse." **Public Opinion,** 2 (October/November): 9-15, 60.

_____. 1980. "Disinterest, Disaffection, and Participation in Presidential Politics." **Political Behavior,** 2 (1): 7-32.

Neuman, W. Russell. 1986. **The Paradox of Mass Politics: Knowledge and Opinion in the American Electorate.** Cambridge, MA: Harvard University Press.

Political Participation

Nie, Norman H., Sidney Verba, and John R. Petrocik. 1979. **The Changing American Voter**. Enlarged ed. Cambridge, MA: Harvard University Press.

Orren, Gary R. 1987. "The Linkage of Policy to Participation." In Alexander Heard and Michael Nelson (eds.), **Presidential Selection**. Durham, NJ: Duke University Press.

Parry, Geraint B. 1972. "The Idea of Political Participation." In Geraint B. Parry (ed.), **Participation in Politics**. Oxford: Manchester University Press.

Pateman, Carole. 1970. **Participation and Democratic Theory**. Cambridge: Cambridge University Press.

Pennock, J. Roland. 1979. **Democratic Political Theory**. Princeton, NJ: Princeton University Press.

Petrocik, John R. 1987. "Voter Turnout and Electoral Preference: The Anomalous Reagan Elections." In Kay L. Schlozman (ed.), **Elections in America**. New York: Allen & Unwin.

Piven, Frances Fox, and Richard A. Cloward. 1988. **Why Americans Don't Vote**. New York: Pantheon Books.

Pomper, Gerald M. 1988. **Voters, Elections, and Parties: The Practice of Democratic Theory**. New Brunswick, NJ: Transaction Books.

Powell, G. Bingham. 1986. "American Voter Turnout in Comparative Perspective." **American Political Science Review**, 80: 17-43.

Ranney, Austin. 1983a. "Nonvoting Is Not a Social Disease." **Public Opinion**, 6 (October/November): 16-19.

_____. 1983b. **Channels of Power: The Impact of Television on American Politics**. New York: Basic Books.

Reiter, Howard R. 1979. "Why Is Turnout Down?" **Public Opinion Quarterly**, 43: 297-311.

_____. 1987. **Parties and Elections in Corporate America**. New York: St. Martin's Press.

Rollenghagen, Rick E. 1984. "Explaining Variation in Concern about the Outcome of Presidential Elections, 1960-1980." **Political Behavior**, 6: 147-157.

Rosenstone, Steven J., and Raymond E. Wolfinger. 1978. "The Effect of Registration Laws on Voter Turnout." **American Political Science Review**, 72: 22-45.

Rusk, Jerrold G. 1970. "The Effect of the Australian Ballot on Split Ticket Voting: 1876-1908." **American Political Science Review**, 64: 1220-1238.

_____. 1974. "Comment: The American Electoral Universe: Speculation and Evidence." **American Political Science Review**, 68: 1028-1049.

Salisbury, Robert H. 1975. "Research on Political Participation." **American Journal of Political Science**, 19: 323-341.

Schattschneider, E. E. 1960. **The Semi-sovereign People.** New York: Holt, Rinehart & Winston.

Shaffer, Stephen D. 1981. "A Multivariate Explanation of Decreasing Turnout in Presidential Elections, 1960-1976." **American Journal of Political Science**, 25: 68-95.

Shortridge, Ray. 1981. "Estimating Voter Participation." In Jerome M. Clubb, William H. Flanigan, and Nancy H. Zingale (eds.), **Analyzing Electoral History.** Beverly Hills, CA: Sage Publications, Inc.

Sigelman, Lee. 1982. "The Nonvoting Voter in Voter Research." **American Journal of Political Science**, 26: 47-56.

_____. 1984. "Doing Discriminant Analysis: Some Problems and Solutions." **Political Methodology**, 10 (1): 67-80.

Silver, Brian D., Barbara A. Anderson, and Paul R. Abramson. 1986. "Who Overreports Voting?" **American Political Science Review**, 80: 613-624.

Smith, Tom W. 1987. "That Which We Call Welfare by Any Other Name Would Smell Sweeter: An Analysis of the Impact of Question Wording on Response Patterns." **Public Opinion Quarterly**, 51: 75-83.

Squire, Peverill, Raymond E. Wolfinger, and David P. Glass. 1987. "Residential Mobility and Voter Turnout." **American Political Science Review**, 81: 45-66.

Tarrance, V. Lance. 1978. "Suffrage and Voter Turnout in the United States: The Vanishing Voter." In Jeff Fishel (ed.), **Parties and Elections in an Anti-Party Age.** Bloomington, ID: Indiana University Press.

Political Participation

Teixeira. Ruy A. 1987. **Why Americans Don't Vote: Turnout Decline in the United States, 1960–1984.** New York: Greenwood Press.

_____. 1988. "Will the Real Nonvoter Please Stand Up?" **Public Opinion,** 11 (July/August): 41–44, 59.

Thompson, Dennis F. 1970. **The Democratic Citizen.** Princeton, NJ: Princeton University Press.

Traugott, Michael W., and John P. Katosh. 1979. "Response Validity in Surveys of Voting Behavior." **Public Opinion Quarterly,** 43: 359–377.

Tucker, Harvey J. 1986. "Contextual Models of Participation in U. S. State Legislative Elections." **Western Political Quarterly,** 39: 68–78.

_____, and Arnold Vedlitz. 1986. "Controversy: Does Heavy Turnout Help Democrats in Presidential Elections?" **American Political Science Review,** 80: 1291–1298.

Verba, Sidney, and Norman H. Nie. 1972. **Participation in America: Political Democracy and Social Equality.** New York: Harper & Row, Publishers.

Wattenberg, Martin P. 1986. **The Decline of American Political Parties 1952–1984.** Cambridge, MA: Harvard University Press.

Wolfinger, Raymond E., and Steven J. Rosenstone. 1980. **Who Votes?** New Haven, CT: Yale University Press.

Wolfinger, Raymond E., and Peter Linquiti. 1981. "Tuning In and Turning Out." **Public Opinion,** 4 (February/March): 56–60.

Woodward, Julian L., and Elmo Roper. 1950. "Political Activity of American Citizens." **American Political Science Review,** 44: 872–885.

Youth and America's Future. 1988. **The Forgotten Half: Non-College Youth in America.** Washington, DC: The William T. Grant Foundation Commission on Work, Family and Citizenship.

DISCUSSION AFTER PROFESSOR BENNETT'S PAPER

GANS: Your paper was good and important, but I have about five comments to augment your argument: One, the age factor, the estimates go from one and one-half percentage points to three in a time when other aspects, such as the liberalization of voting laws, enfranchisement of blacks, should also have had a crosscutting effect. On registration, I have some vested interest in debunking the Cloward and Piven (**Why Americans Don't Vote**) thesis. For example, the state of North Dakota has no registration, yet has greater decline in voter participation than the rest of the nation. In Minnesota and Wisconsin the adoption of election-day registration led to an initial surge in voting, but now registered voters have a greater decline in voting participation than the rest of the nation. In 1984 we had a 2.8 percent increase in registration, but only a .5 percent increase in turnout. This last point needs to be tempered a little bit, because there was between a 60 to 70 percent turnout of new registrants. Their effort was largely counterbalanced by the drop-off among people who were previously registered.

BENNETT: But we normally have had 80 to 85 percent turnout of registered voters.

GANS: Yes, but that's been sliding. Once you go beyond the self-motivated, you have a drop-off in participation of registered voters. This is what a lot of the mobilization campaign found out. This is why there's only one-third as much foundation money in registration this year.

I think you put too much emphasis in your paper on competitiveness. On two levels, senate and governor, we are a more competitive society now than we have ever been. As far as I know on these levels elections are competitive everywhere.

As to state legislatures and probably the House, the situation fluctuates. I suggest that if Dukakis were elected, and he was seen as the person responsible for a recession or a depression, the five percentage point partisan difference in the South, which is a major reason the Democrats are in the majority in the House of Representatives and have a majority in the state legislatures, would evaporate. The natural inclination for the conservative South to vote Republican would take hold.

It should also be noted that in 1986, there were 24 races that were decided between 54 and 46 percent on the statewide basis; in 16 of those 24 turnouts, nevertheless, declined. I oppose bipartisan agreements that gerrymander as many House seats as possible. But I don't think this is much of a factor in the question of turnout.

I also question the word "apathy". I don't like the word, because of it's public connotations. The public connotation says you, you the citizen, are apathetic; you ought to do something. "You are a slacker." Evidence for apathy is very dependent on the type of survey data, and the period in which the survey is made. Surveys in 1976 showed alienation, surveys in 1983 showed more satisfaction.

If you want to use a word, "anomie" might be better. I tend to go back to the Bureau of Labor Statistics, which suggests there are essentially three classes of people: voters, nonvoters, and those out of the voting force. Those people that you are talking about—young, noneducated or noncollege-educated whites—really fit into "out of the voting force." There is one piece of information to buttress that particular case, which is what Peter Hart was doing for People for the American Way this spring—examining focus groups from precisely that group. I could help you get the results of those studies.

What I want to get away from is the word apathy, because of the political connotations. I thought what you said before your paper got to the heavy emphasis on apathy was more important. What we need is longitudinal survey work in the area of participation that uses a sufficiently large sample-size to begin to disaggregate. Because, as a foundation executive said, a person who doesn't vote in Redwood City, California, has very different reasons than the person who doesn't vote in Manhattan.

BENNETT: On surveys, in Los Angeles the Times Mirror Company has been doing these surveys on the people of the press and politics. One of the best parts of the original survey done in April and May 1987 asked a larger number of questions on citizen participation that has ever been put together in one particular survey. It certainly would challenge even the number of questions on participation in the old Verba and Nie study of 1967 (**Participation in America**).

There are serious problems any time we try to cluster participation questions. But at least they give us a basis for beginning anew. I would agree with you about the need for longitudinal data on participation. Our biggest single problem is that we really lack any extended longitudinal analysis over more than six years, other than the Jennings data. That's the one data set. Unfortunately, his data base was the high school senior class of 1965. So we are looking at kids who were seventeen and eighteen years old in 1965. He has interviewed them twice since then—1981 or 1982 was his last sounding.

Let me come back to your point about apathy. To me, anomie carries some of its original sociological connotation of confused norms. I don't think that is what I am talking about. I would give up the use of the word apathy if I could use "indifference" and no one would be upset by that.

I should also point out evidence for some decline in the sense of civic responsibility.

GANS: Absolutely.

BENNETT: This really bothers me. My wife and I are finishing up a book on attitudes about government over the last 35 or 50 years. She just wrote a chapter that looked at young people's attitudes —the baby boom and post-baby boom generations. Part of the general social survey in 1984 asked about the responsibilities of citizens. They included two questions. One, the responsibility to vote, and two, the responsibility to be interested and informed. She found a colossal generational difference between the late boomers, those born after 1955, and the post-boomers. There is a growing indifference to obligations to be attentive and informed. The worst part is that the better educated they are, the less they feel that sense of obligation.

ALMOND: I don't use the word, but you spoke about what many call the elitist approach to participation. I am one of those elitists, at least by reputation. There is a tradition of democratic theory that goes quite far back, and includes people like Aristotle, whose con-

ception of democracy and its problems was very much influenced by
what happened in Athens. It reflects concern about the vulnerabili-
ties and weaknesses of popular mobilization and popular involvement. The same view of democracy was held by Cicero and Polybi-
us, based on the disorders in Rome connected with the collapse of
the Republic. And then, moving up to more recent periods, the
Bagehot people who wrote in the light of the disorders of the French
Revolution and the disorders in England that were accompanied by
the suffrage reforms. This gets brought up to date in connection
with fascism and national socialism, where mobilization or intensity
of involvement are demonstrated to be not unambiguous goods. It
was in the light of that historical background that Schumpeter
wrote, and the idea of "civic culture" was conceived. All these so-
called elitists were writing in light of the lessons of popular mobilization within those decades, and the enormous cost and tragedies
connected with it.

The principal argument is that you cannot look at democracy
and argue that any shortfall from perfection, in the sense that
everybody gets intensely involved, should be viewed as a failure.
On the contrary, coolness of affect, or the ability to remain at a
certain distance from the issues, was the mark of those democracies
that were able to survive difficult experiences.

My collaborator, Sid Verba, and I carry it on our conscience, the
thought that the implication would be drawn, that we rejoiced at the
shortfalls that we brought out in the civic culture. This was not the
case at all. We were looking at a different part of the historical
spectrum. We were looking at the past, and evaluating democracy in
terms of its survival in the crises of the 1930s and the 1940s.

BENNETT: I have always thought that the generation of scholars
from Schumpeter down through **Civic Culture** (Almond and Verba)
took a bad rap in the late 1960s among people who read something
into those writings that was not there. Sid Verba in his **Injury to
Insult** (with Scholzman) made an effort to clear his conscience on
that question.

SIGEL: But the message that comes out is a different one. He
deplores that the electorate is skewed towards the haves. You look
at his second volume and he says that participation is by the well off
for the well off. There is a difference in the point of view there.

This is especially true in the Verba and Nie book. But I agree, **Injury to Insult** is a much more poignant piece of work, and it's speaking to a different kind of poignancy. I read his book as saying why aren't the unemployed mad? Why do they put up with this nonsense? That's how I read it. But I guess everybody reads in it what they want to read in it.

ALMOND: You're quite right. He does ask that continually in later work.

LEVINE: I attended a meeting at the Carnegie Foundation several months ago. I sat there for the whole day asking myself why people participate at all in the United States? I took the other equation. In comparative perspective the United States is very interesting. Our public sector is small, and our options are not particularly open or negotiable. We have all or nothing voting. Life has become very complicated. In post-affluent society, staying up with whatever we think it takes to live is very difficult. This creates demands on us to minimize our attention and commitment to political life. There is a push and a pull. It has something to do with highly modern society. The system works reasonably well; I am shocked that we have such high turnout, and that we do have an attentive public that appears to be about 22 to 23 percent.

As someone who scrambles to make a living in a two-career family, I find it remarkable that other people are able to do it. If I wasn't a political scientist—forget it! I can't keep up: my wife checks off my ballot as I walk out of the door to vote.

ALMOND: In a place like Palo Alto, you have to vote on a dozen issues, as well as two dozen candidates.

GASTIL: Did I understand you correctly Steve? Are you saying that those who are less likely to turn out now are often the ones who are best educated?

BENNETT: No, my wife has been looking at the sense of civic obligation—not participation. We divide the baby boomers up into two sub-cohorts: those who are born between 1946 and 1954, because they went through the Vietnam War as people—at least the male portion—who would be susceptible to the draft, and the late baby boomers, those born from 1955 to 1964, who did not come of age in time to be eligible for the Vietnam draft. We are examining the argument Morris Janowitz made in his book on citizenship that bearing civic obligation in the form of military service has profound implications on people's attitudes about their broader civic responsibilities.

We then looked at the post boomers, those born after 1964. What Linda found, using general social survey data, was that among the late boomers and the post boomers, the better educated one was, the less one was likely to evidence a sense of civic obligation to be politically attentive and informed and to vote—not that they didn't vote, although she also has some data to show that they don't vote either. The data were gathered in the spring of 1984.

What is taught in the schools plays a part. As an old high school social studies teacher for two years in the 1960s, and now conducting some follow-on research for the books that we've been doing, and getting ready to do a new study, I can say that I think that the substance and the format that is being taught in Social Studies in the junior high schools and the high schools is fundamentally different from what I was taught to teach.

(Others agree.)

BENNETT: This has a very direct and palpable bearing on what the majority of students feel are their responsibilities and relationships with public authority.

PENNIMAN: These people are now going on to college. Here their negative views may in some instances be reinforced.

BENNETT: Aren't they being reinforced in 1988? Aren't some people saying, "I shirked my military duty, but I did something anyway, and therefore should be a candidate for the second highest office in the United States?"

PENNIMAN: He's interested in politics!

JENSEN: We've abolished military service, you notice. There is an interesting debate on whether we should have national service. The people who want national service think it's because it would be good for folks, rather than that the country needs the service.

BENNETT: We look into that in the book. What I can tell you is that the better educated the younger people are, the more they reject the idea of any national service.

SIGEL: That brings up what Curtis mentioned before——a problem with survey questions is that they often don't take into consideration the context. The baby boomers you mentioned, derogatorily we call them the "me generation". The "me generation" really had——I sympathize——a good dose of disillusionment. They had Watergate, they had Agnew, they had assassinations, and they had Vietnam. Since most of these very same people were actually better off financially, they said the hell with it. Let me look after myself.

ALMOND: Do you think that was more demoralizing than the depression, the rise of fascism, or the conquest of Europe by the Nazis for the generation that grew up earlier?

SIGEL: Okay, but first of all, we don't have the comparable data.

ALMOND: But the generation that went through that went through the war and didn't come out demoralized.

SIGEL: The depression was horrible. But it was something that hit everybody. It was not really a reflection on government, even though Hoover got blamed and the companies were blamed. Then it was short-lived because we went into the war. After the war you have what Bush is saying now, peace and prosperity. Suddenly all the kids get to be very patriotic, and everybody thinks government is wonderful. Our socialization studies, carried out during Watergate and Vietnam, found young people doubting that government was wonderful, or would always want to help them.

ALMOND: That was the "silent generation" in the '50s.

GANS: It wasn't so silent. The people who were the early leaders of the movements of the 1960's were trained in the 1950s. The Newman Clubs, the United National Student Association, California

233

Democratic Council, Catholic Youth, all are institutions for participation that have atrophied since.

SIGEL: The point I wanted to make is that these guys are very disillusioned. Mr. Levine comes along and says "I've got kids to send through college, or to chauffeur to the hockey games (or whatever). It takes two incomes to pay the mortgage", and so on. Finally the idea is accepted that one might as well live for oneself. And frankly, he is also from the group that is the least affected.

I feel strongly right now about who wins this next election. But basically I don't think it will make one bit of difference to my style of living, or to anything else I am doing. I know that. So, sometimes I say why should I even worry? I worry because I'm interested in politics. But for someone in my position not to worry is very understandable.

I would also note that your figures would look much worse if you had made a cumulative index. You would find out that the people who vote are the same people who work with others in the local community, or give money—they are also the ones who vote.

BENNETT: Yes.

SIGEL: Now, in the Barnes and Kaase study of participation in several democracies, you find the same thing. The people who protest are also the people who vote, and also the people who give money.

ALMOND: That is one of the most powerful findings of the social science research.

SIGEL: That's right. So what we are essentially saying is that for most people, living and keeping a family together is far more interesting than politics. If there are two people working now, when you come home, by the time you fix dinner—how much time do you have to talk about politics? You are going to talk about who is going to take the stuff to the dry cleaner.

JENSEN: Roberta, let me comment on that point. I've done some work on information and activism in the politics of women and men in the 1930s and '40s. What is striking is the extremely low levels among women. Their levels of information were far below men. Even those who were out in the labor force did little better. In the United States during the 1930s and '40s it was very new for women to vote. Indeed, because of the dynamics of 1928, the men had to get them to vote. They needed their votes.

Lazarsfeld and Katz did an interesting study on opinion formation in Decatur, Illinois (**Personal Influence**). They found women to have all sorts of discussion groups and interlocking networks of leadership when it came to fashion, movies, or home affairs. When it came to politics, they almost never took the lead.

ALMOND: What about the League of Women Voters?

SIGEL: That's an upper middle-class group.

GANS: That's a very small group.

OTHERS: But it's influential?

JENSEN: No, they are very peripheral. I would say in the 1930s and '40s, among the vast majority of women, levels of information, interest, and activism were extremely low. Much lower than today.

SIGEL: Yes, but the interesting thing is it's quite possible, according to people I just talked with at the New York Times, that women may vote proportionally more this time. They will because women have a stake in some of the issues. Whether they are pro- or anti-abortion, day care, all the other things——these are women's issues that make it more important. Women are more interested now because it affects them more.

KLEPPNER: Let me add another dimension to what Roberta and Charles said about the difficulty of making a living and giving attention to politics. At this point, to be truly well informed about political issues requires much more knowledge than it ever has in the past. How do you follow, for example, the debate on any environmental issue unless you know a great deal about chemistry and the other technical issues that are being talked about? How do you follow the debate over the stealth bomber versus the B-1 bomber, unless you have a great deal of information about military aircraft, targets, and so on? My colleague, John Miller, argues that there is an increasing specialization of political interest. For example, you will find people who are very well informed on environmental issues, but know very little about defense or other policy areas.

SIGEL: That's true.

LEVINE: We really are male chauvinist pigs. Women have entered the work force, but they continue to do the household work. Men now do a little bit more on the outside of the house, but the women have all the stuff they always had, plus now they have jobs. That really rips into the fabric of attention and family life.

GANS: I have long argued that for enhancing participation the most important technological development was the birth control pill. Although there is a limit, it allows women to participate more politically; yet groups like the League of Women Voters are atrophying because women are working.

(Others agree).

GANS: I don't agree with Roberta, that women will necessarily vote because of women's issues. By and large, conservative women vote on women's issues. Liberal women tend to vote on issues of war and peace, and economics. And in a sense they are classically conservative. They don't want overextension that will kill their sons, and they don't want their present stability in life threatened. If we had relative stability with the Soviet Union, nobody going to war, and economic growth, I don't know if the gender gap would still favor the Democrats? The most recent convention and most recent polls show that the gender gap is very fragile.

On the question of complexity, we have representative democracy. The citizenry, when it votes, delegates to leadership and to elites the decisions as to stealth bomber versus B-1, and which environmental measures ought to be taken. The citizen is going to decide whether or not there is a commitment to do something about air pollution, whether or not the candidate is looking out adequately for our national defense.

KLEPPNER: I wouldn't disagree with that, although people would have to do a great deal of digging even to come up with an answer that satisfies them, such as, "Are we adequately dealing with national defense?" That's not something that they arrive at very quickly or easily.

BENNETT: Several reactions to the comments that have been made. As long as we are touting old books, I suspect everyone has read Walter Lippman's **Public Opinion,** which was published in 1922. A much better book that he did that never received much publicity was called **The Phantom Public,** published in 1925. In this book he discusses the overwhelming problem of becoming informed about complex issues. He writes of the average, ordinary citizen's difficulty in working five or six days a week, and then coming home and trying to decide how to make up his mind about rural credits in Montana, British rights in the Sudan, or what are we going to do about the Manchurian railway. We have always had a sense that the problems we face are the most complex problems that man has ever dealt with at any time. We now look back and say my God, if all you had to worry about was what are we going to do with the Manchurian railway, how much simpler that must have been to deal with. But not to those people at that time. To them it was a pressing issue for those who cared about it.

It is true, Paul, that it takes more time to keep body and soul together for those people who have not had the benefits of a high school diploma or gone on to college. They are young and therefore don't have seniority, they have come up at the time that our basic smokestack industries have been declining—the assembly-line jobs that were high paying with good benefits and perks are gone. These people may feel betrayed by a system that seems to have turned on them and left them to their own resources. For them to withdraw may be understandable. Too often when they have tried to respond they have failed. Remember the busing controversies in Boston a few years ago, and the book that Anthony Lukas did on three working class families in Boston (**Common Ground**). He described how they were denigrated by their own church and their leaders, and simply told that when they won they lost? There have been other instances like that. The Yonkers low-income housing phenomenon that's going on at the present time. When they win, they lose.

JENSEN: That's because the courts are not in the democratic line of action. You can't fight the federal courts.

BENNETT: That's exactly right. Indirectly, they can fight the courts, but they have to do it through voting for a president or a governor who will appoint different judges or something of that nature. They may not have the sophistication to understand that.

Coming back to your point about the gender gap and the participation of women, I would draw your attention to two studies, by Christie Andersen and Ellen Cook (in the American Journal of Political Science, volumes 19 and 29). These show that just going to work will not in and of itself cause an increase in women's participation. What is critical is the quality of the work. If they go into low paying, menial jobs, they are not going to have their degree of political interest or awareness increased. The other study that I would point out is one that Linda Bennett published in Social Science Quarterly in 1986. She showed that the gender gap, as of the early 1980s, disappears into statistical insignificance, if you control for race.

JENSEN: Steve, I'd like to go back to your argument. In terms of the causal relationships between the problems---the normative angle of your paper---you said that the first reason we should be concerned is that ill health in a democracy produces low participation. Therefore, low participation is a fever indicator.

BENNETT: If I said that, I'm sorry, I misspoke myself. What I meant to say is that there are those who argue that low levels of participation indicate a lack of legitimacy in the system. Not that they cause it. They may be reflecting it.

JENSEN: That's what I mean. You say we've got this thermometer---the thermometer doesn't cause the sickness, it indicates that it's there. The system is causing ill health, the system is causing low participation.

In your other two arguments the causality goes in the other direction. Your second argument is that participation itself causes empowerment. Participation is now a positive thing causing some good that you want to see. Thirdly, civic culture is identified with participation, or participation equals civic culture or civic mindedness, that it is itself a good reflected in turnout. So we've got two causalities here. In one direction, participation is good in itself, and causes good things, empowerment and civic culture. On the other hand, and this is the one that I don't buy at all, you first argue that there is some other thing wrong with the system that causes the low participation. I can see a much better argument for two and three, participation is good in itself. I have a hard time seeing your evidence on the first one, that there is something wrong with the polity, the people are alienated, they don't want to be part of it. They are sick of it.

GASTIL: Richard, you are saying, then, that the lack of participation is lack of participation?

JENSEN: I'm saying that Steve has three arguments, two of them I'll buy. The first argument, however, is that there is something else wrong with society. It's not the low participation that is wrong, that is just a thermometer. Something else is wrong. People sense that and don't want any part of it, and opt out.

GASTIL: Are you then positing that there is an uncaused fact, that low participation is only a curious fact? My logic tells me that there must be more meaning than that.

JENSEN: I would like to know what it is about the system that is the ill health.

GANS: Steve, you have the people who have ceased voting at 10 million, I have them at 20 million.

BENNETT: When I used the term 10 million, that was at the time analysts first began to think in those terms. You are right, the numbers have grown since.

GANS: Richard, I see nonparticipation as an active, alienated response to various things in politics that still need to be explained. So, you have both disease and symptom. When I get to my turn I will give more limited and different reasons than Steve on the question of why turnout is important.

Political Participation

JENSEN: Turnout collapsed several years ago.

GANS: That may have a lot to do with the southern phenomenon.

BENNETT: To respond to Dick's question, my paper reviewed the arguments that have been made in the literature; perhaps I didn't make myself clear enough. As Curt has pointed out, there is an element in the American population, ten million, twenty million, a large number, who have evidently quit voting. You could make a good revolution on ten million people, if they were in the right place, doing the right things, at the right time.

But for the system as a whole, as I said in the conclusion of the paper, evidence indicates that low participation has so far not affected the legitimacy of the system in the United States. There are several problems. One of measurement——what do we mean by alienation? All too often we satisfy ourselves by the Michigan battery of questions on trust in government (Cf. note 5, Bennett paper above). I wish we had never gone down that line.

GANS: Right.

BENNETT: But we did. Sometimes our methodology drives us, just like the Titanic's momentum drove it further and further into the water once it struck that little obstacle out there. At any rate, if we are talking about alienation in the sense of profound rejection of the American system, the only place you are going to find that is at the University of California at Berkeley or the University of Chicago. There is very little overt rejection of the system.

If you are talking about alienation in the sense of saying, those boobs in Washington couldn't find their way to the john in a slight fog, there's a lot of that out there. But then, there has always been a sense of cynicism about the capacity of politicians to do something right or honestly the first time. I don't think that this "alienation" is a serious symptom. It can be very useful. You can use it. Vivien Hart wrote a book on democracy and trust about ten years ago. He argues that cynicism, provided it is, "keep an eye on the suckers, see what they are doing," can be very useful as an inducement to get people to the polls.

It appears to me that a certain segment of the public, people who were once regular voters, and are not in their dotage, has

240

simply resigned in disgust. I don't know why. You've heard of resig-nation in protest; I think these people have resigned in disgust. Do you call that alienation? Is that a symptom of concern?

JENSEN: Has anyone ever found these people?

BENNETT: Yes, there have been a number of studies that have found them. The one that I think of is Robert Gilmore and Robert Lamb (**Alienation in Contemporary America**), a book on alienation in American politics. It's old work and has lots of methodological flaws. But certainly they found them. There's another book called, **The Empty Polling Booth,** by a journalist, Arthur Hadley. There are problems with that, but he found some.

POWELL: You don't really see much of it in your data. It is just tinged with discontent.

GANS: You find it in Teeter's data in Hadley's book. The problem with Hadley's book is that he went away from Teeter's data. Tee-ter's data somewhat reinforces the data that we got in 1976, the Hart survey, in which unfortunately we didn't have a control group of voters, which would have been helpful.

ALMOND: Have we forgotten about parochialism? Have we really neglected that? It's really normatively positive. This is my grand-mother who lives her life in a very intimate community. Who doesn't really have significant connections with the larger world outside. We found them in **The Civic Culture.**

BENNETT: Eleven percent of the American public in 1960, right?

ALMOND: You certainly encounter them in other countries. Are we controlling for this? We're talking about indifference, apathy, alienation. But these people aren't any of those things. Many people in the inner cities are parochial rather than alienated.

BENNETT: The recent surveys have not been asking the questions that you people are asking, that would have allowed us to get to that measure. One of the things I'm trying to do is get a group of schol-ars who will insist that we start asking some of those questions.

DISCUSSION OF COMPARATIVE PARTICIPATION

GASTIL: We have with us, luckily, two of the best known authorities on voting outside of this country as well as in this country. I thought it would be useful to have them both speak briefly on the way they would relate their knowledge of voting participation in other countries compared to that in the United States.

POWELL: Let me just make a few comments. I always get a call in election years from some newspaper or other that wants to know what low participation means, whether it threatens the legitimacy of the American system and so forth. The fact is turnout for presidential elections in the United States is now running between 50 and 55 percent. It varies greatly among the contemporary industrialized democracies, from Switzerland, which is down in our area, to Sweden and West Germany, which are 88-90 percent.

The average turnout in the industrialized democracies that don't have compulsory voting is about 78 percent. So we are considering a difference of about 25 percentage points between our national elections and those in other contemporary democracies. You can play with the numbers in a lot of different ways. I think everybody who has studied it thinks that's a reasonable comparison. This is the easy part. Obviously the question is why? There are several points of view, as you might expect. I won't try to review them.

Alongside the difference between turnout averages, there is a difference between the attitudes of Americans and Europeans that goes in the opposite direction. In other words, the attitudes of Americans toward politics, their interest and faith in it, is greater than in other democracies. This difference has declined somewhat, but it is still there.

Therefore, attitude studies in the United States cannot explain the relatively low voter turnout in this country. What they may explain is the decline in voter turnout in the United States in recent decades.

Political Participation

One point stands out in the study of political attitudes. Americans are less apathetic, to use the term we've been using here, than the citizens in practically every other country we know about. If you can poll Danes, or Swedes, or your favorite population, and make a specific comparison, you will find that on average, Americans have the attitudinal advantage, in terms of sense of party identification, interest in politics, and so forth. So the reason for the comparative difference is not fundamentally attitudinal, but institutional.

ALMOND: I did not understand your first point as to what attitudes explain.

POWELL: Studies of attitudes may explain the decline in American turnout from 1960 to 1980, but they don't explain the long-standing difference in turnout between the United States and other democracies.

ALMOND: There's a paradox in what you are saying.

POWELL: It seems paradoxical, but it is not paradoxical. If you go back to the 1960s, when you did **The Civic Culture,** you will find that the attitudinal gap between the United States and other democratic countries of the time was much greater than it is now. American turnout in the institutional sense was even worse, but it was being held up by extremely high levels of attitudinal support. Not compared to what we read in the high school civics books, but extremely high levels in comparative terms.

JENSEN: So American attitudes were much more supportive in 1960 and they are still somewhat more supportive?

POWELL: Yes, but they have declined, and the rest of the world has gained. That's the pattern. In most of the western European countries, education has improved, there's more identification with the party systems, because right after World War II they were all reconstructed. There are many different reasons why. There are country to country variations, but, basically, their attitudinal factors have improved, and ours have declined. Nonetheless we still, on the average, have more supportive attitudes to participation than the average western European country.

244

BENNETT: If you match populations, education for education, the gap becomes even smaller. Because we still have a large educational advantage.

POWELL: That's part of the gap in participation-facilitating factors that has closed. We're still more educated than any western European country. That is helping hold our participation up. If we had the average education level that they have in Britain, we'd have a lot lower turnout than we have right now.

BENNETT: The point I'm making is that change in supportive attitudes in the United States from 1960 to the present becomes even more significant when you consider the fact that our population in the '80s is better educated than the US population of the '60s; and the gap between our population's education and Europe, while it has been closed, still remains fundamental.

POWELL: It may be a paradox, but as far as we can tell, the reason that participation is less in the United States does not have to do with attitudes, it has to do with the institutions. Now, what these institutional factors are is a matter of controversy. It all boils down to the basic problem in comparative politics: many suggested variables, and few cases to look at. You can play all the fancy little statistical games that you want, but you run out of degrees of freedom in a hurry.

Registration has something to do with it––there is both internal and external evidence. It might account for 10 percent––that is, if we adopted European style registration, it would increase our turnout maybe 10 percent. Again, nobody really knows. Nobody has a registration system like ours. I would just point out that a 10 percent increase, suppose it pulled us up from 53 to 63 percent, would still leave a large gap. It still leaves us below most democracies in spite of the attitudinal advantage.

GANS: What about behavioral advantages, like contributing money?

POWELL: Two points about that. It's very hard to know. Every country has a different set of rules about contributing money. There are no precisely similar activities. Parties organize rallies in differ-

Political Participation

ent kinds of ways in different kinds of countries. Britain has a three-week election period.

GANS: How much do you discount lying and misreporting.

PENNIMAN: Most countries do not have reporting systems. For example, you can't find out anything in France.

POWELL: Well, we have surveys, like the nine nations (see Powell in "references" to Bennett paper above). As best one can judge, Americans give more than citizens in other countries. American voting behavior is unusual in comparison to the other sorts of American political activity.

Here I buy the Verba et al argument, which is that the more you look at acts of participation that are relatively institution-free, like talking about politics, trying to follow politics, the clearer the American advantage is. The minute you start to get into those institution-related questions, there is a lot of variation from country to country, depending on exactly what the party system looks like, exactly what the rules are.

We do not have adequate data over time for any place, including the United States. I want to reinforce what Curtis said—apparently people drop in and out of the electorate as they go through different life cycles, and we don't capture this. If we are concerned about democracy, it makes a real difference whether we are talking about a subgroup that is permanently outside the political system, a group that is in and out, or a group that looks pretty much like everybody else and may come cascading in at any time, keeping politicians responsible.

BENNETT: Did you see the study in Kentucky that Sigelman and his people did of registered voters a couple of years ago, in which they had data on recorded votes over about a ten-year period? Now this is just one area, around the University of Kentucky in Lexington. What they saw were some supercitizens, some who went in and out, and then a very substantial group who had dropped out, but were still being carried on the rolls.

POWELL: This is the sort of information we need to answer the types of questions that this seminar is directed toward. We don't have it at all on a cross-national basis. Of course, if in Sweden 90 percent of the people vote in every election, and there is an election every three years, it's pretty likely that almost every Swede has voted every three or four elections. But there is probably a tiny, nonvoting underclass even there. But we don't know that. There isn't any data.

Among other factors influencing voting, one has to do with competitiveness. There is some evidence that in a district-oriented system, of which the electoral college is a good example, there is a tendency for parties to write off certain areas and districts. This tends to depress turnout in those areas. You can see this within nations. There is a good study showing this in Britain, as well as studies about where the American South has changed. Compare this situation to the French presidential election, in which a vote in any part of France is as good as that in any other part of France. Parties need to mobilize every place. Every vote is important. Or consider the proportional representational systems. Internal and external evidence suggests these differences account for three, four percent of the difference in turnout.

Although it is hard to demonstrate fully, the party system is probably the major factor. It has to do with the party system in at least three different ways. First, we should ask how different the parties are. For example in Italy, there is the Christian Democrats or the Liberals or the MSI on one hand, and the Communists on the other. It's a very different party system than that reflected by Mike Dukakis or George Bush. There is reason to think that some people are more likely to vote under Italian conditions.

A related factor is the connections between parties and social groups. The connections are breaking down everywhere, but at very different rates: in most western European countries they have not declined nearly to the American level. In countries like Austria and Italy and Sweden, to know a person's occupation is a very high predictor of what party they vote for. This has a dual effect. Citizens don't have to spend a lot of time gathering information. They know what their party is. Likewise, the parties know who their supporters are. They know where to go and get their supporters to vote.

The third factor, of which we have nothing except the most intuitive knowledge, is organization. We know that the American party organization is very decentralized compared to almost all western European systems. Historically this has been true, and

Political Participation

there is reason to believe that the depth of nationally coordinated mobilizational activity is much greater in most of the western European countries than it is now in the United States. This and other institutional advantages are declining in western Europe a bit, just as their attitudes are improving.

JENSEN: Why do the European countries keep talking about regionalizing? I mean, do they want to undo the national centralization? Italy talks about it. France talks about it. Germany has done it. Are they trying to denationalize in that sense, do you think?

POWELL: There are strong regional pressures in a number of European countries. Let me just leave it there.

SIGEL: But here we not only vote more often, we also have far more issues. First of all, we have primaries. Then, we not only vote for persons, but we always have at least one or two or three referenda to vote on.

POWELL: This is a good example of an institutional factor that there has been a big dispute about. Richard Boyd at Wesleyan, and Richard Rose to some extent, thinks that this is a major reason for low voter turnout. He points to Switzerland, the other country with frequent referenda, and notes its extremely low voter turnout. I myself don't think this is an important factor, because it seems to be that most people who are registered vote in presidential elections (85 to 90 percent). We are not exhausting the vote of the people who are voting in the local elections. Most of the people who are not voting are the nonregistered—they can't be exhausting themselves by voting in the local elections.

But that's just my intuitive response. I could give you fifteen other institutional differences that have been proposed, a multicameral legislature, and so on.

ALMOND: Separation of powers?

POWELL: My opinion is that the verdict is open on this. We need more and different sort of data. Particularly until we get more data on the party organization differences, we are just kidding ourselves that we can get a handle on other institutional factors.

248

ALMOND: Are you unwilling to concede that structural disincentives are concentrated on the American side?

POWELL: No, I agree structural disincentives are the reason for relatively low turnout here. I'm just saying that once you go beyond registration, competition, and something about the party system, then there are many other possible things: having voting spread over two days, or paying people's railway fare home, there are an almost unlimited number of possible factors.

SIGEL: Voting on Sundays.

POWELL: How many percentage points to assign to each of these?

GASTIL: You have focused our attention on and separated two central issues.   One is the decline in American voting in recent years. Most of the discussion that we've been having today has to do with this issue.   The other issue is why Americans vote less than Europeans. You suggest this issue has nothing to do with the former. It has to do with another group of issues which you brought up.

POWELL: Which we haven't really discussed. We talked about party a little.

GASTIL: When you speak about Europeans being below Americans in some indicators, are you referring to data such as that in Steve's first table, and saying that Europeans would have lower responses?

POWELL: There are several different kinds of indicators, obviously. There are attitudinal indicators derived from responses to questions like how interested are you in politics? How much do you know? Do you follow political events on a regular kind of basis? On these it's quite clear the Europeans are substantially below the Americans.

As to what is in Steve Bennett's table, on average, the European figures would be lower. But it depends on the specific item. It's institutionally specific. For example, local politics means different things in different countries——in Britain, there isn't any regional level.

Political Participation

GASTIL: Are all of you satisfied that responses on that first group of questions, those attitudinal questions, are not shifted by European respondents as opposed to American respondents? For example, the same person may say "vaguely interested" in Europe, who would say "very interested" in the United States. Couldn't there be a cultural shift in the way people answer that would account for differences in the figures? Is this something you've satisfied yourself on?

POWELL: That's the kind of very difficult issue that makes it hard to come up with specific numbers. I feel fairly confident of comparability when people say they are absolutely not interested in politics. Once you get into somewhat versus a little versus a lot, it gets harder and harder.

JENSEN: What about those who refuse to answer? Is that still important?

BENNETT: It's less of a problem. There is another problem that Bingham has touched on. Imagine you have a well-designed sample survey questionnaire and a well-selected and comparable German and American sample. You ask the Germans and the Americans how often do you discuss politics with family and friends. Perhaps 68 percent of Americans will say "at least once a week"; perhaps 10 to 15 percent of the Germans will give as high a figure. I haven't seen the latest data on that, but it would be a considerable gap. On the other hand, if you ask the respondents how interested are you, the Germans will appear more interested than the Americans. The problem is that my own data show me that talking politics and saying you are interested in politics are part of the same underlying phenomenon in the United States.

I am trying to get away from just one item indicators, and go to multiple indicators, because I have a lot more faith if there is a pattern of answers all pointing in the same direction. Then I know I've got something that I can write home to Mom about. In the United States, if you ask do you talk politics, are you interested in politics, do you watch media accounts of politics, the answers will pattern. They are part of that unmeasurable thing we call interest. In Germany, on the other hand, they don't pattern. Then you have to ask yourself, why would Germans who are interested in politics not talk politics? Because the social price to be paid, or the economic price to be paid, from talking politics may be greater in Germany, for the very reason you said——the party systems are so much different.

LEVINE: The left versus right dimension there has real meaning. In this country we don't nationalize things. We don't nationalize and renationalize and privatize and all that. We haven't been able to do that since McCullough versus Maryland, if you want a data point. I go back to the stakes issue. That is real stuff for folks there. I was in France during the last election campaign. It is a socially divided country. People have their mind made up. Period. No discussion. They don't have to spend a lot of time on information acquisition.

ALMOND: Ideology just saves a lot of cost.

LEVINE: Yes, exactly.

BENNETT: Yes, it does. The one flaw in that argument, Charles, is the highest turnout in American elections since World War II was 1960, when you had two nice young, attractive boys——remember, we didn't know Nixon's future in those days——who were so close together that Arthur Schlesinger, Jr., had to strong-arm his liberal friends in the ADA (Americans for Democratic Action) to vote for John F. Kennedy, saying yes, it did make a difference, because so few people saw any difference between them.

GASTIL: And the lowest turnout was 1948 that had the four different candidates with very different positions.

BENNETT: Exactly right.

SIGEL: I disagree with you. The Kennedy election was not nonideological. The Protestant South was heavily anti-Kennedy. On the other hand, the well-to-do Irish, who before voted Republican, were apt to vote democratic.

JENSEN: Connections with social groups were much clearer than they had been for a long time.

LEVINE: But not cleavages between the propertied and the rest.

PENNIMAN: As a footnote, from now on that wouldn't be the case. Once we got past electing a Catholic, I doubt if religious affiliation could again make a hell of a lot of difference.

SIGEL: No, it's going to be race.

PENNIMAN: Let me pick up on the question of registration figures. In Europe the registration figures are the figures that come from the government. Sometimes you have to fill in the forms, sometimes the government does it, sometimes at one level, sometimes at another. In any case, the numbers that they find at that point become the numbers for the turnout. From there on, you have that as your base. So it's a percentage of that figure, right?

POWELL: Well, that is not the way I do with my analysis, but that is the way most people do it. The figures I was giving here were not counted that way. I take the turnout and divide it by the population of voting age, using census data.

PENNIMAN: But wherever they use registration, then you've got a very different base.

Second, there is the fact that the Europeans report as having voted the people who went to the polls, but spoiled their ballot or put in a blank ballot. Whereas in the United States, it is the other way around. This group, roughly 2 1/2 percent, is not counted here.

KLEPPNER: No, you are saying that if you cast your ballot and it's spoiled, it's not counted? That may vary by state, but I know you would be in Illinois.

PENNIMAN: But in the figure that comes out, that's not in there.

GANS: Howard's right, in so far as the comparative figures we use. On just votes for president we may have a factual dispute on the amount of additional ballots there are that are cast that are blank or mutilated. I did a recent survey of twenty-nine states that count total ballots, and the factor that I came up with is 1.2 percentage points on average, rather than 2.5. I did it because Jerry Jennings is claiming that this over-reporting is largely a factor of miscount.

And I didn't believe that. I thought it was largely a factor of over-reporting. And for off years, if you use Senate/Governor statistics as the basis of determining turnout then it is 1.6 percent on the average. In the twenty-nine states that count total ballots, this discrepancy accounts for 1.2 percentage points, and 1.6 percentage points in midterm elections.

BENNETT: There is a very tiny percent of survey respondents who will say they voted, but not for president. We tend to lose sight of them. They are seldom more than a percent. Which would be consistent with Curt's figures.

PENNIMAN: You'll get a different set of figures in various places. But 1.3, or 1.5 or whatever it is, in any case, our reports are different from official reports in other countries. Elsewhere, they list them as having voted.

It surprises some, but there are really not very many countries that have compulsory voting. When compulsory voting was abandoned in the Netherlands, voting figures declined by ten percent or more. The four obvious compulsory countries, at least in the group of 28 we covered in Democracy at the Polls, were Australia, Belgium, Greece, and Venezuela. The Australians and the Belgians are the most effective in getting their people out. I don't know whether you noticed the piece a couple of weeks ago saying there are 100,000 Australians overseas who are going to get fined next time if they do not cast their ballot. In most of the other countries, actual sanctions are not very great.

GANS: How about Italy?

PENNIMAN: In Italy for a long period they thought voting was compulsory, but it wasn't. Once voters discovered this, voting percentages began going down. The government pays the cost of getting to the polls. For example, if you were working in Germany, and you come home to vote, you would pay the transportation cost to the Italian border. Once you get to the border you go home free, and you can stay at your home for a week or so. When you go back, the trip is free to the border. All you pay is the cost beyond the Italian border to Germany or wherever you've been working. This has been a very important inducement—for people who live in Sicily, that's an inexpensive way to get home.

PENNIMAN: As to the cost of elections, most countries have few rules on contributions. The British and Canadians have them; where you have rules, the country is often an offshoot of the United Kingdom. Beyond that, in France, for example, you simply can't find the information. Three times I assigned someone to write on the situation there. Then about three weeks later I would get a letter saying, "I'm sorry, but I can't get any figures. I can get estimates." These are not estimates from the people who are getting and paying out the money, but estimates by somebody who knows something about it. Nobody is prepared to call that data very useful in determining what the expenditures were.

The situation is getting better. But you cannot get the figures for France or Greece—certainly not from India or Japan, not from at least two-thirds of the countries we covered.

SIGEL: If you got them, would you trust them?

PENNIMAN: I don't know; we never got them. Expenditures are high in every country. In the case of Venezuela, in the first election I saw down there, 1968, they spent money at a pace that is just enormous by American standards. It was about three or four or five times what ours would be.

ALMOND: That was government supported?

PENNIMAN: Oh, not just government supported. The government puts in a fair amount. But in addition to that, the unions, political parties and others put in large amounts. They will give you a figure, or some of the Americans who go down there and advise them on how to run their campaigns, will give you a figure. You can't be absolutely sure of those figures, but nonetheless they have got to be spending four or five times what we would spend per voter.

The Germans spend an enormous amount. It comes from the government, from trade unions, and from other sources, and again it becomes a very substantial figure. We talk about elections as if we have the most expensive in the world, but per person we must be first, second, or third from the bottom as compared with the other countries in the West.

In New Zealand you don't have regulations. But New Zealand has odd arrangements on a number of things. New Zealand, for example, makes it compulsory that you register. But having registered, you don't have to vote. They get a good turnout. But it's not required by law. So there's no problem in case you decide not to vote. In any case, their records are so bad. In the last election, in 1981, the general population of eighteen years of age and over was roughly two million. They had two million five hundred thousand on the poll list. But when the election took place, they had 25,000 people whose votes were thrown out because they weren't on the list! It's rather casually done.

On the turnout side, it has not been going up in many countries. It went down until the last election in Switzerland by one percentage point every year. This was in a country where four of the little states, or subdivisions, still hadn't given women the right to vote in their own little districts. Then, why did the vote go down? Very likely it went down because their referendums on policies are separated from the general elections. In our case that's not so much of a factor, because we have the issues down at the bottom of the ballot, or it's on a separate ballot. But it is part of our general election. That's not true everywhere in this country. Each state can do it its own way, but most of them do it the way I am saying. And in those cases, if people don't want to vote on the issues, they just ignore this part of the ballot. It doesn't prevent them from voting for governor or senator or congressman or president. Referenda may receive 50 percent or less of the vote for the top offices.

Aside from Switzerland, you have little of this kind of voting in other countries. It's a very, very rare case. You had one in Britain and Ireland when they were voting on how they would deal with the European Parliament.

In general, we are probably very close to the level of voter turnout in most countries, particularly if we calculate for them the relationship between voting age and turnout rather than that between those registered and the turnout (which is the normal system in other countries where they consider participation rates to be a comparison between the number who actually voted and the number registered to vote). But as I understand it, you (Powell) put it on the same basis?

Political Participation

POWELL: Yes, the 53 percent versus 78 percent, is based on taking United Nations census data, the population of voting age, the denominator, and the numerator is the official voting figure.

PENNIMAN: But in much of the literature, they don't do that. And so it has skewed the figures rather considerably in favor of the non-Americans.

GASTIL: But still, Howard, on that point, Bing seems to have given us a 25 percent gap.

PENNIMAN: I didn't mean to suggest that we would be the same. But we would be considerably closer.

POWELL: In most countries it only makes a couple of percent difference because a little over 95 percent of the voting age population is registered. In a few countries it makes a huge difference. Switzerland would be the obvious case, because they disenfranchise the foreign workers, constituting about 20 percent of the voting age population. But for most countries it makes little difference. In the Scandinavian countries, Austria and Germany, when you move into a new community, you automatically have to register with the police, and that automatically puts you on the voting rolls.

GASTIL: Is that true of the guest workers?

POWELL: Everybody, citizens and noncitizens.

JENSEN: Right, but if you are a Turk in Frankfort, Germany, and you are a Turkish citizen and not a German citizen, surely you're not allowed to vote. Are you counted as eligible in these data? Are you counted as part of the denominator?

PENNIMAN: No, but you are on their list of persons of voting age, but it would not show up in their figures.

POWELL: That's how the United Nations reports the population of a country. So by our standards, German turnout is actually a bit higher than reported.

KLEPPNER: If I understand you, your denominator is voting age population? Howard is suggesting that one ought to use, or Howard is using, eligible voting age population.

PENNIMAN: No, I'm saying that the countries themselves use that.

POWELL: Howard is saying that if you just pick up the newspaper, and they give you the government figures, those government figures will often be quite misleading, because they will exclude various parts of the population. My approach assumes that the voting age is correct. So I'll use 18, 17, or 21, depending on the country. But otherwise, I will include everyone.

PENNIMAN: So Bing's figures are down slightly in turnout, percentage-wise, as compared with what they would do.

BENNETT: Very quickly, we need to realize that our population figures are the official Census Bureau figures that include aliens in the voting-age population. There's a political scientist, Walter Dean Burnham, who has systematically tried to get information on legal aliens and get them out of that denominator. He's also tried to guesstimate illegal aliens, and get them out too. His figures are always going to be about 2 or 3 percent higher in terms of the percentage of turnout. For example, in 1984 the official figure was 53.1 percent, his was 55.7.

PENNIMAN: The Bureau of the Census will tell you that there are at the beginning of the election year, for example, 6.5 million legal aliens who can't vote. There are an estimated 2.5 million undocumented aliens that are 18 years of age and older. They will tell you that there are 680,000 persons who will be ineligible because they are in prisons, or in hospitals or something of that sort. But we will count them as not voting.

GANS: There is a small compensatory factor of Americans abroad who are not counted in the eligible vote.

But the point I wanted to make had to do with the reputed panacea of the election day holiday or Sunday voting. The Congressional Research Service has recently done a study for former Congressman Mario Biaggi who wanted an election day holiday. It

257

Political Participation

showed that in those countries that do not have compulsory voting, voter turnout was actually higher by one percentage point on work days than on Sundays or holidays. The results are no different in the few places that have Saturday primaries, as compared to Tuesday primaries. What you lose on a work day, because people do not have time to get to the polls, is probably about balanced by those you lose on a weekend, because people use the day off to go play.

SIGEL: When the United Auto Workers went in for contract negotiations, there was always one clause that the worker would get paid on election day for so many hours to go to the poll. I don't know if they still do that. That would support what you said.

DISCUSSION OF ACTIONS THAT MIGHT INCREASE VOTING

GASTIL: We should tie together today's discussion by going on to what we should really be doing about all this. Since he has been most directly involved in trying to increase voter participation, I have asked Curtis Gans to open this discussion.

GANS: While I consider myself a serious student and provider of data, I also aim at raising the issue of voter participation in the public consciousness, at trying to seek public policy remedies. I am in the world of applied political science rather than theory. This has a number of ramifications. Which is to say when I asked you, Howard, and Austin, to do a comparative study of how other nations regulate their television advertising for political campaigns, it wasn't simply an esoteric exercise. I hoped to find out what could be done about that particular problem in the United States.

When we did this study that you commented on, I believe it was the first longitudinal study on the impact of changes in voting laws on voter turnout that examined actual laws and their impact. If I had been in academia, my finding probably would have been, "impact of voter registration laws significantly less than previous literature indicates." That didn't seem to me to be a very useful way of approaching this problem, and so we ended up with a bipartisan group saying, "six to seven million people blocked by registration laws."

This also led to the effort that Howard and I are involved with, that hopefully will see the light of day this November. This commission headed by Frank Fahrenkopf and Paul Kirk, including the broadest spectrum of American politics that you would want, is coming to some agreement on incentive legislation to encourage the states to liberalize their registration laws and improve the process of purging electoral rolls by making it both more effective and less intrusive.

I start off with an a priori bias that we have a problem. I agree, essentially, with Bing Powell and Raymond's characterization of it as essentially a two-pronged problem. One I would call low voter turnout, which has to do with why we have been the lowest participating democracy, why we had——at the apex of our participation——relatively low turnout. I would only quarrel in degree with the impact of registration laws, based on our studies, which I think are better than others because they are longitudinal and not regression. Secondly, we have the problem of declining voter turnout at a time when demographic and structural changes should have argued for higher turnout.

I am probably more concerned at this point about the decline than the historically low participation. Let me give my own litany of six reasons for this concern.

First, if voter turnout is, as has been shown in almost every study, a lowest common denominator institutional political act, and people who don't vote tend not to participate in anything else, then the more US voter turnout falls, the more our politics comes under the control of intense interest groups——people who are organized, militantly monied, or whatever.

Secondly, public policy will be determined by the heavy voting, large groups, over against the rest of the public that doesn't vote. The example I use, since turnout historically has been a question relatively ignored by the Republican Party, is public employees who constitute one-sixth of the population. If only half the electorate votes, they constitute one-third of the effective population. This will greatly affect the ability of any government to reform the civil service, abolish agencies, and so forth.

Third, I am concerned that young people are the first group that has actually seen a decline in their turnout after enfranchisement. There was a brief blip up in 1984, but by and large a decline——in 1986 their level was 16.6 percent. This doesn't augur well for the American political future, in terms of either participation or leadership.

The fourth is an offshoot of low participation, which is a decline in party allegiance, and the question of cohesion of our society.

The fifth, again, is the lowest common denominator act and the question of volunteerism, upon which our society base depends, and the declining base for that volunteerism.

The sixth is inattention and the potential for demagoguery and greater authoritarianism——the thread that Hadley raises, which is, I think, the least important. The argument is if people aren't trying to work within the system, maybe someday they will work outside it.

For all these reasons, I think we need to be concerned.

I am concerned about voting law for two reasons. First, taking it from your Freedom House brochure, we ought to have an "opportunity society"; anything unnecessary that stands in the way of voters participating or is not necessary to the integrity of the system ought to be removed. Whereas I hold no great hope that we will have a huge surge, especially in this climate, those people who want to participate ought to be able to participate. Second, I would like to get Wolfinger, Rosenstone, and Cloward and Piven (see Bennett references) out from the center stage and begin to deal with some more serious questions.

It may be significant that in this period of declining participation, the last three elections in Chicago for mayor had record high turnouts. The last two elections for senator in North Carolina, both the bitter and highly expensive Hunt-Helms campaign, and the gentle Sanford-Broyhill campaign had high turnouts. The Sanford-Broyhill was the highest since 1950 and Hunt-Helms was the highest ever. The most recent campaign for the senate in Louisiana, after the Republican Party sort of intimidated the blacks, produced the highest turnout for senatorial elections ever. In Fairfax County, Virginia, when the citizens there finally had the opportunity to vote for the issue they cared about——whether growth could continue to go unfettered——they had a record turnout.

All of which suggests there is evidence that the American people will vote when there is something to vote for. This also leads me, without being a rationalist in the classic academic sense, to say there must be something in this decline that is a rational response.

I like the three categories of reasons for decline: decline in efficacy, decline in partisanship, and decline in newspaper reading. What we do, institutionally, is to look at those things that have happened in the last 24 or 25 years that might have contributed to that decline, and try to separate out those that need action and those that need further research, and determine those for which neither is possible.

For instance, there is evidence to indicate that one portion of the decline occurs because since 1964 we have had a series of negative presidential elections. Now, why do I say there is evidence? Because the decline has occurred in each of those elections in one party rather than both. And the expectation level of that party the next time is lower each time. So Reagan's landslide is smaller in terms of his percentage of the eligible vote than Nixon's landslide in 1972.

This is something you can't correct, as you cannot correct Vietnam, Watergate, or Irangate. You can correct a little bit the standards of public service. Charles take note. I don't think "not unfit to serve" need be the minimum criteria for appointive office, and "not indicted" be considered vindication. We can demand higher levels. This is not unimportant for a public that occasionally gives the response that all these guys are crooks.

Getting into your field, Charles, there are two important value shifts that I notice—you probably notice considerably more. But the tendency of demagogic politicians to run against government and create a we/they dichotomy has not been conducive to people feeling that government makes a difference. I also think there's been a generational shift. Our parents went through the depression, or were immigrants. They committed their lives to making the next generation—their children's lives—better. Our generation translated those values into making the society better. We grew up in relative affluence, and we wanted to make our society better.

SIGEL: Can I interrupt you for just a second? I think the difference—that generation was worried about making the world or the country safe for democracy. No one worries about that anymore in this country.

GANS: Okay. This generation right now is into making their own lives better. And they have been encouraged to do so from the bully pulpit of the White House for the last eight years. I think we can ask for a greater commitment.

There are four or five things that have contributed to party weakness. Our parties started getting weaker with the primaries, and nonboss, nonoligarchic selection. They got weaker a second time with the advent of the New Deal, because hiring power went to the federal government, away from the local level. As you people pointed out, that started earlier than that. To a degree we can address this problem. We can bring administration down to lower levels so that not every problem gets solved on the federal level. We have already begun to move in that direction. But it's not going to be the same as patronage, as before.

The third revolution is the consultant revolution, and the essential impact of television on parties. To get elected what you need now is a rich guy, or access to money and a media adviser: that's your entree to politics. There is no way that parties can exert any strength or discipline or cohesion over this process. This problem can be addressed.

The question of alignment, the second part of the party problem, is somewhat harder to address. As I was telling Roberta, I could make a good argument, even as a Democrat, for voting for George Bush. Because he is going to center the Republican Party; by virtue of that, he is going to force the Democratic Party to rethink its agenda. We have said that if the good government Republicans ever took over the Republican Party they could put forward a sensible and popular conservatism that would a) make the debate more rational in our country, and b) force the Democrats to the only constituency they have, the economic have-nots. At last the largest part of our uninvolved might have a party.

I should say, while I am talking about the difference between academic and applied research that although it is overwhelmingly true that poor people are the largest components of the nonvoters, my 1976 survey showed that dropouts were 38 percent educated white collar and professionals. Apparently, by and large, affluent people are keeping pace in terms of their participation or nonparticipation as nonvoters while educated people are increasingly becoming nonvoters.

BENNETT: The class skew to participation has grown substantially just since 1976.

GANS: It depends on where you draw the line. But for $35,000 and up, it's not true. For $10,000 and up in 1972 and $35,000 and up now, it's not true.

JENSEN: Curtis, I am not following you. Are you saying that you can separate out the educational effect from the class effect? That there is a class effect and not an education effect? Or, are you not trying to separate those two out?

GANS: I'm saying it tends to cut across all lines, depending on where you draw your line—with the exception of the occupational line, where it doesn't. But I emphasize middle-class nonparticipation because the middle class is our base of social change in this country, unfortunately. The situation will not change without leadership.

We need to think about how we strengthen and align our parties to enhance participation. We are in a state in which people do not have great allegiance to either party. Whether you agree with getting a handle on the consultant industry, or moderate Republicanism taking hold, this is a question we need to deal with.

Third, the new technology of politics contributes to the problem. It's use is vitiating the impulse to leadership. It is creating a more homogeneous politics. I don't know how we deal with that, but it needs to be talked about in terms of how that technology could be used for the exercise of leadership and choice rather than used to vitiate that leadership.

I disagree with you, Richard, because I think we are in a period of ideological interregnum. I'm not sure we have come to the next forward thrust, whatever that is and whichever party it is. And I think there is a great deal that needs to be defined there. You may be right. We may be in for Republican dominance for thirty years. It's still an open question.

But in the absence of that, we do need a replacement for the shared national goals we had in the period of the 1940s to 1960s.

I'm not going to give my standard talk about television. I'm going to distribute to you an article that appeared four weeks to six weeks ago in **Arts and Leisure.** Television is a fundamental change that has occurred in American politics. We can't change the institution, but we can change viewing habits, and many other things having to do with it.

We also have the question of education, civic education, which is, I know, one of the places you want this conference to go. We are a far cry from where we were with John Dewey, Robert Maynard Hutchins, or Frank Porter Graham in terms of our sense of mission for education, for the development of citizenship. We have moved away from the sort of mediating institutions that I talked about in the 1950s that led to leadership in the 1960s.

JENSEN: Curtis, do you see a difference between Fahrenkopf and Kirk? At the national party level, do the two parties take a different approach to this?

GANS: The only agenda I've gotten Fahrenkopf and Kirk to agree on is a series of voting law reforms. There were several causes. First, what the Republicans did in Louisiana and New Jersey and a couple of other places on ballot security and their own set of embarrassments about that. Second, the polling data with which Wirthlin and Peter Hart—or Teeter and Peter Hart—would absolutely agree, namely that the majority of the electorate is up for grabs. Given this, at this point there is no partisan interest on either side in holding the electorate. This, together with the Democratic Party's historic recent history of expanding the electorate, made the basis for a political deal. Otherwise, Kirk sees the world in one way and Fahrenkopf sees it another. Neither one of them is a political theorist at all. By and large, both are decent men.

GASTIL: I would like to get the sense of the group on some basic questions. The first question is whether we should really be worried about low participation in this country. In some sense, everybody is going to be a little bit worried. But I mean worried enough to make a big effort. Now I took it that some of the remarks that Gabriel was making earlier suggested not as deep a worry as some other people. Is it something to really worry about?

BENNETT: A paper that a colleague of mine and I did earlier this spring went into the question, does nonvoting threaten American democracy? We looked at it from basically four different dimensions. One dimension that we need not go into is if you got a sudden surge of nonvoters into the polls, would it change the mix of policy opinion that elites hear? Would it change the partisan makeup of the electorate? Would it have made a difference in any recent presidential election's outcome? (We were not talking about outcomes below the presidency, where it probably would have.)

The three other dimensions were: would new voters be the yahoo crowd, a question scholars influenced by the events in Germany have every right to be concerned about. What we found is that strictly speaking, for the United States, the nonvoters who were interviewed—that's an important caveat—would not constitute an anti-democratic, anti-civil libertarian yahoo mob.

The one case we had to look at, which was frustrating because there were so few of them, was where George Wallace's voters came from in 1968, and where they went in 1972. A lot of people have

Political Participation

asked the question, where did Wallacites come from? They came out of the woodwork. They were mostly people who had not voted before, especially very young southern males who had never voted because they were just coming of age or were still in their mid-20s.

SIGEL: In Wisconsin, it was a labor vote that went for Wallace.

BENNETT: Yes, but most of that was southern. Even in Wisconsin, if you go back into the Wisconsin data from 1964, when Wallace first ran in the primary, and then in 1968, you see that there is a southern tie—either first generation in Wisconsin, or second generation in Wisconsin.

SIGEL: I didn't know that.

BENNETT: The interesting thing is where did the Wallacites go? They went to Richard Nixon. But 15 percent of them voted for George McGovern in 1972. The overwhelming percentage of them stayed in the electorate. Of those who stayed, most voted for Richard Nixon in 1972, but one out of every six voted for George McGovern in '72.

So our conclusion was, at least in the American context of the present period, we don't need to worry about a group of anti-civil libertarian anti-democratic yahoos who are going to tip the balance in terms of changing the political context of this country. We can't say, however, that they wouldn't change it at the lower levels. Even Wolfinger admits that easing the franchise is going to have some minor 2 percent here or 2 percent there partisan impact. But—of those who agreed to be interviewed—they would not constitute a danger to American democratic institutions.

GASTIL: What percentage did not agree to be interviewed?

BENNETT: Tom Smith at National Labor Relations Council has done a study of people who refused to be interviewed, and they are as much as 25 percent of those who were contacted in the first wave of the survey. Obviously people refuse to be interviewed in surveys for a lot of reasons. But the yahoo vote would be in this group—if there is one.

GASTIL: Okay, Steve, so you are giving a kind of negative reply: More voting wouldn't hurt us.

BENNETT: In this one very narrow sense I don't think the future of American democracy would be adversely affected if these people suddenly started voting.

GASTIL: No, but that doesn't show a great interest in doing something about nonvoting.

BENNETT: No, but there are other issues that are very fundamental. For example, the issue of representation for those people who are outside the electorate. Their interests are being systematically either discounted or ignored. That's a much different question altogether.

GASTIL: Steve, how can that be if you told me just a minute ago that we wouldn't really change much if more people voted?

GANS: If you look at economic, social, and cultural issues, the nonvoter has very different attitudes than the voters.

GASTIL: Then it would make a difference?

GANS: It wouldn't at this point, given the nature of our parties, which is what you have to always include. It would not necessarily make a partisan difference. The Democrats have backed off. Cloward and Piven argue that if you got everybody to vote, the American polity would be transformed. That's crazy. At least it's crazy in the absence of leadership that would want to transform it. At this point, there is no leadership to really represent the nonvoter.

SIGEL: It's a circular argument. This is a problem, and it's why I can't get excited about turnout. Although I know I should be here. As long as the two parties are tweedledee and tweedledum, a lot of people have very little incentive to vote. If, on the other hand, and this is where I don't quite agree with you, Curtis, if you did polarize the parties a little bit more, I don't think that you'd have enough people to make the second party a truly competitive party. Mondale proved that. You tell it to them straight, and offer a different agenda, and people ignore you.

PENNIMAN: The problem of lack of competition is greater lower down. We are talking as if the president owned the place, so to speak. And yet, as a matter of fact, the people in Congress can get elected with virtually no effort, with no real competition. Talking to people in the last week or so, we were talking about possibly a six- or seven-seat change in Congress as a result of this election. What are we going to do there?

GASTIL: I agree with that point, but I'm trying to move on to a series of questions. I'm not too clear about whether the group as a whole feels it's really important to do something about voter participation per se.

BENNETT: It is fundamental. And one of the things that Curtis said is that that's your base for voluntary forms of participation.

PENNIMAN: It can be crucial for the question of the Congress. More crucial, maybe, for the Congress than it is for the Presidency.

GANS: All I wanted to do was respond to Roberta when she said she wasn't concerned that participation was so low, because it was probably a rational response to the choices people have. That's what you were saying, right?

SIGEL: Yes.

GANS: That doesn't mean Roberta likes the level low. What she's hoping for is better political choices. And I didn't say I wanted very narrowly ideological parties. It's not going to happen in this country in any case. But I tend to think that Mondale is a bad example, because Mondale appeared as a panderer to begin with, and a whole series of other things. Secondly, whereas you had a real choice in 1984, it wasn't a choice that addressed large coalitions on either side.

ALMOND: This is a simpleminded question. In these figures, are the same people turning out, or is there turnover?

GANS: There is turnover.

ALMOND: All right, over a period of time, let's say three or four elections, how many people, let's say, would have ever voted?

GANS: The answer is, we don't have that longitudinal data. We don't really know.

ALMOND: So we don't even know what the scope of the turnover problem is?

GANS: We do know a little.

ALMOND: Do you know that it's very small?

GANS: In 1984, the only date I've got any data for, there were eleven million new registrants, 70 percent of whom voted. This includes 18 to 20-year olds, all the way up. The eleven million represented a 2.8 percent increase in registration. The vote increased 0.5 percent.

BENNETT: The social psychologist Angus Campbell developed back in the 1950s a way to talk about the oscillations between high turnouts, again in relative contexts, in presidential elections and the lower turnouts in congressional off-year elections. He noticed there was a core electorate, and these were people who would vote come hell or high water. Supercitizens is what we would call them today. There was a group of people who wouldn't vote if God incarnate were on the ballot. And there was that peripheral element of people who would vote in high stimulus presidential elections, but who dropped out when the presidency was no longer at the head of the ticket.

He had panel data, where the same people were reinterviewed in 1956, 1958, 1960. There has been only one other panel we can use on a national level, and it was from 1972, 1974, 1976.

There have been two or three studies that have shown that relatively the core electorate has shrunk a little bit, while the size of the nonvoting element, those who never get in, has remained about constant. What has happened is that the size of the peripheral voters has increased a little. What we are getting is more of the people who will vote on an irregular basis, but fewer people who are the Roberta Sigels of this world, who always vote, even if the dog-catcher is the only thing on the ballot.

SIGEL: Yes, but I've got to modify what I said. It just occurred to me, it was really dumb what I said. Partially I believe it. But partially it does make a difference whom you recruit. The expansion of black voting in the South is the reason that, from my point of view, thank God, Mr. Bork is not sitting on the Supreme Court (although I am not sure we did much better with Mr. Kennedy). But the southern senators who ordinarily would not have dared vote against him had a lot of their support from the blacks. If they had to rely on southern whites, they wouldn't have been elected. They were smart enough to know on what side their bread was buttered. But that means the opposite of what you want, because it really means drawing into the electorate a group of people who have been left out and who would give a different result.

ALMOND: But who is moving out? That is my question. Who is moving out and for how long?

BENNETT: Young, white, working-class, noncollege-educated.

ALMOND: It seems to me this is priority number one for your conference. Let's find out what is really happening here. Turnout is a very ambiguous concept. Let's break it down. Let's operationalize it and really try to ascertain it.

JENSEN: Would it help the system if everyone was paid $50 if they showed up to vote, and our turnout jumped to 88 percent? Would we have a better society?

ALMOND: You never can tell. You get them to vote, you might crank them up, so to speak, and they might continue.

JENSEN: I can imagine that as a remedy. That's a theoretical possibility. I can't possibly see how that would help the American political system.

GASTIL: So the point that Richard is making, and a point that I was trying to make before, is that increase in voting per se doesn't seem to be very high on anybody's agenda here.

BENNETT: If we don't change anything else.

GASTIL: Right. Increasing voting along with other things may be very important.

BENNETT: And if E. E. Schattschneider was right, you've got to change the other things before you are going to get the transformation or increase in voting.

GASTIL: Okay. Let me go on to the next issue that I'd like a consensus on. Are most of you convinced that it would be useful to make some of what Curtis would see as the relatively easy and shorter range changes, like making registration easier? Does everybody more or less agree that those would be good things to do even though they are very neutral as far as what Richard was saying?

JENSEN: It is hard to believe that changes in the registration system will change the political system in any favorable fashion. If people are alienated that's a serious problem. If they don't bother to register, that indicates they're on the fringe of the system. Our system is a voluntary one and that's one of its glories. It's not that Americans are inactive, they participate in an enormous number of activities of which registering to vote is one of the easiest and simplest and cheapest in the 1980s. If they choose not to invest that amount of time, that's a signal that they would rather not. I think they feel no problem in that regard.

LEVINE: I'll take the other position. I think you can bring a horse to water, draw in a little more interest, induce some people to say now I've registered, I better get myself a little bit educated. I don't think that hurts.

GASTIL: I take it that Charles represents the majority position, but there is another position that Richard has just described.

Political Participation

BENNETT: Maybe there's a middle position. From reading the studies that Bingham and others have done, and from listening to Curt and reading other things that he has done, changes in registration and other laws would have an impact. But it would very quickly begin to have diminishing returns. I tend to doubt we'll get nine, ten, or sixteen percent increases. Those estimates are made on the basis of a given motivational pattern to turnout now. I can see instances in which Archie Six Pack is sent an automatic registration form. Harriet, what is this thing? And it goes right into the trash. You must change Archie Six Pack's motivational environment. I think Curt's right, it's the party system that will have to do that. In the longer run the education system will have to change.

GANS: The evidence is clearly that when registration is liberalized, voting increases, but then it goes down again. All I'm saying is we need to create the necessary condition for that person who may get motivated 15 days before the election instead of 30 to be able to vote; and that persons who may have low motivation and didn't vote in the last election shouldn't be kicked off the rolls because they exercised their right not to vote.

GASTIL: In addition to registration and other easier voting ideas, Curtis provided us with an extensive list of thoughts that really summarized many things that had been said today in regard to parties and attitudes. I take it everybody in the group more or less agrees that this is the important area to work in. The problem for me in listening to the discussion is that the action agenda becomes very vague. Just what is to be done to change, let's say, the impact of television to make the parties more competitive, or to implement some of the other suggestions that have been made? Is there an agenda that can be implemented?

GANS: The answer is some approaches can be followed now, and some need more research.

GASTIL: Give us a couple of specifics, Curtis, things that could be done in the next few years that would help.

GANS: First, we ought not to be the only country that doesn't regulate advertising on television. It has a lot to do with the con-

272

sulting question. It has a lot to do with the money question, and it has a lot to do with some of the public attitude questions.

Nineteen eighty-six was an election year in which neither party put forward a program. It was run almost entirely on the statewide level by essentially negative advertising. The Republican National Committee supplied me with figures that showed there was a ten percent increase in negative attitude to the candidates, corresponding almost precisely with the ten percent decline in voter turnout. There were plenty of other examples of the effect of the new methods. My favorite example is California's relatively close race in 1982 between Jerry Brown and Pete Wilson. Twelve million dollars was spent; seven million on television. You had a much closer race between Cranston and Schau in 1986 with $24 million spent, about $14 million on television exclusive of the $5 million or so that was spent on fund raising. And you had the sharpest decline and lowest turnout in California history in 1986.

GASTIL: How do you answer the argument that the only way to increase competition is to make it possible for people to raise large amounts of money?

GANS: Understand, I am opposed to limits on contributions. I'm opposed to limits on spending. I do want public financing as a floor to provide access to the polity and to provide insulation to the officeholder from those people who give money and want to make demands on the recipient. I am in favor of doing something about television spending, but this is a different issue. After doing some market testing on both the question of constitutionality and the question of political salability, my thoughts are embodied in the Inouye-Rudman bill that is essentially an offshoot of the French uniform format regulation that requires the purchaser of the TV ad or an identified spokesperson to speak to the camera for its duration.

GASTIL: Okay, here are some specifics. Are these statements that you've been making politically identifiable or would there be general consensus on most of them? It seems to me you are making two kinds of statements. One having to do with regulating television, and the other having to do with putting a base under campaign funding. Are these regulations that the rest of you think will help?

GANS: I want the television regulation because it will be four scandals and thirty years before legislation on public financing is possible. Public financing is the surest way to kill a campaign finance measure. I think all the other reforms of campaign financing having to do with limits are pernicious. Spending limits are very much incumbent protection. Contribution limits vitiate pluralism. Therefore, my concern about campaign finance cost control as well as television in terms of politics, and consultants in terms of parties, has to do with TV ad regulation. You kill all three birds with that stone. You create a more competitive system with the rest. If you are taking all other campaign devices, as far as I know, there is a limit as to what can be spent.

GASTIL: I'm not really interested right now in political practicability, but rather whether a group like this concerned with these matters can come together on some broad areas of agreement on what could actually be done that would make a difference. I want reactions from the group.

KLEPPNER: Intuitively, I'm inclined to agree with Curt about some control over television advertising. In fact, I really don't know that the research has been done to show that negative advertising has this kind of effect.

GANS: All we have is indicative data. In nineteen eight-six, three statewide campaigns—California, Missouri, and Texas —were similar or identical to those in 1982. In each case there was higher spending on television, a closer race, and substantially lower turnout. You had a situation in Wisconsin in which you had over fifty percent negative attitudes to both candidates.

JENSEN: Curtis, do you want to prohibit negative campaigns?

GANS: No, I don't want to prohibit them.

JENSEN: You want to prohibit them on television.

GANS: No. I want ads to be answerable and verbal rather than emotive and unanswerable. Constitutionally, you cannot ban negative ads because that would be content regulation. Secondly, somebody else's record, character, and advisors should be subject to legitimate commentary. But the commentary ought to be in a form that is answerable, debatable, and does not lead to an arms race of ever more slick demagogic commercials on increasingly irrelevant topics. Let us debate. Let time be given to everyone to say whatever they want to say so long as others get the chance to effectively answer.

GASTIL: You're saying that we should raise the level of campaigning through some process of regulation. Has that ever been done successfully in another country?

GANS: Sure. Every other country in the world regulates its television advertising, either by time or format. Many other countries do not permit—Howard probably has the details, I haven't looked back at that study recently—any form of paid advertising.

GASTIL: I understood you to say something rather different. You seemed to be saying not that you want to stop things being done on television, but that you want things done in such a way that arguments were answered. Isn't that what you were saying?

GANS: I'm talking about three phenomena: cost, public attitudes, and consultants. (There are other things such as independent expenditures and things like that that are of more concern to officeholders.) For these there are four effective means of regulation. One is to abolish television ads altogether.

JENSEN: You're not talking about newspaper ads?

GANS: No. Newspaper ads are answerable. They don't reach the emotions in the same way. They don't cost as much. It's just like direct mail. It's defensible. This stuff isn't. The second is to abolish paid ads and to provide grants of free time, as in Britain. The third is, as Charles Guggenheim suggested, essentially to have a time regulation. You can't have thirty-second to five-minute spots, everything's got to be longer, or longer than two minutes or something like that. This way you force some substantive content, and it's not quite a captive audience. The fourth is this format regulation. Number one, abolishing the ads altogether, won't happen. Number three buys you the legitimate opposition of the broadcasters because they cannot plan their program time. Number two, free time, buys you the political opposition of the broadcasters, and also buys you allocation problems because free time should be meaningful time, which should be prime time. You take a market area like New York with four parties, and primaries and general elections in thirty congressional districts. There are probably two senatorial races, a mayoral race, and something else up all at the same time. With all this, you are not talking about meaningful time.

JENSEN: You're arguing: a) that in the 1986 election there was a lot of negative campaigning, which indeed there was, b) that it had the effect of depressing turnout, as the voters got upset with both candidates and therefore turnout went down, c) that this is tied in with the heavier than usual use of television, and d) that one of the solutions to declining turnout is controls or regulations that would restructure television ads. But the turnout has been low regardless of high, medium, or low use of television over the last thirty-some years.

GANS: That's not true.

JENSEN: It was low in 1948 before we had television.

ALMOND: I just wanted to give a preview of what I'm going to say tomorrow: I'll begin but not develop the argument. I think that what we were discussing in the last couple of minutes doesn't come anywhere near in importance to pure rational choice considerations in the problem of voting: information and transaction costs, what it costs the voter to vote, to get and analyze information in the American system, and the transaction costs, actually casting the vote. The benefits are too low. I'm going to argue that.

GANS: I don't dispute that.

ALMOND: To cope with that problem is going to take some fundamental constitutional changes. We're talking about changes that would bring the American voter into a situation where the cost that he incurs or the cost benefit ratio in voting is like that of the British and the French who vote in much larger numbers.

BENNETT: Let me make two quick suggestions. Curt, you are much closer to the real world than I am in terms of doability. I buy Dick Boyd's research that shows that a decoupling of state and local election calendars from national calendars has had an adverse impact on turnout.

GANS: Has it had an adverse impact on presidential turnout? I don't think it has.

BENNETT: A new study has just been done that shows there have been substantial declines in turnout in local elections, too.

GANS: Absolutely. I agree that there should be fewer elections.

BENNETT: I think we should recouple election calendars across the board. And in the process, I come back to something that Howard talked about, and I know Curtis does not agree with, that is, to increase the impact of voting on house seat outcomes. It's incredible to find out that you can have substantial shifts in voting in terms of the partisan makeup of the turnout, with very little effect on shifting seats in the House. I got some data from the U. S. Statistical Abstract that show that since 1970 the percentage of House seats decided by 60 percent of the vote or more has never fallen below 50 percent. And in 1986, 80 percent of House seats were decided by a two-party vote of 60 percent or better.

GANS: The reason I haven't dealt with that issue here is not simply because I think the senatorial and gubernatorial races are increasingly competitive, as I think by the way presidential races are in terms of individual states. But it is also the fact that dealing with the competitiveness of districts is much like dealing with negative elections for the past twenty years. At one point David Cohen, when he was president of Common Cause, tried to convince one state in which he had substantial backing and organization not to gerrymander their state along partisan lines. He wanted them to create competitive districts as a good government act. It did not work. It's like public financing right now; it is not something that's going to happen.

There are other things that can happen. We can do something about questions of civic education. We can do something about values. We can do something about at least getting people concerned about technology. On a different level, we ought to be concerned about the whole question of information, just straight information, or how we take people away from a television society and give them better information. On the other hand, I should say about my advertising proposal, the current system of political advertising will dominate rational information in the absence of long-term teaching.

GASTIL: Thank you, I am afraid we will have to continue this tomorrow morning.

DISCUSSION OF PARTICIPATION IN GOVERNMENT SERVICE

GASTIL: This morning we begin with a discussion of declining participation in public service. When I originally conceived the idea of
doing something in this area I noticed an Op Ed piece in The New
York Times by a couple of people from Harvard's Kennedy School.
Following up on that I found that they had been working for some
time on the problem of participation and, as they saw it, it was one
that involved both voter participation and participation in the public
service. This led me to assume there was something in common in
these issues; they were both obviously important. Charles Levine
and Pete Zimmerman will begin by giving us some thoughts on this.

LEVINE: I'm involved in something called the National Commission
on the Public Service, chaired by Paul Volcker. This is what he calls
the quiet crisis. This commission has been up and running for a little
over a year, and it's your typical Washington commission with a
typical cast of characters. Volcker, Ford, Mondale, Tower, Mathias,
Muskie. There are 37 members, and I think Volcker's favorite line is
that the commission covers all the leagues, the Ivy League, the
Urban League, the League of Women Voters, and, when we added
Walter Haas who owns the Oakland A's, the American League. Funding comes from eight foundations, all grants of reasonable size,
nothing enormous, and three corporations. It has a small staff
headed by Bruce Laingen who was charge d'affaires in Iran; he is an
eloquent spokesman for issues of public service.

We started with the idea that something might be wrong with
the federal civil service and with the concept of public service more
generally in the United States in the mid-80s. This has turned out to
be an illusive linkage. Pete will describe why it is illusive; it's
fraught with paradoxes and ironies. But by and large the commissioners were drawn to the idea that the best and the brightest no
longer seem to be attracted to government. And I will add to that,
"if they ever were." Maybe the golden era was not so golden after
all.

But the history of who came into government and why over 200 years is interesting, as is the history of the American people's relationship to their civil servants. I will just quote from the Declaration of Independence where it was observed that King George III had "erected a multitude of new offices and sent hither swarms of officers to harass our people and"—the most graphic line—"eat out their substance."

This is how we began, to eat out our substance. There's no question that American suspicion of the civil service has always been high and probably with some appropriateness. But the concept of public service, noblesse oblige, has waxed and waned in this country. Jefferson certainly spoke eloquently about it. Later on the progressives had this as a major theme. There are some people trying to revive it now. People talk of the "campus compact" and other things that are working quite well around the country. At the same time, as government grew the discriminatory forces in our workplace made the government an excellent place for first generation immigrants, for blacks making the first run into the lower middle class, and providing what Joe Biden would call a "platform" for development. Finally, we wind up with a government that is technologically very sophisticated, in which expertise is very much a part of the demands of handling the details of government in the 1980s and beyond.

This gets back to the issue, what do we do about making the government and public service generally more attractive to the American people, or government employment more attractive to young people, or how do we make the people who work in government feel better about their work?

When you talk about bureaucrats you really are talking about lambs in sheep's clothing. The idea that powerful career civil servants such as existed formerly in several agencies still exist is largely false. (You mentioned yesterday the Social Security Administration from the late thirties right on through the mid-60s.) We have transformed the situation through the imposition of political appointees —there are now 3,000 of them at the top—and the development of much stronger congressional staffs than ever before.

The way we have recruited people and the kinds of people we have recruited has produced a group of narrow technocrats who do not perceive themselves as players in a political system or as major shapers of policy. That's not everywhere; there is no question that the uniformed military and the State Department remain bastions of the career civil servant with immense political power to shape the policy agenda.

We now come to at least five conclusions or observations about where we're at. First, you should not join government employment anymore and shouldn't even think about it, for wealth, power, or prestige. What has always worked best in government is the idea that you can make a difference. You can still make a difference either by making people's lives better, by working on a piece of hardware, or by doing something in foreign affairs. The idea that government might be a place to make a difference as opposed to getting rich we think is important.

Second, perhaps because of our strange history, maybe because of what government does, maybe because of all the political noise, or the way the media covers government, even when public servants do make a difference they are not perceived to do so, and the difference they make is too often perceived to be negative.

Furthermore, the concept that civil service might be public service has totally disappeared in the United States. Civil service jobs are just other jobs in a marketplace full of opportunities. If public service is not part of the equation and if you're not perceived to make any special kind of difference, then pay becomes very much a part of the calculus, and the government simply doesn't pay a competitive wage anymore.

Finally, for a whole generation of people, mostly the young, even those who would like to do some good and make a difference, public employment is too often seen as a place where they cannot do that. We have copious correspondence and communication from college students, from people in government, from younger people, expressing their frustration. They are frustrated by the management systems, by political systems, by the generally low prestige of their work—perhaps even by the way the government budgets.

We're talking about a group that perceives itself to be powerless, overworked, underappreciated, underpaid, and furthermore, not given the tools in a timely fashion to do the work they want to do. For example, the way we acquire computer equipment often gives them the wrong hardware, the wrong software, and the wrong tasks at the wrong time. This is not everywhere but it's too common.

More affirmatively, we think change should be focused on creating the conditions that will allow public employees to enjoy the satisfaction of making a difference. We should work on freeing up, loosening up, and deregulating the incredible array of rules and regulations and layers of political appointees that get in the way of the sort of satisfaction we are talking about.

A public relations campaign is one approach. I will tell you, though, having been in this business for fifteen months now, the American people are not interested in a public relations campaign on "be kind to bureaucrats." Paul Volcker was on the Larry King show two nights ago and, just as we predicted, the first phone call after he got through making the public service pitch was about interest rates. The second phone call was about international monetary this and that. And the third phone call was what does the Federal Reserve do?

One last step. We think increasingly that to encourage initiative in the civil service, to build back respect, that government must build from strength, and that strength is increasingly lower down in the government firmament, in its agencies where traditions of excellence exist. Where you do not have such traditions of excellence, start working in that direction. I could go on to some management fixes.

We also have fixes that relate to others of our task force, and I'll just tick them off. The pay and compensation task force, which Jim Ferguson, CEO of General Foods, chairs, is talking about a scheme for location pay as well as trying to do something about top executive salaries. L. A. Richardson chairs a task force on career political relations that is trying to find ways to build more cooperative, as opposed to hostile, relationships between those two cadres of people. We have a recruitment and retention task force chaired by Rocco Siciliano that is trying to take a look at not only entry level college people, but, further down the road, what it takes to keep the good people you get, and keep them motivated.

We have a new retirement system in the federal government. About forty percent of federal employees are presently covered by this new retirement system. It's portable. The old golden handcuffs that kept people in government after they hit about eight or nine years are now gone. So government better be a fully competitive employer at the middle levels. Likewise, government better be able to attract good people at the middle levels to replace those who leave by attrition. These are systems that simply to not exist now.

Derek Bok chairs the task force on education, and Pete staffs it out. And, finally, the slipperiest of all, the image and public perception task force chaired by Bob Schaetzel, former ambassador to the European Economic Community, and Leonard Marks, former director of USIA. Frankly, it's been murder. What does it take to turn around public perceptions and the image of the civil servant in this country? We have gone to Dan Yankelovich. We've gone to Louis Harris. We've talked to some of the best and brightest gurus on this issue, and at a minimum they say this is a tough struggle. We've done some research on Roper and Gallup polls over time on this issue. Today the American public is not hostile, but it is not supportive either. It is by and large indifferent to the civil service at all levels. People seem to be a little stronger in support of police and local government services; then state, and finally the Feds. The fact that the federal government no longer delivers more than three or four different kinds of services doesn't help anything. It makes it all the more difficult to develop proposed systems in which government employees will be closer to the people. There are just too many links in that chain now.

GASTIL: You started to develop the question of whether there's been any change. Has there? Is there anybody who has actually tried to look at changes in the status of civil servants over the years?

LEVINE: Two observations. First, there has been major change in the last twelve years with Carter and Reagan coming in and bashing the bureaucracy. After 200 years of experience, I conclude that if the president doesn't lead on this issue, isn't affirmative about his work force, you are in deep trouble. This is where the indifference starts. If the president turns on his own work force, then civil servants are really in trouble. The press looks to the president to lead. Congress looks to the president to lead. Carter had his problems, but with Reagan it got worse. Not only was he indifferent to the bureaucracy, but he turned loose a junkyard dog in Don Devine who understood things——I've seen him footnoted in a couple of the papers here on civic culture. He turned the guns of the administration on the civil servants. This created serious problems of morale. It also created serious problems in the way the media covered the civil service for a time. It is hard to turn this around unless the president steps forward and starts saying good things about civil service, starts doing the symbolic stuff.

GASTIL: I was thinking of a longer time scale, let's say, from 1920 to the present.

LEVINE: No question that the president saying affirmative things about government employees is number one. It is hard to find presidential speeches about civil service but they are there—I have tracked them since the 1920s. Every once in a while it doesn't hurt for your boss to say we appreciate your work. This administration has not done that.

Second, there's been a great ethnic and generational change in this country; this really affected the quality of people who came into the civil service. If we think about the civil servants who came into government in the 1930s and World War II, we're really talking about first-class people recruited from first-class places who were the first generation to go to college. Particularly the European ethnics; it's not only Jewish, it was Italian, Irish, and several other ethnic groups that brought their best and brightest. These came along with the children of school teachers. They regarded government as a totally appropriate place to make a career. They did not have corporate connections, so when the corporate job market was tight they came to government. They did well. They were ambitious and aggressive.

The government has not been getting their children. When we look at the entry-level classes of government employees, a small number will come through the public administration track; in government, they will move into a sidetrack, essentially the administrative cone of the departments, such as the administrative cone of the State Department. When you start looking in the technical and policy areas you find narrow technicians who do not consider their jobs governmental. It's just another job in their specialty. That may be okay, but where does the leadership come from?

As to leadership, we used to talk about iron triangles of bureaucrats, interest groups, and Congress or congressional staff. Well, the bureaucrats that are there are this cadre of 1,500 political appointments—there are another 1,500 that carry spears but don't do much. These people are coming in and out, twenty-one months apiece. So the real stability is shifting to the congressional staffs.

This is the general argument. The really powerful career civil servants aren't there anymore in most departments.

SIGEL: The way you characterize the group that came in beginning with the New Deal, that's right on target. There was a feeling you could make a difference. It was a new era. You'd really change the system. But if you leave this out for a minute, and go as far back as the founding of the country, civil servants in the United States never had much respect, any more than there was for school teachers. They were seen as "pencil pushers".

LEVINE: That wasn't true in the beginning, not until 1828.

ALMOND: There was a great pride in the New Deal period, and then in World War II, and up to the early 1960s. They saw themselves as "government", not bureaucracy.

LEVINE: That's right.

ALMOND: But since that time political parties have been running against government personified in terms of bureaucrats.

PENNIMAN: On top of that there is the vast difference that size makes. When I came into the State Department back in 1948, one of the first stories I heard was from a guy who had come into the State Department as a foreign service officer in 1924. His first job was to go up and talk with the Chief Justice of the Supreme Court. He was a GS-7 at that time. This was his function. This was how small the place was. Within that small a world you could be somebody. But when you multiply that world by ten, fifteen, whatever it is, then these possibilities are just gone. GS-7s, there are a billion of them.

GASTIL: You're really talking about the administrative bureaucracy. There is also a technical bureaucracy. I'm thinking that, for example, people in the Bureau of American Ethnography and the Agricultural Department and others on the technical side used to be very important players.

PENNIMAN: That's right.

Political Participation

GASTIL: In some fields that's still true.

LEVINE: Decreasingly so.

ALMOND: If they are, he's talking about policy communities and issue networks and iron triangles. Are those concepts meaningless? If they mean anything, then they've got a bureaucratic component.

LEVINE: They do.

ALMOND: If they have a bureaucratic component, then you've got community.

LEVINE: I think it's a legitimate observation and one I keep going back and forth on. Once upon a time the leaders in some of these technical fields were in the government. They were tied into a network of like-minded people in their professional and scientific communities and around the country. They were tied into congressional committees; we had networks that worked and they were very much a part of it. At the National Institute of Health that still exists, and in a few places like that. But increasingly career people do not have authority within their own agencies to shape policy. So they have to go through a backyard route and they are not part of the bargain.

Furthermore, you have some contested agencies where in order to break the policy networks, particularly in the domestic areas, recent administrations brought in "antis" from these policy communities, and they did their damndest. Their mission was to destroy the networks that already existed. In environment, education, civil service and public administration, networks were destroyed.

GASTIL: McNamara did that in the Defense Department, didn't he?

LEVINE: Yes.

JENSEN: Charles, you did not mention privatization. That was brought up briefly, in regard to the National Institute of Health a year or so ago. Is that a possibility?

286

LEVINE: I don't think so. What drove privatization was not that privatization would yield greatly improved health research. It would simply allow the government to pay special salary rates for health workers. So it's a way to be consistent.

JENSEN: Well, that was a major issue. If university research communities pay $150,000 a year to top biomedical researchers and the National Institute of Health pays half that or whatever it is.

LEVINE: No, they pay much better, now $90,000.

JENSEN: That's still well below what universities pay for the exact same job as far as that goes.

GANS: We are a long distance from the concept of the British public service.

KLEPPNER: The British are coming closer to us, thanks to Mrs. Thatcher.

GANS: To some extent the traditional British concept is what we have to sell in this country; that's the sales job. I think it's somewhat inhibited by the stringency of civil service regulations on the lowest levels. Both the people in the bureaucracy and the people outside the bureaucracy who have to deal with it are dealing with a lot of incompetence.

LEVINE: The solution is not to penalize them by paying them less.

GANS: But you have to be able to remove and replace them.

JENSEN: In the New Deal period they used to say government jobs give you security. The New Deal was a depression era phenomenon, when job security was a very attractive feature. My impression is that in the private sector job security is much less than it was ten or twenty years ago. What's job security like in the civil service? Is it ironclad?

GANS: Part of the public reaction to civil service is due to the people they confront on the other end of the telephone.

Political Participation

ZIMMERMAN: It is worth pointing out that if you look at public perceptions of bureaucracy or government in the aggregate you get negative associations. When you disaggregate them, and ask about the civil services most people actually deal with, whether it's the police or the school system or things like that, you get much higher public ratings of capability.

GANS: But that's not true on the federal level.

LEVINE: No. And if you happen to live in the District of Columbia that is also not true on lower levels.

ZIMMERMAN: What I thought I might do is begin by saying a bit about my sense of what young people are thinking of, or reacting to, in regard to their interest in public service. The signs are mixed and slightly confusing. Maybe you can help us sort them out. Then I will come back to the bureaucracy question and say a bit about the mood in the bureaucracy, and then discuss some intermittently hopeful signs. Our work suggests that if we took some plausible and reasonable actions, this would make a difference in terms of our capacity to attract talented young people to government. Some of these actions, like pay, will be hard, but many are quite straightforward. This is the way we've been focusing—much of the time working with Charley, Volcker, and others.

Let me say a word about the campus situation. Many of you are familiar with (Alexander) Astin's ongoing survey of college freshmen. For twenty-five years or so he has been asking an essentially consistent set of questions to a national sample of college freshmen.

A couple of things emerge from this data. One is that financial security is a life goal for young people; this is now the number one goal for sixty to seventy percent of college freshmen. (Next to that is something with a kind of quaint sixtyish label that they call "having a meaningful philosophy of life." This now seems a little anachronistic and cutesy, but twenty years ago it seemed just right. Now it may be telling us less than Astin and others are trying to make of it.) If you think about when this generation has grown up and the economic shocks of the 1970s and early 1980s, it may be a first derivative of the kind of shocks that our parents had growing up in the depression that made them perhaps very conscious of financial security. Business as an undergraduate major is booming. Close to one-quarter of undergraduates now major in business. This leads to a big fight: many schools don't like undergraduate vocational programs in business, public administration, criminal justice, or whatever.

Astin also asks questions related to perceptions of government. When you ask young people about their ability to get ahead in government, only 45 percent say the opportunities are excellent or good. In a Roper poll, 37 percent of college-educated people would agree. The implication is that the better educated really see the bureaucracy for what it is in terms of prospects for future growth.

According to Astin, keeping up with political affairs is something that people do in an avocational sense. In 1965, which is a little before or at the edge of the Vietnam, urban, and other crises, 58 percent said keeping up with political affairs was important or very important to them; in 1985, twenty years later, 38 percent gave these replies.

That's one side of a ledger that could be interpreted as the Wall Street view---the "greed-is-good" view.

One other thing that came out of the National Association of Educational Assessment. There was an article that just blew me away. Only one-third of high school graduates could describe the freedoms in the Bill of Rights. Of the two-thirds who could not, half had no interest in knowing what they were. For those of us who have grown up in a tradition of studying politics and government that's a real shocker.

On the other side, there's been a dramatic turnabout in college attitudes toward community service or public service in the broadest sense. Just a small data point from Harvard: from 1983 to 1987 the career affairs office at Harvard did an exit interview with about 90 percent of graduating seniors. They asked the seniors about their college experience. During that time the percentage of students who participated in some form of volunteer community service had gone from 38 to 53 percent. That's just four years. Bok interprets this as a sign that what he's been doing to promote community is paying dividends.

There are other activities. The "Campus Compact" is a declaration of intent now signed by over 100 university presidents to promote public service and community service on their campuses. There's an operation called COOL, which means something like Campus Outreach Opportunity League. It is aimed at generating opportunities for young people to participate in shelters, workshops, tutoring young kids and things like that. Another is called ACCESS, which is trying to create a job market to make opportunities and job information available to graduating students who want to work in the nonprofit sector. So there are encouraging signs. From some of the same Roper data I cited earlier, younger students have a very positive association with government. If you ask a question such as, "If you knew that a young person was considering a career in government, would you encourage them to do so?" About eighty percent would. I think the age range was 18 to 24 for this particular question.

In Astin's survey of college freshmen, if you ask about the government's role or ask questions that may elicit some indications about government's role, such as "Is government doing enough about disarmament?" or "Is government doing enough about the environment?", "Are we spending too much on defense, or too little on defense?", you get signals that they want a more activist government in the environmental area, more disarmament, less defense. Over the last five years even the percentage of college freshmen who support forced busing to achieve integration has gone up by eight or ten percent. This runs against a general perception that some people have of college campuses being hotbeds of conservatism.

GANS: I don't think that is the general perception. They were for Reagan in '84, but I don't think that's the general perception.

ZIMMERMAN: It's also the case that by self-description they don't label themselves significantly more conservative today than they did twenty years ago. But many fewer label themselves "liberal." So the middle of the road bunch is what's gone up in this twenty-year period.

BENNETT: On that point, if you ever cross-index self-labelings on ideology by interest in politics, the middle of the road is a great haven for the apathetics.

ZIMMERMAN: That's a good point.

JENSEN: Do you have figures on career intentions or considering civil service-type jobs?

ZIMMERMAN: That's turned out to be one of the problems with the data. There are only indications. This goes back to the point Charley made about "what is the civil service?" There's not really a career called public service. There are careers called engineering, teaching, foreign affairs, things like that. The general answer is that we've been mining some of this data trying to figure out if we can get a clearer picture of what people think about public service as a career, but we only get fragments. So the answer is no.

Two other notes of a more anecdotal character. I don't know whether it would surprise you to know that the most visible government agency on college campuses is the CIA. They recruit everywhere, and they are doing very well. They are the most widely visible, and recruiting the largest numbers. We did a survey of about 75 universities, sent it to presidents and deans to get information on things like who comes to your campus and how do you compare government recruiting to business recruiting. We were quite surprised. In this sample of university campuses, the CIA is by far the government agency most commonly seen. Others are more specialized. At Michigan State there would be somebody from the Agriculture Department, but you wouldn't see that person at Yale. But at both Michigan State and Yale you see the CIA.

GASTIL: How does this visibility compare with the number of people that are going to be hired?

ZIMMERMAN: This relates to some of the other points made about the generation that came into government in the 1930s and '40s. Bob Gates, the Deputy Director of the CIA, told me last night that fully seventy-five percent of their employees have been with the CIA less than ten years. He was very concerned about a loss of continuity and historical context, because few analysts have a memory of 1948, '58, or even '62.

BENNETT: Is the fact that so many of them have served for less than ten years, is that from the purge in the 1970s?

Political Participation

ZIMMERMAN: That's a small part of the explanation. Natural attrition is the major explanation.

ALMOND: Are there alternate career paths for spies in some sector?

JENSEN: No, I think we've had a core or a cadre of people in the CIA for a long period of time most of whom reached retirement at about the same time.

PENNIMAN: The OSS (Office of Strategic Services) people had already retired. This is the group that followed the OSS people. So there is some continuity, but they lost a lot at the wrong time.

ALMOND: I wonder if the visibility isn't really controversiality rather than visibility? You're not talking about perceptions, you're talking about actual visible presence?

ZIMMERMAN: Actual campus visits. Maybe visibility was the wrong word, it certainly has visibility in the controversial sense as well.

LEVINE: Pete pointed out to me today that most government agencies do not bother to show up at our better universities.

ZIMMERMAN: At MIT in 1987, 404 institutions showed up to recruit---fourteen were government agencies. This is in a period when the government was crying about the need for scientific and technical talent. They say we can't compete at MIT; our return rate is going to be low. Therefore, we're not going to go to the top engineering schools. We'll go to the second ten or the third ten. Here the cost benefit calculus says we can do better.

ALMOND: Oh, we're better treated, too.

ZIMMERMAN: And we're better treated perhaps, yes.

JENSEN: Where our mediocre recruiter can meet some mediocre students and get a mediocre job.

GASTIL: That's the point I was going to make. Bouncing around looking at different colleges, one of the things that suddenly struck me was that a political science department, for example, in a small college is not going to want to have a better academic than one now on the faculty.

BENNETT: That's not always true.

GASTIL: There is a tendency not to want a person who is of a higher status than you are and is going to come in and suddenly be the star and push you aside. I think for government agencies it's the same thing. If you have a group of people, all of whom have come out of let's say Kentucky State, they are not going to go to MIT and Harvard to recruit people, because they really want people from Kentucky State.

ZIMMERMAN: I wouldn't put it in the affirmative. I think it is more insecurity. One of the things I spent time doing was a series of three- or eight-week programs for government executives—federal, state, and local. There's no question that the first day these government executives show up, the fact that they are at Harvard means a lot to them. In some cases it's bound up in personal histories and roots, and aspirations. Harvard is one of those icons that no matter what you think about it, it matters a lot. In some ways it is less what we teach; it is the validating character of kind of club, or it seems to be that. I think there's a feeling that if I'm graduated from a small or less prestigious school, I'd be nervous going to Harvard or Stanford or Berkeley, and have to talk to professors whose books I had to read.

One other point relating to Richard's question. In our querying of folks on campus that are involved in career counseling, they say that if you ask people about student's perceptions of government the modal answer is that government is just not very relevant, or it's boring. I've been trying to understand how is it that these kids would want to go to work in shelters for homeless or battered women, or go into prisons and work with convicts, but are not interested in government. Because in my generation there was an assumption that that was part of what government was about. This has changed.

Let me just say a word about the government side of this, in a preparatory kind of way. My own working notion about the bureaucracy is that it's a very immature profession. If you think of law, medicine, or business as major professions, government is a very immature profession. It hasn't found a professional identity yet. The enormous expansion of government really began only a couple of generations ago. And there, we are talking even less about the federal than we are about state and local.

JENSEN: You're leaving the military out.

ZIMMERMAN: Even the military. We had a very small military until World War II. We had a very small military in the 1930s compared to the permanent establishment that was set up after Korea.

PENNIMAN: And not highly respected.

JENSEN: You wouldn't call it immature.

ZIMMERMAN: No, I wouldn't call it immature as a profession. I take that point. But it was very modest in scope and scale. And the military is quite different in the way it thinks about issues such as recruiting, placement, or career development, the way to build identity.

JENSEN: They never call themselves civil servants, do they?

ZIMMERMAN: That's right. They are distinct. If you walk into the Pentagon, you see civil servants who have one set of complaints sitting alongside military officers who have a very different set. They're working in the same government system, under the same general fabric of laws and political authority, but they have a very different life. The military has its own complaints, but they don't feel nearly as aggrieved as the civil servants. And often they are literally side by side doing similar jobs.

ALMOND: They don't call themselves civil servants. What do they call themselves?

ZIMMERMAN: Career officers or career noncoms.

ALMOND: But in the government service as a whole, do people say "I'm in government service"?

ZIMMERMAN: No, they say I'm a lawyer, I'm an economist. I'm an electronics engineer.

ALMOND: And they just happen to be employed in government?

ZIMMERMAN: Yes.

ALMOND: Would this be true of the nonprofessional levels as well?

ZIMMERMAN: I don't know the answer to that. That's a good question. The thing I was going to note is that there's enormous striving on the part of procurement folks and the personnel types and things like that to acquire professional trappings. All of these communities want to have their own education requirements. They would like to see universities adopt programs to teach subjects such as personnel, procurement, or grants management. The lawyers seem to be part of a different class—or the economists, or the historians.

JENSEN: No, not the historians. We're like procurement agents.

ZIMMERMAN: On the mood of the bureaucracy, one of the things that has been bandied about quite a lot is a survey that was done by what's called the Senior Executive Association, a professional group of the top six thousand or so civil servants. Half, or maybe sixty percent, of those eligible belong to it. According to the survey, the majority of them said they would discourage their children from following public service careers.

SIGEL: Elected officials say the same thing. Congressmen and other elected officials say they wouldn't want their kids to go into politics.

ZIMMERMAN: In a different survey, fifty-nine percent of these same senior executives believe subjectively that the new hires joining their agencies are either marginally or a lot worse.

JENSEN: Then that's more than oblique. That's a very expert observation, wouldn't you say?

ZIMMERMAN: I actually have a suspicion that it's self-serving. You know, "These kids, they're not like we were."

LEVINE: Some of it is tinged with a heavy reaction to affirmative action.

BENNETT: It's not just specific to government employment. I've had occasion in the last two years to speak to a fairly wide sampling, although not systematic, of departmental chairmen in political science. They're convinced to a person that the people who are coming in as newly minted Ph.D.'s in political science do not have the same background, training, or capabilities of those before. I'm wondering if what we are seeing in that data point that you mentioned is perhaps indicative of a broader decline in the quality of higher education of K through 16?

GANS: That's a question. How do you feel about the quality of your students longitudinally?

BENNETT: In the eighteen years I have taught at the University of Cincinnati, and I'm speaking strictly in terms of one campus, I've seen a major decline in the quality of the students coming to us.

GANS: My brother-in-law teaches at Wesleyan and feels that very strongly.

JENSEN: The younger generation's not as good.

ALMOND: When did it begin to deteriorate? I have the longest memory of all here. I think it began to decline in the late '60s and '70s. The first generation of Ph.D.'s after World War II were special, unusual.

SIGEL: If there is a difference, there is also a reason. I'm not talking about emigres now. A colleague of mine worked for Exxon for a couple of years, and they did a study. The study found that the young people who used to go into political science, the smart kids who wanted to go into law, are going into business administration now.

GANS: We don't have anybody here from a business school, so we don't know what they would say.

LEVINE: The business schools are getting the cream, and they artificially ration enrollments. This creates two things. One is a certain prestige—if you can get into the business school you become part of an elite. Secondly, this dumps the less gifted into kindred fields, one of which happens to be political science. If you don't make a three point, there's always political science.

SIGEL: Exactly.

ALMOND: There is a very powerful indicator that really gets to this whole problem. In all the major universities that do Ph.D. training in political science, recruitment to the subfield of American government is at an all time low.

BENNETT: Exactly. That's right.

ALMOND: The subfields that they opt for are Third World, Latin American Studies, International Relations, and Theory of Disarmament.

BENNETT: Theory?

ALMOND: I would say that the political theory subfield has remained constant at a relatively high level.

BENNETT: But they have reached such a low point.

ALMOND: You've got critical theory, you can play around with things like Marxism and you can really be interesting and progressive by doing that kind of theory. Or you can be involved in questions of arms control by going into international relations, or you can be for the South against the North by going into third world studies. American studies is for the birds.

LEVINE: Let me say that parents are putting enormous pressures on the kids to go into business, or other professional fields. "I've got $60,000 to $80,000 invested in this degree from Georgetown, and I want something out of it."

GASTIL: Charles, is it true that if you go to the average business school professor, he'll say students now are much better than they were ten years ago?

LEVINE: I hope so, because he's getting the best.

ZIMMERMAN: If you go to certain military academies, they would answer that affirmatively, and they can document it. They're getting better students. Now that's partly as a rebound from the anti-military feelings in the 1970s. But they will tell you that they're getting much, much better students.

JENSEN: Business used to have very low prestige.

ZIMMERMAN: Yes, that's right.

BENNETT: My comment about the poor quality of students did not simply relate to who we're getting in M.A., Ph.D., or M.B.A. programs. I'm speaking about introductory government courses, this includes the business types. I'm sorry to say, the worst of the lot are the education majors and the communications majors. Those people, where they have been I do not know and do not wish to speculate.

KLEPPNER: Read the publication called, What Our Seventeen Year Olds Know. It was put out by ETS (Educational Testing Service). One of the interesting data points is that about thirty percent of the 17-year olds identified one of the consequences of the Spanish American War as the destruction of the Spanish Armada.

ZIMMERMAN: It is worth noting that the number of M.B.A. degrees has about doubled in ten or fifteen years. About 70-75,000 M.B.A.'s are awarded annually. In public administration, public policy, things like that the number of masters degrees is more like 6,000, and enrollments have actually dropped. That's an order of magnitude difference. Yet if you look at the work force, about twenty to twenty-five percent of the work force in America is in the public sector, another sixty to sixty-five percent is in the business sector.

JENSEN: What are the annual flows in and out of the civil service?

LEVINE: Two hundred thousand new hires a year.

ZIMMERMAN: If you include postal employees, it's 350,000 a year out of a population of about three million. New hires are on average about ten to fifteen percent.

BENNETT: There was an article by William Mitchell, called "The Ambivalent Status of the American Politician," published about thirty years ago. If I recall correctly, it drew on some sociological studies of prestige ratings of various occupations. I think August Hollingshead's status ranking (in **Elmstown Youth**) was one key data point. What it showed is that the highest status was Supreme Court Justice. The president was quite high. But then you got down into congressmen, used-car salesmen or something like that. The civil servant was rated very low. Have there been any follow-on studies like that?

JENSEN: I think the politicians have come down even further in the language.

LEVINE: May I scale that for you? When I used to work for the CRS (Congressional Research Service), I'd play this game with people. I'd go to a party and somebody'd ask me where I worked. If I really wanted to turn them off, I'd say I worked for the government, and I'd end the conversation. If I wanted to turn them off slightly less, I'd say I'm a political scientist who works for the government. Snore. Then I would go to the next stage and answer, "Congressional Research Service." Then I'd say Congress. With these answers I would be getting better. Finally, I'd say "Library of Congress". Oooh!

ZIMMERMAN: Let me offer a slightly hopeful point. I am coming to believe that there are a lot of things we can do to change the likelihood that talented people will want careers in government. Look at what's happened to public school teaching over the last twenty-odd years. Richard, this gets to your question earlier. One of the career preferences Astin's survey asks freshmen about is school teaching. A generation ago this was chosen by twelve to fifteen percent. It bottomed out in 1983 at 4.7 percent, at the same time a "nation at risk" and a whole wave of states—such as, Texas, Florida, Tennessee, Mississippi—made attempts to make some improvements in public education. It is now up to 8.0 percent as of 1987. Another thing happened: If you look at the relationship between average salaries paid to graduates who go into public school teaching, the federal government, trainees at Citibank, insurance companies, things like that, they were fairly close together fifteen years ago—fifteen percent differences. This difference opened up quite a bit in '77 to '82. Public school teachers have come up since 1982 dramatically and closed the gap at least with the Feds. In relative terms, they are now closer to the federal civil service than they were a decade ago. The business folks, of course, are still way out front. Some of the business school people will tell you that there is some attenuation of demand in terms of the salaries they are seeing offered. Not Harvard, Sloan, or Stanford, they won't tell you that. But go down a bit and question those M.B.A. programs that got started fifteen years ago—they're seeing some fall off.

Many school systems have job fairs. Recruiters come from all over. You get somebody from the school district in Tupelo, Mississippi, coming to Boston College, prepared to sign people up on the spot. It's not just salary. Such offers greatly reduce the transaction costs, the encumbrances and impediments to going to work and making a decision. Even though Tupelo might not pay as much as Citibank, what the student hears is, "I want you. We had a good talk. I've looked at your background. I've seen your recommendations. We want to offer you a contract." It's very similar to what the student who was interviewed by Citibank hears. When you talk to folks on the college campuses about problems of government recruiting, the number one problem is you can't get an answer. People come to the campus and they're interested in you and you're interested in them. Then they say fill out the standard form, submit it to the civil service commission or the OPM (Office of Personnel Management), and in sixty to ninety days maybe we'll be able to tell you something.

JENSEN: It's notorious. But it's been that way for I suppose fifty years, hasn't it?

ZIMMERMAN: I don't think it's been quite as bad. In any event, the government is now making an effort to change that. They're just starting pilot programs that will make it possible to say yes within seventy-two hours, even twenty-four hours, so they can be more competitive recruiters. My own view is that the transaction costs or encumbrances around hiring are as important to deal with as the $24,000 versus $32,000 wage differential for somebody coming out of college—not to diminish that. One can be too obsessed by starting salaries.

As to the point Charley made, when you have 300,000 people a year coming in, the implication is there's a lot of people leaving, which is also true. You've got mobility in the system. The Department of Defense did a study of quit rates for engineers. They found that there was a higher quit rate associated with engineers whose undergraduate SAT scores were above 650 in a quantitative test than the group that was below 650.

JENSEN: Charles described a very unattractive set of jobs. If the Volcker Commission has a little pamphlet I hope government recruiters don't use it. Here's frustration, low prestige, low income, negative opportunity for you.

LEVINE: We're clever enough that our brochure doesn't look like that. However, we are also clever enough to know you have to establish the problem before you can establish a program.

SIGEL: Charles, you mentioned the kind of people that you get on the telephone or when you go to an agency or the post office, and you mentioned affirmative action. I think one of the confusions in the public mind is that we confuse the secretary at an office with the career service. I personally don't mind that you get the wrong answer on the telephone. I get it from American Express, and Bloomingdale's. Actually I think one of the great virtues of both the City of New York and the Johnson administration is to let the great unwashed masses into the stream where they can become telephone operators and secretaries. While I think they're terrible, let me tell you, the mailman in Italy or Germany is no pleasure to deal with either. The problem that I see is an American problem that is only aggravated in the civil service. This is the lack of respect for people who don't do something—where doing something means something material that you can see. In a later survey than the one you mentioned, it was university presidents and university professors who were at the top. Actually physicians and university people are way down now because what do they do? Of course, lawyers are even lower. It is a general cultural phenomenon that we don't respect these kind of people.

GASTIL: This leads me, Roberta, to a question I want to ask Charles and Pete. It seems to me there's two problems. One is getting people interested in public service, serving the government. The other is getting people interested in going into the civil service or the bureaucracy. I wonder if that's the right strategy. I wonder if it wouldn't be preferable to push the idea that the person who goes into these positions is a lawyer, is a computer operator, and so forth. He's something else, you have a lot more respect for a person if he's some kind of specialist.

ZIMMERMAN: Let me argue with that a moment. Who are some of the most admired people in America today? Rock stars, athletes, Lee Ioccoca, or Donald Trump.

GASTIL: Also scientists.

ZIMMERMAN: The swashbuckling entrepreneurs, the Steven Jobs, one of the things that has been drawing people toward business. This is the immaturity of the public service profession. The notion that you care about how the phone is answered at the Social Security Administration, that's not something lawyers or engineers or most of the other professional groups are going to be able to think about. In business that's something people are beginning to think about. It still means that when I call Aetna like you, or American Express, you still wind up pretty frustrated.

SIGEL: After you get through, you stay on the line and listen to Muzak.

GASTIL: The point I'm making is if you call up that government office person and you get an ignorant response or don't get any response, you identify that with the civil service. Now you're asking people to want to go into something that's identified with that kind of thing.

ZIMMERMAN: We're challenging people to change that image.

GANS: Several points. First, we are paying an enormous price for the retreat from commitment to constructive government. Our politicians don't have the guts, this includes right now Dukakis, not only to defend, but to recruit people for government. It is inexcusable. However much the polls may show something else, at some point you have to stand up. Second, we've paid an enormous price for a lack of commitment to quality and competence. I'm for some degree of affirmative action, the levels vary, but we have to demand performance. When I talked about the person you got on the phone, it's not only the person you get on the phone. When you're sitting in a middle-level bureaucratic position and you want a secretary who can either type or spell, you've got about a forty percent chance of getting one. (General agreement.)

This isn't going to get anybody to enter, or stay in, public service. Employees feel the frustration of not being able to get anything done, of not being able to continue to hire personnel. You've got to change standards, you've got to change attitudes. The lack of demand for quality throughout our country must be changed.

SIGEL: It's not just government.

LEVINE: I mentioned affirmative action. Let me say that 200 years from now somebody will figure out that the black middle class in the United States was built on public employment, and that the integration of our society overall was made possible by public employment.

BENNETT: In the early 1980s, it's about seventy percent of the black middle class.

LEVINE: That's in the long run. In the short run, there's a real problem. But check out the military academies. The military academies have a much higher percentage of blacks than you'd guess. And they're doing fine.

303

Political Participation

ZIMMERMAN: They really are. I'd just like to second that. If you look over the last twenty-five years, who has done a better job at integrating women and minorities into the senior ranks of the work force? The political appointees who every year appoint a few hundred or a few thousand, or the career civil service? Answer, it doesn't matter whether it's Reagan or Kennedy or Johnson or Nixon or Carter, the military does a much better job of finding reasonably talented, competent women and minorities. One might think of the career services as a place where people rise to the top. But the senior executive service is still as much as 92 to 94 percent white male. These are the top ranked. On the military side, in the Department of the Army, comparing the civilian component of the Army and the general officer ranks of the Army, there are more black generals than there are black civil servants in the same cohort of 400 top civil servants and 400 generals. These are guys now who have been in the system for twenty-five years, who have had terrific training, education, and development. The military program is very impressive; it is paying dividends.

BENNETT: On the political side of affirmative action, one of the things that needs to be done in this country is to get congress to stop exempting itself from its own affirmative action laws.

GANS: I agree with that.

JENSEN: The military throws people out very gracefully, with a nice handshake and a nice pension. This twenty-year retirement— would that help the bureaucracy?

ZIMMERMAN: Conceivably. The average age of military retirees in the United States today is something like thirty-nine.

CONCLUSIONARY DISCUSSION OF GENERAL ISSUES

GASTIL: I thought it would be useful at this point in the program to have comments from two people who have spent many years of their professional lives thinking about attitudes and values in relation to these issues. Therefore, I've asked Gabriel Almond and Roberta Sigel to make some remarks to move us into the general question of whether there is an overall problem that involves both of these kinds of issues and how we might approach that.

ALMOND: I really hadn't focused on the government service aspect of this. I was concentrating on the voting problem. But my argument may bear on both government employment and the act of voting, on both citizenship and the public service.

The general point that can be made is that the net benefit, after cost, has declined in respect to voting as well as in joining the public service. Attitudes in the sense of values, sentiments, feelings are relatively less important, although not completely unimportant. From a professional point of view, this is an acknowledgment that I come rather reluctantly, since I've been unhappy with the rational choice, public choice, trend in the social sciences, the imperialism of economics in recent decades. But on these questions you can really see how it's not so much a case of fundamental values or feelings of obligation or moods and sentiments, but rather pretty hard-headed calculation. Maybe a lot of people, let's say at the level of voting, solve the problems intuitively. They intuit that the net benefit of voting after costs makes voting an activity with a relatively low value.

As a preface to this argument, in regard to attitudes let me mention two bodies of evidence.

First, major studies, such as the Lipset-Schneider book, **The Confidence Gap**, that as of 1980 or so summarized the results of about 1500 surveys on attitudes toward not only government service but elites of all kinds, including military traditions, chart a substantial trend over time, particularly after the Vietnam-Watergate period, toward declining trust and confidence in government and its various parts. Of course, this decline differs from one agency to the next, from one type of public service to the next. In the middle of the first Reagan administration these trends began to change. There was some evidence that Reagan had given some positive blip to confidence in government. I haven't followed the trend in the last few years. But certainly if we're now thinking of the last several decades, there has been substantial decline on the order of maybe fifteen or twenty percentage points, even larger in regard to some government units.

The second body of literature which I've been closer to was, of course, the civic culture study that established the high point in the '50s and '60s of the American and British civic culture, but particularly the American civic culture—its extraordinary high level of the sense of obligation to participate. **Civic Culture Revisited,** written in the latter part of the 1970s, showed substantial evidence of the decline in the civic culture and its various components, and decline in trust, both in the United States and Britain.

These trends stand in contrast to what we might have expected from the demographic changes of that period: particularly, radically rising educational levels in the United States. We have known that for a long time one payoff of higher education is higher participant patterns. So we can speak of the nonvoting paradox, because rates of participation should be going up. Some kinds of participation rates have gone up. But I don't want to get into that.

Going back to the question of how important attitudes are, the most important point I want to make is that even in the period of the height of the civic culture, in the late 1950s and the 1960s, American participation rates were relatively low by comparison with other advanced industrial democracies. So, what we have to explain is not the decline in voting rates in the post-Vietnam, Watergate era, but the consistently low voting rates through the entire post World War II period.

Here I come to the argument that it isn't changing attitudes and values that have been the important factors. It is really hard-headed, calculating, self-interested rationality that can explain the decline in voting and I would assume in government service. The cost of voting in the broadest sense has been rising, and the benefits have been falling. The cost/benefit ratio, in other words, has been declining, the net benefit after costs. I would group costs under two headings: information costs and transaction costs. The number of times people have to vote, primaries and frequent elections, the number of things that people have to vote on—federal, state, local, executive, legislative, judicial, policy issues, initiative, referendum——and in the American context the absence of information-economizing devices like ideology and disciplined, coherent parties. You could have a heavy load of information but you could have convenient ways of making decisions, "decision-cost economizers." As far as transaction costs are concerned, perhaps one of the most important ones is registration. Before you can vote, you've got to register.

On the benefit side, I would place the sense of efficacy and effectiveness, whatever you want to call it, that one gets in the exercise of the suffrage, or on the government employment side, efficacy in the sense of being in a job that makes a difference. My colleague, David Brady, an econometric political historian——a new breed of political scientist——has charted the history of American government from the point of view of its policy-making effectiveness (**Critical Elections and Congressional Policy Making**). What he points to is the unlinking of the partisan connection between the presidency and the congress, and a decline of partisan cohesiveness in the American government due to the reform of the party system, the rise of electronic media, and rising educational levels. He speaks of the disappearance of the presidential coattails. It has become increasingly difficult for the voter to view the act of voting as productive or of policy benefit. The connection between voting and policy output has become attenuated. The normal situation is one of a divided government, such as a president of one party and a congress dominated by the other. Even in the situation, let's say, in which you might have a Democratic president and a Democratic house and senate, the composition of the Democratic house and senate would be such that it would be immobilist. It would be very difficult to crank policy up, even in that context.

We used to talk about the Weimar Republic and the Third and the Fourth Republic of France as being immobilist political systems, stalemated political systems. Today the United States may be the best exemplar of an immobilist and stalemated government. France is moving along well. West Germany is a model of effective political performance. In the United States, you would have to say that the effectiveness of the vote has declined. Its actual instrumental effectiveness is low.

What American voters may be telling us, and what potential candidates for public office, public or government positions, may be telling us is that the costs are too high, and it isn't worth it. It's as simple as that.

The issue becomes how to reduce costs and how to increase benefits to get at both problems. This is kind of simpleminded. I don't claim any great originality in putting that in front of you. But let's say you're thinking of what would be the actions that would have the largest payoff to reduce the input of effort. To shorten the ballot would be one obvious move in that direction. Just make it much more difficult to call on people to actually legislate, as in the initiative and referendum. Why should there be judicial elections? Make registration automatic. Cut the transaction costs. When you have a change of address there ought to be automatic reregistration. As far as increasing the benefit side, I turn to the Committee on the Revision of the Constitution connected with the 200th anniversary. Among the recommendations that they proposed for constitutional amendments, one of the most valuable from this point of view would be to give members of the House of Representatives four-year terms, and have them elected co-terminously with presidents. That would increase the length of the presidential coattail to some extent. That's one example of a measure that might streamline the relationship such that the voter might more often conclude that it makes a difference.

SIGEL: Last night after you told me what you wanted me to do, I was going to question whether turnout has really dropped so much. But I've learned a lot from what you people said. I don't buy it 100 percent, but let's let that rest. I also don't think I want to talk about structural problems, since Gabe did it now, although I think there are some other things we have to think about. When you read Richard Fenno's book, **Homestyle,** you get a good feeling for some of that. Our districts are very large, and lots of congressmen have little contact with their own constituency. Congressmen rely on their polls to determine what the public thinks it wants. This cannot take the place of real contact. There is much less of an attempt to go into the district and offer leadership and educate people. But I want to let all this rest and concentrate on a few things that might account for it.

We haven't looked enough at the change in the composition of the electorate. We have eighteen-year olds voting now, and we have people who vote who are eighty-five and older, or who could vote. We used to say it is a curvilinear turnout, and the young ones don't vote as much, but the young ones then were between twenty-one and thirty. Any of you who have ever had teenage kids know there is a big difference between and eighteen-year old who is entering college and a twenty-one-year old who is thinking of a career. By twenty-eight there is much more change. So the drop-off should have been more than you would just anticipate by clumping all the young ones together.

Secondly, the old adage that the old don't vote as much really isn't true. The old in general are becoming a larger part of the population, but many in their sixties and seventies are as active as they were when they were fifty. It's only the so-called old-old who are eighty-five and older, often in nursing homes or otherwise physically handicapped, who are less likely to vote. They are also predominantly female, and females of a generation prior to women's suffrage. Thus, the very youngest and oldest groups may have suppressed the figures a bit more than we realize.

I will advance a somewhat unpopular thesis, and say it's not just costs. There's a psychological plus when you vote, you feel virtuous. I think one of the reasons we don't have as much voting is we don't have basic cleavages in this country. We have one group of people who are left out, the constituency for whom Jesse Jackson speaks. That's why he was so appealing. You may call it "false consciousness" if you are a Marxist, but basically very few feel left out of the system. We don't have partisan newspapers similar to those in Europe that can drum up votes. Few feel an incentive to make sure that the "Laborites don't get in", or Mrs. Thatcher's people don't get in. These feelings are lessening in the UK, too.

You're right when you talk about the '50s and the early '60s, how different they were. The first time I was able to vote was 1948. At that time we came out of a war that we thought was a good war, which we fought for righteousness. We had just undergone what we thought was a social revolution under Roosevelt, and the United Nations was founded. It was a period of rising expectations. We thought there would be no more war. There would be social welfare.

You had the Beveridge Plan in England. So everybody thought that the world would be a better place. Why anyone ever thought that the world would ever be a better place, that's a different question. But it was a period of euphoria.

We were bound for a letdown. What interests us in the '60s and '70s? Several things to shake this harmony. You have the new life-styles of the kids from the long hair to the flower children to what Raymond calls the significant others. I remember so distinctly when my oldest son came home and brought a young lady, she stayed on the third floor. When my son asked if he could go up and visit her, my husband said absolutely not. When it came time for his brother to bring a girl home, he didn't even ask; he brought the girl home and that was it. All I said was "What are we going to say if grandma comes?" So by now nobody minds this anymore.

In addition, we get Vietnam, we get Watergate, and so forth. So you have new lifestyles by which some people still feel very threatened, and you have signs that government is not as nice as it was. But then you have a third thing. Take the right-to-life people: they so scared one major party, and sent quivers through the second party, with such issues as prayer in schools, that a presidential candidate gets up and says "I don't belong to the ACLU, and I never will". None of this could have been as influential if it weren't for the new electronic media. Every time you have twenty people standing at an abortion clinic, the TV is there because they tell them beforehand. Where would Phyllis Schafly have gotten all of this impetus if there weren't Viguerie with his direct mail? So you suddenly have a group that feels extremely threatened by what is going on, and a group that is disillusioned with what has happened. The mass media bear a lot of responsibility for this.

On the lack of cleavages, let us consider an engineer or a computer scientist who works for New Jersey Bell. He's got a good job. Unless he doesn't do his job well, he's going to be equally well-off under Bush or under Dukakis. He isn't going to get himself excited about voting. For the inner-city kids and the rural poor, they're left out anyway, so they don't have any interest. The stakes in voting are not that high.

Does this apathy mean that they're alienated or indifferent? I think there is a group of people that is alienated. I hear it particularly among very well-educated blacks who are saying not much is being done for the inner-city school system, for the homeless, and so on. I have some friends right now who are debating whether they are even going to vote. They have voted all their lives, very well-educated college professors, deans and so on. They're acting on behalf of these constituencies. But if you leave that group out, most people who may or may not vote are indifferent because we don't have any debate about what I call basic issues. There is no debate in our country about redistribution of wealth in a real sense. We may say we want to tax a little bit more. Dukakis wants to tax the rich a little more, but we don't talk about the redistribution of wealth.

Have you ever heard a discussion on television, for instance, about whether the family is an outmoded institution, or whether religion isn't such a hot idea? We don't talk about these things. We talk about how we are a Christian nation. Nobody questions that. Are we a Christian nation or a secular nation? What I'm saying is everything is muted not because there are conflicts, but because we take everything for granted. Do you remember when Roosevelt came out with the idea of a $25,000 limit on incomes? The public was against it then; it's going to be against it now.

ALMOND: The studies of Herbert McClosky and Sidney Verba show that people are quite content with equality of opportunity.

SIGEL: Most people still believe that if you want to work you can get a job, they're quite content. I want to talk a little bit about our own research, which by now is outdated, but I think it's indicative. First, there is a difference between attitudes towards the system and attitudes towards those who administer it. Basically, most Americans still think this is the best country on earth.

ALMOND: Best system, right.

SIGEL: They are no longer convinced. These socialization studies that were done by Easton and Dennis, first of all, were all done with white middle-class kids, which is really funny or sad, whichever way you want to put it. They were done in the days of Eisenhower. Of course, there were problems with the studies. But if you take away all the methodological faults, the overwhelming feeling was one of trust in government. The adult population, while it was less trustful, was also more trusting than today.

Political Participation

One of the questions they asked was, "Are you proud to be an American?" When we tried to do cross-national research, we wanted to use that same question, in Germany and Canada. They laughed and said you can't use that question. This is silly. In 1974 we asked 1000 high school students, randomly selected in Pennsylvania, if they were proud to be an American. I think ninety percent said yes. But then at a different point we said to them, "Are you proud of your country all the time, most of the time, some of the time, or never?" They split between most of the time and some of the time. We had virtually nobody who said never and virtually nobody who said all the time. We then gave them a card chart where we said, "Here are some civil rights, tell us if the country is doing a very good job, and adequate job, or could do better?" And we made them sort them, and then do the same thing with regard to services. In both sets, there were very few kids who thought the country was doing a very good job, except for athletics.

At that time the erased tape of Nixon hadn't come up. They were relatively sure we were doing a good job guaranteeing basic rights. On social services and crime and taking care of the elderly and taking care of the sick, the kids were very critical. We asked about eleven services, and on only one did the United States come out as very good. We followed this up by another question, "Compared to other countries how do we rank on these things?" Now, those kids didn't know anything about other countries, but we wanted to know how they felt. It was a very mixed picture. On many things like safety and services they thought we didn't do as well as other countries. On freedom and beauty of the country they thought we were doing very well. Americans are proud, but it's a relative pride. Compared to other countries they think we are still pretty good, but that we still have a long way to go. According to the Michigan feeling thermometer (see Bennett, note 5) the flag, which after all is a symbol, America is in the very warm category. Everything else is lukewarm.

All of these things; the lack of real cleavages—the two parties trying so hard to appeal to everybody that they don't offer alternate programs. You see that right now. Dukakis is a Democratic Tom Dewey. "I can do it better." But you can't afford the lack of participation. We also asked our sample to define democracy. The most frequent answer had nothing to do with politics. It's, "I can pick any job I want to. I can make as much money as I want to. I can travel whenever I want to."

ALMOND: It's really freedom they're talking about.

SIGEL: It's very egocentric.

BENNETT: Self-absorbed.

SIGEL: If that's all you're interested in, and the system doesn't keep you from traveling to Florida tomorrow, what is going to make you into a real citizen? So, what you find is selective citizenship. In my neighborhood, because New Jersey is having trouble with landfills, every time you have a new development, people are worried about the sewage system, they're worried about the toxic dump, and you get everybody out. I've been a pollwatcher for the Democratic party, and checked voters off. We don't get anybody out to vote. It is a strongly Republican upper-class area. But if a new developer wants to come in and they want to reduce zoning from two acre to one acre, you've got every homeowner out.

More generally, there is a change in attitude toward saying, "It really doesn't make that much difference who is in." The fact that voting is consistently overreported in polls, according to the University of Michigan, means that people basically still believe citizens should vote. There should be much more of an attempt made to show people that it does make a difference who is in. The schools are doing a dismal job. They are worse now. At least fifteen years ago we were trying to raise problems of democracy and some social issues. But now, when you're supposed to only teach patriotism and so on in schools, the kids are absolutely bored with what they learn in school.

One exception is women. Women are voting more than they used to. They are voting more not because they love the government more or feel more enthused about it, but because through the women's movement and other things, they've been mobilized to see they have an interest.

ALMOND: And they are getting more out of it.

Political Participation

JENSEN: Roberta, you touched on a matter that Steve referenced yesterday, namely what's being taught in the schools. I presume you're referring here to the high schools, or even junior high. Do you know of any systematic studies that have taken textbooks now and compared them systematically with what textbooks were ten or twenty years ago?

SIGEL: I don't think any of them have been done since the famous one by John Patrick and Howard Mehlinger. I'm having a conference in late October, an international one, to which I've invited people from abroad. They're having the same problem. They're particularly interested in citizenship education in multiethnic settings---the Dutch, the British, and the Germans. They are deliberately developing programs to do away with the old-fashioned European type of instruction. But I don't work in this area anymore, so I don't know.

LEVINE: Let me get back to a couple of themes. One is the stakes theme. Everybody you talk to who is involved in the policy process sees less and less room for movement. The deficit has killed off any kind of domestic initiative. Then something else is going on, on a totally different level. I'm not sure how many people understand this or whether I'm just whistling when I see this. The developed countries that are competing in the international arena tradewise or otherwise are all in one big game because there's so much interdependence now, so much rapid feedback, so many time-sensitive problems. I'm just wondering how the state steers its military and economic systems when major policy choices are very much determined by the fine tuning of the international order or relationships?

GASTIL: Let me ask a question along that line that was bothering me yesterday. It seems to me that it's always been the case that it is irrational to vote. If you look at an individual facing the high probability that one vote will not make the difference between his candidate winning or losing, his cost, to go back to Gabriel's point, in getting the information, going to register, going to the polls, and so forth is much higher than the expected benefit from this effort. The only way he might rationally make the decision to vote, leaving aside emotional factors and a sense of citizenship, would be if he identified with a group of people so that when he thought of his vote he would think of it not as one vote but as a hundred or a thousand, as a part of a block, then it might make sense because it could make a difference.

ALMOND: If he were a retrospective voter, it might make a difference, too.

GASTIL: Let me ask if anyone in doing studies of participation asked, along with questions about participation, what groups or organizations the respondent identifies with?

BENNETT: Yes, they've been asked a number of times from the '50s through the '80s, although the questions have changed, and the contexts have changed. Starting with 1972, there have been questions about identification with a wide variety of groups. The makeup of those groups changes periodically from questionnaire to questionnaire. A follow-up question would be, "Which of these groups do you feel closest to?" Then they ask specific questions, such as, "Do you think your group is gaining power, or losing power?" There are problems here. My wife has done a study of whom women identify with; she finds that ten percent of women say they identify most closely with women. Now you might say, good Lord, that means ninety percent don't. If not that, perhaps it means only ten percent identify with the women's movement. No, that's not what they mean. They mean identify with my mother, identify with my sister or whatever, not the feminist movement. Most people will identify with the middle class or the working class, or blacks will identify with blacks. You also get a smaller percentage identifying with the working class, or working men and women, or with business people, and so on.

KLEPPNER: So they identify with a category that is really not a psychological grouping.

BENNETT: Only a very small percentage of the public is willing to say, "I don't identify with any group." So there is group identification out there.

GASTIL: Has there been any change in these percentages?

JENSEN: Not in ten or twenty years, but over 100 years there have been drastic changes.

SIGEL: They identify, but the trouble is they don't relate this to politics. I remember when in the 1960 election we polled in Detroit (Detroit was a United Auto Workers stronghold in those days). When we asked them if they belonged to any political organizations, the people would say no. Later on we gave them a list of organizations, and these people would say UAW——they might even be officers in the UAW. They didn't think of this as a political organization. This is very tricky. Even the question that I thought was getting closer to what you had in mind, namely when you ask people the issues that are most important their answers don't mean it will affect their vote. People will say, for example, that the environment is the second most important issue. But they don't really know where the candidates stand on the environment. One group that is an exception, and that's why I am so broadmindedly angry or narrowmindedly prejudiced, is the anti-abortionist: Is a candidate for or against abortion? That is a litmus test for them. There is nothing you can do about that.

GANS: The question you raised is very important, one often discussed in terms of Rousseau. The voting act in the American context has not been rational, but it has expressed the general will ——either assent or withdrawal of assent. Voting has been essentially religious, although expressing a secular religion. One of the problems of our time is that the secular faith has been declining and nobody has replaced Reinhold Niebuhr, for instance, in our cosmology. If there is any message to what I have had to say in the last day and a half, it is that both Gabriel and Roberta are right. It is a question both of rational response and changing attitudes, and the changing attitudes are based in reality. Probably we are moving from alienation to indifference.

ALMOND: Or the other way around.

GANS: If alienation implies active feelings and indifference inactive, I think we're moving from alienation to indifference. The message I have had for twelve years is that there is no simple answer to this. There isn't one thing you've got to do to try to reverse it but a complex of things. My list starts with values; they must be taught someplace. The second issue is the nature and direction of education. And then finding places to use that education, civic education, both within the educational community and out, in finding a leadership function. This has to do with the rise of modern media. That needs to be addressed. It has to do with three aspects of government: responsiveness, effectiveness, and in the present context, the nature or complexity of the issues. Issues now demand an anticipatory government, while previously we responded ad seriatim to crises. This argues for not only enhancement of participation but for a new collective elite, a new "senate." The question that you raised quite correctly, Roberta, the question of parties, is important—parties in terms of organizing the debate, parties in terms of mobilizing people. I don't think anybody who is looking at the 1988 election can say that it's an important election. The Court may be important. The business climate may be important. But by and large nothing major is going to change by this election, because there's nothing major being debated. We need to deal with the registration question, and we need to find a middle ground between the prolixity of the California ballot, with its many propositions, and the other extreme where, as in Virginia, there are no propositions unless someone can persuade an extraordinarily conservative legislature to hold a referendum. We need to have fewer elections. But eventually we will need to address larger substantive questions. Participation is both problem and symptom.

ALMOND: I would like to follow up on that. An enormous opportunity was lost in connection with the 200th anniversary of the Constitution which produced an outpouring of the most complacent self-congratulatory activity. Anything having to do with basic faults in our political system and the Constitution that lies behind it was not discussable.

GANS: There are two different things. The official celebration has been in the hands of Ronald Reagan and Warren Burger and the Committee for the Constitutional System, of which I tend to be a dissenting board member. Lloyd Cutler and others are also members.

Political Participation

ALMOND: What they were doing was viewing it as a secular problem. There are serious problems with the functioning of our government as we are acknowledging quite clearly. How to get back to this, so that we would look at questions. This business of four-year terms for congressmen makes eminent sense from a variety of points of view.

PENNIMAN: Except for the congressman who doesn't want it that way. He would no longer have control of his district, because the president represents new votes.

KLEPPNER: He'd like four-year terms but just not elected at the same time as the presidential election.

BENNETT: One of the things that has happened, and correct me if I'm wrong, Curtis, is that in campaigning for the national legislature I think the individual candidates often disassociate themselves from parties. If you look at their advertisements, whether they be on billboards or in the media, especially on television, one sees "Smith for Congress, return justice to the American way." All right Smith, what are you, Republican, Democrat? "I ain't going to tell you." If you happen to be in a Democratic state or locality, you put "Dem." on it; if you're a Republican in that same district you say vote the man not the party. When you get down to the level of some state legislatures or city councils, party becomes increasingly important. There they vote for party rather than the man because the men aren't visible.

JENSEN: It's information that's more available.

SIGEL: Television time gives everything in such a short superficial form that I disagree with you, Gabe—I don't think the cost of information is very high anymore. The quality is awful but the information is so simplistic and our candidates don't do much more when they talk about it. So really in many ways it's easier.

ALMOND: But that increases information cost because "information" assumes accurate information.

BENNETT: On the question of the irrationality of voting, I find problems with the rational choice literature. Clearly, when there are going to be about 180 million people who will be of voting age in 1988, and some 90 million of them are going to vote, the probabilities of one single vote tipping an election are infinitesimal. People are smart enough to know that. Yet when people are asked if they agree or disagree with a statement like, "So many other people vote that it doesn't make much difference whether I vote or not," ninety to ninety-five percent will disagree. They are expressing a sense of civic obligation that has remained fairly high, at least for the population as a whole. Two things are alarming. One, they've stopped asking those questions on a regular basis; you can no longer track them with some degree of regularity. Second, from the few relevant questions that continue to be asked we can surmise that among young people that sense of civic obligation has begun to wane. From the early 1960s to the late 1980s, there has been a ten to fifteen percent decline in the percentage of young people who agree that voting is a civic duty.

GASTIL: Steve, could I ask a question about this? I've been thinking about something that came up earlier this morning, and perhaps should be looked into more. That is, you the pollster, whoever is going out and looking for this information, would tend to be perceived in most cases to be looking for a certain kind of answer. Respondents are bound to size up who is asking them questions, and then decide what answer will make the interviewer happier. Some of the change we're talking about here, couldn't it be a change in the attitude of respondents toward saying things that appeal to the person who is asking them? There may be a generational change in openness, to use that expression.

BENNETT: There's always the danger of eliciting the socially approved response pattern. Some of the more sophisticated survey agencies have tried to take that into consideration. For example, the question on voting is one that elicits misreporting. Maybe it's lying and maybe it's not. I tend to give my fellow citizens some benefit of the doubt: they may have honestly intended to vote but forgot, or can't remember what they did on election day. To reduce this problem, polltakers ask the question in a disarming manner, prefacing it with a statement that many people don't have the opportunity to vote because they're ill or they were away or they were busy or the lines were too long, or whatever. So they set up a context in which okay, Charley, if you didn't vote, we're not going to put you on the rack.

GASTIL: Has that been shown to actually improve the accuracy?

BENNETT: Not a lot. But there are other questions where we've not changed the wording or the contexts of the questions, and yet seen major changes in attitudes relevant to the act of voting. For instance, beginning in 1964 they asked the question, "How much do you think that having elections makes government pay attention to what the people think? A good deal, some, or not much?" In 1964, 65 percent of the voting-age population interviewed said having elections makes a good deal of difference by making government pay attention. Only about six percent said it didn't make much difference. There has been a steady erosion in answers to that question; by 1980 it was down to 50 percent saying it makes a good deal of difference. Even though there was that blip upward in other trust questions in the first four years of the Reagan administration, those giving a positive answer dropped down to 43 percent by 1984. Fourteen percent now said it made no difference whatsoever. So there was almost a doubling in the perception that elections are ineffective as institutions of democratic government.

GASTIL: Steve, this is the point I'm trying to make. If you had been sitting on a bar stool next to the person you were asking the question of in 1964 you might have gotten more than six percent saying that government wasn't going to listen to the votes.

JENSEN: They use focus groups and talk this out. Not with large samples, but they do that.

BENNETT: We no longer just use survey data. We have a few studies. For example, the one that Bob Lane did with working-class respondents in New Haven——he called it Eastport. He even went into their homes in some instances because some of the guys he contacted wouldn't talk with him otherwise. He had a tape recorder going and he talked with them over four, five, six or seven months sometimes. He also asked them some of the standard survey questionnaire type items so that he could match their responses in the interview context. Sometimes they would make it very clear that the answers they were giving on those surveys were what they really felt. These were the guys you would find on the bar stool. A couple of colleagues and I were fascinated by this problem of what respondents mean when they tell us how interested they are—just that question—either in elections or in government per se. We fiddled around with where that question was on the questionnaire, we put it in one context, we put it in another context. We asked them before or after a series of questions on interest. We got differences in reported interest, but they were always within just three to five percent. When you're only working with 400 to 500 cases to start with, the figures could bounce around and oscillate that much just through a sampling error.

The question is can these questions be trusted? Do they have a basis of veracity? I think there is good evidence they do.

JENSEN: We should be summing up the conference rather than getting bogged down in survey research methods.

GASTIL: I agree, Richard, but we have been kind of bombarded during this entire conference with the idea of attitudinal change toward government. Insofar as we're going to want to come out of here in various directions saying this is what should be done, we should be very clear about the data base, about what we're dealing with and how to deal with it.

ALMOND: A good research agenda could come out of these discussions.

SIGEL: You mentioned the increased use of focus groups for unstructured discussion used prior to developing a questionnaire. This gives a tremendous advantage. When you go in with a typical Harris or other survey (they don't do it this way anymore, but they used to), you set the agenda and you ask the questions. When I am asked if I am interested in politics, I think, well if this guy is asking me this must be important. Whereas in a focus group if the people don't mention an issue the investigator assumes that it isn't an issue.

For instance, a year ago we finished a study of women. I now have a much better understanding of what an answer in a telephone survey means by having heard the women talk in these focus groups. For example, as political scientists we wanted to know whether or not they were angry and whether they wanted to use political organizations to bring on change. We were absolutely flabbergasted when we watched these women in the focus group. I watched the group along with male colleagues and graduate assistants. They said they never felt so dumped on when they listened to what these women had to say about men—men at work and men at home. These women were furious at the lack of empowerment and the lack of respect in the male dominated society. Yet, even when the moderator, against our instructions, tried to bring it into the political arena, asking what would you do about it, is there anything that can be done about it with the parties, these women would turn him off. The only political thing they can think of, other than their own activities on the job, is suing.

The idea of doing things through the political process was absent. This makes me think that if I had another grant, I would ask even fewer political questions. Our questionnaire was full of political questions, and they gave us answers. Sure, they were nice and they did just what you said, they were nice. The answers were meaningless.

GASTIL: Let's follow what Richard would like to do and see if we as a group, or any of you individually, have drawn any conclusions. Gabriel and Curtis essentially gave us lists of conclusions. I'm really asking the rest of you to evaluate these and add your own.

KLEPPNER: I'll begin by distinguishing the short term things that I might do given our participation problem versus the long term things that I would do. Among the short term things, I think the sort of procedural changes that Professor Almond outlined are useful— shorten the ballot, have some form of automatic registration, link congressional elections with presidential elections, give representatives longer terms. One also might attempt to persuade states to have gubernatorial elections at the same time as presidential elections. All of those kinds of things probably will contribute incrementally to an increase in turnout. These are short term moves to reduce the costs of participation.

GASTIL: Before you go further, I wanted to ask a question about the four-year term. Where does that leave the senatorial elections?

KLEPPNER: Where they are now, staggered.

GASTIL: So that senators will sometimes be elected when they will be by themselves on the ballot?

ALMOND: There will be the possibility for some political change in their terms.

KLEPPNER: In the longer term, I'm increasingly impressed with the notion that what one has to do is look very hard at the kind of civic education people are receiving in grade schools and high schools, and work to improve that.

ALMOND: Shouldn't we say in that connection that political science has been looking down its nose at formal civic instruction from the word go? As a matter of fact, political science has been trying to separate itself from civic instruction because that was one of the things it was before it became professionalized. As a consequence we have neglected it. We don't really know what can be done with it. Socialization theory would tend to minimize this.

LEVINE: I have the same problem with the personnel people who have tried to professionalize their work.

KLEPPNER: We've also neglected to find out what the quality and character of civic education is. We've neglected to participate in it on both sides. In any case, these, it seems to me, are the long- and short-term things one might be moved to do.

Ultimately, I hope with Roberta and Professor Almond that all of this would lead eventually to a re-energized linkage between partisan positions and the kinds of cleavages that do exist in the society. Roberta said there are no fundamental cleavages in the society. I disagree with her phrasing. I don't think she really meant that cleavages don't exist. What she meant to say was that the relevance of these cleavages to political action isn't clear to most people. The cleavages are there. It's a question of the parties representing contrasting positions on those cleavages. And they don't, they generally muddy the waters.

SIGEL: I would go further. There are some terrible cleavages, but people at the bottom of the totem pole have no chance of using the system. I'm much more cynical in that respect.

GASTIL: On that, there have been studies over the years that show that policy has been somewhat different under Republicans and Democrats in the last fifty years. One of the things that people need to be taught is to not be so interested in what's going to happen next year. One reason why Curtis was saying, and to some extent Roberta, that there isn't any choice this time—"The '88 election has no meaning"—was an overemphasis on short-term gains. In other words, if one thought in longer terms what it means to have Democrats in the White House and in Congress versus having Republicans, I think there is an actual difference.

KLEPPNER: But in your very phrasing you run counter to approximately 200 years of notions of value in this society. You're saying that people ought to value the party more than the candidate. I agree with that. But we're stuck with what I refer to in a very pejorative sort of way with the League of Women Voters' concept of what one ought to do. Namely, vote the candidate, not the party.

BENNETT: That's a value that is very widely subscribed to.

KLEPPNER: Of course it is. Probably it was a very influential one in terms of the older civic education, if not contemporary civic education. It's what the textbooks teach.

PENNIMAN: So much of the electoral process does deal with individuals, not with parties.

JENSEN: There are three levels that we are mixing up in this discussion. When the country was founded the founding fathers had a strong sense of what historians refer to as "republicanism." It's a sense of the importance of civic duty. This has been a motif through the whole conference; there's a sense that to be a citizen of the nation one ought to a) participate, and b) have a sense that one ought to participate. That was very much the enlightenment, our founding fathers', ideal. Nineteenth century politics were structured in quite a different fashion. Historians have recently been writing about the decline of republicanism and how it happened. The rise of a role-oriented political system. This is why I was talking about the "armies", or put it in Professor Almond's terms, the cost/benefit ratio, who benefits?

The founding fathers were talking about benefiting the nation. The nineteenth century machine-oriented, army-oriented politics was talking about benefiting your group, your social or religious group, your racial group, ethnic group, maybe a region, your labor union, your occupational group. A person's identity was suppressed —you voted as part of an army. The soldier doesn't fight for himself. He may fight for the nation. Much more likely he will fight for his buddies, for his group, for his team. That was the main motif of the strong, intense partisanship of the nineteenth century, fight for your group. That's closely related to the existence of the cleavages in society. The Europeans still have a much stronger sense of an identity with one's religious, class, geographical, ethnic, linguistic, or other group.

In the United States in the twentieth century, especially in the last ten or twenty years, we have strongly moved away from emphasis on groups and roles. Affirmative action is an excellent example of strongly insisting that age, sex, and especially race should not be taken into account, and have to be neutralized. Ethnicity has disappeared. Since 1960 religion has virtually disappeared as a powerful force in group identity. Religion is still powerful for individuals but as group identity, identifying as a Catholic and so on, it is vastly weaker. The only strong remaining identifier is race. And not among whites. Whites used to have a strong race identity in the United States. Only blacks do now—maybe some of the Asians, I'm not too clear about that. The sense of identification with class, ethnicity, religion, geographical region, sex, race, and with party has drastically declined. We've become much more individualistic than ever before.

The founding fathers say who benefits? The nation benefits. The nineteenth century says who benefits? Your group benefits. You should vote and participate to help your group. It may be your labor union, your ethnic group, and so forth. Today, who benefits? Yourself, and hardly anyone else. (General agreement.)

No one ever says the group anymore. And instead, why do we participate in government? What do I get out of it? The answer is the individual doesn't get very much out of it, and there's no way to rig the system whereby the individual gets very much. Change in basic values from the nation to the group to the individual is what's happened to us. The problem is on the benefit side, not on the cost side nearly as much. These are very deep basic social transformations. You can see it happening in other countries. You can see it happening in Russia of all places, causing a severe system crisis in that country right now. You can see it happening in most of Western Europe too. It is deeply ingrained. Nobody even talks about undoing it, for example, of going back and making your geographical region important. Fifty years ago in politics the state a person came from, a candidate's home district and what not, these were important issues. Now they are minor. Even in the case of Texas, it's not clear. We don't even talk about a candidate's religion anymore, although as late as 1960 that was a central issue. One voted in 1960 to put a Catholic in or keep him out, to express your group.

PENNIMAN: You're vastly exaggerating this for 1960. Of course, there were some Catholics who voted for Kennedy because he was a Catholic, and some who voted against him because he was, but this was surely not the majority.

JENSEN: I'm saying it was much stronger in 1960 than today. It was much stronger in 1928.

PENNIMAN: That's right.

JENSEN: Nineteen-sixty was the last time religion was a notable factor in American politics. Race remains today and only among blacks, as a remnant of a group sense. Why do blacks vote? "To express our racial unity and pride." And they do have that sense. And Jesse Jackson articulated that very well indeed. There are hardly any other groups like that.

PENNIMAN: The blacks need to win once, then it would cease to be a major issue. If in 1928 the Catholics had won, people wouldn't have worried about it anymore. After Kennedy, it ceased to be an issue because he didn't do anything different than one of another religion would have done.

GASTIL: I thought Richard's statement was right on target. It's a dismal picture in a way that doesn't lead easily to action. I wanted him to add to this if he had any thoughts as to how to reverse this course.

JENSEN: One thought is going back to that original civic sensibility—republicanism. What we should not try to do, and don't want to do, is go back to the group basis of nineteenth and early twentieth century politics. We're strongly moving away from that. The other alternative is going back to civic republicanism.

ALMOND: What about de Tocqueville's mid-nineteenth century idea of "self-interest rightly conceived" as a solution?

JENSEN: That's what people do. They see self-interest rightly conceived. America has always been more individualistic than other countries. It's just that we keep getting more and more individualistic. We keep stripping ourselves of these identities. The student movement was very dramatic in stripping class away. Thirty or forty years ago, the middle class dressed differently, talked differently, deliberately kept itself different. That class difference has drastically weakened as well.

GASTIL: Is there any going forward, Richard? There's always a problem in my mind about going back. Is it possible to go forward?

ALMOND: I think it would be along the lines of examining how one thinks about self-interest in a constructive way. There has to be the forward development of this notion of citizenship in the republican sense. That really ought to be the center of civic instruction. We need the elaboration of an argument as to why one should be concerned with voting and with civic participation, with recruiting the very best into the public service.

GASTIL: Howard, do you have some thoughts?

PENNIMAN: No. I don't get moved by these things as much as some people do. Voter turnout doesn't bother me in the way it bothers a lot of people. If we come to the point at which it's important to people, they will come out as they have at various times throughout our history. Voting sags back again when there isn't something that will bring people out. I do agree with Gabriel that if you could—I don't think you can, but at least it's worth trying—change the timing of elections, I would strongly support that.

ZIMMERMAN: Could I just toss in something a little bit from left field? Business has been trying to understand what allows Japan to focus human resources on discrete problems. Today, there is a lot of interest in stakeholder models and things like that. This still has the underlying character of individualism as a dominant driving interest, but it also involves a corporatist view very different from the traditional virtues in American business.

SIGEL: And they don't think of just today. I like the question you asked in the beginning about the short range versus long range. When they think now about competing with Japan, they don't ask themselves just about the minichips but they ask what's going to happen in the next ten or twenty years?

ZIMMERMAN: This goes back to your point and Gabriel's, about making the stakes visible. Trying through aggressive training and various kinds of mechanisms to define what the stakes are, to get people to change the discount rates a little bit if you want to use economic jargon. This would make the discussion more respectable than the purely exhortatory debate it was originally.

BENNETT: I'd like to pick up on the point Peter just made and add two thoughts very quickly. One, there is one aspect of all this that we have not really brought out very much, except Curtis when he talked about negative advertising on television. It is not coincidental that at the very time turnout has gone down since the early 1960s, people's patterns of media dependence for information about politics have changed fundamentally from print media and face-to-face contacts to television. Someone once said television does a wonderful job of covering politics, but does a lousy job covering government. Television is great at playing up Dan Quayle's problems with his resume, military service, and so on—or who's winning, who's losing. But it does a lousy job of conveying the deeper stakes that are present. Whether this is an unimportant election or an important election will make a difference to some people.

There have been some studies by Michael J. Robinson that show that the consequence of dependence on television for information is less and less participation and interest and more cynicism toward the political process. I agree so much with what you've said, we've got to reinvigorate that sense of civic responsibility. We'll have to do it through the schools, and that's going to be a slow process. We can start asking the media to play their role more constructively. They are operating in the area of civic responsibility, public necessity and convenience. We can ask them to start being a little more sensitive to what they can do in that regard. When you talk to members of the media they'll say yes, but how do we do it? And that's a good question.

ALMOND: That's a point that Curtis made earlier in private conversation. This was the absence of a journal of opinion that would be kind of a post-New Republic that would reach the American intelligentsia, including the media people.

SIGEL: The one program on television that tries to do this (Mac-Neil-Lehrer) has a much smaller audience than Dan Rather or any of the others.

ALMOND: But it's in the millions.

LEVINE: Yes, you know what we're really talking about is the necessity for specific myth making in a society that has gone to schools where teachers are behaviorally trained scientists who see their role as demystification and debunking. Then, after graduation, students get hit by a third layer, television. Well you know, bang, bang, bang, expose after expose. So the new generation takes a look at the whole thing, and they say it's junk. "It's all mythology. My father's generation got conned; I'm not going to be conned." And you get the "wise civic citizen". Can you ever go back and teach myth, make it respectable? That's the question.

ZIMMERMAN: We don't need to teach myths, we need to get in and teach appreciation. At Kennedy we have a curriculum that is heavily economic in its underlying disciplinary origins——after they've done econometrics and data analysis and decision analysis and modeling simulation, a year of microeconomic theory, we start to tell our students about how organizations of people work. Their first reaction is, "Oh, my God. It's all politics." They develop a premature cynicism, because it's a more subtle field in some ways. Human behavior is a more subtle field than number crunching abstractions. We work hard to try to give them appreciation for what's at stake.

BENNETT: One of the things you have to be careful about is that cynicism that is so on the cuff is an excuse to be apathetic and ignorant.

LEVINE: The free market and the efficiency of the American business firm or any business firm is so easy to teach in the abstract and so easy to grasp. Yet it has so little to do with what's really going on out there. But nobody asks that question. We do not have the equivalent behavioral study in openness in the private sectors, as we do of the public sector.

ZIMMERMAN: That sort of stuff in the private sector is much more governed by myths. The Lee Ioccocas and the Steven Jobs are mythical figures. You look in vain for the public sector equivalents. We look more closely at public leaders. All we can see is their warts and bumps.

BENNETT: I recall something that V. O. Key wrote in that great book, **American Democracy and Public Opinion,** in which he said that ultimately the success of democracy rests on belief in the myth. But he went on to say that those clerics who have the greatest degree of success in getting their supplicants to believe in the myths are those who every so often have a success. To put it into a sports metaphor, we've had many losing seasons, or too many seemingly losing seasons in American government and politics. We've fired managers and we've traded players around and we've changed the rules to let more of the amateurs play along with the pros. Yet, with the exception of that one very brief period in the second part of the early Reagan administration, carried on over into '85 and '86, the history of the last twenty-five years is not a happy one from the point of view of what the public sees.

Professor Almond asked the question, where has the trust gone? Well, compared to 1986, the 1987 general social survey (the NORC, or National Opinion Research Center, annual opinion survey) showed an evaporation of trust of about fifteen or twenty percent in the leadership of the executive branch. The interesting thing is that it also carried over and had an impact on the legislative branch and on the judiciary and the military, despite Ollie's doing well—that was a passing moment. It would be useful if we could convey, some of the successes along with the failures. There have been successes. We've done some things right. We tend not to tell that news. Well, maybe it should be.

ZIMMERMAN: Moving toward proscription, let me make one point. Myth making is an important part of it. The social sciences are not very comfortable with myth making, for many obvious reasons. We do know that participation has a self-reinforcing quality, whether it's volunteerism or whatever. One of the things going on on all these campuses is trying to wrestle with the individualistic—"I'll get it in 30 seconds from Dan Rather" view—the isolating impulse and trend. We're in the myth-making business to some extent. We've been going around looking at state and local governments. I think it would be worth thinking about how one might disaggregate this national problem. In most states most of the time, political action is on a level where people can identify plausibly with a housing program, a drug program, with programs to clean up the neighborhood—that particular neighborhood or that street corner. Maryland has passed or at least considered passing a law mandating some kind of active, voluntary activity for high school students outside school classroom activity. Some state legislatures have considered laws equivalent to the national public service legislation that's floating around. Pushing this to try to build habits of participation and to get people past the crudest kind of myths, and the crudest kind of individuals can make a difference.

There's nothing like showing a person that he or she can make a difference in at least one person's life. My wife is a public school teacher and she's had a number of years doing special education with kids. These are kids with very limited horizons and prospects. Me, I'm off talking to hundreds of people about more abstract ideas and

331

things like that, and I just feel like I'm dropping raindrops into big lakes in terms of trying to make a difference. But she's got a target rifle on one person and can really see a tangible difference. If there is a way to help people get that kind of experience, then you might begin to at least counteract the worst, the most divisive trends that Richard is talking about.

JENSEN: Peter, you're talking about micro, and I think you're right. And I'd say a word for macro solutions, too. One we have mentioned is patriotism. One of the interesting changes in the business environment is a strong, brand new sense of international competitiveness. We're no longer isolated. The Japanese scare the hell out of us. That's led to rather drastic changes and spills over into government. There was a trade bill last week. Historically patriotism has been a major sort of differentiation. It's often been tied into a cold war or hot war context. But today there's a strong sense in which the United States as an entity has to be competitive economically in the world. As the Europeans are moving, and the Japanese, and various other countries, there has developed a "we can't fall behind" attitude. This is basically a patriotic line of thought, but one that ties the individual's own long-term self-interest to the nation-state. That's one of the chief uses of patriotism. This is giving it an economic slant, but it could tie in with a lot of different things, with student exchange programs, for example. The best way for students to learn about the United States is to send them to some other country for six months. There is a small amount of movement in that direction. The business community and the financial community have taken the lead because they are in an international market like they've never experienced before.

ZIMMERMAN: They have gotten very sophisticated at blurring the patriotic line you are describing. I take it the burden of your argument would be to reinforce that. Sophisticated businesses, both Japanese and American, are blurring that line with acquisitions and stakes, both minority stakes and majority stakes. Japanese buying plants in America and that sort of thing blurs those lines. It's hard to decide who is benefiting. When you want to do the cost/benefit calculation you can't quite figure out where the costs and benefits line up.

332

JENSEN: The U.S. has lost its economic isolation. Our economy is increasingly integrated with Europe, Canada, and Japan. That means that decisions made in London, Toronto, or Tokyo affect us almost as much as those made in New York, Chicago, or San Francisco. One response—a dangerous one—is protectionism and nativism. You could see flashes of this in 1988 when Gephardt, Dukakis, and Bentsen attacked foreign ownership of American securities and factories. An antidote to economic nativism may appear as more Americans actually work for British-owned oil companies, Canadian real estate firms, or Japanese auto plants. I don't think this will blur anyone's sense of patriotism. It may add perspective to what it means to be an American.

GASTIL: Evaluating the costs and benefits of internationalizing the American economy to the structure of social identifications necessary for political participation will be as hard as analyzing the economic benefits for the country. But certainly whatever new myth making we might propose to help us recapture past levels of participation will only succeed if it takes into account this fundamental restructuring of economic relationships. With this thought we have certainly moved to a new "macro-level" of discussion. Perhaps this is just the right level to end on. Thank you all very much.

PART III

Country Summaries

INTRODUCTION

The following country descriptions summarize the evidence that lies behind our ratings for each country. They first bring together for each country most of the tabular material of Part I. Then, political rights are considered in terms of the extent to which a country is ruled by a government elected by the majority at the national level, the division of power among levels of government, and the possible denial of self-determination to major subnationalities, if any. While decentralization and the denial of group rights are deemphasized in our rating system, these questions are not ignored. The summaries also contain consideration of civil liberties, especially as these include freedom of the media and other forms of political expression, freedom from political imprisonment, torture, and other forms of government reprisal, and freedom from interference in nonpublic group or personal life. Equality of access to politically relevant expression is also considered, as well as economic conditions and organization in their relation to freedom. In some cases the summaries will touch on the relative degree of freedom from oppression outside the government arena, for example, through slavery, labor bosses, capitalist exploitation, or private terrorism: this area of analysis is little developed at present.

At the beginning of each summary statement the country is characterized by the forms of its economy and polity. The meanings of the terms used in this classification may be found in the discussion of the relation of political-economic systems to freedom and its accompanying Table 8. The classification is highly simplified, but it serves our concern with the developmental forms and biases that affect political controls. As in Table 8, the terms inclusive and noninclusive are used to distinguish between societies in which the economic activities of most people are organized in accordance with the dominant system and those dual societies in which they remain largely outside. The system should be assumed to be inclusive unless otherwise indicated.

Each state is categorized according to the political positions of the national or ethnic groups it contains. Since the modern political form is the "nation-state," it is not surprising that many states have a relatively homogeneous population. The overwhelming majority in these states belong to roughly the same ethnic group; people from this group naturally form the dominant group in the state. In relatively homogeneous states there is no large subnationality (that is, with more than one million people or twenty percent of the population) residing in a defined territory within the country: Austria, Costa Rica, Somalia, and West Germany are good examples. States in this category may be ethnically diverse (for example, Cuba or Colombia), but there are no sharp ethnic lines between major groups. These states should be distinguished from ethnically complex states, such as Guyana or Singapore, that have several ethnic groups, but no major group that has its historic homeland in a particular part of the country. Complex states may have large minorities that have suffered social, political, or economic discrimination in the recent past, but today the governments of such states treat all peoples as equals as a matter of policy. In this regard complex states are distinguishable from ethnic states with major nonterritorial subnationalities, for the governments of such states have a deliberate policy of giving preference to the dominant ethnic group at the expense of other major groups. Examples have been Burundi or China (Taiwan).

Another large category of states is labeled ethnic states with (a) major territorial subnationalities(y). As in the homogeneous states there is a definite ruling people (or Staatsvolk) residing on its historic national territory within the state. But the state also incorporates other territories with other historic peoples that are now either without a state, or the state dominated by their people lies beyond the new border. As explained in Freedom in the World 1978 (pp. 180-218), to be considered a subnationality a territorial minority must have enough cohesion and publicity that their right to nationhood is acknowledged in some quarters. Often recent events have forged a quasi-unity among quite distinct groups—as among the peoples of southern Sudan. Typical countries in this category are Burma and the USSR. Ethnic states with major potential territorial subnationalities fall into a closely related category. In such states—for example, Ecuador or Bolivia—many individuals in prenational ethnic groups have merged, with little overt hostility, with the dominant ethnic strain. The assimilation process has gone on for centuries. Yet in these countries the new consciousness that accompanies the diffusion of nationalistic ideas through education may reverse the process of assimilation in the future, especially where the potential subnationality has preserved a more or less definable territorial base.

There are a few truly multinational states in which ethnic groups with territorial bases coexist in one state without an established ruling people. In such states the several "nations" normally have autonomous political rights, although these do not in law generally include the right to secession. India and Nigeria (when under civilian rule) are examples. One trinational and a few binational states complete the categories of those states in which several "nations" coexist.

The distinction between truly multinational states and ethnic states with territorial subnationalities may be made by comparing two major states that lie close to the margin between the categories—the ethnic Russian USSR and multinational India. In the USSR, Russian has been in every way the dominant language. By contrast, in India Hindi speakers have not achieved dominance. English remains a unifying lingua franca, the languages of the several states have not been forced to change their script to accord with Hindi forms, and Hindi itself is not the distinctive language of a "ruling people"—it is a nationalized version of the popular language of a portion of the population of northern India. (The pre-British ruling class used a closely related language with Arabic, Persian, and Turkish infusions; it was generally written in Persian-Arabic script.) Unlike Russians in the non-Russian Soviet Republics, Hindi speakers from northern India do not have a special standing in their own eyes or those of other Indians. Calcutta, Bombay, and Madras are non-Hindi speaking cities, and their pride in their identities and cultures is an important aspect of Indian culture. By contrast, many officially non-Russian Soviet Republics have been dominated by Russian speakers. As with much else in the Soviet Union, this situation may be changing, at least in some Republics.

Finally, transethnic heterogeneous states, primarily in Africa, are those in which independence found a large number of ethnically distinct peoples grouped more or less artificially within one political framework. The usual solution was for those taking over the reins of government to adopt the colonial approach of formally treating all local peoples as equal, but with the new objective of integrating all

339

equally into a new national framework (and new national identity) as and when this would be possible. Rulers of states such as Senegal or Zaire may come from relatively small tribes, and it is in their interest to deemphasize tribalism. In some cases the tribes are so scattered and localistic that there is no short-term likelihood of secession resulting from tribalism. However, in other cases portions of the country have histories of separate nationhood making the transethnic solution hard to implement. In a few countries recent events have placed certain ethnic groups in opposition to one another or to ruling circles in such a way that the transethnic state remains only the formal principle of rule, replaced in practice by an ethnic hierarchy, as in Cameroon, Togo, or Zimbabwe.

The descriptive paragraphs for political and civil rights are largely self-explanatory. Subnationalities are generally discussed under a subheading for political rights, although the subject has obvious civil liberties aspects. Discussion of the existence or nonexistence of political parties may be arbitrarily placed in one or the other section. These paragraphs only touch on a few relevant issues, especially in the civil liberties discussion. An issue may be omitted for lack of information, because it does not seem important for the country addressed, or because a particular condition can be inferred from the general statement of a pattern. It should be noted that we have tried where possible to incorporate the distinction between a broad definition of political prisoners (including those detained for violent political crimes) and a narrow definition that includes those arrested only for nonviolent actions—often labeled "prisoners of conscience." Obviously we are primarily concerned with the latter.

Under civil liberties there is often a sentence or two on the economy. However, this is primarily a survey of politically relevant freedoms and not economic freedoms. In addition our view of economic freedom depends less on the economic system than the way in which it is adopted and maintained. (See Lindsay M. Wright, "A Comparative Survey of Economic Freedoms," in Freedom in the World 1982, pages 51-90.)

At the end of each country summary we have included an overall comparative statement that places the country's ratings in relation to those of others. Countries chosen for comparison are often neighboring or similar ones, but juxtaposing very different countries is also necessary for tying together the system.

Human rights, in so far as they are not directly connected with political and civil liberties, are given little attention in the following summaries. Capital punishment, torture, denial of refugee status, or food and medical care are issues that are less emphasized in this treatment than they would be in a human rights report. The summaries take little account of the oppressions that occur within the social units of a society, such as family and religious groups, or that reflect variations in the nonpolitical aspects of culture. The reader will note few references in the following summaries to the relative freedom of women. Democracies today have almost universally opened political and civic participation to women on at least a formal basis of equality, while most nondemocratic societies that deny these equal rights to women also deny effective participation to most men. In such societies granting equal rights has limited meaning. There is little gain for political and most civil rights when women are granted equal participation in a totalitarian society. For a rating system relating to women's rights see Table 10 above.

AFGHANISTAN

Economy: noninclusive socialist
Polity: communist one-party
Population: 14,500,000 (est.)*

Political Rights: 6
Civil Liberties: 6
Freedom Rating: 12

An ethnic state with major territorial subnationalities

Political Rights. Afghanistan's ruling communist party is show-ing faint signs of emerging from under the tutelage and direct control of the Soviet Union. An attempt has been made to hold legislative elections and consultative assemblies to add legitimacy, but with little success. The rule of this very small party has no electoral or traditional legitimization. Soviet and government forces controlled the major cities in 1988, but their control is con-tested by a variety of resistance movements throughout the country. In many areas local administration is in the hands of traditional or ad hoc resistance leaders. This anarchical situation provides a degree of local self-determination. Subnationalities: The largest minority is the Tajik (thirty percent), the dominant people of the cities and the western part of the country. Essentially lowland Per-sians, their language remains the lingua franca of the country. The Persian speaking Hazaras constitute five to ten percent of the population. Another ten percent belong to Uzbek and other Turkish groups in the north.

Civil Liberties. In government-controlled areas the media are primarily government owned and controlled. Antigovernment organ-ization or expression is forbidden. Limited discussion of alternatives occurs, especially in transitional or neutral areas. In a condition of civil war and foreign occupation, political imprisonment, torture and execution have been common, in addition to war deaths and massa-cres. Resources have been diverted to the Soviet Union as payment for its military "assistance".

Comparatively: Afghanistan is as free as Djibouti, less free than Iran, freer than Iraq.

-----

* Most population estimates are based on data from Population Reference Bureau, Washington, DC, 1988. Especially doubtful population totals, such as Afghanistan's, are followed by (est.). Several million Afghanistanis are refugees in Pakistan and Iran.

A L B A N I A

Economy: socialist
Polity: communist one-party
Population: 3,100,000

Political Rights: 7
Civil Liberties: 7
Freedom Rating: 14

A relatively homogeneous population

Political Rights. Albania is a traditional Marxist-Leninist dicta-torship. While there are a number of elected bodies, including an assembly, the parallel government of the communist party (4.5 percent of the people) is decisive at all levels; elections offer only one list of candidates. Candidates are officially designated by the Democratic Front, to which all Albanians are supposed to belong. In recent years extensive purges within the party have maintained the power of the top leaders.

Civil Liberties. Press, radio, and television are completely under government or party control, and communication with the outside world is minimal. Media are characterized by incessant propaganda, and open expression of opinion in private conversation may lead to long prison sentences. There is an explicit denial of the right to freedom of thought for those who disagree with the govern-ment. Imprisonment for reasons of conscience is common; torture is frequently reported, and execution is invoked for many reasons. All religious institutions were abolished in 1967; religion is outlawed; priests are regularly imprisoned. Apparently there are no private organizations independent of government or party. Only party leaders live well. Most people are required to work one month of each year in factories or on farms; there are no private cars. Attempting to leave the state is a major crime. Private economic choice is minimal.

Comparatively: Albania is as free as Cambodia, less free than Yugoslavia.

A L G E R I A

Economy: socialist
Polity: socialist one-party
Population: 23,000,000

Political Rights: 5
Civil Liberties: 6
Freedom Rating: 11

343

An ethnic state with a potential subnationality

Political Rights. Algeria has combined military dictatorship with one-party socialist rule. Elections at both local and national levels are managed by the party; they allow little opposition to the system, although choice among individuals is encouraged. Late 1988 saw demonstrations that forced a referendum, real discussion and voting in parliament and considerable revamping of the system. Subnationalities: Fifteen to twenty percent of the people are Berbers, who have demonstrated a desire for enhanced self-determination.

Civil Liberties. Opposition expression is controlled and foreign publications are closely watched, but the government media have become increasingly critical. Private conversation appears relatively open. Although not fully independent, the regular judiciary has established a rule of law in some areas. Demonstrations and human rights discussion have emerged in spite of attempted repressions. Many prisoners of conscience are detained for short periods; a few for longer terms. There are no appeals from the decisions of special courts for state security and economic crimes. Land reform has transformed former French plantations into collectives. Although the government is socialist, the private sector has received increasing emphasis. Travel is generally free. Eighty percent of the people are illiterate; many are still very poor, but extremes of wealth have been reduced. The right to association is limited; unions have slight freedom. Islam's continued strength provides a counterweight to governmental absolutism. There is freedom of religious worship.

Comparatively: Algeria is as free as Kuwait, freer than Iraq, less free than Morocco.

ANGOLA

Economy: noninclusive socialist
Polity: socialist one-party
Population: 8,200,000

Political Rights: 7
Civil Liberties: 7
Freedom Rating: 14

A transethnic heterogeneous state with major subnationalities

Political Rights. Angola is ruled by a small, elitist, Marxist-Leninist party, relying heavily on Soviet equipment and Cuban troops to dominate the civil war and to stay in power. The parliament is elected, but the party controls the selection of candidates. Subnationalities: The party is not tribalist, but is opposed by groups relying on particular tribes or regions—especially in Cabinda, the northeast, and the south-central areas. The UNITA movement, strongest among the Ovimbundu people, actively controls much of the south and east of the country.

Civil Liberties. The nation remains in a state of war, with power arbitrarily exercised, particularly in the countryside. The media in controlled areas are government owned and do not deviate from its line. Political imprisonment and execution are common; repression of religious activity has moderated, and church leaders speak out on political and social issues. Travel is tightly restricted. Private medical care has been abolished, as has much private property—especially in the modern sectors. Strikes are prohibited and unions tightly controlled. Agricultural production is held down by peasant opposition to socialization and lack of markets.

Comparatively: Angola is as free as Mongolia, less free than Zambia.

ANTIGUA AND BARBUDA

Economy: capitalist
Polity: centralized multiparty
Population: 82,000

Political Rights: 2
Civil Liberties: 3
Freedom Rating: 5

A relatively homogeneous population

Political Rights. Antigua is a parliamentary democracy with an elected house and appointed senate. The opposition's inability to compete may indicate deficiencies in the electoral or campaign system. Corruption and nepotism are problems of the government. The secessionist island of Barbuda has achieved special rights to limited self-government.

Civil Liberties. Newspapers are published by opposing political parties, but an opposition paper has been repeatedly harassed, especially by libel cases. Radio and television are either owned by the state or the prime minister's family—both have been charged with favoritism. The effectiveness of the rule of law is enhanced by an inter-island court of appeals for Antigua and five of the other small former British colonies in the Antilles. Rights to organization and demonstration are respected; unions are free, have the right to strike, and are politically influential.

Comparatively: Antigua and Barbuda is as free as India, freer than Guyana, less free than Dominica.

A R G E N T I N A

Economy: capitalist-statist
Polity: centralized multiparty
Population: 32,000,000

Political Rights: 2
Civil Liberties: 1
Freedom Rating: 3

A relatively homogeneous population

Political Rights. Argentina has a functioning constitutional democracy under a strong president. The president is elected by electors, but as in the United States it is essentially a direct election. Two successful elections and the well-publicized trials of the country's previous military junta leaders for murder and torture have exemplified democratic rule. Yet continued worry about the military reduces the government's options. Elected provincial governments show increasing independence.

Civil Liberties. Private newspapers and both private and government broadcasting stations operate. The media freely express varying opinions. The government has used the broadcasting media to serve its purposes, but only in exceptional circumstances. Political parties organize dissent, and public demonstrations are frequent. Courts are independent. The church and trade unions play a strong political role. Human rights organizations are active. The economy includes a large government sector.

Comparatively: Argentina is as free as Finland, freer than Bolivia, less free than Costa Rica.

AUSTRALIA

Economy: capitalist
Polity: decentralized multiparty
Population: 16,500,000

Political Rights: 1
Civil Liberties: 1
Freedom Rating: 2

A relatively homogeneous population with small aboriginal groups

Political Rights. Australia is a federal parliamentary democracy with strong powers retained by its component states. With equal representation from each state, the Senate provides a counterbalance to the House of Representatives. The British-appointed governor-general retains some power in constitutional deadlocks. Constitutional referendums add to the power of the voters. The states have separate parliaments and premiers, but appointed governors. Corporatist tendencies exist in the close relationship of business, government, and labor. The self-determination rights of the aborigines are recognized through limited self-administration and return of property; recently, the rights of Torres Straits Melanesians have also become an issue.

Civil Liberties. All newspapers and most radio and television stations are privately owned. The Australian Broadcasting Commission operates government radio and television stations on a basis similar to BBC. As in the UK, strict libel laws can restrict discussion. Freedom of assembly is generally respected, although it varies by region. Freedom of choice in education, travel, occupation, property, and private association are perhaps as complete as anywhere in the world. Relatively low taxes enhance this freedom.

Comparatively: Australia is as free as the United Kingdom, freer than France.

AUSTRIA

Economy: mixed capitalist
Polity: centralized multiparty
Population: 7,600,000

Political Rights: 1
Civil Liberties: 1
Freedom Rating: 2

A relatively homogeneous population

Political Rights. Austria's parliamentary system has a directly elected lower house and an upper (and less powerful) house elected by the provincial assemblies. The president is directly elected, but the chancellor (representing the majority party or parties in parliament) is the center of political power. The two major parties have alternated control since the 1950s, but the government often seeks broad consensus. In 1987 it was again governed by a "grand coalition" of the two major parties. The referendum is used on rare occasions. The provinces have popularly elected governors and legislatures. Subnationalities: Fifty thousand Slovenes in the southern part of the country have rights to their own schools.

Civil Liberties. The press in Austria is free and varied, although foreign pressures have exceptionally led to interference. Radio and television are under a state-owned corporation that by law is supposed to be free of political control. Its geographical position and constitutionally defined neutral status places its media and government in a position analogous to Finland's, but the Soviets have put less pressure on Austria to conform to Soviet wishes than on Finland. The rule of law is secure, and there are no political prisoners. Banks and heavy industry are largely nationalized.

Comparatively: Austria is as free as Belgium, freer than Greece.

BAHAMAS

Economy: capitalist-statist
Polity: centralized multiparty
Population: 245,000

Political Rights: 2
Civil Liberties: 3
Freedom Rating: 5

A relatively homogeneous population

Political Rights. The Bahamas have a parliamentary system with a largely ceremonial British governor-general. The House is elective and the senate appointed. The ruling party has a large majority, but there is an opposition in parliament. Government power is maintained in part by discrimination in favor of supporters and control over the broadcast media. There has not been a change in government since independence. Most islands are administered by centrally appointed commissioners. There is no army.

Civil Liberties. Independent and outspoken newspapers are constrained by strict libel laws. The Speaker of the House has, on occasion, compelled the press not to print certain materials. Radio and television are government owned and often fail to disseminate opposition viewpoints. Labor and business organization are generally free; there is a right to strike. A program of Bahamianization is being promoted in several sectors of the economy. Rights of travel, occupation, education, and religion are secure. Corruption is widely alleged, and may reach the highest governmental levels.

Comparatively: Bahamas is as free as India, freer than Mexico, less free than Barbados.

BAHRAIN

Economy: capitalist-statist
Polity: traditional nonparty
Population: 442,000

Political Rights: 5
Civil Liberties: 5
Freedom Rating: 10

The citizenry is relatively homogeneous

Political Rights. Bahrain is a traditional shaikhdom with a modernized administration. A former British police officer still directs the security services. Direct access to the ruler is encouraged. The legislature is dissolved, but powerful merchant and religious families place a check on royal power. There are local councils. Subnationalities: The primary ethnic problem has been the struggle between the Iranians who once ruled and the Arabs who now rule; in part this is reflected in the opposition of the Sunni and majority Shi'a Muslim sects.

Civil Liberties. The largely private press seldom criticizes government policy. Radio and television are government owned. There is considerable freedom of expression in private, but informers are feared. Rights to assembly and demonstration are limited, but a human rights organization functions. The legal and educational systems are a mixture of traditional Islamic and British; the population has a high literacy rate. Short-term arrest is used to discourage dissent, and there are long-term political prisoners. In security cases involving violence, fair and quick trials are delayed and torture occurs. Rights to travel, property, and religious choice

349

Comparative Survey

are secured. There is a record of disturbances by worker groups, and union organization is restricted. Many free social services are provided. Citizenship is very hard to obtain; there is antipathy to foreign workers (but unlike neighboring shaikhdoms most people in the country are citizens).

Comparatively: Bahrain is as free as Guyana, freer than Saudi Arabia, less free than India.

BANGLADESH

Economy: noninclusive
    capitalist-statist
Polity: centralized dominant-party
    (military dominated)
Population: 109,500,000

Political Rights: 4

Civil Liberties: 5

Freedom Rating: 9

An ethnically and religiously complex state

Political Rights. Bangladesh has a military-dominated political and economic system. Political parties are active. Parliamentary and presidential elections have been seriously marred by violence, widespread abstention, and government interference. Local elective institutions are functioning, and have been expanded by well-contested subdistrict level elections. Subnationalities: Non-Muslim hill tribes have been driven from their lands, tortured, and killed.

Civil Liberties. The press is largely private and party. The papers are intermittently censored, and there is pervasive self-censorship through both government subsidy and pressure. International news is closely controlled. Radio and television are government controlled, but are not actively used for mobilization. In a violent context, there have been recurrent executions and imprisonments, and considerable brutality. Opposition leaders are frequently detained, but there are few if any long-term prisoners of conscience. Political parties organize and mobilize the expression of opposition, and large rallies are frequently held—and as frequently banned. Civilian courts can decide against the government, but judicial tenure is insecure. In spite of considerable communal antipathy, religious freedom exists. Travel is generally unrestricted. Although they do not have the right to strike, labor unions are active and strikes occur. Over half of the rural population are laborers or tenant farmers; some illegal land confiscation by local groups has been reported. The country is plagued by continuing large-scale corruption and extreme poverty.

Comparatively: Bangladesh is as free as Morocco, freer than Burma, less free than Indonesia.

BARBADOS

Economy: capitalist
Polity: centralized multiparty
Population: 252,000

Political Rights: 1
Civil Liberties: 1
Freedom Rating: 2

A relatively homogeneous population

Political Rights. Barbados is governed by a parliamentary system, with a ceremonial British governor-general. Elections have been fair and well administered. Power alternates between the two major parties. Public opinion has a direct and powerful effect on policy. Local governments are also elected.

Civil Liberties. Newspapers are private and free of censorship. Both the private and government radio stations are largely free; the only television station is organized on the BBC model. There is an independent judiciary, and general freedom from arbitrary government action. Travel, residence, and religion are free. Although both major parties rely on the support of labor, private property is fully accepted.

Comparatively: Barbados is as free as Costa Rica, freer than Jamaica.

BELGIUM

Economy: capitalist
Polity: decentralized multiparty
Population: 9,900,000

Political Rights: 1
Civil Liberties: 1
Freedom Rating: 2

A binational state

Political Rights. Belgium is a constitutional monarchy with a bicameral parliament. Elections lead to coalition governments, generally of the center. Continual instability due to linguistic controversies has enhanced the power of the bureaucracy. Subnationalities: The rise of nationalism among the two major peoples —Flemish and Walloon—has led to increasing transfer of control over cultural affairs to the communal groups. However, provincial governors are appointed by the national government.

Civil Liberties. Newspapers are free and uncensored. Radio and television are government owned, but independent boards are responsible for programming. The full spectrum of private rights is respected; voting is compulsory. Property rights, worker rights, and religious freedom are guaranteed.

Comparatively: Belgium is as free as Switzerland, freer than France.

B E L I Z E

Economy: capitalist	Political Rights: 1
Polity: centralized multiparty	Civil Liberties: 2
Population: 168,000	Freedom Rating: 3

An ethnically complex state

Political Rights. Belize is a parliamentary democracy with an elected house and indirectly elected senate. The governor-general retains considerable power. Elections are competitive and fair. Competitive local elections are also a part of the system. However, the increasing identification of parties with the two main ethnic groups is bringing new bitterness to the political system. A small British military force remains because of non-recognition by Guatemala.

Civil Liberties. The press is generally free and varied. Radio is government controlled and may not be fair in time allotments to opposition. Television is private, diverse, but may be interfered with. Organization and assembly are guaranteed, as is the rule of law. The opposition is well organized, and can win in the courts. However, harassment of the opposition occurs; a newspaper has been silenced by litigation. Private cooperatives have been formed in several agricultural industries. Unions are independent and diverse; strikes have been used to gain benefits.

Comparatively: Belize is as free as Venezuela, freer than Honduras, less free than Costa Rica.

BENIN

Economy: noninclusive socialist

Political Rights: 7

Polity: socialist one-party
(military dominated)

Civil Liberties: 7

Population: 4,500,000

Freedom Rating: 14

A transethnic heterogeneous state

Political Rights. Benin is a military dictatorship buttressed by a one-party organization. Regional and tribal loyalties may be stronger than national. Elections are single list, with no opposition. Local assemblies are closely controlled.

Civil Liberties. All media are rigidly censored; most are owned by the government. Opposition is not tolerated; criticism of the government often leads to a few days of reeducation in military camps. There are few long-term political prisoners, but the rule of law is very weak. Detainees are mistreated. Private schools have been closed. Although there is general freedom of religion, some sects have been forbidden. Independent labor unions are banned. Permission to leave the country is closely controlled. Economically, the government's interventions have been in cash crops and external trade, and industries have been nationalized; control over the largely subsistence and small entrepreneur economy remains incomplete. Widespread corruption aggravates already large income disparities.

Comparatively: Benin is as free as Iraq, less free than Zimbabwe.

BHUTAN

Economy: preindustrial

Political Rights: 5

Polity: traditional nonparty

Civil Liberties: 5

Population: 1,500,000

Freedom Rating: 10

Comparative Survey

An ethnic state with a significant subnationality

Political Rights. Bhutan is a hereditary monarchy in which the king rules with the aid of a council and an indirectly elected National Assembly. There are no legal political parties, and the Assembly does little more than approve government actions. Villages are traditionally ruled by their own headmen, but districts are directly ruled from the center. The Buddhist hierarchy is still very important in the affairs of the country. Bhutan remains heavily under Indian influence in defense, foreign policy, and other areas. Subnationalities: The main political party operates outside the country, agitating in favor of the Nepalese and democracy. Although they may now be a majority, the Nepalese are restricted to one part of the country.

Civil Liberties. The only papers are government and private weeklies. There are many small broadcasting stations. Outside media are freely available. There are few if any prisoners of conscience. No organized opposition exists within the country. The legal structure exhibits a mixture of traditional and British forms. There is religious freedom and freedom to travel. Traditional agriculture, crafts, and trade dominate the economy.

Comparatively: Bhutan is as free as Bahrain, freer than Swaziland, less free than Nepal.

BOLIVIA

Economy: noninclusive capitalist-statist	Political Rights: 2
Polity: centralized multiparty	Civil Liberties: 3
Population: 6,900,000	Freedom Rating: 5

An ethnic state with major potential subnationalities

Political Rights. Bolivia is a parliamentary democracy with a directly elected president. The traditional power of the military and security services has been curtailed, but not eliminated. Union power expressed through massive strikes has become a major challenge. Provincial and local government is controlled from the center. Subnationalities: Over sixty percent of the people are

Indians speaking Aymara or Quechua; these languages have been given official status alongside Spanish. The Indian peoples remain, however, more potential than actual subnationalities. The Spanish-speaking minority still controls the political process.

Civil Liberties. The press and most radio stations are private and are now largely free. But fear remains in the presence of private security forces and mob action; torture has occurred. The Catholic Church retains a powerful and critical role. The people are overwhelmingly post-land reform, subsistence agriculturists. The major mines and much of industry are nationalized; the workers have a generous social welfare program, given the country's poverty. While union leaders are frequently ousted, this results more from the often violent political struggle of union and government than from the simple repression of dissent.

Comparatively: Bolivia is as free as India, freer than Guyana, less free than Venezuela.

BOTSWANA

Economy: noninclusive capitalist
Polity: decentralized multiparty
Population: 1,300,000

Political Rights: 2
Civil Liberties: 3
Freedom Rating: 5

A relatively homogeneous population

Political Rights. The republican system of Botswana combines traditional and modern principles. The assembly is elected for a fixed term and appoints the president who rules. There is also an advisory House of Chiefs. Nine district councils, led either by chiefs or elected leaders, have independent power of taxation, as well as traditional control over land and agriculture. Elections continue to be won overwhelmingly by the ruling party, as they were before independence, yet there are opposition members in parliament and the opposition controls town councils. There is economic and political pressure from both black African and white neighbors. Subnationalities: The country is divided among several major tribes belonging to the Batswana people, as well as minor peoples on the margins. The latter include a few hundred relatively wealthy white farmers.

Civil Liberties. The radio and the daily paper are government owned; there are private and party papers. Opposition party and foreign publications are available. However, 1987 saw an opposition editor arrested on vague charges. Courts appear independent. Rights of assembly, religion, and travel are respected but regulated. Passport controls may be restrictive, and have been applied in the past to the opposition. Prisoners of conscience are not held. Unions are independent, but under pressure. In the modern society civil liberties appear to be guaranteed, but most people continue to live under traditional rules. (Government support is firmest in rural areas of great inequality.)

Comparatively: Botswana is as free as Cyprus (T), freer than Gambia, less free than Mauritius.

B R A Z I L

Economy: capitalist–statist
Polity: decentralized multiparty
Population: 144,400,000

Political Rights: 2
Civil Liberties: 3
Freedom Rating: 5

A complex but relatively homogeneous population with many very small, territorial subnationalities

Political Rights. Although still in a transitional stage, in which the president has not been directly elected, the fully open process by which he came to power was effectively democratic. The legislature is popularly elected. The military remains politically powerful. Political party activity is free, but political power depends on individuals. There are independently organized elected governments at both state and local levels. Subnationalities: The many small Indian groups of the interior are under both private and governmental pressure on their lands, culture, and even lives.

Civil Liberties. The media are private, except for a few broadcasting stations. The powerful and critical press is free of censorship, however government control of most industry, and thus advertising, limits freedom to criticize government. While radio and television are generally free, government control of access during campaigns has been criticized. Private concentration in the media, in the absence of a tradition of neutrality, may limit full freedom.

Rights of assembly and organization are recognized, and prisoners of conscience are not held. Massive opposition demonstrations have become a recent feature of political life. Private violence against criminals, suspected communists, peasants, and Indians continues outside the law. The courts are beginning to move actively against officers and others accused of killing or corruption. Union organization is powerful and strikes are widespread, though sometimes repressed. In spite of large-scale government ownership of industry, rights to property are respected. Freedom of religion, travel, and education exists. Extreme regional, class, and racial differences in living standards continue to imperil democracy.

Comparatively: Brazil is as free as India, freer than Mexico, less free than Argentina.

BRUNEI

Economy: capitalist-statist
Polity: monarchy
Population: 236,000

Political Rights: 6
Civil Liberties: 6
Freedom Rating: 12

An ethnic state with a major nonterritorial subnationality

Political Rights. Brunei is ruled in the traditional manner as an absolute monarchy with little delegation of authority. The cabinet is dominated by the Sultan and his relatives. Religious questions are decided by the government's religious department. Considerable reliance on the military forces and advice of the United Kingdom and Singapore continues.

Civil Liberties. Little or no dissent is allowed in the nation's strictly censored media. Radio and television and a major paper are government owned. However, many students attend schools overseas, and foreign media of all kinds are widely available. Opposition parties are dissolved, their leaders jailed. Formally the judicial system is patterned on the English model. The position of Chinese non-citizens (many long-term residents) has declined since independence. All land is government owned, as is most of the oil wealth.

Comparatively: Brunei is as free as Laos, freer than Vietnam, less free than Indonesia.

BULGARIA

Economy: socialist
Polity: communist one-party
Population: 9,000,000

Political Rights: 7
Civil Liberties: 7
Freedom Rating: 14

A relatively homogeneous population

Political Rights. Bulgaria is governed by its Communist Party, although the facade of a parallel government and two-party system is maintained. The same man has essentially ruled over the system since 1954; elections at both national and local levels have little meaning, but have recently allowed the local election of individuals in neither party. Soviet influence in the security services is decisive. Subnationalities: The government has destroyed the cultural identity of Muslim and other minorities.

Civil Liberties. All media are under absolute control by the government or its Party branches. Citizens have few if any rights against the state. There are hundreds or thousands of prisoners of conscience, many living under severe conditions. Brutality and torture are common. Those accused of opposition to the system may also be banished to villages, denied their occupations, or confined in psychiatric hospitals. Believers are subject to discrimination. Hundreds have been killed in enforcing name changes. Citizens have little choice of occupation or residence. Political loyalty is required to secure many social benefits. The most common political crimes are illegally trying to leave the country, criticism of the government, and illegal contacts with foreigners. However, there have been openings through a new spirit of independence and attempts at deconcentration in the economic sphere.

Comparatively: Bulgaria is as free as Mongolia, less free than Hungary.

B U R K I N A   F A S O
(UPPER VOLTA)

Economy: noninclusive mixed
    socialist
Polity: military nonparty
Population: 8,000,000 (est.)

Political Rights: 7

Civil Liberties: 6

Freedom Rating: 13

A transethnic heterogeneous state

Political Rights. The country remains under dictatorial military government, accompanied by experiments in mass organization.

Civil Liberties. The media are government-controlled means of indoctrination. Censorship is the rule, although private criticism remains common. Government opponents are imprisoned. External travel is restricted. The economy remains dependent on subsistence agriculture, with the government playing the role of regulator and promoter of development. Unions may have limited independence.

Comparatively: Burkina Faso is as free as Congo, freer than Albania, less free than Sierra Leone.

B U R M A

Economy: noninclusive mixed
    socialist
Polity: socialist one-party
    (military dominated)
Population: 41,100,000

Political Rights: 7

Civil Liberties: 6

Freedom Rating: 13

An ethnic state with major territorial subnationalities

Political Rights. Although shaken by rebellion in 1988, Burma remains governed by a small military elite. Elections have been held at both national and local levels: the "former" ruling party chose the slate of candidates. By fall 1988, the ostensibly new military regime appeared transitional, but the promised free elections seemed unlikely to occur. Subnationalities: The government represents essentially the Burmese people that live in the heartland of the country. The Burmese are surrounded by millions of non-

Burmese living in continuing disaffection or active revolt. Among the minorities on the periphery are the Karens, Shan, Kachins, Mon, and Chin. Many Muslims have been expelled, encouraged to leave, or imprisoned indefinitely.

Civil Liberties. All media are government owned; both domestic and foreign publications are censored. The media are expected to actively promote government policy. Massive arrests have brought the Buddhist hierarchy under control. During and after the 1988 revolt hundreds were killed, yet in spite of massive repression a slight increase in free expression appeared to be achieved by the time it was over. Racial discrimination has been incorporated in government policy. Emigration or even travel outside the country is very difficult. Living standards have progressively declined as the country falls into ruin.

Comparatively: Burma is as free as Vietnam, freer than North Korea, less free than Bangladesh.

BURUNDI

Economy: noninclusive mixed capitalist	Political Rights: 7
Polity: socialist one–party (military dominated)	Civil Liberties: 6
Population: 5,200,000	Freedom Rating: 13

An ethnic state with a major, nonterritorial subnationality

Political Rights. Burundi is under military rule. Subnationalities: The rulers and nearly all military officers continue to be from the Tutsi ethnic group (fifteen percent) that has traditionally ruled; their dominance has been reinforced by massacres of Hutus (eighty-five percent). However, in late 1988 after another massacre, many Hutus were appointed to the cabinet as a gesture of reconciliation.

Civil Liberties. The media are all government controlled and closely censored, as are often the foreign media. Lack of freedom of political speech or assembly is accompanied by political imprisonment and reports of brutality. Under current conditions there is little guarantee of individual rights, particularly for the

Hutu majority. However, in recent years the exclusion of the Hutu from public services, the Party, and other advantages has been relaxed. There are no independent unions, but short wildcat strikes have been reported. Traditional group and individual rights persist on the village level: Burundi is not a highly structured modern society. Travel is relatively unrestricted. Although officially socialist, private or traditional economic forms predominate.

Comparatively: Burundi is as free as Czechoslovakia, freer than Somalia, less free than Kenya.

CAMBODIA

Economy: noninclusive socialist
Polity: communist one-party
Population: 6,700,000 (est.)

Political Rights: 7
Civil Liberties: 7
Freedom Rating: 14

A relatively homogeneous population

Political Rights. Cambodia is divided between the remnants of the Pol Pot tyranny and a less tyrannical, Marxist-Leninist regime imposed by the Vietnamese. Although the Vietnamese have reestablished a degree of civilized life, the people have little part in either regime. More democratic rebel groups also exist.

Civil Liberties. The media continue to be completely controlled in both areas; outside publications are rigorously controlled, and there are no daily papers. Political execution has been a common function of government. Reeducation for war captives is again practiced by the new government. There is no rule of law; private freedoms are not guaranteed. Buddhist practices are again allowed. Cambodians continue to be one of the world's most tyrannized peoples. At least temporarily much of economic life has been decollectivized.

Comparatively: Cambodia is as free as Mongolia, less free than Indonesia.

C A M E R O O N

Economy: noninclusive capitalist

Polity: nationalist one-party

Population: 10,500,000

Political Rights: 6

Civil Liberties: 6

Freedom Rating: 12

A transethnic heterogeneous state with a major subnationality

Political Rights. Cameroon is a one-party state ruled by the same party since independence in 1960. The government has steadily centralized power. Referendums and other elections have little meaning; all candidacies must be approved by the ruling party; campaigns must avoid policy issues. Provincial governors are appointed by the central government. Attempts have been made to incorporate all elements in a government of broad consensus. A recent party election at several levels introduced a degree of democracy. Subnationalities: The most significant opposition has come from those opposing centralization. Politics is largely a struggle of regional and tribal factions.

Civil Liberties. The largely government-owned media are closely controlled; copy must pass elaborate pre-publication censorship. Works of critical authors are prohibited, even university lectures are subject to government censorship. In addition, self-censorship is common in all media. A number of papers have been closed, and journalists arrested. Freedom of speech, assembly, and union organization are limited, but there is increasingly open discussion. A private human rights group has been established. Freedom of occupation, education, and property are respected. Prisoners of conscience are detained without trial and may be ill-treated. Many have recently been released. Internal travel and religious choice are relatively free; foreign travel may be difficult. Labor and business organizations are closely controlled. Although still relatively short on capital, private enterprise is encouraged wherever possible.

Comparatively: Cameroon is as free as Central African Republic, freer than Ethiopia, less free than South Africa.

CANADA

Economy: capitalist
Polity: decentralized multiparty
Population: 26,100,000

Political Rights: 1
Civil Liberties: 1
Freedom Rating: 2

A binational state, with small territorial groups in the north

Political Rights. Canada is a parliamentary democracy with alternation of rule between leading parties. A great effort is made to register all eligible voters. The provinces have their own democratic institutions with a higher degree of autonomy than the American states. Subnationalities: French has linguistic equality, and French is the official language in Quebec. In addition, Quebec has been allowed to opt out of some national programs and maintains its own representatives abroad. Rights to self-determination for Indian and Eskimo groups in the North have been emphasized recently.

Civil Liberties. The media are free, although there is a government-related radio and television network. The full range of civil liberties is respected, except for linguistic rights. In Quebec, education in the English language is available only to those with an English heritage, and the written use of English is otherwise restricted. The new Charter of Rights and Freedoms includes the right of judicial review. There has been evidence of the invasion of privacy by Canadian security forces in recent years, much as in the United States. Many judicial and legal structures have been borrowed from the United Kingdom or the United States, with consequent advantages and disadvantages. Some provinces limit employment opportunities for nonresidents.

Comparatively: Canada is as free as the United States of America, freer than France.

CAPE VERDE

Economy: noninclusive mixed
  socialist
Polity: socialist one-party
Population: 334,500

Political Rights: 5

Civil Liberties: 6
Freedom Rating: 11

Comparative Survey

An ethnically complex state

Political Rights. The single ruling party enlists no more than four percent of the population. Although elections are controlled, choice is allowed, and there are extensive consultations. Abstention and negative votes are common. The resulting assembly includes independents and has demonstrated considerable freedom.

Civil Liberties. Nearly all media are government owned; all are controlled to serve party purposes. Foreign print and broadcast media are freely available, and a Catholic publication exists. Rights to organize opposition, assembly, or political expression are not respected, but little political imprisonment or mistreatment takes place. The judiciary is weak. Drought and endemic unemployment continue to lead to emigration. Fishing, farming, small enterprises, and most professions are private. Land reform has emphasized land-to-the-tiller programs. Religion is relatively free, although under political pressure; labor unions are government controlled. Travel is relatively free.

Comparatively: Cape Verde is as free as Zambia, freer than Equatorial Guinea, less free than Gambia.

CENTRAL AFRICAN REPUBLIC

Economy: noninclusive
    capitalist–statist
Polity: nationalist one–party
    (military dominated)
Population: 2,800,000

Political Rights: 6

Civil Liberties: 6

Freedom Rating: 12

A transethnic heterogeneous state

Political Rights. The Central African Republic is a military dictatorship with an elected one-party parliament. The loosely organized single party allows for choice. The current system has been approved by referendum. French–style prefects are appointed by the central government, but there is some elected local government. Heavily dependent on French economic and military aid, France has influenced or determined recent changes of government; French forces are still present.

Civil Liberties. All media are government owned or closely controlled, but some de facto free expression exists. There are prisoners of conscience. Party affiliation is voluntary. Religious freedom is generally respected. The judiciary is not independent. Movement is occasionally hampered by highway security checks. Most economic activity is private with limited government involvement; workers are not free to organize. Corruption is particularly widespread.

Comparatively: Central African Republic is as free as Tanzania, freer than Somalia, less free than Senegal.

CHAD

Economy: noninclusive capitalist
Polity: military nonparty
Population: 4,800,000 (est.)

Political Rights: 6
Civil Liberties: 7
Freedom Rating: 13

A transitional collection of semi-autonomous ethnic groups

Political Rights. The central government is under control of a military-factional leader. However, the government now includes leaders from a variety of ethnic and factional groups. France's participation in the defense of the present government has reduced its independence in inter-state relations. Subnationalities: The primary ethnic cleavage is between the southern Negroes (principally the Christian and animist Sara tribe) and a number of northern Muslim groups (principally nomadic Arabs). Political factionalism is only partly ethnic.

Civil Liberties. Media are government owned and controlled. Free expression has had little opportunity to develop; criticism of the government is dangerous. Many have been imprisoned without due process; judicial independence does not exist beyond the local level. Labor and business organizations exist with some independence. Religion is relatively free. Not an ideological area, traditional law is still influential. The economy is predominantly subsistence agriculture with little protection of property rights.

Comparatively: Chad is as free as Ethiopia, freer than Somalia, less free than Tanzania.

C H I L E

Economy: capitalist	Political Rights: 5
Polity: military nonparty	Civil Liberties: 4
Population: 12,600,000	Freedom Rating: 9

A relatively homogeneous population

Political Rights. The government of Chile is led by a self-appointed military dictator assisted by a junta of military officers. A 1988 referendum supported the opposition's call for free elections and a change of government. For now, power is concentrated at the center; there are no elective positions.

Civil Liberties. All media have both public and private outlets; newspapers are primarily private. Although under pressure, the media express a range of opinion, including direct criticism of government policy. Limited party activity is allowed. Students, church leaders, former political leaders, and human rights organizations regularly express criticism and dissent, sometimes massively and in the face of violent government repression. While one can win against the government, the courts are under government influence. Prisoners of conscience are still commonly taken for short periods; torture, political expulsion, internal exile, and assassination of government opponents continue. Violent confrontations lead repeatedly to repressions, only to be followed by new periods of relaxation. Unions are restricted but have some rights, including a limited right to strike and organize at plant levels. Many nationalized enterprises have been resold to private investors, with government intervention in the economy now being limited to copper and petroleum.

Comparatively: Chile is as free as Egypt, freer than Paraguay, less free than Peru.

C H I N A (Mainland)

Economy: mixed socialist	Political Rights: 6
Polity: communist one-party	Civil Liberties: 6
Population: 1,087,000,000	Freedom Rating: 12

An ethnic state with peripheral subnationalities

Political Rights. China is a one-party communist state under the collective leadership of the Politburo. A National People's Congress is indirectly elected within party guidelines, but its discussions are now relatively open and competitive. Still, national policy struggles are obscured by secrecy, and choices are sharply limited. Some local elections have allowed limited competition. Party administration is decentralized. Subnationalities: There are several subordinated peripheral peoples such as the Tibetans, Uygurs, Mongols, and the much acculturated Zhuang. These are granted a limited degree of separate cultural life. Amounting to not more than six percent of the population, non-Chinese ethnic groups have tended to be diluted and obscured by Chinese settlement or sinification. Nationalist expression in Tibet continues to be strongly repressed. However, minority peoples have been given a special dispensation to have more children than Han Chinese.

Civil Liberties. The mass media remain closely controlled tools for mobilizing the population. There is limited non-political cultural and scientific freedom. Many local papers not entirely under government control have developed recently. Although there is movement toward "socialist legality" on the Soviet model, court cases are often decided in political terms. There are unknown thousands of political prisoners, including those in labor-reform camps; the government has forced millions to live indefinitely in undesirable areas. Political executions are still reported. Political-social controls at work are pervasive.

Compared to traditional communist states, popular opinions and pressures have played a major role in internal politics. Occasional poster campaigns and demonstrations, as well as private conversation, show that pervasive factionalism has allowed elements of freedom and consensus into the system; recurrent repression, including imprisonment, equally shows the government's determination to keep dissent from becoming a threat to the system or its current leaders. Rights to travel and emigration are limited, as are religious freedoms. Economic pressures have forced some, not wholly successful, rationalization of economic policy, including renunciation of guaranteed employment for youth. Introduction of private sector incentives has increased economic freedom, especially for small entrepreneurs and farmers. Small local strikes and slowdowns have been reported concerning wage increases and worker demands for greater control over choice of employment. Inequality derives from

367

differences in political position and location rather than direct income.

Comparatively: China (Mainland) is as free as Kenya, freer than Mongolia, less free than China (Taiwan).

C H I N A (Taiwan)

Economy: capitalist–statist
Polity: centralized dominant party
Population: 19,800,000

Political Rights: 5
Civil Liberties: 3
Freedom Rating: 8

A quasi–ethnic state with a majority nonterritorial subnationality

Political Rights. Taiwan has been ruled by a single party organized according to a communist model (although anticommunist ideologically), and under strong military influence. Parliament includes some representatives from Taiwan, but most parliamentarians are still persons elected in 1947 as representatives of districts in China where elections could not be held subsequently because of communist control. Several opposition parties have been formed. Campaigns have been limited, particularly because the media are overwhelmingly pro–government. The indirect presidential election is pro forma. Some local and regional positions are elective, including those in the provincial assembly that are held by Taiwanese. Subnationalities: The people are eighty–six percent native Taiwanese (speaking two Chinese dialects); opposition movements in favor of a truly independent Taiwan nation–state have been repressed, but native Taiwanese have become increasingly important in the political system. Small indigenous ethnic groups often are discriminated against.

Civil Liberties. The media include government or party organs, but are mostly in private hands. Newspapers and magazines are subject to censorship or suspension, but are now relatively free and critical. Martial law was ended in 1987, but replaced by a law that greatly reduced the meaning of its repeal. Government thought-police and their agents also operate overseas. Television is one-sided. Rights to assembly are limited, but are sporadically granted. Nearly all political prisoners have been released. Unions have achieved increased independence. Private rights to property, education, and religion are generally respected. Rights to travel overseas, including mainland China, have been liberalized.

Comparatively: China (Taiwan) is as free as Tonga, freer than Indonesia, less free than South Korea.

COLOMBIA

Economy: capitalist
Polity: centralized multiparty
Population: 30,600,000

Political Rights: 2
Civil Liberties: 3
Freedom Rating: 5

A relatively homogeneous population with scattered minorities

Political Rights. Colombia is a constitutional democracy. The president is directly elected, as are both houses of the legislature. Power alternates between the two major parties. Both have well-defined factions. The largest guerrilla group now participates in electoral politics. The provinces are directly administered by the national government. The military and police are not firmly under government control; violence limits political rights at all levels.

Civil Liberties. The press is private, with most papers under party control, and quite free. Radio includes both government and private stations; television is a government monopoly. All media have been limited in their freedom to report subversive activity. Personal rights are generally respected; courts are relatively strong and independent. However, endemic violence curbs expression through fear of assassination by right or left—or gangsters more connected with the drug trade than ideology. Assemblies are often banned for fear of riots. In these conditions the security forces have infringed personal rights violently, especially those of leftist unions, peasants, and Amerindians in rural areas. Many persons are rounded up in antiguerrilla or antiterrorist campaigns, and may be tortured or killed. However, opponents are not given prison sentences simply for the nonviolent expression of political opinion, and the government and courts have attempted to control abuses. Human rights organizations are active. The government encourages private enterprise where possible; union activity and strikes for economic goals are legal.

Comparatively: Colombia is as free as India, freer than Guyana, less free than Venezuela.

C O M O R O S

Economy: noninclusive capitalist
Polity: nationalist one-party
Population: 460,000 (est.)

Political Rights: 6
Civil Liberties: 6
Freedom Rating: 12

A relatively homogeneous population

Political Rights. The present Comoran dictator returned to power with the aid of mercenaries in 1978, and they continue to protect him. 1987 assembly elections were prefaced by consultations with the people on candidates for the ruling party. Although an opposition party participated in the subsequent election, the election was marked by use of the courts to exclude much of the opposition, credible accusations of widespread fraud, and hundreds of arrests. All, or nearly all, seats in the weak assembly are now controlled by the ruling party. Each island has an appointed governor and council. (The island of Mahore is formally a part of the Comoros, but it has chosen to be a French dependency.)

Civil Liberties. Radio is government owned and controlled. There is no independent press, but some outside publications and occasional underground dissident writings are available. People are detained for reasons of conscience, and there are many political prisoners. Pressure is reported against the opposition, but private criticism is allowed. There is a new emphasis on Islamic customs. The largely plantation economy has led to severe landlessness and concentrated wealth; emigration to the mainland for employment is very common. The concentration of wealth in a few hands closely connected to the government reduces choice.

Comparatively: Comoros is as free as Tanzania, freer than Mozambique, less free than Madagascar.

C O N G O

Economy: noninclusive mixed
    socialist
Polity: socialist one-party
    (military dominated)
Population: 2,200,000 (est.)

Political Rights: 7

Civil Liberties: 6

Freedom Rating: 13

A formally transethnic heterogeneous state

Political Rights. Congo is an arbitrary military dictatorship with a very small ruling party based primarily in one section of the country. One-party elections allow little opposition, but criticism is aired in parliament. Two thousand Cuban troops help to maintain the regime.

Civil Liberties. The press and all publications are heavily censored. Broadcasting services and most of the press are government owned. Criticism may lead to imprisonment, yet there is some private discussion and limited dissent. Executions and imprisonment of political opponents have occurred, but conditions have improved. The only union is state sponsored; strikes are illegal. Religious organization is generally free; however, government and party are officially atheist and some church functions or services have been abolished. There is little judicial protection; passports are difficult to obtain. At the local and small entrepreneur level private property is generally respected; most large-scale commerce and industry are either nationalized or controlled by expatriates. Literacy is high for the region.

Comparatively: Congo is as free as Syria, freer than Iraq, less free than Kenya.

C O S T A   R I C A

Economy: capitalist
Polity: centralized multiparty
Population: 2,900,000

Political Rights: 1
Civil Liberties: 1
Freedom Rating: 2

A relatively homogeneous population

Political Rights. A parliamentary democracy, Costa Rica has a directly elected president and several important parties. No parties are prohibited, and intraparty democracy is highly developed. Much of the society and economy is administered by a large and diffuse network of autonomous public institutions. This structure is supplemented by an independent tribunal for overseeing elections. Elections are fair; rule alternates between parties. Lacking a regular army, politics are not under military influence. Provinces are under the direction of the central government.

Civil Liberties. The media are notably free, private, and varied; they serve a society ninety percent literate. A surprisingly onerous licensing requirement for journalists is a stain on the country's well-known freedoms. The courts are fair, and private rights, such as those to movement, occupation, education, religion, and union organization, are respected.

Comparatively: Costa Rica is as free as Australia, freer than Venezuela.

C O T E   D ' I V O I R E
(IVORY COAST)

Economy: noninclusive capitalist
Polity: nationalist one-party
Population: 11,200,000

Political Rights: 6
Civil Liberties: 6
Freedom Rating: 12

A transethnic heterogeneous state

Political Rights. Cote d'Ivoire is ruled by a one-party, capitalist dictatorship in which a variety of political elements have been integrated. Assembly elections have recently allowed choice of individuals, including nonparty, but not policies. Rates of voter participation are quite low. Provinces are ruled directly from the center. Contested municipal elections occur. The French military, bureaucratic, and business presence remains powerful.

Civil Liberties. Although the legal press is party or government controlled, it presents a limited spectrum of opinion. Foreign publications are widely available. While opposition is discouraged, there is no ideological conformity. Radio and television are government controlled. Major events may go unreported. Short-term imprisonment and conscription are used to control opposition. Travel and religion are generally free. Rights to strike or organize unions are quite limited. All wage earners must contribute to the ruling party. Economically the country depends on small, private or traditional farms; in the modern sector private enterprise is encouraged.

Comparatively: Cote d'Ivoire is as free as Mauritania, freer than Guinea, less free than Senegal.

C U B A

Economy: socialist
Polity: communist one-party
Population: 10,400,000

Political Rights: 7
Civil Liberties: 6
Freedom Rating: 13

A complex but relatively homogeneous population

Political Rights. Cuba is a one-party communist state on the now-dated Soviet model. Real power lies, however, more in the person of Fidel Castro and in the Russian leaders upon whom he depends than is the case in other noncontiguous states adopting this model. Popular election at the municipal level is closely supervised. Provincial and national assemblies are elected by municipalities but can be recalled by popular vote. The whole system is largely a show: political opponents are excluded from nomination by law, many others are simply disqualified by Party fiat; no debate is allowed on major issues; once elected the assemblies do not oppose Party decisions.

Civil Liberties. All media are state controlled and express only what the government wishes. Although the population is literate, publications, foreign or domestic, are in very short supply. Cuba may have the longest serving prisoners of conscience in the world. Torture has been reported in the past; hundreds who have refused to recant their opposition to the system continue to be held in difficult conditions, and new arrests are frequent. There are hundreds of thousands of others who are formally discriminated against as opponents of the system. There is freedom to criticize policy administration through the press and the institutions of "popular democracy," but writing or speaking against the system, even in private is severely repressed. There are reports of psychiatric institutions also being used for incarceration. Independent human rights organizations are not allowed to function. Freedom to choose work, education, or residence is greatly restricted; new laws force people to work harder. It is generally illegal to leave Cuba, but some have been forced to leave.

Comparatively: Cuba is as free as Czechoslovakia, less free than Hungary, freer than Bulgaria.

C Y P R U S (G)

Economy: capitalist
Polity: centralized multiparty
Population: 520,000 (est.)

Political Rights: 1
Civil Liberties: 2
Freedom Rating: 3

An ethnic state

Political Rights. The "Greek" portion of Cyprus is a fully functioning parliamentary democracy on the Westminster model. Elections have been fair and highly competitive. Recently, local elective government has been instituted. However, the community continues to be under considerable political influence from mainland Greece. The atmosphere of confrontation with the Turkish side of the island may restrict freedoms, especially for the small number of remaining citizens of Turkish background.

Civil Liberties. The newspapers are free and varied in both sectors, but generally support their respective governments. Radio and television are under the control of governmental or semigovernmental bodies. The usual rights of free peoples are respected, including occupation, labor organization, and religion. Because of communal strife and invasion, property has often been taken from members of one group by force (or abandoned from fear of force) and given to the other. Under these conditions rights to choose one's sector of residence or to travel between sectors have been greatly restricted.

Comparatively: Cyprus (G) is as free as Malta, freer than Brazil, less free than Denmark.

C Y P R U S (T)

Economy: capitalist
Polity: centralized multiparty
Population: 160,000 (est.)

Political Rights: 2
Civil Liberties: 3
Freedom Rating: 5

An ethnic state

Political Rights. "Turkish" Cyprus was created after Turkish troops intervened to prevent a feared Greek takeover. A large section of the island, including much territory formerly in Greek hands, is protected by Turkish military power from the larger Greek portion of the island, as well as the much larger Greek population. Turkey supports a large share of the country's budget. In spite of these limitations, parliamentary forms are functioning fairly in the Turkish sector. However, the continuing confrontation restricts choice for some, particularly the few remaining Greek Cypriots in the Turkish sector.

Civil Liberties. Publications are free and varied. Radio and television are under governmental or semigovernmental control. The usual rights of free peoples are respected, including occupation, labor, organization, and religion. However, political use of the courts against an opposition party is claimed, and travel between the sectors and the transfer of property is restricted. Many people formerly resident in the Turkish part of the island have lost their property.

Comparatively: Cyprus (T) is as free as Bahamas, freer than Turkey, less free than Greece.

C Z E C H O S L O V A K I A

Economy: socialist
Polity: communist one-party
Population: 15,600,000

Political Rights: 7
Civil Liberties: 6
Freedom Rating: 13

A binational state

Political Rights. Czechoslovakia is a Soviet style, one-party communist state, reinforced by the presence of Soviet troops. Elections are noncompetitive and there is essentially no legislative debate. Polls suggest passive opposition of the great majority of the people to the governing system. Subnationalities: The division of the state into separate Czech and Slovak socialist republics has only slight meaning since the Czechoslovak Communist Party continues to rule the country (under the guidance of the Soviet Communist Party). Although less numerous and poorer than the Czech people, the Slovaks are granted at least their rightful share of power within this framework.

Civil Liberties. Media are government or Party owned and rigidly censored. There is a general willingness to express dissent in private, and there are many serious, if small, underground publications. Freedoms of assembly, organization, and association are denied, although moderately large opposition demonstrations do occur. Heavy pressures are placed on religious activities, especially through holding ministerial incomes at a very low level and curtailing religious education. There are a number of prisoners of conscience; exclusion of individuals from their chosen occupations and short detentions are more common sanctions. The beating of political suspects is common, and psychiatric detention is employed. Successful defense in political cases is possible, but lawyers may be arrested for overzealous defense. Human rights groups are persecuted. Travel to the West and emigration are restricted. Independent trade unions and strikes are forbidden. Rights to choice of occupation and to private property are restricted.

Comparatively: Czechoslovakia is as free as East Germany, freer than Bulgaria, less free than Poland.

D E N M A R K

Economy: mixed capitalist
Polity: centralized multiparty
Population: 5,100,000

Political Rights: 1
Civil Liberties: 1
Freedom Rating: 2

A relatively homogeneous population

Political Rights. Denmark is a constitutional monarchy with a unicameral parliament. Elections are fair. Since a wide variety of parties achieve success, resulting governments are based on coalitions. Referendums may be used to decide major issues. Districts have governors appointed from the center and elected councils; local administration is under community control.

Civil Liberties. The press is free (and more conservative politically than the electorate). Radio and television are government owned but relatively free. Labor unions are powerful both socially and politically. All other rights are guaranteed. The very high tax level constitutes more than usual constraint on private property in a capitalist state, but has provided a fairly equitable distribution of social benefits. Religion is free; most churches are state supported.

Comparatively: Denmark is as free as Norway, freer than Finland.

DJIBOUTI

Economy: inclusive capitalist
Polity: nationalist one–party
Population: 360,000 (est.)

Political Rights: 6
Civil Liberties: 6
Freedom Rating: 12

A binational state with subordination

Political Rights. Djibouti is formally a parliamentary democracy under French protection. Only one party is allowed, and in recent elections there has been little if any choice. The party is tightly controlled by a small elite. Although all ethnic groups are carefully balanced in single-party lists, ethnic strife simmers. French influence, backed by a large French garrison, is critical.

Civil Liberties. The media are government owned and controlled and there is no right of assembly. However, some opposition literature is distributed. There have recently been prisoners of conscience and torture. Unions are under a degree of government control, but there is a right to strike. An extremely poor country, its market economy is still dominated by French interests.

Comparatively: Djibouti is as free as Tanzania, freer than Somalia, less free than North Yemen.

D O M I N I C A

Economy: capitalist
Polity: centralized multiparty
Population: 82,000 (est.)

Political Rights: 2
Civil Liberties: 2
Freedom Rating: 4

A relatively homogeneous population with a minority enclave

Political Rights. Dominica is a parliamentary democracy with competing political parties. After violent attempts to overthrow the government, the military was disbanded. The dissolution of the army has been accepted by the voters. There are local assemblies. Rights of the few remaining native Caribs may not be fully respected.

Civil Liberties. The press is private; radio is both private and public. The press is generally free and critical, and the radio presents alternative views. Rights of assembly and organization are guaranteed. There is rule of law and no prisoners of conscience. States of emergency have recurrently limited rights to a small extent. Personal rights to travel, residence, and property are secured, as are the union rights of workers.

Comparatively: Dominica is as free as Nauru, freer than Guyana, less free than Grenada.

D O M I N I C A N   R E P U B L I C

Economy: capitalist
Polity: centralized multiparty
Population: 6,900,000

Political Rights: 1
Civil Liberties: 3
Freedom Rating: 4

A complex but relatively homogeneous population

Political Rights. The Dominican Republic is a presidential democracy on the American model. Elections are free and competitive. Direct military influence is now minimal. Provinces are under national control, municipalities under local.

Civil Liberties. The media are generally privately owned, free, and diverse, but government advertising may be denied unfavored papers, and stations may be closed for defamation. Communist materials are restricted. Broadcasting is highly varied, but subject to government review. Public expression is generally free; the spokesmen of a wide range of parties quite openly express their opinions. There are no prisoners of conscience; the security services seem to have been responsible for disappearances and many arbitrary arrests in recent years. The courts appear relatively independent, and human rights groups are active. Labor unions operate under constraints and strikes have been repressed. Travel overseas is sometimes restricted. State-owned lands are slowly being redistributed.

Comparatively: Dominican Republic is as free as Uruguay, freer than Colombia, less free than Belize.

ECUADOR

Economy: noninclusive capitalist	Political Rights: 2
Polity: centralized multiparty	Civil Liberties: 2
Population: 10,200,000	Freedom Rating: 4

An ethnic state with a potential subnationality

Political Rights. Ecuador is governed by an elected president and congress. Elections are fair, highly competitive, and lead to the alternation in power of loosely organized parties. There have been minor restrictions on party activity and nominations. Provinces and municipalities are directly administered, but local and provincial councils are elected. Subnationalities: Forty percent of the population is Indian, most of whom speak Quechua. This population at present does not form a conscious subnationality in a distinct homeland.

Civil Liberties. Newspapers are under private or party control and quite outspoken. Radio and television are mostly under private control. Human rights organizations are active. Torture is alleged. The court system is not strongly independent. Land reform has been hampered by resistance from landed elites. Although there are state firms, particularly in major industries, Ecuador is essentially a capitalist and traditional state.

Comparatively: Ecuador is as free as Uruguay, freer than Guatemala, less free than Venezuela.

E G Y P T

Economy: mixed socialist
Polity: dominant-party
    (military dominated)
Population: 53,300,000

Political Rights: 5
Civil Liberties: 4

Freedom Rating: 9

A relatively homogeneous population with a communal religious minority

Political Rights. Egypt is a controlled democracy. Within limits political parties may organize: communist and religious extremist parties are forbidden. The ruling party makes sure of overwhelming election victories by excluding groups and individuals from the competition, harassment of opponents, limited campaigns, election-period arrests, and general domination of the media. Participation rates are very low; electoral laws greatly favor the government party. The military is largely autonomous and self-sufficient. Neither house of parliament plays a powerful role. Subnationalities: Several million Coptic Christians live a distinct communal life.

Civil Liberties. The Egyptian press is mostly government owned, but presents critical discussions in many areas; weekly party papers are relatively free and increasingly influential. Radio and television are under governmental control. A fairly broad range of literary publications has recently developed. There is limited freedom of assembly. Severe riot laws and a variety of laws restricting dissent have led to large-scale imprisonment or banning from political or other organizational activity. Many prisoners of conscience have been held in the last few years, but very seldom for long periods. Women's rights have improved. In both agriculture and industry considerable diversity and choice exists within a mixed socialist framework. Unions have developed some independence from the government, but there is no right to strike. The secular court system is increasingly independent. Travel and other private rights are generally free. More substantial democratic development is retarded by corruption, poverty, population growth, and Islamic fundamentalism.

Comparatively: Egypt is as free as Malaysia, freer than Algeria, less free than Brazil.

EL SALVADOR

Economy: capitalist
Polity: centralized multiparty
    (military influenced)
Population: 5,400,000 (est.)

Political Rights: 3
Civil Liberties: 3

Freedom Rating: 6

A relatively homogeneous population

Political Rights. El Salvador is ruled by an elected president and parliament. The 1984 election was fair, but the armed opposition did not participate. In the countryside a bloody struggle between government and guerrilla forces continues. On the government side, armed killers have prevented the establishment of normal political or civil relationships. Recent elections have legitimized the power of the civil, elected government and confirmed the political weakness of the guerrillas. But the army continues to operate outside government control, even in the area of rural development.

Civil Liberties. Newspapers and radio are largely in private hands. Newspapers continue to provide a limited, rightist perspective. Legal and illegal opposition papers and broadcasts appear, but no major critical voice on the left has developed since violence ended earlier efforts. However, radio and television have become increasingly open, and revolutionary leftists now have legal access to the public. The rule of law is weak and assassination common. Conscription by both sides has been a major rights problem. Atrocities are committed by both sides in the conflict, probably frequently without the authorization of leaders. On the government side, no military officer has yet been successfully tried for a human rights offense. Human rights organizations are active. The Catholic church remains a force. The university has reopened, but faculty and students continue to live under threat. Union activities are common, and strikes, legal and illegal, have become a major means of political expression for groups on the left. Although still a heavily agricultural country, rural people are to a large extent involved in the wage and market economy. Banking and foreign trade of export crops have been nationalized; land reform has had limited but significant success.

Comparatively: El Salvador is as free as Guatemala, freer than Nicaragua, less free than Dominican Republic.

EQUATORIAL GUINEA

Economy: noninclusive
    capitalist-statist
Polity: military nonparty
Population: 331,000 (est.)

Political Rights: 7

Civil Liberties: 7
Freedom Rating: 14

An ethnic state with a territorial minority

Political Rights. Equatorial Guinea is a military dictatorship in which power has been concentrated in one family or clan. A popular coup replaced the former dictator, but the population as a whole played and plays little part. The partially elected assembly seems irrelevant; elections are single-list, 99 percent, public relations approval exercises. A Moroccan bodyguard protects the incumbent. The local army is recruited from only one ethnic group.

Civil Liberties. The media are very limited, government owned, and do not report opposition viewpoints. Many live in fear. The rule of law is tenuous; there are political prisoners, but perhaps none of conscience. Police brutality is common, and execution casual. Compulsory recruitment for plantation and other work occurs. Opposition parties are not tolerated, and there are no unions. Religious freedom was reestablished in 1979, and private property is recognized. Plantation and subsistence farming is still recovering from near destruction under the previous government.

Comparatively: Equatorial Guinea is as free as Iraq, less free than Tanzania.

ETHIOPIA

Economy: noninclusive socialist
Polity: communist one-party
    (military dominated)
Population: 48,000,000 (est.)

Political Rights: 6
Civil Liberties: 7

Freedom Rating: 13

An ethnic state with major territorial subnationalities

Political Rights. Ethiopia is ruled by a Marxist-Leninist military committee that has successively slaughtered the leaders of the ancien regime and many of its own leaders. A spectrum of mass organizations has been established on the model of a one-party socialist state. Establishing locally elected village councils has been the primary effort to mobilize the people. Membership in the communist party remains secret. In 1987, extended open discussions of the proposed constitution before its enactment led to important changes (such as dropping a ban on polygamy). Subsequent assembly elections under the new constitution allowed a restricted choice of individuals.

Subnationalities. The heartland of Ethiopia is occupied by the traditionally dominant Amhara and acculturated subgroups of the diffuse Galla people. In the late nineteenth century Ethiopian rulers united what had been warring fragments of a former empire in this heartland, and proceeded to incorporate some entirely new areas. At that time the Somali of the south came under Ethiopian rule; Eritrea was incorporated as the result of a UN decision in 1952. Today Ethiopia is crosscut by linguistic and religious conflicts: most important is separatism due to historic allegiances to ancient provinces (especially Tigre), to different experiences (Eritrea), and to the population of a foreign nation (Somalia). Perhaps one-third of the country remains outside government control, with the Eritrean secessionists increasingly able to establish a rural administration. New constitutional proposals may give some self-determination to major territorial groups—if peace can be restored.

Civil Liberties. The media are controlled, serving the mobilization needs of the government. Individual rights are unprotected under conditions of despotism and anarchy. Political imprisonment, forced confession, execution, disappearance, and torture are common. There are no rights to assembly. Many thousands have been killed aside from those that died in civil war. Education is totally controlled. What freedom there was under the Ethiopian monarchy has been largely lost. Initially, land reform benefited many, but the subsequent villagization policy seriously disrupted agriculture. Choice of residence and workplace is often made by the government; forced transport to state farms and the forced transfer of ethnic groups are reported. In all, the government expects fifteen million to have been "regrouped" by the end of 1989. Religious groups have been persecuted, and religious freedom is limited. Peasant and worker organizations are closely controlled. Travel outside the country is strictly controlled; hostages or guarantors are often required before exit. The words and actions of the regime indicate little respect for private rights in property. The economy is under increasing government control through nationalizations, state-sponsored peasant cooperatives, and the regulation of business licenses. Starvation has been a recurrent theme, with government ineffectiveness playing a part both before and after the accession of the present regime. Starvation is also used as a tool in the struggle against dissident peoples.

Comparatively: Ethiopia is as free as South Yemen, freer than Somalia, less free than Sudan.

EUROPEAN COMMUNITY

Economy: capitalist-statist
Polity: decentralized multiparty
Population: 322,300,000

Political Rights: 2
Civil Liberties: 1
Freedom Rating: 3

An ethnically heterogeneous community of independent states

Political Rights. The members of the Community are democracies, and in this way governance at this supranational level is democratic. Otherwise, the system represents a mixture of elitist and democratic elements.

The Community has evolved a variety of institutions since World War II for the managing of economic and political affairs. As in most international organizations, major decision making is made through an international bureaucracy or commission representing the member countries, and through the periodic meeting of representatives of their respective governments—the Council of Ministers and European Council. However, the Community has also developed a directly elected parliament that is growing in influence, and a Community Court of Justice. Increasingly, the law made by these institutions is coming to be considered superior to the national law of member countries. In addition, other institutions in Western Europe reinforce the operation of a system of free institutions within the Community itself.

Civil Liberties. The availability of information to the publics of the Community is characteristic of the free nature of these societies. In addition, the Council of Europe's court of human rights has striven to raise the level of respect for civil liberties.

Comparatively: The European Community is as free as France, less free than Denmark, freer than Turkey.

F I J I

Economy: noninclusive capitalist
Polity: military nonparty
Population: 700,000 (est.)

Political Rights: 5
Civil Liberties: 4
Freedom Rating: 9

A binational state

Political Rights. A military leader overthrew the democratic political system in 1987. New institutions have not yet been established, although handpicked civilian leaders have been reinstated with limited authority. Clearly, the power of the armed forces and the traditional council of chiefs have been enhanced. Local government is organized both by the central government and by a Fijian administration headed by the council of chiefs. Subnationalities: The Fiji Indian community, slightly larger than the native Fijian, has become economically dominant, even with sharp restrictions on the rights of its members to own land. Many native Fijians, dominant in the army, intend to prevent Indian political dominance for all time by forcing through a new constitution that rules out this eventuality.

Civil Liberties. The private press practices self-censorship. All broadcasting is closely controlled. Privately, much of the open discussion of a free society continues. Judges have been arbitrarily dismissed; union and political party activity curtailed, and rights to employment and emigration restricted. There is still little political imprisonment. Rights to property have been sacrificed to guarantee special rights of inalienability of land granted the Fijians. The country may be about evenly divided between a subsistence economy, based on agriculture and fishing, and a modern market economy.

Comparatively: Fiji is as free as Indonesia, freer than Burma, less free than Vanuatu.

FINLAND

Economy: mixed capitalist
Polity: centralized multiparty
Population: 4,900,000

Political Rights: 1
Civil Liberties: 2
Freedom Rating: 3

An ethnic state with a small territorial subnationality

Political Rights. Finland has a parliamentary system with a strong, directly elected president. Since there are many relatively strong parties, government is almost always by coalition. Elections have resulted in shifts in coalition membership. By treaty foreign policy cannot be anti-Soviet, but recent elections suggest a weakening of the Soviet veto on the political process. The provinces have centrally appointed governors. Subnationalities: The rural Swedish minority (seven percent) has its own political party and strong cultural ties to Sweden. The Swedish-speaking Aland Islands have local autonomy and other special rights.

Civil Liberties. The press is private, diverse, and uncensored. Government-press relations can be so hostile as to restrict communications. Most of the radio service is government controlled, but there is an important commercial television station. The government network has been manipulated at times. Discussion in the media is controlled by a political consensus that criticism of the Soviet Union should be circumspect. There is a complete rule of law; private rights are secured, as is freedom of religion, business, and labor.

Comparatively: Finland is as free as France, freer than Turkey, less free than Sweden.

FRANCE

Economy: mixed capitalist
Polity: centralized multiparty
Population: 55,900,000

Political Rights: 1
Civil Liberties: 2
Freedom Rating: 3

An ethnic state with major territorial subnationalities

Political Rights. France is a parliamentary democracy with many features of the American system, such as a strong presidency and a check and balance of several centers of power. Either the Senate or the more powerful Assembly can check the power of government. If the president's party does not control parliament, experience in 1986 suggested that the prime minister can exercise powers comparable to those of the president. The constitutional council oversees elections and passes on the constitutionality of assembly or executive actions on the model of the United States Supreme Court. Referendums can also be used to test sentiment. Regional and local power has recently been greatly increased: communes, departments, and regions now have elected governments. Subnationalities: Territorial subnationalities continue to have limited rights as ethnic units, but the ethnic and self-determination rights of such groups as the Bretons, Corsicans, and Basques are increasingly observed.

Civil Liberties. The French press is generally free. There is government involvement in financing and registration of journalists; press laws restrict freedom more than in other Western states. Criticism of the president and top officials is muted by government threats and court actions. The news agency is private. Radio is now free and plural; the government television monopoly has ended, but new owners seem equally intrusive. In spite of recent changes there is still an authoritarian attitude in government-citizen relations, publications may be banned at the behest of foreign governments, and arrest without explanation still occurs, particularly of members of subnationalities. Police brutality is commonly alleged. Information and organization about conscientious objection is restricted. France is, of course, under the rule of law, and rights to occupation, residence, religion, and property are secured. A new Secretary of State for Human Rights, concerned primarily with internal issues, should improve governmental performance. Both through extensive social programs and the creation of state enterprises France is quite far from a pure capitalist form.

Comparatively: France is as free as Spain, freer than India, less free than Italy.

GABON

Economy: noninclusive capitalist
Polity: nationalist one-party
Population: 1,300,000 (est.)

Political Rights: 6
Civil Liberties: 6
Freedom Rating: 12

A transethnic heterogeneous state

Political Rights. Gabon is a moderate dictatorship operating in the guise of a one-party state, with controlled elections characteristic of this form. Candidates must be party approved, but there is limited competition, particularly at the local level. The system remains dependent on the French (French military garrison, French army officers in the army, and French bureaucrats in the government). The dictator attempts to incorporate potential opposition leaders and individuals from a variety of ethnic groups in successive cabinets.

Civil Liberties. All media are government owned and controlled; few legitimate opposition voices are raised; journalists may be arrested for expression. Some critical items appear in local or available foreign media. Prisoners of conscience are held and mistreatment is alleged. The right of political assembly is not respected; only one labor union is sanctioned. Membership in the governing party is compulsory. The authoritarian government generally does not care to interfere in private lives, and respects religious freedom, private property, and the right to travel. The government is taking a more active role in the economy and is gradually replacing foreign managers with Gabonese.

Comparatively: Gabon is as free as Libya, freer than Angola, less free than Sudan.

GAMBIA

Economy: noninclusive capitalist
Polity: dominant party
Population: 765,000 (est.)

Political Rights: 3
Civil Liberties: 3
Freedom Rating: 6

A transethnic heterogeneous state

Political Rights. This is a parliamentary democracy in which the same party and leader have been in power since independence in 1965; elections are won with substantial margins. In a recent election the opposition candidate campaigned from prison. There is limited local, mostly traditional, autonomy. Since its confederation with Senegal, Senegalese troops protect the government.

Civil Liberties. The private and public newspapers and radio stations are generally free, but are subject to self-censorship. In campaigns, the government may misuse its control of the radio. Arrests for antigovernment pamphlets occur. However, opposition organizational expression is freely allowed, and the independent judiciary maintains the rule of law. A threatening law against treason was passed in 1986. Labor unions operate within limits. The agricultural economy remains traditionally organized and is largely dependent on peanuts, the export of which is a state monopoly. Internal travel is limited by document checkpoints.

Comparatively: Gambia is as free as Vanuatu, freer than Sierra Leone, less free than Botswana.

GERMANY, EAST

Economy: socialist
Polity: communist one-party
Population: 16,600,000

Political Rights: 7
Civil Liberties: 6
Freedom Rating: 13

A relatively homogeneous population

Political Rights. East Germany is in practice a one-party communist dictatorship. No electoral competition is allowed that involves policy questions; all citizens are compelled to vote; the government-selected list of candidates may offer limited choice. In addition, the presence of Soviet troops and direction from the Communist Party of the Soviet Union significantly reduces the sovereignty (or group freedom) of the East Germans.

Civil Liberties. Media are government-owned means of indoctrination. Dissidents are repressed by imprisonment and exclusion; the publication or importation of materials with opposing views is officially forbidden, although a small dissident church and underground press is developing. One may be arrested for private criticism of the system, but complaints about policy implementation occur in all the media; a few favored dissidents have managed to exist and publish outside the country. Among the thousands of prisoners of conscience, the most common offenses are trying to leave the country illegally (or in some cases even seeking permission to leave), or propaganda against the state. Prisoners of conscience may be severely beaten or otherwise harmed. Political reeducation may be a condition of release. The average person is not allowed freedom of occupation or residence. Once defined as an enemy of the state, a person may be barred from his occupation and his children denied higher education. Particularly revealing has been the use of the "buying out scheme" by which West Germany has been able intermittently to obtain the release of prisoners in the East through cash payments and delivering goods such as bananas and coffee. There is considerable religious freedom, with the Catholic and Protestant hierarchies possessing some independence, as does the peace movement at times. Freedom exists within the family, although there is no right to privacy or the inviolability of the home, mail, or telephone. Agriculture is highly collectivized; virtually all industry is state controlled. Membership in unions, production cooperatives, and other associations is compulsory.

Comparatively: East Germany is as free as Saudi Arabia, freer than Bulgaria, less free than Poland.

G E R M A N Y, W E S T

Economy: capitalist
Polity: decentralized multiparty
Population: 61,200,000

Political Rights: 1
Civil Liberties: 2
Freedom Rating: 3

A relatively homogeneous population

Political Rights. West Germany is a parliamentary democracy with an indirectly elected and largely ceremonial president. The weak Senate is elected by the assemblies of the constituent states and loyally defends states' rights. Successive national governments have been based on changing party balances in the powerful lower house. The recent success of the "Greens" at all levels suggests the system's openness to change. The states have their own elected assemblies; they control education, internal security, and culture.

Civil Liberties. The papers are independent and free, with little governmental interference. Radio and television are organized in public corporations under the usually neutral direction of the state governments. Generally the rule of law has been carefully observed, and the full spectrum of private freedoms is available. Terrorist activities have led to tighter security regulations, invasions of privacy, and less acceptance of nonconformity. Arrests have been made for handling or producing inflammatory literature, for neo-Nazi propaganda, or for calling in question the courts or electoral system. Anti-census literature has been confiscated. Government participation in the economy is largely regulatory; in addition, complex social programs and mandated worker participation in management have limited certain private freedoms while possibly expanding others.

Comparatively: West Germany is as free as Portugal, freer than Greece, less free than the United States of America.

GHANA

Economy: capitalist-statist
Polity: military nonparty
Population: 14,400,000

Political Rights: 6
Civil Liberties: 6
Freedom Rating: 12

A transethnic heterogeneous state with subnationalities

Political Rights. A small military faction has managed to institutionalize an authoritarian system and gain increasing public support. On the local level, traditional sources of power are minimal. Local and district councils are elected with limited respect for democratic freedoms. Subnationalities: The country is composed of a variety of peoples, with those in the south most self-conscious. The latter are the descendants of a number of traditional kingdoms, of which the Ashanti are the most important. A north-south, Muslim-Christian opposition exists but is weakly developed, because of the numerical and economic weakness and incomplete hold of Islam in the north. In the south and center of the country a sense of Akan identity has developed among the Ashanti, Fanti, and others; since they include forty-five percent of the people, this amounts to strengthening the ethnic core of the nation. The one million Ewe in the southeast (a people divided between Ghana and Togo) play a major role in the new revolutionary government.

Civil Liberties. Radio and television and most of the press are government owned. All are under close government scrutiny. However, a degree of independence is suggested by the periodic suspension and banning of semi-independent publications. Private opinion is restrained. Recent improvements must be seen against a background in which there have been hundreds of political arrests and political trials, and many professionals have been murdered for "revolutionary" reasons. Papers and universities have been closed. Peoples' courts have been used to counter the previous judicial system. Government control is decisive in some areas of the economy—especially in cocoa production, on which the economy depends, and in modern capital-intensive industry. The assets of many businesses have been frozen. Some groups, including the strong women's marketing associations, have resisted government attempts to impose price ceilings on all goods. Labor unions are controlled, but union leaders have become outspoken critics of the government. Like Senegal, Ghana has a relatively highly developed industry and agriculture dependent on world markets. There is religious freedom; travel is controlled.

Comparatively: Ghana is as free as Cote d'Ivoire, freer than Romania, less free than Sudan.

GREECE

Economy: mixed capitalist
Polity: centralized multiparty
Population: 10,100,000

Political Rights: 2
Civil Liberties: 2
Freedom Rating: 4

A relatively homogeneous state

Political Rights. Greece is a parliamentary democracy with an indirectly elected president. The development and extension of free institutions has proceeded rapidly, and recent elections have been competitive and open to the full spectrum of parties. However, governmental actions in elections and parliament have led to serious accusations of misuse of authority. Provincial administration is centrally controlled; there is local self-government.

Civil Liberties. Newspapers are private and the judiciary is independent. Most broadcast media are government owned and controlled, but private and opposition radio stations were established in 1987; television favors the government viewpoint. Government interference in journalism, broadcasting, and universities has recently been reported. There are no known prisoners of conscience. Because of the recent revolutionary situation, all views are not freely expressed (a situation similar to that in post-fascist Portugal). One can be imprisoned for insulting the authorities or religion. The courts are not entirely independent. Pressures have been reported against the Turkish population in Western Thrace, in regard to education, property, and free movement. Union activity is under government influence, particularly in the dominant public sector. Private rights are respected.

Comparatively: Greece is as free as Mauritius, freer than Turkey, less free than France.

GRENADA

Economy: capitalist-statist
Polity: centralized multiparty
Population: 114,000

Political Rights: 2
Civil Liberties: 1
Freedom Rating: 3

A relatively homogeneous population

Political Rights. Parliamentary rule has been effectively reestablished. The 1984 elections were free and fair, and included all major political forces. The legislature governs. There is no local government. Direct United States influence has been reduced to that characterizing the region as a whole.

Civil Liberties. The newspapers are independent, varied, and free. Radio is government controlled—the government has been accused of restricting the development of private radio. There are no prisoners of conscience. All groups have full rights of expression and organization. The judiciary and trade unions are strong and independent. The economy is largely private.

Comparatively: Grenada is as free as St. Lucia, freer than Panama, less free than Barbados.

GUATEMALA

Economy: noninclusive capitalist   Political Rights: 3
Polity: centralized multiparty   Civil Liberties: 3
   (military influenced)
Population: 8,700,000   Freedom Rating: 6

An ethnic state with a major potential territorial subnationality

Political Rights. Guatemala is formally under an elected democratic government. However, military and other security forces maintain extra-constitutional power at all levels. The provinces are centrally administered; local government under elected officials is important in some areas. Subnationalities: Various groups of Mayan and other Indians make up half the population; they do not yet have a subnationalist sense of unity, but are involved both forcibly and voluntarily in guerrilla and antiguerrilla activity.

Civil Liberties. The press and a large portion of radio and television are privately controlled. Until recently self-censorship has been common because of the threat of torture and murder by political opponents. Expression is now relatively free, although many killings continue to occur. The struggle against rural guerrillas has led to frequent attacks on recalcitrant peasants or Indians by security forces. Tens of thousands have been killed in the last few years, primarily by the security forces. Thousands have sought refuge internally and in border areas. The judiciary is under both leftist and governmental pressure in political or subversive cases and has been relatively ineffective in these areas. Rights of assembly and demonstration are vigorously expressed. Political parties are active, and unions are reestablishing their strength.

Comparatively: Guatemala is as free as Thailand, freer than Mexico, less free than Ecuador.

GUINEA

Economy: noninclusive
      mixed capitalist
Polity: military nonparty
Population: 6,900,000

Political Rights: 7

Civil Liberties: 6

Freedom Rating: 13

A formally transethnic heterogeneous state

Political Rights. Guinea is under military rule. Local elective councils with very limited powers have been established.

Civil Liberties. The government controls all media; free expression is limited by fear of dismissal. However, critical foreign publications are available. Unions are under government direction, but some independence has been achieved. Many political detainees have been tortured and executed after secret political trials. Industry is heavily nationalized.

Comparatively: Guinea is as free as Mali, freer than Equatorial Guinea, less free than Cote d'Ivoire.

GUINEA-BISSAU

Economy: noninclusive socialist
Polity: socialist one-party
      (military dominated)
Population: 900,000

Political Rights: 6

Civil Liberties: 7

Freedom Rating: 13

A transethnic heterogeneous state

Political Rights. Guinea-Bissau is administered by one party; other parties are illegal. Regional council elections lay the basis for indirect election of the assembly; party guidance is emphasized at all levels. Public pressure has caused the replacement of some local officials. Increasingly violent struggle among top leaders has resulted in many deaths.

Civil Liberties. The media are government controlled; criticism of the system is forbidden. Human rights are not protected by an adequate rule of law; many have been executed without adequate trial or died in detention. Union activity is government directed.

Land ownership is public or communal. The small industrial sector remains mixed, but the continuing economic crisis has virtually halted all private sector activity. An additional block to further decollectivization is the Soviet and Cuban presence. Religion is relatively free, as are travel and other aspects of private life.

Comparatively: Guinea-Bissau is as free as Mozambique, freer than Somalia, less free than Libya.

G U Y A N A

Economy: mixed socialist
Polity: dominant party
Population: 816,000

Political Rights: 5
Civil Liberties: 5
Freedom Rating: 10

An ethnically complex state

Political Rights. Guyana is a parliamentary democracy with a strong executive and an increasingly dominant ruling party. However, on occasion parliament can express its independence. In recent elections the government has been responsibly charged with irregularities that resulted in its victory. In the last election, the opposition was often excluded from the polling stations both to vote and observe the process. Opposition parties are denied equal access to the media, and their supporters are discriminated against in employment. Administration is generally centralized, but some local officials are elected.

Civil Liberties. Radio is government owned. Several opposition newspapers have been nationalized; the opposition press is under continuing pressure. However, a variety of foreign news media are still available. There is a right of assembly, but harassment occurs. Opposition parties remain well organized. There is an operating human rights organization. All private schools have been nationalized, and the government has interfered with university appointments. It is possible to win against the government in court, although the government appears in practice not to respect the independence of the judiciary. There are no long-term prisoners of conscience, but internal exile may be used against political opponents. Art and music are under considerable government control. The independence of unions has been greatly abridged. The private sector is stagnating under official intimidation and extensive state control of productive property, although a black market thrives. The opposition is terrorized by armed gangs and the police; the general public suffers under arbitrary and severe controls. Political patronage is extensive and some social benefits are allocated on a preferential basis.

Comparatively: Guyana is as free as Liberia, freer than Zambia, less free than Nicaragua.

H A I T I

Economy: noninclusive capitalist
Polity: military nonparty
Population: 6,300,000 (est.)

Political Rights: 7
Civil Liberties: 5
Freedom Rating: 12

A relatively homogeneous population

Political Rights. Currently, government by military faction has replaced normal civilian institutions.

Civil Liberties. The media are private and public, highly varied and sporadically free. The prisons have been emptied. The main human rights problems are those of anarchy—many have been killed or persecuted without trial. Fear has become a major control over expression or assembly. Union activity remains restricted. Corruption and extreme poverty has seriously infringed rights to political equality.

Comparatively: Haiti is as free as Lesotho, freer than Malawi, less free than Guyana.

H O N D U R A S

Economy: noninclusive capitalist
Polity: centralized multiparty
    (military influenced)
Population: 4,800,000

Political Rights: 2
Civil Liberties: 3

Freedom Rating: 5

A relatively homogeneous population

Political Rights. The government is a parliamentary democracy with an elected president. The relationships between the president, congress, the supreme court, and the military are still in question. Military leaders have retained influence, as does the United States government. Provincial government is centrally administered; local government is elected.

Civil Liberties. The media are largely private and free of prior censorship. Licensing requirements for journalists can limit freedom. Human rights organizations are active. Militant peasant organizations are quite active, and the struggle of peasants for land often leads to violence. The spreading of guerrilla war from neighboring countries has led to repressions of refugees and others. Most private rights are respected—in so far as government power reaches. Private killings, especially of leftists and with the involvement of security forces, have often been reported. Labor unions have suffered oppression, but are relatively strong, especially in plantation areas. There is freedom of religion and movement.

Comparatively: Honduras is as free as Colombia, freer than Panama, less free than Uruguay.

HUNGARY

Economy: socialist
Polity: communist one-party
Population: 10,600,000

Political Rights: 5
Civil Liberties: 4
Freedom Rating: 9

A relatively homogeneous population

Political Rights. Hungary is ruled as a one-party communist dictatorship. Although there is an elective national assembly as well as local assemblies, all candidates must be approved by the party, and the decisions of the politburo are decisive. Within this framework recent elections have allowed choice among candidates. Independents have been elected and in many cases runoffs have been required. Parliament has come to take a more meaningful part in the political process. The group rights of the Hungarian people are diminished by the government's official acceptance of the right of the Soviet government to intervene in the domestic affairs of

Hungary by force. A council to represent the special interests of the large gypsy community has been established.

Civil Liberties. Media are under government or party control. Basic criticism of top leaders, communism, human rights performance, or the Soviet presence is inadmissible, but some criticism is allowed; this is expressed through papers, plays, books, the importation of foreign publications, or listening to foreign broadcasts. Radio and television give relatively balanced presentations, even of news. Major public organizations such as the writers' union and the Academy of Sciences have defied the government. Opposition marches for democracy are held. Informally organized dissident groups are allowed to exist. Individuals are regularly detained for reasons of conscience, though usually for short periods. Control over religious affairs is more relaxed than in most communist states. Although private rights are not guaranteed, in practice there is considerable private property, and permission to travel into and out of the country is easier to obtain than in most of Eastern Europe. The border with Austria is essentially open. Unions are showing increasing independence—some small strikes have been successful.

Comparatively: Hungary is as free as Egypt, freer than Czechoslovakia, less free than Mexico.

I C E L A N D

Economy: capitalist
Polity: centralized multiparty
Population: 232,000

Political Rights: 1
Civil Liberties: 1
Freedom Rating: 2

A relatively homogeneous population

Political Rights. Iceland is governed by a parliamentary democracy. The relatively powerless president is popularly elected, but usually without opposition. Recent years have seen important shifts in voter sentiment, resulting successively in right- and left-wing coalitions. Although a small country, Iceland pursues an independent foreign policy. Provinces are ruled by central government appointees.

Civil Liberties. The press is private or party and free of censorship. Radio and television are state owned but supervised by a state board representing major parties and interests. There are no political prisoners and the judiciary is independent. Private rights are respected; few are poor or illiterate.

Comparatively: Iceland is as free as Norway, freer than Portugal.

INDIA

Economy: noninclusive
    capitalist-statist
Polity: decentralized multiparty
Population: 817,000,000

Political Rights: 2

Civil Liberties: 3

Freedom Rating: 5

A multinational and complex state

Political Rights. India is a parliamentary democracy in which the opposition has an opportunity to rule. The strong powers retained by the component states have been compromised in recent years by the central government's frequent imposition of direct rule. However, control of the states by regional political parties has increased. Use of criminal elements in politics in some local areas is a threat to fair participation.

Subnationalities. India contains a diverse collection of mostly territorially distinct peoples united by historical experience and the predominance of Hinduism. India's dominant peoples are those of the north central area that speak as a first language either the official language, Hindi (Hindustani), or a very closely related dialect of Sanskrit origin. The other major subnational peoples of India may be divided into several groups: (1) peoples with separate states that are linguistically and historically only marginally distinct from the dominant Hindi speakers (for example, the Marathi, Gujerati, or Oriya); (2) peoples with separate states that are of Sanskrit background linguistically, but have a relatively strong sense of separate identity (for example, Bengalis or Kashmiris); (3) peoples with separate states that are linguistically and to some extent racially quite distinct (for example, Telegu or Malayalam); and (4) peoples that were not originally granted states of their own, and often still do not have them. These peoples, such as the Santali, Bhuti-Lepcha, or Mizo, may be survivors of India's pre-Aryan peoples. The Indian federal system accords a fair amount of democratic rights to its peoples. Several peoples from groups (2), (3), and (4) have shown through legal (especially votes) and illegal means a strong desire by a significant part of the population for independence or greater autonomy (notably Kashmiris, Nagas, and Gurkhas), and the government has accommodated many of these demands. In 1986, after a long struggle, the Mizos were granted a greater degree of self-determination. Sikh extremists continue to impede the successful reestablishment of elected state government in the Punjab. The Northeast is inflamed by hatred of encroaching Bengalis from both Indian Bengal and Bangladesh. This accounting leaves out many nonterritorial religious and caste minorities, although here again the system has granted relatively broad rights to such groups for reasonable self-determination.

Civil Liberties. The Indian press is diversified, independent, but often not strongly critical or investigative. Governmental pressure against opposition papers became a critical issue for Indian democracy in 1987-88. In the face of unified press opposition, the government was forced to abandon passage of a more restrictive defamation law in 1988. Radio and television are government controlled in this largely illiterate country, and they serve government interests. There is freedom of organization and assembly, but there have been illegal arrests, questionable killings, and reports of torture by the police, which have often been out of control. Journalism can be dangerous. There is a remarkable extent of private political organization at many social levels and for a variety of causes. The judiciary is generally responsive, fair, and independent. The frequent approach to anarchy in Indian society offers many examples of both freedom and repression. There are few if any prisoners of conscience, but hundreds are imprisoned for real or "proposed" political violence; demonstrations often lead to fatalities and massive detentions. Due to the decentralized political structure, operation of the security laws varies from region to region. Kashmir and Bihar have especially repressive security policies in relation to the press and political detention; Sikkim is treated as an Indian colony. Assam, the Punjab, and other areas of violent opposition are necessarily under stricter supervision. Indians enjoy freedom to travel, to worship as they please, and to organize for mutual benefit, especially in unions and cooperatives. Lack of education, extreme poverty, and surviving traditional controls reduce the meaning of such liberties for large numbers.

Comparatively: India is as free as Peru, freer than Malaysia, less free than Japan.

INDONESIA

Economy: noninclusive capitalist-statist

Political Rights: 5

Polity: centralized dominant-party (military dominated)

Civil Liberties: 5

Population: 177,000,000

Freedom Rating: 10

A transethnic complex state with active and potential subnationalities

Political Rights. Indonesia is a controlled parliamentary democracy under military direction. Recent parliamentary elections allowed some competition but severely restricted opposition campaigning and organization. The number and character of opposition parties are carefully controlled, parties must refrain from criticizing one another, candidates of both government and opposition require government approval, and the opposition is not allowed to organize in rural areas. All parties must accept the broad outline of state policy and the state ideology. All civil servants are expected to vote for the government. In any event parliament does not have a great deal of power. Regional and local government is under central control, although there is limited autonomy in a few areas. Local and regional assemblies are elected. Military officers are included in most legislatures and play a major part in the economy as managers of both public and army corporations.

Subnationalities. Indonesia includes a variety of ethnic groups and is divided by crosscutting island identities. Although the island of Java is numerically dominant, the national language is not Javanese, and most groups or islands do not appear to have strong subnational identifications. Both people of Chinese background and Chinese culture are discriminated against. Otherwise, civilian and military elites generally attempt to maintain religious, ethnic, and regional balance, but government-sponsored settlement of Javanese on outer islands results in the destruction of minority cultures and the denial of self-determination. In recent years groups demanding independence existed in Sulawesi, the Moluccas, Acheh, Timor, and West Irian. Active movements exist now only in the latter two areas among peoples with little in common with most Indonesians.

Civil Liberties. Most newspapers are private. All are subject to fairly close government supervision; there is heavy self-censorship and censorship. Criticism of the system is muted by periodic suppressions. Radio and television are government controlled, whether or not private. Freedom of assembly is restricted, but citizens are not compelled to attend meetings. All organizations must now conform to the official ideology. There are prisoners of conscience. Thousands of released prisoners remain in second-class status, especially in regard to residence and employment. In this area the army rather than the civilian judiciary is dominant. The army has been responsible for many thousands of unnecessary deaths in its suppression of revolt in, or conquest of, East Timor. Union activity is closely regulated, but labor organization is widespread and strikes occur. Many people are not allowed to travel outside the country for political reasons. Movement, especially to the cities, is restricted; other private rights are generally respected. The Indonesian bureaucracy has an unenviable reputation for arbitrariness and corruption—practices that reduce the effective expression of human rights. The judiciary is not independent. There are many active human rights organizations. Much of industry and commercial agriculture is government owned; sharecropping and tenant farming are relatively common, particularly on Java.

Comparatively: Indonesia is as free as Tunisia, freer than China (Mainland), less free than Singapore.

IRAN

Economy: noninclusive
        capitalist-statist
Polity: quasi-dominant party
Population: 51,900,000

Political Rights: 5

Civil Liberties: 6

Freedom Rating: 11

An ethnic state with major territorial subnationalities

Comparative Survey

Political Rights. Iran has competitive elections, but the direction of the nonelective, theocratic leadership narrowly defines who may compete in the elections. Those who oppose the overall system on fundamentals are silenced or eliminated. Political parties are poorly defined. However, parliament is an open and disputatious body with considerable influence. The Council of Guardians and a new review board provides constitutional and theological checks on parliament—in addition to the overall policy guidance of the nonelective Faqih (currently Khomeini). Elections are increasingly important on the local level. Subnationalities: Among the most important non-Persian peoples are the Kurds, the Azerbaijani Turks, the Baluch, and a variety of other (primarily Turkish) tribes. Many of these have striven for independence in the recent past when the opportunity arose. Although their political desires have been thwarted, Kurds now enjoy considerable cultural freedom within Iran.

Civil Liberties. Newspapers are semi-private or factional, and all are closely controlled, particularly in foreign and defense matters. However, strong criticisms of government leaders (other than Khomeini) appear in major publications, along with critical discussions of internal issues. The other media are largely government-owned propaganda organs. Parliamentary debates are broadcast in full. The right of assembly is denied to those who do not approve of the new system. There are many prisoners of conscience, and executions for political offenses—often nonviolent—have been frequent. Unions have been suppressed. Vigilante groups compete with the official security system; many private rights have become highly insecure, as the goal of the Islamic system is control over most aspects of life. This is especially so for the Bahais and other religious minorities. Legal emigration is quite difficult. Education is subject to religious restrictions; the freedom and equality of women is radically curtailed. However, privacy has recently been reemphasized and there appears to be a good deal of freedom in the home. Diversity and choice still characterize economic activity.

Comparatively: Iran is as free as South Africa, freer than Iraq, less free than Egypt.

I R A Q

Economy: noninclusive socialist
Polity: socialist one-party
Population: 17,600,000

Political Rights: 7
Civil Liberties: 7
Freedom Rating: 14

An ethnic state with a major territorial subnationality

Political Rights. Iraq is a one-party state under dictatorial leadership. Elections allow some choice of individuals, but all candidates are carefully selected, and no policy choices are involved in the process. Resulting parliaments have little if any power. Provinces are governed from the center. Subnationalities: In spite of institutions ostensibly developed for them, many Kurds fight against the regime whenever opportunity arises. Because of the remarkably secular nature of the regime, Christians, Yezidis, and secularists live in greater social freedom than similar groups in neighboring states.

Civil Rights. Newspapers are public or party and are closely controlled by the government; foreign and domestic books and movies are censored. Radio and television are government monopolies. The strident media are emphasized as governmental means for active indoctrination. Major events go unrecorded. Political imprisonment, brutality, and torture are common, and execution frequent. Poisoning on release from prison is reported. The families of suspects are often imprisoned. Rights are largely de facto or those deriving from traditional religious law. Religious freedom or freedom to organize for any purpose is very limited. Education is intended to serve the party's purposes. Iraq has a dual economy with a large traditional sector. The government has taken over much of the modern petroleum-based economy; land reform is, however, now expanding private choice.

Comparatively: Iraq is as free as Bulgaria, less free than Lebanon.

IRELAND

Economy: capitalist
Polity: centralized multiparty
Population: 3,500,000

Political Rights: 1
Civil Liberties: 1
Freedom Rating: 2

A relatively homogeneous population

Political Rights. Ireland is a parliamentary democracy that successively shifts national power among parties. The bicameral legislature has an appointive upper house with powers only of delay. Local government is not powerful, but is elective rather than appointive. Referendums are also used for national decisions.

Civil Liberties. The press is free and private, and radio and television are under an autonomous corporation. Strong censorship has always been exercised over both publishers and the press, but since this is for social rather than political content, it lies within that sphere of control permitted a majority in a free democracy. The rule of law is firmly established and private rights are guaranteed.

Comparatively: Ireland is as free as Canada, freer than France.

ISRAEL

Economy: mixed capitalist
Polity: centralized multiparty
Population: 4,400,000

Political Rights: 2
Civil Liberties: 2
Freedom Rating: 4

An ethnic state with microterritorial subnationalities

Political Rights. Israel is governed under a parliamentary system. Recent elections have resulted in increasingly uneasy or unstable coalitions. Provinces are ruled from the center, although important local offices in the cities are elective. Subnationalities: National elections do not involve the Arabs in the occupied territories, but Arabs in Israel proper participate in Israeli elections as a minority grouping. Arabs both in Israel and the occupied territories must live in their homeland under the cultural and political domination of twentieth century immigrants.

Civil Liberties. Newspapers are private or party. Jewish papers are free of censorship except for restrictions relating to the always precarious national security; Arabic papers must submit all material to censors—some have been closed. Radio and television are governmentally owned. In general the rule of law is observed, although Arabs in Israel are not accorded the full rights of citizens, and the orthodox Jewish faith holds a special position in the country's religious, customary, and legal life. Detentions, house arrest, and brutality have been reported against Arabs opposing Israel's Palestine policy. Because of the war, the socialist-cooperative ideology of its founders, and dependence on outside support, the role of private enterprise in the economy has been less than in most of Euro-America. Arabs are, in effect, not allowed to buy land from Jews, while Arab land has been expropriated for Jewish settlement. Unions are economically and politically powerful and control over twenty-five percent of industry. The Survey's rating of Israel is based on its judgment of the situation in Israel proper and not that in the occupied territories.

Comparatively: Israel is as free as Uruguay, freer than Turkey, less free than Malta.

I T A L Y

Economy: capitalist-statist
Polity: centralized multiparty
Population: 57,300,000

Political Rights: 1
Civil Liberties: 1
Freedom Rating: 2

A relatively homogeneous population with small territorial subnationalities

Political Rights. Italy is a bicameral parliamentary democracy. Elections are free. Since the 1940s governments have been dominated by Christian Democrats, with coalitions shifting between dependence on minor parties of the left or right. Recently premiers have often been from these smaller parties. At the same time, major parties have improved their internal democracy and legitimacy. The fascist party is banned. Referendums are used increasingly to supplement parliamentary rule. Opposition parties often achieve local political power. Regional institutions are developing, and the judiciary's moves against mob influence at this level improves the legitimacy of the system.

Civil Liberties. Italian newspapers are free and cover a broad spectrum. Radio and television are both public and private and provide unusually diverse programming. Laws against defamation of the government and foreign and ecclesiastical officials exert a slight limiting effect on the media. Freedom of speech is inhibited in some areas and for many individuals by the violence of extremist groups or criminal organizations. Since the bureaucracy does not respond promptly to citizen desires, it represents, as in many countries, an additional impediment to full expression of the rule of law. The judiciary has recently shown strong independence and determination. Detention may last for years without trial. Unions are strong and independent. Catholicism is no longer a state religion but remains a favored religion. Major industries are managed by the government, and the government has undertaken extensive reallocations of land.

Comparatively: Italy is as free as Austria, freer than Greece.

J A M A I C A

Economy: capitalist-statist
Polity: centralized multiparty
Population: 2,500,000

Political Rights: 2
Civil Liberties: 2
Freedom Rating: 4

A relatively homogeneous population

Political Rights. Jamaica is a parliamentary democracy in which power changes from one party to another. However, political life is violent; election campaigns have been accompanied by hundreds of deaths. The general neutrality of the civil service, police, and army preserves the system. Because of massive abstention, anomalously, the current parliament has only one party. Both major parties have recently moved toward the center. Public opinion polls are becoming an increasingly important part of the political process. Regional or local administrations have little independent power, but local elections have taken an increasing national significance.

Civil Liberties. The press is largely private; the broadcasting media largely public. Critical media are widely available to the public. Freedom of assembly and organization are generally respected. The judiciary and much of the bureaucracy retain independence, although the police and legal system have been accused of countenancing brutality and severe punishments. The number of criminals shot by the police is remarkably high. However, political violence has declined. Some foreign companies have been nationalized, but the economy remains largely in private hands. Labor is both politically and economically powerful.

Comparatively: Jamaica is as free as Mauritius, freer than Guatemala, less free than Barbados.

JAPAN

Economy: capitalist
Polity: centralized multiparty
Population: 122,700,000

Political Rights: 1
Civil Liberties: 1
Freedom Rating: 2

A relatively homogeneous population

Political Rights. Japan is a bicameral, constitutional monarchy with a relatively weak upper house. The conservative-to-centrist Liberal Democratic Party has ruled since the mid-1950s, either alone or in coalition with independents. Concentrated business interests have played a strong role in maintaining Liberal Party hegemony through the use of their money, influence, and prestige. In addition, weighting of representation in favor of rural areas tends to maintain the Liberal Party position. Opposition parties are fragmented. They have local control in some areas, but the power of local and regional assemblies and officials is limited. Nevertheless, the government almost never forces through major legislation unless a nongovernmental party supports it. The Supreme Court has the power of judicial review, but its voice is not yet powerful. Subnationalities: Some people in the Ryukyu Islands (including Okinawa) regard themselves as occupied by a foreign people.

Civil Liberties. News media are generally private and free, although many radio and television stations are served by a public broadcasting corporation. Television is excellent and quite free. Investigative reporting remains anemic. Courts of law are not as important in Japanese society as in Europe and America. Although the courts and police appear to be relatively fair, nearly all of those arrested confess and are convicted. A high rate of involuntary admissions to mental hospitals is reported. Travel and change of residence are unrestricted. By tradition public expression and action are more restricted than in most modern democracies. Japanese style collectivism leads to strong social pressures, especially psychological pressures, in many spheres (unions, corporations, or religious-political groups, such as Soka Gakkai). Control over education is highly centralized and restrictive. Most unions are company unions. Human rights organizations are very active. Discrimination against Koreans and other minority groups remains a problem.

Comparatively: Japan is as free as Australia, freer than Argentina.

JORDAN

Economy: capitalist
Polity: limited monarchy
Population: 3,800,000

Political Rights: 6
Civil Liberties: 5
Freedom Rating: 11

A relatively homogeneous population

Political Rights. Although formally a constitutional monarchy, Jordan has had few elections and a very weak parliament. Its parliamentary system is currently suspended. Provinces are ruled from the center; elected local governments have limited autonomy. The king and his ministers are regularly petitioned by citizens.

Civil Liberties. Papers are mostly private, but self-censored and occasionally suspended. Television and radio are government controlled. Free private conversation and mild public criticism are allowed. Under a continuing state of martial law, normal legal guarantees for political suspects are suspended, and organized opposition is not permitted. There are prisoners of conscience and instances of torture. Labor has a limited right to organize and strike. Private rights such as those of property, travel, or religion appear to be respected. The government has partial control over many large corporations.

Comparatively: Jordan is as free as Iran, freer than South Yemen, less free than Egypt.

410

K E N Y A

Economy: noninclusive capitalist
Polity: nationalist one-party
Population: 23,300,000

Political Rights: 6
Civil Liberties: 6
Freedom Rating: 12

A transethnic heterogeneous state with active and potential subnationalities

Political Rights. Kenya is a one-party nationalist state. Only members of the party can run for office, and political opponents are excluded or expelled. All civil servants have been ordered to join the party, which includes a large part of the population. Election results can express popular dissatisfaction, but candidates avoid discussion of basic policy or the president. Selection of top party and national leaders is by acclamation. In this increasingly dictatorial state both parliament and judiciary have become subservient to the president. The administration is centralized, but elements of tribal and communal government continue at the periphery. Subnationalities: Comprising twenty percent of the population, the Kikuyu are the largest tribal group. In a very heterogeneous society, the Luo are the second most important subnationality.

Civil Liberties. The press is private, but little criticism of major policies is allowed. Radio and television are under government control. Opposition statements are either ignored or declared treasonous. Rights of assembly, organization, and demonstration are severely limited, particularly for students and faculty. Although under great pressure, the churches still manage to express some opposition. There are hundreds of prisoners of conscience, and torture is common. Defending them in court is itself dangerous. Courts are no longer independent: the government always wins. Unions are now under party direction: strikes are de facto illegal. Private rights are generally respected. Land is gradually coming under private rather than tribal control.

Comparatively: Kenya is as free as Tanzania, freer than Ethiopia, less free than Sudan.

KIRIBATI

Economy: noninclusive
    capitalist-statist
Polity: decentralized nonparty
Population: 66,000 (est.)

Political Rights: 1

Civil Liberties: 2

Freedom Rating: 3

A relatively homogeneous population with a territorial subnationality

Political Rights. Kiribati has a functioning parliamentary system. Although there are no formal parties, both the legislature and president are elected in a fully competitive system. In his attempt to retain the presidency, the incumbent has been charged with stretching the constitution. Local government is significant.

Civil Liberties. The press is private; radio government owned. Public expression appears to be free and the rule of law guaranteed. The modern economy is dominated by investments from the now virtually depleted government-run phosphate industry. A free union operates, and most agriculture is small, private subsistence; land cannot be alienated to non-natives.

Comparatively: Kiribati is as free as Portugal, freer than Western Samoa, less free than New Zealand.

KOREA, NORTH

Economy: socialist
Polity: quasi-communist one-party
Population: 21,900,000

Political Rights: 7
Civil Liberties: 7
Freedom Rating: 14

A relatively homogeneous state

Political Rights. North Korea is a hard-line communist dictatorship in which the organs and assemblies of government are only a facade for party or individual rule. The communism and Marxism-Leninism on which the governing system is based seems to have been replaced by the ruler's personal ideology. National elections allow no choice. The politburo is under one-man rule; the dictator's son is the dictator's officially anointed successor. Military officers are very strong in top positions.

Civil Liberties. The media are all government controlled, with glorification of the leader a major responsibility. External publications are rigidly excluded, and those who listen to foreign broadcasts severely punished. No individual thoughts are advanced publicly or privately. Individual rights are minimal. Everyone is given a security rating that determines future success. Opponents are even kidnapped overseas. Rights to travel internally and externally are perhaps the most restricted in the world: tourism has been virtually unknown––even to communist countries. Social classes are politically defined in a rigidly controlled society; differences between the standard of living of the elite and the general public are extreme. Thousands are long-term prisoners of conscience; torture is reportedly common. There are also reeducation centers and internal exile. There is no private business or agriculture.

Comparatively: North Korea is as free as Albania, less free than Vietnam.

K O R E A, S O U T H

Economy: capitalist-statist
Polity: centralized multiparty
Population: 42,600,000

Political Rights: 2
Civil Liberties: 3
Freedom Rating: 5

A relatively homogeneous state

Political Rights. South Korea is now a parliamentary democracy with a directly elected president. Recent elections have been disputed, but in the last year the process has appeared relatively fair. Although not united, the opposition now controls a majority of legislative seats. Local government is not independent.

Civil Liberties. Most newspapers are private, as well as much of radio and television. All media now operate with relatively little restriction. Most, if not all, prisoners of conscience have been released. Rights of organization and assembly are generally respected, although a history of violent confrontations between students and security forces still affects what is allowed in the streets. Human rights organizations are active. Religious freedom is respected. Rapid capitalistic economic growth has been combined with a relatively egalitarian income distribution. Government controls most heavy industry; other sectors are private. Unions have achieved increasing independence; significant strikes now occur.

Comparatively: South Korea is as free as Philippines, freer than China (Taiwan), less free than Israel.

KUWAIT

Economy: mixed capitalist-statist
Polity: traditional nonparty
Population: 1,700,000

Political Rights: 6
Civil Liberties: 5
Freedom Rating: 11

The citizenry is relatively homogeneous

Political Rights. Kuwait's limited parliament was again dissolved in 1986 when its criticisms of the government became too threatening to the ruling family. Citizens have access to the monarch. More than half the population are immigrants: their political, economic, and social rights are inferior to those of natives; they very seldom achieve citizenship for themselves or their children.

Civil Liberties. Although the private press presents diverse opinions and ideological viewpoints, papers are subject to suspension for "spreading dissension," or for criticism of the monarch, Islam, or friendly foreign states. Radio and television are government controlled. Imported media are censored. Freedom of assembly is curtailed. Public critics or pamphleteers may be detained, expelled, or have their passports confiscated. Formal political parties are not allowed. Private discussion is open; prisoners of conscience are seldom detained for long. Most private freedoms are respected, and independent unions operate. However, many have been expelled or prevented from leaving for security reasons. There is a wide variety of enabling government activity in fields such as education, housing, and medicine that is not based on reducing choice through taxation.

Comparatively: Kuwait is as free as South Africa, freer than Oman, less free than Egypt.

L A O S

Economy: noninclusive socialist
Polity: communist one-party
Population: 3,800,000

Political Rights: 6
Civil Liberties: 6
Freedom Rating: 12

An ethnic state with active or potential subnationalities

Political Rights. Laos has established a traditional communist party dictatorship in which the party is superior to the external government at all levels. The small cadre party enlists little more than one percent of the population. The government is subservient, in turn, to the desires of the Vietnamese communist party, upon which the present leaders must depend. Vietnam continues to maintain five divisions in the country; it is represented in nearly every government ministry. Resistance continues in rural areas, where many groups have been violently suppressed. Local and district elections with some choice—and only 50 percent turnout—have been held. The first communist national legislative elections are to be held in early 1989. Subnationalities: Pressure on the Hmong people has caused the majority of them to flee the country.

Civil Liberties. The media are all government controlled, although Thai TV is now available. There are prisoners of conscience; thousands have spent as long as a decade in reeducation camps. Few private rights are accepted, but there is relaxed opposition to traditional ways, particularly Buddhism. Collectivization has been halted since 1979 because of peasant resistance; most farms continue to be small and individually owned. The limited industry is nationalized. Travel within and exit from the country are highly restricted.

Comparatively: Laos is as free as Paraguay, freer than Cambodia, less free than Malaysia.

L E B A N O N

Economy: capitalist
Polity: decentralized multiparty
Population: 3,000,000 (est.)

Political Rights: 6
Civil Liberties: 5
Freedom Rating: 11

A complex, multinational, microterritorial state

Political Rights. In theory Lebanon is a parliamentary democracy with a strong but indirectly elected president. After the calamities of the last decade, the constitutional government has almost ceased to exist—in late 1988 even the presidency was vacant. The parliament is elected, although the last general election was in 1972. Palestinians, local militias, Syrian and Israeli forces have erased national sovereignty in much of the country. Subnationalities: Leading administrative and parliamentary officials are allocated among the several religious or communal groups by complicated formulas. These groups have for years existed semi-autonomously within the state, although their territories are often intermixed.

Civil Liberties. Renowned for its independence, the press still offers a highly diverse selection to an attentive audience. Most censorship is now self-imposed, reflecting the views of locally dominant military forces. Radio is government and party; television is part government and now officially uncensored. Widespread killing in recent years has inhibited the nationwide expression of most freedoms and tightened communal controls on individuals. In many areas the courts cannot function effectively, but within its power the government secures most private rights. Few if any prisoners of conscience are detained by the government. Unions are government-supervised and subsidized, but have become increasingly active in the cause of peace. Government seldom intervenes in the predominantly service-oriented economy. There is an active human rights organization.

Comparatively: Lebanon is as free as Panama, freer than Syria, less free than Morocco.

LESOTHO

Economy: noninclusive capitalist
Polity: military nonparty
Population: 1,600,000

Political Rights: 6
Civil Liberties: 6
Freedom Rating: 12

A relatively homogeneous population

Political Rights. After an early 1986 coup, Lesotho has been ruled by a military council with the apparent endorsement of the king. There is some local government, and the chiefs retain limited power at this level. Although there are frequent expressions of national independence, the country remains under heavy South African economic and political pressure. Lesotho is populated almost exclusively by Basotho people, and the land has never been alienated. A large percentage of the male citizenry works in South Africa.

Civil Liberties. The media are government and church; criticism is dangerous and muted. Political activity or assembly is banned; some members of the previous government have been detained—or killed under mysterious circumstances. The judiciary preserves considerable independence vis-a-vis the government: one can win against the government in political cases. Limited union activity is permitted; some strikes have occurred. Most private rights are respected, but political opponents may be denied foreign travel.

Comparatively: Lesotho is as free as Togo, freer than Angola, less free than Madagascar.

LIBERIA

Economy: noninclusive capitalist
Polity: dominant party
   (military dominated)
Population: 2,500,000

Political Rights: 5
Civil Liberties: 5

Freedom Rating: 10

A transethnic heterogeneous state

Political Rights. Liberia's election of president and assembly in 1985 was marred by the exclusion of important candidates and parties from the process. Credible accusation of falsification led to an attempted coup in the aftermath and the subsequent detention of opposition leaders. However, opposition parties continue to operate in and out of parliament, and parliament has successfully opposed government bills. There is some traditional local government.

Civil Liberties. The press is private, exercises self-censorship, but represents a variety of positions. Papers may be suspended or closed. Radio and television are largely government controlled. Lack of legal protection characterizes society; anarchical conditions are common; courts are controlled. Executions, coups, and accusations of coups are frequent. Disappearances and torture are reported. Prisoners of conscience are detained. Travel and other private rights are generally respected. Only blacks can become citizens. Religion is free. Union organization is partly free; illegal strikes have occurred, often without government interference. Most industry is government or foreign owned.

Comparatively: Liberia is as free as Sierra Leone, freer than Togo, less free than Senegal.

L I B Y A

Economy: mixed socialist

Polity: socialist quasi one–party
     (military dominated)

Population: 4,000,000

Political Rights: 6

Civil Liberties: 6

Freedom Rating: 12

A relatively homogeneous state

Political Rights. Libya is a military dictatorship with institutions for popular participation. The effort to mobilize and organize the entire population for state purposes has imitated Marxist-Leninist methods. The legislature is the indirectly elected General People's Congress. Elections held at local levels reflect local interests and are relatively fair; some have been nullified by the central government on the basis that they too closely reflected "outworn" tribal loyalties. Recently the legislature has successfully opposed governmental initiatives. Institutional self-management has been widely introduced in the schools, hospitals, and factories. Sometimes the system works well enough to provide a meaningful degree of decentralized self-determination.

Civil Liberties. The media are government-controlled means for active indoctrination. Political discussion at local and private levels may be relatively open. Many political prisoners have recently been released, and capital punishment officially abolished. The use of military and people's courts for political cases suggests little respect for the rule of law, yet acquittals in political cases occur. All lawyers must work for the state. At least until recently, torture and mistreatment have been frequent, as have executions for crimes of conscience——even in foreign countries through assassination. Although ideologically socialist some of the press remains in private hands. Oil and oil-related industries are the major areas of government enterprise. Economic policy is currently very mixed, with both socialist and private initiatives. Respect for Islam provides some check on arbitrary government.

Comparatively: Libya is as free as Afghanistan, freer than Czechoslovakia, less free than Tunisia.

L U X E M B O U R G

Economy: capitalist
Polity: centralized multiparty
Population: 366,000

Political Rights: 1
Civil Liberties: 1
Freedom Rating: 2

A relatively homogeneous state

Political Rights. Luxembourg is a constitutional monarchy on the Belgian model, in which the monarchy is somewhat more powerful than in the United Kingdom or Scandinavia. The legislature is bicameral with the appointive upper house having only a delaying function. Recent votes have resulted in important shifts in the nature of the dominant coalition.

Civil Liberties. The media are private and free. The rule of law is thoroughly accepted in both public and private realms. Rights of assembly, organization, travel, property, and religion are protected.

Comparatively. Luxembourg is as free as Iceland, freer than France.

M A D A G A S C A R

Economy: noninclusive mixed
    socialist
Polity: dominant party
    (military dominated)
Population: 10,900,000

Political Rights: 5
Civil Liberties: 5
Freedom Rating: 10

A transethnic heterogeneous state

Political Rights. Madagascar is essentially a military dictatorship with a very weak legislature. Legislative elections have been restricted to candidates selected by the former political parties on the left grouped in a "national front"; resulting parliaments have played a small part in government. The presidential election in late 1982 allowed vigorous opposition. Although the opposition candidate was later arrested, he subsequently won a seat in the 1983 parliamentary elections. Emphasis has been put on developing the autonomy of local Malagasy governmental institutions. The restriction of local elections to approved "front" candidates belies this emphasis, but contests are genuine. 1987 saw a breakup of the national front—with unpredictable consequences. Opposition party organization remains vigorous. Although tribal rivalries are very important, all groups speak the same language.

Civil Liberties. There is a private press, but papers are carefully censored and may be suspended. Broadcasting is government controlled. Movie theaters have been nationalized. There is no right of assembly; still, election processes allow periods of intense criticism, and vocal, organized opposition persists. There are few long-term prisoners of conscience; short-term political detentions are common, often combined with ill-treatment. The rule of law is weak, but political prisoners may be acquitted. Labor unions are not strong and most are party-affiliated. Religion is free, and most private rights are respected. Public security is very weak. Overseas travel is restricted. While still encouraging private investment, most businesses and large farms are nationalized. Corruption is widespread.

Comparatively: Madagascar is as free as Liberia, freer than Mozambique, less free than Morocco.

MALAWI

Economy: noninclusive capitalist
Polity: nationalist one-party
Population: 7,700,000

Political Rights: 6
Civil Liberties: 7
Freedom Rating: 13

A transethnic heterogeneous state

Political Rights. Malawi is a one-man dictatorship with party and parliamentary forms. Elections allow some choice among individuals. Administration is centralized, but there are both traditional and modern local governments.

Civil Liberties. The private and religious press is under strict government control, as is the government-owned radio service. Even private criticism of the administration remains dangerous. Foreign publications are carefully screened. The country has been notable for the persecution of political opponents, including execution and torture. There are prisoners of conscience, and even slight criticism can lead to severe penalties. Asians suffer discrimination. Corruption and economic inequality are characteristic. The comparatively limited interests of the government offer considerable scope for individual rights. There is some protection by law in the modernized sector. Small-scale subsistence farming is dominant, with much of the labor force employed in southern Africa.

Comparatively: Malawi is as free as Burkino Faso, freer than Somalia, less free than Zambia.

M A L A Y S I A

Economy: capitalist   Political Rights: 4
Polity: decentralized   Civil Liberties: 5
     dominant-party
Population: 17,000,000   Freedom Rating: 9

An ethnic state with major nonterritorial subnationalities

Political Rights. Malaysia is a parliamentary democracy with a weak, indirectly elected and appointed senate and a powerful lower house. The relatively powerless head of state is a monarch; the position rotates among the traditional monarchs of the constituent states. A multinational front has dominated electoral and parliamentary politics. By such devices as imprisonment, the banning of demonstrations, and very short campaigns, the opposition is not given an equal opportunity to compete in elections; in 1987-88 many opposition leaders were imprisoned. Traditionally, the ruling party has incorporated a wide variety of parties and interests, but in 1988 most of the internal opposition was thrown out of the party. The states of Malaysia have their own rulers, parliaments, and institutions, but it is doubtful if any state has the power to leave the federation. Elected local governments have limited power. Subnationalities: Political, economic, linguistic, and educational policies have favored the Malays (forty-four percent) over the Chinese (thirty-six percent), Indians (ten percent), and others. Malays dominate the army. Traditionally the Chinese had been the wealthier and better-educated people. Although there are Chinese in the ruling front, they are not allowed to question the policy of communal preference. Increasingly, Chinese voters are voting for the opposition.

Civil Liberties. The press is private and varied, but papers may be suspended or closed for a variety of reasons. "Undesirable" publications, defined in the broadest terms, may not be printed or distributed. Radio is mostly government owned, television entirely so: both present primarily the government's viewpoint. Academics are restrained from discussing sensitive issues. In many areas discrimination against non-Malays is official policy. The atmosphere of fear in academic, opposition, and minority political circles has worsened recently through many arrests. Some are clearly prisoners of conscience; several have held responsible political positions. The independence of the courts has been seriously compromised. Confessions are often forcibly extracted. Nevertheless, significant criticism appears in the media and in parliament. The government regularly interferes with Muslim religious expression, restricting both those too modernist and too fundamentalist. Christians cannot proselytize. Chinese must convert to Islam before marrying a Muslim. Unions are permitted to strike and have successfully opposed restrictive legislation. Although the government has begun to take control of strategic sectors of the economy, economic activity is generally free, except for government favoritism to the Malays.

Comparatively: Malaysia is as free as Bangladesh, freer than Brunei, less free than Thailand.

MALDIVES

Economy: noninclusive capitalist
Polity: traditional nonparty
Population: 197,000

Political Rights: 5
Civil Liberties: 6
Freedom Rating: 11

A relatively homogeneous population

Political Rights. Maldives has a parliamentary government in which a president (elected by parliament and confirmed by the people) is predominant. The presidential election is pro forma. The elected parliament has gained some freedom of discussion. Regional leaders are presidentially appointed, but there are elected councils. Both economic and political power are concentrated in the hands of a very small, wealthy elite. Islam places a check on absolutism.

Civil Liberties. Newspapers are private, but writers are subject to prosecution for expressing even modest criticism. The radio station is owned by the government. Foreign publications are received; political discussion is limited. Several persons have been arrested for their political associations since a coup attempt. The legal system is based on traditional Islamic law. There is no freedom of religion. No unions have been formed. Most of the people rely on a subsistence economy; the small elite has developed commercial fishing and tourism.

Comparatively: Maldives is as free as Iran, freer than Seychelles, less free than Mauritius.

MALI

Economy: noninclusive mixed socialist

Polity: nationalist one-party (military dominated)

Population: 8,700,000

Political Rights: 6

Civil Liberties: 6

Freedom Rating: 12

A transethnic heterogeneous state

Political Rights. Mali is a military dictatorship with a recently constructed political party to lend support. The regime appears to function without broad popular consensus. Assembly and presidential elections allow choice among preselected candidates. Military officers have a direct role in the assembly. Subnationalities: Although the government is ostensibly transethnic, repression of northern peoples has been reported.

Civil Liberties. The media are nearly all government owned and closely controlled. Antigovernment demonstrations are forbidden. Private conversation is relatively free, and foreign publications enter freely. There are prisoners of conscience, and reeducation centers are brutal. Student protests are controlled by conscription and detention. Religion is free; unions are controlled; travelers must submit to frequent police checks. There have been reports of slavery and forced labor. Private economic rights in the modern sector are minimal, but collectivization has recently been deemphasized for subsistence agriculturists—the majority of the people. Corruption, particularly in state enterprises, is widespread and costly.

Comparatively: Mali is as free as Ghana, freer than Burundi, less free than Liberia.

M A L T A

Economy: mixed capitalist-statist
Polity: centralized multiparty
Population: 352,000 (est.)

Political Rights: 1
Civil Liberties: 2
Freedom Rating: 3

A relatively homogeneous population

Political Rights. Malta is a parliamentary democracy in which power alternates between the two major parties. There is little local government. A major party agreement and subsequent election in 1987 established the power of the majority to rule, but also introduced an element of broad consensus into major decisions.

Civil Liberties: The press is free and highly partisan. Radio and television are government controlled. In an often inflamed and partisan atmosphere, individuals are likely to have felt constrained by those about them. Rights to assembly and organization are fully respected. Rights to personal and religious freedom now appear fully guaranteed. The unions are free and diverse.

Comparatively: Malta is as free as France, freer than Turkey, less free than Italy.

MAURITANIA

Economy: noninclusive
    capitalist-statist
Polity: military nonparty
Population: 2,100,000

Political Rights: 6

Civil Liberties: 6

Freedom Rating: 12

An ethnic state with a major territorial subnationality

Political Rights. Mauritania has been ruled by a succession of military leaders without formal popular or traditional legitimation. Local elections provide an authentic competitive opportunity for a variety of political groupings. Subnationalities: There is a subnational movement in the non-Arab, southern part of the country.

Civil Liberties. The media are government owned and censored, but foreign publications and broadcasts are freely available. There are few if any long-term prisoners of conscience. Arrests are common, particularly for voicing opposition to Arabicization. Conversation is free; no ideology is imposed, but no opposition organizations or assemblies are allowed. Travel may be restricted for political reasons. Internal exile has been imposed on some former officials. Union activity is government controlled. There is religious freedom within the limits of an Islamic country. The government controls much of industry and mining, as well as wholesale trade, but there have been recent moves to reduce government involvement. The large rural sector remains under tribal or family control. Only in 1980 was there a move to abolish slavery.

Comparatively: Mauritania is as free as Tanzania, freer than Malawi, less free than Kuwait.

MAURITIUS

Economy: capitalist
Polity: centralized multiparty
Population: 1,100,000

Political Rights: 2
Civil Liberties: 2
Freedom Rating: 4

An ethnically complex state

Political Rights. Mauritius is a parliamentary democracy. Recent elections have shifted control from one party to another. However, the weakness of parties and political allegiances inhibits the development of stable and thoroughly legitimate government. A variety of different racial and religious communities are active in politics. There are guarantees in the electoral system to make sure no major group is unrepresented in parliament. The major elected local governing bodies are dominated by the opposition.

Civil Liberties. The press is private or party, pluralistic and uncensored. Nevertheless, there has been a struggle between journalists and the government over the imposition of restrictions, and rights of reply on television. Broadcasting is government owned; opposition views are aired. Opposition parties campaign freely and most rights are guaranteed under a rule of law. The security services have been accused of violating the privacy of dissenters. The labor union movement is quite strong, as are a variety of communal organizations. Strikes are common, but restrictive laws make most strikes both illegal and costly to the participants. There is religious and economic freedom; social services are financed through relatively high taxes.

Comparatively: Mauritius is as free as Jamaica, freer than Honduras, less free than Portugal.

M E X I C O

Economy: capitalist–statist	Political Rights: 3
Polity: decentralized	Civil Liberties: 4
dominant–party	
Population: 83,500,000	Freedom Rating: 7

An ethnic state with potential subnationalities

Political Rights. Mexico is ruled by a governmental system formally modeled on that of the United States; in practice the president is much stronger and the legislative and judicial branches much weaker. The states have independent governors and legislatures, as do local municipalities. The ruling party's near monopoly of power on all levels since the 1920s was seriously challenged in 1988. Although unfair in some respects, and with results subject to manipulation, 1988 elections came close to turning out the ruling PRI. They also produced the first serious opposition in the legislature. Plausible accusations include adding fictitious names, stuffing the ballot boxes, excluding opposition observers, and fraudulent counting. Government pressure on the bureaucracy and media for support is overwhelming. The clergy are not allowed to participate in the political process. Subnationalities: There is a large Mayan area in Yucatan that has formerly been restive; there are also other smaller Indian areas.

Civil Liberties. The media are mostly private, but operate under a variety of direct and indirect government controls (including subsidies and takeovers). Free of overt censorship, papers are subject to government "guidance." Literature and the arts are free. The judicial system is not strong. However, decisions can go against the government; it is possible to win a judicial decision that a law is unconstitutional in a particular application. Religion is free. Widespread bribery and lack of control over the behavior of security forces greatly limits freedom, especially in rural areas. Disappearances occur, detention is prolonged, torture and brutality have been common. Private economic rights are respected; government ownership predominates in major industries, graft is legendary. Access to land continues to be a problem despite reform efforts. Nearly all labor unions are associated with the ruling party. Their purpose is as much to control workers for the system as to represent them. There is a right to strike. Some union and student activity has been repressed. Critical human rights organizations exist.

Comparatively: Mexico is as free as Sri Lanka, freer than Nicaragua, less free than Colombia.

MONGOLIA

Economy: socialist
Polity: communist one-party
Population: 2,000,000

Political Rights: 7
Civil Liberties: 7
Freedom Rating: 14

A relatively homogeneous population

Political Rights. A one-party communist dictatorship, Mongolia has recently experienced a change of leader through a mysterious politburo shift of power. Power is organized at all levels through the party apparatus. Those who oppose the government cannot run for office. Parliamentary elections offer no choice and result in 99.9 percent victories. Mongolia has a subordinate relationship to the Soviet Union; 25,000 Soviet troops are maintained in the country. It must use the USSR as an outlet for nearly all of its trade, and its finances are under close Soviet supervision.

Civil Liberties. All media are government controlled. Religion is restricted; Lamaism is nearly wiped out. Freedom of travel, residence, and other civil liberties are denied. As in many communist countries, all typewriting and duplicating machines must be registered annually. Employment is assigned; workers' committees are extensions of the party.

Comparatively. Mongolia is as free as Bulgaria, less free than China (Mainland).

M O R O C C O

Economy: noninclusive
    capitalist-statist
Polity: centralized multiparty
Population: 25,000,000

Political Rights: 4

Civil Liberties: 5

Freedom Rating: 9

An ethnic state with active and potential subnationalities

Political Rights. Morocco is a constitutional monarchy in which the king has retained major executive powers. Parliament is active and competitive, but not powerful. Referendums have been used to support the king's policies. Recent elections at both local and national levels have been well contested. Many parties participated; the moderate center was the chief victor. The autonomy of local and regional elected governments is limited.

Subnationalities. Although people in the newly acquired land of Western Sahara participate in the electoral process, it has an important resistance movement——mostly in exile. In the rest of the country the large Berber minority is a subnationality whose self-expression is restricted.

Civil Liberties. Newspapers are private or party, and quite diverse. Recently there has been no formal censorship, but government guidance is common, and backed up with the confiscation of particular issues and the closing of publications. Monarchical power must not be criticized. Broadcasting stations are under government control, although they have recently been opened to the parties for campaign statements. In the past the use of torture has been quite common and may continue; the rule of law has also been weakened by the frequent use of prolonged detention without trial. There are many political prisoners; some are prisoners of conscience. Private organizational activity is vigorous and includes student, party, business, farmer, and human rights groups. There are strong independent labor unions in all sectors; religious and other private rights are respected. State intervention in the economy is increasing, particularly in agriculture and foreign trade.

Comparatively: Morocco is as free as Sudan, freer than Algeria, less free than Spain.

MOZAMBIQUE

Economy: noninclusive socialist
Polity: socialist one-party
Population: 15,000,000 (est.)

Political Rights: 6
Civil Liberties: 7
Freedom Rating: 13

A transethnic heterogeneous state

Political Rights. Mozambique is a one-party communist dictatorship in which all power resides in the "vanguard party." All candidates are selected by the party at all levels, but there is some popular control of selection at local levels. Discussion in party congresses and other meetings can be quite critical. Regional administration is controlled from the center. Southerners and non-Africans dominate the government. Much of the country is under guerrilla control.

Civil Liberties. All media are rigidly controlled. Rights of assembly and foreign travel do not exist. There are no private lawyers. Secret police are powerful; thousands are in reeducation camps, and executions have occurred. Police brutality is common. Unions are prohibited. Villagers have been forced into communes, leading to revolts in some areas. However, the system is moderating, and may be in transition. The emigration of citizens is restricted, although seasonal movement of workers across borders is unrecorded.

Comparatively: Mozambique is as free as Malawi, freer than Equatorial Guinea, less free than Gabon.

N A U R U

Economy: mixed capitalist–statist
Polity: traditional nonparty
Population: 8,500 (est.)

Political Rights: 2
Civil Liberties: 2
Freedom Rating: 4

An ethnically complex state

Political Rights. Nauru is a parliamentary democracy in which governments change by elective and parliamentary means. All members of parliament have been elected as independents, although parties are forming. The country is under Australian influence.

Civil Liberties. The media are free of censorship but little developed. The island's major industry is controlled by the government under a complex system of royalties and profit-sharing. No taxes are levied; phosphate revenues finance a wide range of social services. The major cooperative and union are independent.

Comparatively: Nauru is as free as Mauritius, freer than Tonga, less free than New Zealand.

N E P A L

Economy: noninclusive capitalist
Polity: traditional nonparty
Population: 18,300,000

Political Rights: 3
Civil Liberties: 4
Freedom Rating: 7

An ethnic state with active and potential subnationalities

Political Rights. Nepal is a constitutional monarchy in which the king is dominant. A relatively free referendum held in 1980 rejected a move toward party government, but the new constitution opened the system to direct elections for most members of parliament. Although neither king nor government determines who is elected, the king appoints many MPs. Although parliament acts independently, and is able to change governments, as in Morocco the king has almost unlimited power to make final decisions. Recently, local elections have gained in significance.

Subnationalities. There are a variety of different peoples, with only fifty percent of the people speaking Nepali as their first language. Hinduism is a unifying force for the majority. Historically powerful Hindu castes continue to dominate.

Civil Liberties. Principal newspapers are public and print only what the government wishes; private journals carry criticism of the government but not the king. Some offending publications have been suspended in the recent past. Radio is government owned. Private contacts are relatively open. Political detention is common, sometimes probably for little more than expression of opinion. Parties are officially banned as the result of the referendum, but they continue to maintain offices and organization. Human rights organizations function. Union organization is under government control. The judiciary is not independent. Religious proselytizing and conversion is prohibited, and the emigration of those with valuable skills or education is restricted. The population is nearly all engaged in traditional occupations; sharecropping and tenant farming is common. Illiteracy levels are very high.

Comparatively: Nepal is as free as Sri Lanka, freer than Bhutan, less free than Thailand.

N E T H E R L A N D S

Economy: mixed capitalist
Polity: centralized multiparty
Population: 14,700,000

Political Rights: 1
Civil Liberties: 1
Freedom Rating: 2

A relatively homogeneous population

Political Rights. Netherlands is a constitutional monarchy in which nearly all the power is vested in a directly elected legislature. The results of elections have periodically transferred power to coalitions of the left and right. There is some diffusion of political power below this level, but not a great deal. The monarch retains more power than in the United Kingdom through the activity of appointing governments in frequently stalemated situations, and through the advisory Council of State.

Civil Liberties. The press is free and private. Radio and television are provided by private associations under state ownership. Commercial services have been introduced. A wide range of views is broadcast. The courts are independent, and the full spectrum of private rights guaranteed. Non-European immigrants are not well accepted by the society. The burden of exceptionally heavy taxes limits some economic choice, but benefits offer the opportunity to choose not to work.

Comparatively: The Netherlands is as free as Belgium, freer than Portugal.

NEW ZEALAND

Economy: capitalist
Polity: centralized multiparty
Population: 3,300,000

Political Rights: 1
Civil Liberties: 1
Freedom Rating: 2

A relatively homogeneous state with a native subnationality

Political Liberties. New Zealand is a parliamentary democracy in which power alternates between the two major parties. There is elected local government, but it is not independently powerful. Subnationalities: About ten percent of the population are Maori, the original inhabitants. Their rights are now a growing concern; the seriousness with which they are taken is suggested by the growing impediment to development presented by Maori land claims.

Civil Liberties. The press is private and free. Television and most radio stations are government owned, but without reducing their independence significantly. The rule of law and private rights are thoroughly respected. Since taxes (a direct restriction on choice) are not exceptionally high, and industry is not government owned, we label New Zealand capitalist. Others, emphasizing the government's highly developed social programs and penchant for controlling prices, wages, and credit, might place New Zealand further toward the socialist end of the economic spectrum.

Comparatively: New Zealand is as free as the United States, freer than Argentina.

NICARAGUA

Economy: mixed capitalist
Polity: dominant-party
Population: 3,500,000 (est.)

Political Rights: 5
Civil Liberties: 4
Freedom Rating: 9

A relatively homogeneous population

Political Rights. Government is in the hands of the Sandinista political-military movement. Major opposition parties chose not to participate in the November 1984 elections, because of Sandinista controls on the media and harassment of the opposition campaigns. Detailed Sandinista controls over livelihood makes a free vote impossible. Still, there is a small, legal, elected opposition in the legislature. The legislature has little significance in the political system; in the Marxist-Leninist style, the government is controlled by the Party rather than the legislature. Subnationalities: Miskito and related Indian groups struggle for greater autonomy with limited success.

Civil Liberties. Most newspapers and radio stations are under direct or indirect government control; private television is not allowed. However, a major opposition newspaper and a religious radio station exist—the latter with only limited freedom. Government gangs break up opposition rallies; arrests and detentions further inhibit expression. Political activity by parties outside the Sandinista movement is restricted. Neighborhood watch committees have been established. Killing and intimidation occur, especially in rural areas, and thousands of disappearances have been reported. With the war in recess, violent repression in rural areas by the government and the contras has declined. The independence of the judiciary is not well developed, although the government does not always win in court. A parallel judiciary has constricted the rule of law. Foreign travel is restricted for some political opponents. Internal travel is restricted in much of the country. Nongovernmental labor unions are restricted. A private human rights organization is active, but its publications have been censored and then suspended. The Catholic Church retains its critical independence, as do many individuals and small groups. Some enterprises and farms have been nationalized; much of the economy remains formally private, though supplies must generally be bought from, and products sold to, the government.

Comparatively: Nicaragua is as free as Singapore, freer than Panama, less free than Honduras.

N I G E R

Economy: noninclusive capitalist
Polity: military nonparty
Population: 7,200,000

Political Rights: 6
Civil Liberties: 6
Freedom Rating: 12

A transethnic heterogeneous state

Political Rights. Niger is a military dictatorship with no elected assembly or legal parties. After considerable consultation, new institutions were approved in an unopposed referendum in 1987, but have not yet been implemented. Elections are promised. All districts are administered from the center. The Songhai ethnic group (25 percent) controls the system.

Civil Liberties. Niger's very limited media are government owned and operated, and are used to mobilize the population. Dissent is seldom tolerated, although ideological conformity is not demanded, and foreign publications are available. There is little overt censorship, but also no barrier to censorship. A military court has taken the place of the suspended Supreme Court; a few political prisoners are held under severe conditions. Unions and religious organizations are relatively independent but nonpolitical. Foreign travel is relatively open; outside of politics the government does not regulate individual behavior. The economy is largely subsistence farming based on communal tenure; direct taxes on the poor have been abolished; agriculture has been honestly supported.

Comparatively: Niger is as free as Rwanda, freer than North Korea, less free than Uganda.

NIGERIA

Economy: capitalist-statist
Polity: military nonparty
Population: 110,000,000 (est.)

Political Rights: 5
Civil Liberties: 5
Freedom Rating: 10

A multinational state

Political Rights. After successive coups, Nigeria is under the direct rule of the military. The full spectrum of political positions has been replaced by the military command. However, a complex plan to return the country to democracy has been widely accepted in this relatively open and consensual society. The first steps, the establishment of local elected bodies and the subsequent forming of an indirectly elected constituent assembly, have been taken. Subnationalities: Nigeria is made up of a number of powerful subnational groupings. The numerical dominance of Muslims, and agitation for an Islamic state, makes full majoritarian democracy unattractive to many non-Muslims. Speaking mainly Hausa, the people of the north are Muslim. The highly urbanized southwest is dominated by the Yoruba; and the east by the Ibo. Within each of these areas and along their borders there are other peoples, some of which are conscious of their identity and number more than one million persons. Strong loyalties to traditional political units—lineages or kingdoms—throughout the country further complicate the regional picture.

Civil Liberties. The status of civil liberties remains in flux. Television and radio are now wholly federal or state owned, as are all but two of the major papers, in part as the result of a Nigerianization program. Still, the media have limited editorial independence, and, between clampdowns, express diverse and critical opinions. Political organization, assembly, and publication are largely eliminated. The universities, secondary schools, and trade unions are under close government control or reorganization in the last few years. The national student association has been banned. The courts have demonstrated their independence on occasion. Police are often brutal, and military riot control has led to many deaths. There is freedom of religion and travel, but rights of married women are quite restricted. The country is in the process of moving from a subsistence to industrial economy—largely on the basis of govern-

ment-controlled oil and oil-related industry. Government intervention elsewhere in agriculture (cooperatives and plantations) and
industry has been considerable. Since private business and industry
are also encouraged, this is still far from a program of massive
redistribution. General corruption in political and economic life has
frequently diminished the rule of law. Freedom is respected in most
other areas of life.

Comparatively: Nigeria is as free as Liberia, freer than Cote
d'Ivoire, less free than Senegal.

NORWAY

Economy: mixed capitalist   Political Rights: 1
Polity: centralized multiparty   Civil Liberties: 1
Population: 4,200,000   Freedom Rating: 2

A relatively homogeneous population with a small Samer minority

Political Rights. Norway is a centralized, constitutional monarchy. Labor remains the strongest party, but other parties have
formed several governments since the mid-1960s. Norway appears
to lead the world in the acceptance of women in high government
position. There is relatively little separation of powers. Regional
governments have appointed governors, and cities and towns their
own elected officials.

Civil Liberties. Newspapers are privately or party owned; radio
and television are state monopolies, but are not used for propaganda.
This is a pluralistic state with independent power in the churches
and labor unions. Relatively strong family structures have also been
preserved. Norway is capitalistic, yet the government's control over
the new oil resource and general reliance on centralized economic
plans reduce the freedom of economic activity. Wages are equalized
to an unusual degree; private hospitals are all but forbidden.

Comparatively: Norway is as free as the United Kingdom, freer
than West Germany.

O M A N

Economy: noninclusive
    capitalist–statist
Polity: centralized nonparty
Population: 1,400,000 (est.)

Political Rights: 6

Civil Liberties: 6

Freedom Rating: 12

An ethnic state with a territorial subnationality

Political Rights. Oman is an absolute monarchy with no political parties or elected assemblies. There is an appointed consultative assembly. Regional rule is by centrally appointed governors, but the remaining tribal structure at the local and regional level gives a measure of local autonomy. British influence remains strong. Subnationalities: The people of Dhofar constitute a small regional subnationality.

Civil Liberties. Broadcasting is government owned; the daily papers are government owned, weeklies are subsidized. There is little or no criticism. Foreign publications are censored regularly. Although the preservation of traditional institutions provides a check on arbitrary action, the right to a fair trial is not guaranteed in political cases. Freedom of assembly is curtailed, and there are no independent unions. With all this, there are few if any prisoners of conscience. Travel is not restricted; private property is respected. Proselytizing for non-Muslim faiths is illegal. The population is largely involved in subsistence agriculture.

Comparatively: Oman is as free as Tanzania, freer than Saudi Arabia, less free than the United Arab Emirates.

P A K I S T A N

Economy: noninclusive
    capitalist–statist
Polity: multiparty
Population: 107,500,000

Political Rights: 3

Civil Liberties: 3

Freedom Rating: 6

A multinational state

Political Rights. Pakistan is apparently in rapid transition from military-civilian rule to full parliamentary government. 1988 legislative elections were decisively won by the opposition, which then formed the government. The role of the president and the military in the new system remains unclear. Local elections of increasing significance have been held. Military officers have positions throughout the bureaucracy and private industry.

Subnationalities. Millions of Pathans, Baluch, and Sindis have a long record of struggle for greater regional autonomy or independence. Provincial organization has sporadically offered a measure of self-determination, but at least the Baluch and Sindis continue to feel oppressed.

Civil Liberties. The previously censored and self-censored newspapers became largely free by the end of 1988. Radio and television are government controlled. For ordinary crimes punishments are often severe; torture is alleged, and executions have been common. Rights of assembly and demonstration are respected, at least for the moment. Union activity has been restricted. Emphasis on Islamic conservatism has curtailed private rights, especially freedom of religion and women's rights: religious minorities suffer discrimination. Teaching has had to conform to Islam. Much of this Islamic fundamentalism is likely to be abandoned under the new regime. Private property is respected; some basic industries have been nationalized. Over half the rural population consists of sharecroppers and tenant farmers.

Comparatively: Pakistan is as free as Thailand, freer than Malaysia, less free than India.

PANAMA

Economy: capitalist-statist	Political Rights: 6
Polity: centralized multiparty	Civil Liberties: 5
(military dominated)	
Population: 2,300,000	Freedom Rating: 11

A relatively homogeneous population with small subnationalities

Political Rights. Formally organized as a democracy on the American model, Panama has again become essentially a military dictatorship. In 1985 the military forced the resignation of the president they had chosen; his relatively unknown replacement was subsequently also dismissed. Yet to a degree the legislature and civilian government continues to function. The provinces are administered by presidential appointees, with elected councils; there is considerable local power in Indian areas.

Civil Liberties. No regularly appearing media oppose the system. Through regulation, sanctions, threats, and special arrangements, the government ensures a preponderance of pro-government reporting. Occasional opposition announcements or publications appear——including those of the church. Opposition rallies are held, but demonstrations are restricted in an atmosphere of confrontation between the civilian opposition and often violent security forces. Detentions are frequent, but generally last for only a few days. The judiciary is not independent; the rule of law is weak in both political and nonpolitical areas. There are few if any long-term prisoners of conscience, but individuals dangerous to the military's interests may be eliminated. Labor unions are under some restrictions. There is freedom of religion, although foreign priests are not allowed. In general, travel is free and private property respected. Major firms are state owned; land reform has been largely ineffective in reducing inequities in land ownership.

Comparatively: Panama is as free as Cape Verde Islands, freer than Brunei, less free than Guyana.

PAPUA NEW GUINEA

Economy: noninclusive capitalist
Polity: decentralized multiparty
Population: 3,700,000

Political Rights: 2
Civil Liberties: 3
Freedom Rating: 5

A transethnic heterogeneous state with many subnationalities

Political Rights. Papua New Guinea is an independent parliamentary democracy, although it remains partially dependent on Australia economically, technically, and militarily. In spite of many irregularities, elections are broadly fair and seats are divided among a number of major and minor parties. With a very large number of candidates in many single-member districts, some candidates are elected with less than ten percent of the vote. Since party allegiances are still fluid, there is considerable party-switching after elections. Parties are weakened by the overwhelming desire of politicians for government positions and their perquisites. Because of its dispersed and tribal nature, local government is in some ways quite decentralized. Elected provincial governments with extensive powers have been established, but only a few have firm public support. Subnationalities: The nation is being created from an amalgam of small tribal peoples with similar racial and cultural backgrounds. Development of provincial governments has quieted secessionist sentiments in Bougainville, Papua, and elsewhere.

Civil Liberties. The press is free, but not highly developed. Radio is government controlled but presents critical views; Australian stations are also received. There are no political prisoners. Rights to travel, organize, demonstrate, and practice religion are secure. The legal system adapted from Australia is operational. However, a large proportion of the population lives in a preindustrial world with traditional controls, including frequent violence, that limit freedom of speech, travel, occupation, and other private rights. In the cities wide disparities in income and violent crime are major social issues; in the country, continued tribal warfare. Land ownership is widely distributed.

Comparatively: Papua New Guinea is as free as Philippines, freer than Vanuatu, less free than Australia.

PARAGUAY

Economy: noninclusive capitalist-statist	Political Rights: 6
Polity: centralized dominant-party (military dominated)	Civil Liberties: 6
Population: 4,400,000	Freedom Rating: 12

A relatively homogeneous state with small Indian groups

Political Rights. Paraguay has been ruled as a modified dictatorship since 1954. In addition to an elected president, there is a parliament that includes members of the "cooperative opposition". Presidential election results determine parliamentary representation. Elections are regularly held, but their meaning has evaporated: the ruling party receives about ninety percent of the vote, a result guaranteed by direct and indirect pressures on the media, massive government pressure on voters, especially in the countryside, interference with opposition party organization, and perhaps electoral fraud. The more serious opposition refuses to participate. The most important regional and local officials are appointed by the president. Subnationalities: The population represents a mixture of Indian (Guarani) and Spanish peoples; ninety percent continue to speak Guarani as well as Spanish—a bilingualism the government has promoted. Several small tribes of primitive forest people are under heavy pressure from both the government and the public.

Civil Liberties. The government closely controls both press and broadcasting; nongovernmental stations and papers have very limited editorial independence. Dissenting opinion is expressed, especially by the church hierarchy, but it is very hard to disseminate within the country. Opposition political organization continues, as do human rights organizations, but there is open discrimination in favor of members of the ruling party in education, government, business, and other areas. A limited right of assembly and demonstration is exercised. Imprisonment, torture, and execution of political opponents, particularly peasants, have been and, to a limited extent, still are an important part of a sociopolitical situation that includes general corruption and anarchy. Mobs are often used by the government to intimidate the opposition. Political opponents or dissident writers may also be refused passports or exiled. There are now few if any long-term prisoners of conscience, but the rule of law is very weak. Most unions are dominated by the ruling party, but some demonstrate independence. Beyond the subsistence sector, private economic rights are restricted by government intervention, control, and favoritism. A large proportion of peasants work their own land, partly as a result of government land reform.

Comparatively: Paraguay is as free as Haiti, freer than Cuba, less free than Guatemala.

P E R U

Economy: noninclusive	Political Rights: 2
capitalist–statist	
Polity: centralized multiparty	Civil Liberties: 3
Population: 21,300,000	Freedom Rating: 5

An ethnic state with a major potential territorial subnationality

Political Rights. Peru is ruled by an elected multiparty parliamentary system. Complete civilian control over security forces has not yet been achieved. Provincial administration is not independent, but local elections are significant. Subnationalities: Several million people speak Quechua in the highlands, and it is now an official language. There are other important Indian groups.

Civil Liberties. The media are largely private. Censorship has been abolished. Essentially all positions are freely expressed, but there is still the shadow of the military and the recent past. There is little if any imprisonment for conscience, but many are killed or imprisoned in the course of antiguerrilla and antiterrorist campaigns; torture occurs. Although thousands of members of the security forces have been censored or arrested for excesses, few, if any, have actually been punished. Periodic states of emergency reduce freedoms, especially in certain areas. Travel is not restrained, and rights to religion and occupation are generally respected. Labor is independent and politically active; strikes are common. The public sector remains dominant; except in banking, private property has regained governmental acceptance.

Comparatively: Peru is as free as Colombia, freer than Mexico, less free than Ecuador.

P H I L I P P I N E S

Economy: noninclusive	Political Rights: 2
capitalist–statist	
Polity: centralized multiparty	Civil Liberties: 3
Population: 63,200,000 (est.)	Freedom Rating: 5

A transethnic heterogeneous state with active and potential subnationalities

Political Rights. The governmental system is modeled on that of the United States. Although there have been problems in recent elections, the results were broadly reflective of popular sentiment. Threats to the system from radical leftists, the armed forces, and vigilante groups continue. Subnationalities: The Philippines includes a variety of different peoples of which the Tagalog-speaking are the most important (although a minority). A portion of the Muslim (Moro) subnationality is in active revolt along the front of Christian-Muslim opposition. There are several major potential subnationalities that may request autonomy in the future on the basis of both territorial and linguistic identity.

Civil Liberties. Newspapers and broadcasting are largely private, free, and pluralistic. Diverse foreign publications are available. Radio is free and varied, but television seems to continue under more government influence. Demonstrations by groups from the far right to the far left have been massive. Unions are again developing independence, and strikes occur. Deaths and disappearances are increasing in both urban and rural areas, because of the activities of both left and right. Labor leaders, human rights activists, and police have been special targets. The Catholic Church maintains its independence. Glaring class discrepancies and rampant corruption also reduce rights. The private economy is marginally capitalist, but rapid growth in government intervention, favoritism, and direct ownership of industries by government and government favorites brings the economy closer to capitalist-statist.

Comparatively: Philippines is as free as Bolivia, freer than Singapore, less free than New Zealand.

POLAND

Economy: mixed socialist
Polity: communist one-party
    (military dominated)
Population: 38,000,000

Political Rights: 5
Civil Liberties: 5

Freedom Rating: 10

A relatively homogeneous population

Political Rights. Poland is a one-party communist and military dictatorship. Assembly elections in 1985 allowed some competition. All candidates must support the system. More generally, in recent years a few nonparty persons have gained election to the assembly, and parliament sometimes refuses to go along with the government. In 1987 the government allowed itself to be defeated on a major referendum. There are elected councils at provincial levels, and remarkably low turnouts for a communist country are reported. Although party and military hierarchies operating from the top down are the loci of power, the Catholic Church, academics, peasants, and workers must be considered by any government. The Soviet Union's claim to a right of interference and continual pressure diminishes Poland's independence.

Civil Liberties. The Polish newspapers are both private and government; broadcasting is government owned. Censorship is pervasive, but legal media have opened their discussion to a wide range of opinions. Underground publication on a massive scale exists in a variety of fields. Private expression is relatively free. Although there are no formal rights of assembly or organization, the government has accepted tacitly the concept of a legitimate opposition, even perhaps of opposition parties. The courts have also begun to accept the concept of the accountability of government officials to the courts. The Church remains a major independent voice, as do the leaders of the formally disallowed Solidarity. The international writers society—PEN—has been reestablished. Detention, beating, and harassment are common means of restricting opposition. Illegal attempts to leave Poland have frequently led to arrest, but opponents have been forced into exile. For most people passports are now relatively easy to obtain. Most agriculture and considerable commerce remain in private hands; industry is fully nationalized.

Comparatively: Poland is as free as Yugoslavia, freer than USSR, less free than Hungary.

PORTUGAL

Economy: mixed capitalist
Polity: centralized multiparty
Population: 10,300,000

Political Rights: 1
Civil Liberties: 2
Freedom Rating: 3

A relatively homogeneous population

Political Rights. Portugal is a parliamentary democracy with a more powerful president than is common in Europe. There is vigorous party competition over most of the spectrum (except the far right), and fair elections. The overwhelming majority of voters are centrist. Elections are competitive and power is shared by several groups. Provincial government is centrally directed.

Civil Liberties. In spite of government or party ownership of most major papers, journalism is now quite free. Radio and television are government owned, except for one Catholic station. They are both relatively free editorially. The government has restored the rule of law. There are few if any prisoners of conscience, yet one can be imprisoned for insult to the military or government. Long periods of detention without trial occur in isolated instances. Imprisonment for "fascist" organization or discussion was promulgated in 1978. The Catholic Church, unions, peasant organizations, and military services remain alternative institutions of power. Although there is a large nationalized sector, capitalism is the accepted form for much of the economy.

Comparatively: Portugal is as free as France, freer than Brazil, less free than United Kingdom.

QATAR

Economy: mixed capitalist-statist
Polity: traditional nonparty
Population: 323,000 (est.)

Political Rights: 5
Civil Liberties: 5
Freedom Rating: 10

A relatively homogeneous citizenry

Political Rights. Qatar is a traditional monarchy. The majority of the residents are recently arrived foreigners; of the native population perhaps one-fourth are members of the ruling family. Open receptions are regularly held for the public to present grievances. Consensus plays an important role in the system.

Civil Liberties. The media are public or subsidized private, and loyalist. Discussion is fairly open; foreign publications are controlled. Political parties are forbidden. This is a traditional state

445

still responsive to Islamic and tribal laws that moderate the absolutism of government. The family government controls the nation's wealth through control over oil, but there are also independently powerful merchant and religious classes. There are no income taxes, and many public services are free. There are no organized unions or strikes. The rights of women and religious minorities are quite limited: only native Muslim males have the full rights of citizens.

Comparatively: Qatar is as free as the United Arab Emirates, freer than Saudi Arabia, less free than Morocco.

R O M A N I A

Economy: socialist
Polity: communist one-party
Population: 23,000,000

Political Rights: 7
Civil Liberties: 7
Freedom Rating: 14

An ethnic state with territorial subnationalities

Political Rights. Romania is a traditional communist state. Assemblies at national and regional levels are subservient to the party hierarchy. Although the party is not large, all decisions are made by a small elite and especially the dictator. Elections involve only candidates or issues chosen by the party or dictator; for some assembly positions the party may propose several candidates. Soviet influence is relatively slight. Subnationalities: The Magyar and German minorities are territorially based. If offered self-determination, one Magyar area would surely opt for rejoining neighboring Hungary; many of the Germans evidently wish to migrate to Germany, and many have. In Romania the cultural rights of both groups are narrowly limited.

Civil Liberties. The media include only government or party organs; self-censorship committees replace centralized censorship. Private discussion is guarded; police are omnipresent. Dissenters are frequently imprisoned. Forced confessions, false charges, and psychiatric incarceration are characteristic. Treatment may be brutal; physical threats are common. Many arrests have been made for attempting to leave the country or importing foreign literature (especially Bibles and publications in minority languages). Contacts with foreigners must be reported if not given prior approval. Religious and other personal freedoms, such as the right not to have children, are unusually restricted. Outside travel and emigration are not considered rights; potential emigrants may suffer economic discrimination, but many have been allowed to leave the country. Private museums have been closed. Independent labor and management rights are essentially nonexistent. Attempts to form a trade union in 1979 were crushed, as was a major coal strike in 1981. Pressure on workers and consumers to provide a greater surplus is heavy. Central planning is pervasive throughout the highly nationalized economy.

Comparatively: Romania is as free as Albania, less free than the USSR.

R W A N D A

Economy: noninclusive mixed socialist
Polity: nationalist one-party (military dominated)
Population: 7,100,000

Political Rights: 6

Civil Liberties: 6

Freedom Rating: 12

An ethnic state with a minor nonterritorial subnationality

Political Rights. Rwanda is a military dictatorship with an auxiliary party organization. Elections are not free and candidates are preselected, but voters have some choice. Districts are administered by the central government. Everyone must belong to the party, but party elections and deliberations have some competitive and critical aspects. There are elected local councils and officials. Subnationalities: The former ruling people, the Tutsi, have been persecuted and heavily discriminated against, but the situation has improved.

Civil Liberties. The weak media are governmental or religious; Only the mildest criticism is voiced; there is no right of assembly. Political prisoners are held. The courts have some independence. Hundreds of followers of religious sects were sentenced in 1986 for crimes such as failing to salute or to pay mandatory party contributions. Travel is restricted both within the country and across its borders. Labor unions are very weak. There are no great extremes of wealth. The government is socialist in intent, but missionary cooperatives dominate trade, and private business is active in the small nonsubsistence sector. Traditional ways of life rather than government orders regulate the lives of most.

Comparatively: Rwanda is as free as Tanzania, freer than Burundi, less free than Zambia.

ST. KITTS-NEVIS
(ST. CHRISTOPHER AND NEVIS)

Economy: capitalist
Polity: decentralized multiparty
Population: 47,000

Political Rights: 1
Civil Liberties: 2
Freedom Rating: 3

A relatively homogeneous state

Political Rights. St. Kitts-Nevis has a fully functioning parliamentary system in which the smaller Nevis has a relatively large share of power, internal self-government, and an open option to secede. Both unicameral parliaments include several appointed senators.

Civil Liberties. Although television is government owned, the media are free. There is a constitutional rule of law with the full spectrum of democratic rights. However, recently a libel suit and accusation of sedition against an opposition leader raised a question as to the willingness of the government to freely allow the full spectrum of expression.

Comparatively: St. Kitts-Nevis is as free as Venezuela, freer than Jamaica, less free than Costa Rica.

ST. LUCIA

Economy: capitalist
Polity: centralized multiparty
Population: 143,000

Political Rights: 1
Civil Liberties: 2
Freedom Rating: 3

A relatively homogeneous state

Political Rights. This is a functioning parliamentary democracy in which power alternates between parties, most recently in 1982. Elections are extremely close. There are also elected local governments.

Civil Liberties. The papers are largely private or party controlled, and uncensored. Radio is government and private; television private. Organization and assembly are free, but harassment and violence accompany their expression. There are strong business, labor, and religious organizations. Massive strikes played a role in forcing the resignation of the prime minister in early 1982. Personal rights generally are secured, although travel to Libya has been limited for potential dissidents.

Comparatively: St. Lucia is as free as Belize, freer than Solomon Islands, less free than the United States.

ST. VINCENT AND THE GRENADINES

Economy: capitalist
Polity: centralized multiparty
Population: 113,000

Political Rights: 1
Civil Liberties: 2
Freedom Rating: 3

A relatively homogeneous state

Political Rights. St. Vincent is an operating multiparty state. In a 1984 election the ruling party was defeated.

Civil Liberties. Weekly papers present a variety of uncensored opinion, although there may be some government favoritism. Radio is government owned and favors government releases. Foreign media are readily available. There is a full right to assembly and organization; effective opposition to government policies is easily organized and often successful. There is a rule of law, but accusations of police brutality. Much of economic activity is based on agriculture.

Comparatively: St. Vincent is as free as Finland, freer than Colombia, less free than Barbados.

SAO TOME AND PRINCIPE

Economy: socialist
Polity: socialist one-party
Population: 113,000

Political Rights: 6
Civil Liberties: 7
Freedom Rating: 13

A relatively homogeneous population

Political Rights. Sao Tome and Principe are governed under strongman leadership by the revolutionary party that led the country to independence. There is an indirectly elected assembly. Popular dissatisfaction and factional struggles occasionally appear, but no public opposition is allowed. Liberalization of the system is occurring: members of the former opposition are now in government. Local elections allow greater freedom. Angolan troops maintaining the regime are leaving.

Civil Liberties. The media are government owned and controlled; opposition voices are not heard; there is no effective right of political assembly. Labor unions are not independent. The rule of law does not extend to political questions; persons are detained for expression of wrong opinions; many opponents are in exile. There is little evidence of brutality or torture. Union activity is minimal and controlled. The largely plantation agriculture has been socialized, as has most of the economy. Illiteracy is particularly high.

Comparatively: Sao Tome and Principe is as free as Guinea-Bissau, freer than Angola, less free than Comoros.

SAUDI ARABIA

Economy: capitalist-statist
Polity: traditional nonparty
Population: 14,200,000 (est.)

Political Rights: 6
Civil Liberties: 7
Freedom Rating: 13

A relatively homogeneous population

Political Rights. Saudi Arabia is a traditional family monarchy ruling without representative assemblies. Political parties are prohibited. The right of petition is guaranteed, and religious leaders provide a check on arbitrary government. Foreign contract soldiers help support the system. Regional government is by appointive officers; there are some local elective assemblies.

Civil Liberties. The press is both private and governmental; strict self-censorship is expected. Radio and television are mostly government owned, although ARAMCO also has stations. Private conversation is relatively free; there is no right of political assembly or political organization. Islamic law limits arbitrary government, but the rule of law is not fully institutionalized. There are political prisoners, and torture is reported; there may be prisoners of conscience. Citizens have no freedom of religion——all must be Muslims, and must observe Muslim rites. Strikes and unions are forbidden. Private rights in areas such as occupation or residence are generally respected, but marriage to a non-Muslim or non-Saudi is closely controlled. Women may not marry non-Muslims, and suffer other special disabilities, particularly in the right to travel. The economy is overwhelmingly dominated by petroleum or petroleum-related industry, which is directly or indirectly under government control. The commercial and agricultural sectors are private, but connection to the royal family may be critical for success. Extreme economic inequality is maintained by the political system.

Comparatively: Saudi Arabia is as free as Ethiopia, freer than Iraq, less free than Bahrain.

SENEGAL

Economy: mixed capitalist
Polity: centralized
    dominant-party
Population: 7,000,000

Political Rights: 3
Civil Liberties: 4

Freedom Rating: 7

A transethnic heterogeneous state

Political Rights. Although elections are fairly open and parties represent a variety of positions, one party continues to dominate elections, and not without help from the government. Opposition parties have not been allowed to form coalitions——a regulation that is frequently tested——and election regulations do not provide for adequate supervision. Contested elections occur on the local level. Subnationalities: Ethnically eighty percent are Muslims; the Wolof

people represent thirty-six percent of the population, including most
of the elite, the urban population, and the more prosperous farmers.
However, regional loyalties, both within and outside of this linguistic
grouping, seem to be at least as important as communal groupings in
defining potential subnationalities.   Rapid assimilation of rural
migrants in the cities to Wolof culture has reduced the tendency
toward ethnic cleavage, but a separatist movement in the far south
has shown increasing activity.

Civil Liberties.   The press is predominantly public; the independence of private publications is somewhat constrained, although
opposition papers and journals appear. Although radio and television
are under an autonomous government body, they are not impartial.
Rights of assembly and demonstration are often denied. There are
at least separatist prisoners of conscience.   Unions have gained
increasing independence. Religion, travel, occupation, and other
private rights are respected. The government sometimes loses in
the courts. Although much of the land remains tribally owned,
government-organized cooperatives, a strong internal private market, and dependence on external markets have transformed the
preindustrial society. Many inefficient and corrupt state and quasi-
public enterprises are now being dismantled.

Comparatively: Senegal is as free as Nepal, freer than Cote
d'Ivoire, less free than Botswana.

S E Y C H E L L E S

Economy: mixed socialist
Polity: socialist one-party
Population: 71,000 (est.)

Political Rights: 6
Civil Liberties: 6
Freedom Rating: 12

A relatively homogeneous population

Political Rights. Seychelles is a one-party state allowing little
political competition for parliament and none for president. The
former ruling party is said to have "simply disappeared." Tanzanian
military support has largely been replaced by North Korean. There
is no local government.

Civil Liberties. Aside from an occasional, mildly critical Catholic publication, there is no independent opinion press; radio is gov-

ernment owned. No opposition in publication or even conversation is legal. Individuals have little judicial protection. There is no right of political assembly, and the security services have broad powers of arrest. Opposition party activities are banned; people have frequently been arrested on political charges. Critics are often urged to leave, exiled, or refused permission to leave. Labor and government are interconnected. Private rights, including private property, are generally respected. Religious institutions maintain some independence. Quasi-governmental enterprises are being established; state monopolies control the marketing of all export crops. Government services in this largely impoverished country are extensive.

Comparatively: Seychelles is as free as Djibouti, freer than Vietnam, less free than Maldives.

S I E R R A   L E O N E

Economy: noninclusive capitalist
Polity: socialist one-party
    (military dominated)
Population: 4,000,000

Political Rights: 5
Civil Liberties: 5

Freedom Rating: 10

A formally transethnic heterogeneous state

Political Rights. Sierra Leone's one-party system has coopted many members of the previous opposition. The 1985 presidential election allowed no choices; participation was suspiciously high. The 1986 parliamentary election allowed choice, but many candidates were arbitrarily excluded. Military influence in government is critical. There are some elected and traditional local governments.

Civil Liberties. The press is private and governmental. Radio is government controlled. There is occasional independence in the press, but it is under pressure; still there is considerable freedom of private speech. The courts do not appear to be very powerful or independent. Special emergency powers have sporadically given the government untrammeled powers of detention, censorship, restriction of assembly, and search. There may now be no prisoners of conscience. Identity cards have recently been required of all citizens. Labor unions are relatively independent, and travel is freely permitted. The largely subsistence economy has an essentially capitalist modern sector. Corruption is pervasive and costly.

Comparatively: Sierra Leone is as free as Madagascar, freer than Gabon, less free than Gambia.

SINGAPORE

Economy: mixed capitalist
Polity: centralized
      dominant-party
Population: 2,600,000

Political Rights: 4
Civil Liberties: 5

Freedom Rating: 9

An ethnically complex state

Political Rights. Singapore is a parliamentary democracy in which the ruling party traditionally wins all, or nearly all, legislative seats. Economic and other pressures against all opposition groups (exerted in part through control of the media) make elections very unfair. Opposition leaders have been sentenced and bankrupted for such crimes as defaming the prime minister during the campaign. The opposition still obtains over thirty percent of the vote. There is no local government.

Civil Liberties. The press is nominally free, but owners of shares with policy-making power must be officially approved—in some cases the government owns the shares. By closing papers and imprisoning editors and reporters, the press is kept under close control. Government argues that the press has a duty to support government positions. Letters to the editors do express opposition opinion. Broadcasting is largely a government monopoly and completely controlled. The prime minister has publicly pressed the law society to expel members of which he disapproves. University faculties are under pressure to conform. Rights of assembly are restricted. Most opposition is treated as a communist threat and, therefore, treasonable. Prisoners of conscience are held; in internal security cases the protection of the law is weak—prosecution's main task appears to be obtaining forced confessions of communist activity. Torture is alleged. Trade union freedom is inhibited by the close association of government and union. Private rights of religion, occupation, or property are generally observed, although a large and increasing percentage of manufacturing and service companies are government owned. Natalist policy favors the better educated. Many youths have reportedly been forcibly drafted into construction brigades.

Comparatively: Singapore is as free as Sudan, freer than Indonesia, less free than China (Taiwan).

S O L O M O N   I S L A N D S

Economy: noninclusive capitalist
Polity: decentralized multiparty
Population: 286,000

Political Rights: 2
Civil Liberties: 2
Freedom Rating: 4

A relatively homogeneous state with subnational strains

Political Rights. The Solomon Islands are a parliamentary democracy under the British monarch. Elections are intensely contested; party discipline is weak. There is some decentralization of power at the local level; further decentralization to the provincial level is planned.

Civil Liberties. Radio is government controlled; the limited press is both private and governmental. There is no censorship. Although some pressures against journalists have been reported, discussion in both media is varied and critical. The rule of law is maintained in the British manner alongside traditional ideas of justice. Published incitement to inter-island conflict has led to banishment for several persons. Union activity is free, and strikes occur. The government is involved in major businesses. Most land is held communally but farmed individually.

Comparatively: The Solomon Islands are as free as Mauritius, freer than Vanuatu, less free than New Zealand.

SOMALIA

Economy: noninclusive mixed
    socialist

Political Rights: 7

Polity: socialist one-party
    (military dominated)

Civil Liberties: 7

Population: 8,000,000 (est.)

Freedom Rating: 14

A relatively homogeneous state

Political Rights. The Somali Republic is under one-man military rule combining glorification of the ruler with one-party socialist legitimization. Elections with ninety-nine percent approval allow no choice. Ethnically the state is homogeneous, although until the military coup in 1969 the six main clan groupings and their subdivisions were the major means of organizing loyalty and power. While politics is still understood in lineage terms, in its centralizing drive the government has tried to eliminate both tribal and religious power. Opposition guerrilla activity is frequently reported.

Civil Liberties. The media are under strict government control, private conversation is controlled, and those who do not follow the government are considered to be against it. There are many political prisoners, including prisoners of conscience. There have been jailings for strikes and executions for reasons of conscience. Travel is restricted. Some state farms and industries have been established beyond the dominant subsistence economy. A large black market circumvents official distribution channels; corruption is widespread in government and business.

Comparatively: Somalia is as free as Cambodia, less free than Kenya.

SOUTH AFRICA

Economy: capitalist-statist

Political Rights: 5

Polity: centralized multiparty

Civil Liberties: 6

Population: 30,000,000 (est.)

Freedom Rating: 11

An ethnic state with major territorial and nonterritorial subnationalities

Political Rights. South Africa is a parliamentary democracy in which the black majority is excluded from participation in the national political process because of race. Recent constitutional changes have added ten percent or more of the population to the legally politically participant population at the national level. The great majority of the population, the black population, remains excluded. For the nonblack population elections appear fair and open. There is a limited scope for blacks to influence affairs within their own communities. Subnationalities: Most of the black majority is ascribed to a variety of "homelands" that they may or may not live in, although thousands have been forced to move to these limited areas. Several of these have become independent states in the eyes of South Africa, but they have not received such recognition elsewhere. (Except for Transkei, we see these as dependent territories; because of their close integration into South Africa politically and economically we treat these states as part of South Africa for most purposes. The dependent governments of these states are generally unpopular and tyrannical, although this is less so in Bophuthatswana. Geographically and historically Transkei has a reasonable claim to statehood, in spite of the purposes for which it was brought into being. Its dependency is comparable to that of Lesotho, Swaziland, or, further afield, states such as Bhutan or Mongolia.) In the homelands that have not yet separated from the country officially, black leaders have some power and support from their people. Most black political parties are banned; Indians and people officially recognized as mulattos have political parties representing the interests of their peoples and have gained very limited legislative power. Regionally, government within the white community includes both central government officials and elected councils.

Civil Liberties. The white South African press is private and quite outspoken, although censored and restricted. Restrictions apply to reportage and access to information rather than expression of opinion. The nonwhite press is closely restricted, but nevertheless shows critical independence on occasion. Broadcasting is under government control. The courts are independent on many issues, including apartheid, but have not effectively controlled the security forces. There are political prisoners and torture—especially for black activists, who live in an atmosphere of terror. Nevertheless, black organizations regularly denounce the government's racial and economic policies, hold conferences, and issue statements. Academ-

457

ic groups publish highly critical well-publicized studies of the system. Private rights are generally respected for whites. Blacks have rights to labor organization, although political activity is restricted. Legal separation of the races remains, but has been relaxed in a number of ways. Rights to choice of residence and occupation have improved for nonwhites, but hundreds of thousands have been forcibly moved, and such expulsions continue. Human rights organizations are active in both white and black communities. Church organizations have become centers of opposition to apartheid. Escalating violence and counterviolence, and the emergency powers that accompany the violence, obscure these gains.

Comparatively: South Africa is as free as Zimbabwe, freer than Tanzania, less free than Morocco.

SPAIN

Economy: capitalist
Polity: centralized multiparty
Population: 39,000,000

Political Rights: 1
Civil Liberties: 2
Freedom Rating: 3

An ethnic state with major territorial subnationalities

Political Rights. Spain is a constitutional monarchy with a fully functioning democratic system. In the last few years it has managed to largely overcome or pacify military, far right, and Basque dissidence. Elected regional and local governments are of increasing importance. Referendums are also used for major issues. Subnationalities: The Basque and Catalan territorial subnationalities have had their rights greatly expanded in recent years.

Civil Liberties. The press is private and is now largely free. The television network and some radio stations are government owned. National television is controlled by an all-party committee, but there are autonomous and private regional channels. There are few prisoners of conscience; imprisonment still threatens those who insult the security services, the courts, the state, or the flag. Short detention periods are often used with little legal redress. Police brutality and torture still occur, and the government has been slow to punish the civil guardsmen often responsible. Criticism of the government and of suspected human rights violators are quite freely expressed both publicly and privately. Private freedoms are re-spected. Continued terrorism and reactions to terrorism affect some areas. Union organization is free and independent.

Comparatively: Spain is as free as France, freer than Uruguay, less free than Netherlands.

SRI LANKA

Economy: mixed capitalist–statist
Polity: centralized multiparty
Population: 16,600,000

Political Rights: 3
Civil Liberties: 4
Freedom Rating: 7

An ethnic state with a major subnationality

Political Rights. Sri Lanka is a parliamentary democracy in which opposition groups have been partially excluded. From 1982 to 1988 a questionable referendum and other measures were used to guarantee continuation of the government in power. At the end of 1988 local, regional, and national elections, and preparations for these, laid the basis for reestablishing the country's democratic system. (December's presidential election came too late to be reflected in this annual.) Regional government has been centrally controlled, although this is now changing; local government is by elected councils. Indian troops operating against guerrillas in the northeast have reduced government sovereignty there, at least tem-porarily. In all areas, the effectiveness of the government has been greatly reduced by anarchy; it is unclear the degree to which current reforms and policies will be able to overcome this burden. Subna-tionalities: For historical reasons and because of recent persecu-tions, the Tamil minority constitutes a serious secessionist tendency. Their violent national movement in the northeast so strained the country's security forces that India was asked to send soldiers to contain it. Recent agreements grant the Tamils major regional authority in the east and north, if and when the agreements can be successfully implemented.

Civil Liberties. The government-owned press is dominant and under strong pressure to follow the governmental line. However, a broad range of independent journals is also available. Government-controlled broadcasting presents a narrow range of views. The rule

459

of law is threatened by communal violence. Courts remain independent of the government; an important human rights movement supports their independence. However, their decisions can be overruled by parliament. There is freedom of assembly but not demonstration. Private rights to movement, residence, religion, and occupation are respected in theory; in practice, nationalist and leftist gangs and the army have denied these rights to many through widespread looting, destruction, and killing, especially in Tamil areas. Strikes in public services are restricted, but unions are well developed and politically influential. Extensive land reform has occurred, and the state has nationalized a number of enterprises in this largely plantation economy. The system has done an excellent job in providing for the people's basic nutrition, health, and educational needs.

Comparatively: Sri Lanka is as free as Nepal, freer than Indonesia, less free than India.

S U D A N

Economy: noninclusive mixed
        capitalist
Polity: multiparty
Population: 23,000,000 (est.)

Political Rights: 4

Civil Liberties: 5

Freedom Rating: 9

An ethnic state with major but highly diverse subnationalities

Political Rights. Elected, multiparty parliamentary government functions only in the northern two-thirds of the country. The unstable system is beset by periodic breakdowns and continual threats; much of the south is effectively under rebel or military control. Subnationalities: The peoples of the south are ethnically and religiously distinct. The national government remains overwhelmingly northern. A war for southern independence is again underway with atrocities on both sides—southerners on both sides. Other major ethnic groups have achieved increasing regional autonomy in their own areas.

Civil Liberties. The largely government-owned press is remarkably free, and rebel tracts are readily available. Radio and television are government controlled. Arrests for expression still occur, however, and violence or its threat limits expression elsewhere. Worker and professional organizations are politically effective. The greatest limitation on freedom is extreme starvation, now endemic in the south, and abetted by both government and rebels. (The Survey normally avoids this understanding of what limits freedom, but it seems justified in this case.)

Comparatively: Sudan is as free as Egypt, freer than Ethiopia, less free than Turkey.

S U R I N A M E

Economy: capitalist
Polity: multiparty
   (military dominated)
Population: 388,000

Political Rights: 3
Civil Liberties: 2

Freedom Rating: 5

An ethnically complex state

Political Rights. Suriname is now a functioning parliamentary democracy, although it still might not be able to fully control its military forces. The president is indirectly elected by the assembly. A minority area continues its insurgency against the regime.

Civil Liberties. The press and radio are largely private and varied, and have full freedoms. Political organization and assembly are unrestricted. The courts and unions are strong and independent. In rural areas many have been senselessly gunned down in the course of antiguerrilla operations.

Comparatively: Suriname is as free as South Korea, freer than Thailand, less free than Dominica.

S W A Z I L A N D

Economy: noninclusive capitalist
Polity: traditional nonparty
Population: 690,000 (est.)

Political Rights: 5
Civil Liberties: 6
Freedom Rating: 11

A relatively homogeneous population

Country Summaries

Political Rights. Swaziland is ruled by a king. Indirect elections for part of an advisory legislature are held, but only one party is allowed. Local councils invite popular participation. South African political and economic influence is pervasive.

Civil Liberties. Private media exist alongside the dominant government media; little criticism is allowed; South African and other foreign media provide an alternative. Opposition leaders have been repeatedly detained, and partisan activity is forbidden. Criticism is common in parliament and other councils, but public assemblies are restricted, unions limited, emigration difficult. The rule of law is very insecure. Religious, economic, and other private rights are maintained. The traditional way of life is continued, especially on the local level. Several thousand whites in the country and in neighboring Transvaal own the most productive land and business.

Comparatively: Swaziland is as free as South Africa, freer than Mozambique, less free than Botswana.

S W E D E N

Economy: mixed capitalist
Polity: centralized multiparty
Population: 8,400,000

Political Rights: 1
Civil Liberties: 1
Freedom Rating: 2

A relatively homogeneous population

Political Rights. Sweden is a parliamentary democracy in which no party monopolizes power, and the king's power has been all but extinguished. Referendums are held. Although there are some representative institutions at regional and local levels, the system is highly centralized. Resident aliens have a right to vote in local elections. The tendency of modern bureaucracies to regard issues as technical rather than political has progressed further in Sweden than elsewhere.

Civil Liberties. The press is private or party; broadcasting is by state-licensed monopolies. Although free of censorship; the media are accused of presenting a narrow range of views, but this may be changing as politics become polarized. There is the rule of law. The defense of those accused by the government may not be as spirited as elsewhere, but, on the other hand, the ombudsman office gives special means of redress against administrative arbitrariness. Most private rights are respected. State interference in family life is unusually strong, with many children unjustly taken from their parents. The national church has a special position. In many areas, such as housing, individual choice is restricted more than in other capitalist states—as it is of course by the very high tax load. Unions are a powerful part of the system. The state intervenes in the economy mainly through extensive business regulation rather than direct ownership.

Comparatively: Sweden is as free as Italy, freer than West Germany.

SWITZERLAND

Economy: capitalist
Polity: decentralized multiparty
Population: 6,600,000

Political Rights: 1
Civil Liberties: 1
Freedom Rating: 2

A trinational state

Political Rights. Switzerland is a parliamentary democracy in which all major parties are given cabinet positions on the basis of the size of the vote for each party. The president and vice-president are elected on a rotating basis from this cabinet. Parties that increase their vote above a certain level are invited to join the government, although such changes in party strength rarely occur. The lack of a decisive shift in power from one party to another in the last fifty years is a major limitation on the democratic effectiveness of the Swiss system. However, its dependence on the grand coalition style of government is a partial substitute, and the Swiss grant political rights in other ways that compensate for the lack of a transfer of power. Many issues are decided by the citizenry through national referendums or popular initiatives. After referendums, in keeping with the Swiss attitude, even the losing side is given part of what it wants if its vote is sufficiently large. Subnationalities: The three major linguistic groups have separate areas under their partial control. Their regional and local elected governments have autonomous rights and determine directly much of the country's business. National governments try to balance the representatives of the primary religious and linguistic groups; this is accomplished in another way by the upper house that directly represents the cantons (regions) on an equal basis.

Civil Liberties. The high-quality press is private and independent. Broadcasting is government operated, although with the considerable independence of comparable West European systems. Unions are free. Strikes are few because of a 1937 labor peace agreement requiring arbitration. The rule of law is strongly upheld; as in Germany it is against the law to question the intentions of judges. 1985 saw a major extension of women's rights. Private rights are thoroughly respected.

Comparatively: Switzerland is as free as the United States, freer than France.

S Y R I A

Economy: mixed socialist
Polity: centralized dominant-party
    (military dominated)
Population: 11,300,000 (est.)

Political Rights: 6
Civil Liberties: 7

Freedom Rating: 13

A relatively homogeneous population

Political Rights. Syria is a military dictatorship assisted by an elected parliament. The election of the military president is largely pro forma; in assembly elections a variety of parties and independents compete within and without the National Front, organized under the leadership of the governing party. Many "independents" serve in the cabinet, but their independence is minimal. Because of its control of the army, the Alawite minority (ten percent) has a very unequal share of national power. Provinces have little separate power, but local elections are contested.

Civil Liberties. The media are in the hands of government or party. Broadcasting services are government owned. The media are used as governmental means for active indoctrination. Medical, bar, and engineering associations have been dissolved. Thousands have been arrested and many executed. Other thousands have been killed in punitive expeditions. The courts are neither strongly independent nor effective in political cases where long-term detention without trial occurs. Political prisoners are often arrested following violence, but there are also prisoners of conscience. Political opponents may even be killed overseas. Torture has frequently been employed in interrogation. Religious freedom is restricted. Rights to choice of occupation or residence are generally respected; foreign travel and emigration are closely controlled for certain groups. Much of industry has been nationalized; the commercial sector remains private. Land reform has successfully expanded private ownership. There is no independent labor movement.

Comparatively: Syria is as free as Saudi Arabia, freer than Somalia, less free than Kuwait.

T A N Z A N I A

Economy: noninclusive socialist
Polity: socialist one-party
Population: 24,300,000

Political Rights: 6
Civil Liberties: 6
Freedom Rating: 12

A transethnic heterogeneous nation in union with Zanzibar

Political Rights. Tanzania is an unequal union of two states. The single parties of each state have joined to form one all-Tanzanian party. Elections offer choice between individuals, but no issues are to be discussed in campaigns; all decisions come down from above, including the choice of candidates. Over half of the MP's are appointed. The resulting parliament is not, however, simply a rubber stamp. Local government is an extension of party government. Subnationalities: Ethnically, the country has many peoples (none larger than thirteen percent); most are not yet at the subnational level. The use of English and Swahili as national languages enhances national unity. Still, high government and military positions are dominated by the Kuria people.

Civil Liberties. Civil liberties are subordinated to the goals of the socialist leadership. No contradiction of official policy is allowed to appear in the media, nearly all of which is government owned, or in educational institutions; private and limited criticism of implementation appears. The people learn only of those events the government wishes them to know. There is no right of assembly or organization. Millions of people have been forced into communal villages; people from the cities have been abruptly transported to the countryside; forced labor on the farms is still a problem. Thousands have been detained for political crimes. There are prisoners of conscience. Lack of respect for the independence of the judiciary and individual rights is especially apparent in Zanzibar. Union activity is government controlled. Neither labor nor capital have legally recognized rights——strikes are illegal. Most business and trade and much of agriculture are nationalized. Religion is free, at least on the mainland; overseas travel is restricted.

Comparatively: Tanzania is as free as Seychelles, freer than Malawi, less free than Zimbabwe.

THAILAND

Economy: noninclusive capitalist
Polity: centralized multiparty
    (military dominated)
Population: 54,700,000

Political Rights: 3
Civil Liberties: 3

Freedom Rating: 6

An ethnic state with a major territorial subnationality

Political Rights. Thailand is a constitutional monarchy with continuing military influence. Both parties and parliament are, however, significant. The politics are those of consensus. Provincial government is under national control; there are elected and traditional institutions at the local level. Subnationalities: There is a Muslim Malay community in the far south, and other small ethnic enclaves in the north.

Civil Liberties. The press is private, but periodic suppressions and warnings lead to limited self-censorship. Casting doubt on the monarchy is illegal. Most broadcasting is government or military controlled. Some books are banned as subversive. There are few long-term prisoners of conscience, but many are periodically detained for communist activity. Human rights and other public interest organizations are active. Labor activity is relatively free, strikes frequent. Private rights to property, choice of religion, or residence are secure; foreign travel or emigration is not restricted. However, corruption limits the expression of all rights. Government enterprise is quite important in the basically capitalist modern economy.

Comparatively: Thailand is as free as Turkey, freer than Sri Lanka, less free than India.

T O G O

Economy: noninclusive mixed
    socialist
Polity: nationalist one-party
    (military dominated)
Population: 3,300,000

Political Rights: 6

Civil Liberties: 6

Freedom Rating: 12

A transethnic heterogeneous state

Political Rights. Attaining power by military coup, Togo's dictator now rules in the name of a one-party state. In this spirit there is a deliberate denial of the rights of separate branches of government, including a separate judiciary, or even of private groups. National elections allow choice among party-approved candidates. Campaigns allow no policy discussion. Essentially everyone can join the party and there is some discussion in parliament and party organs. An effort has been made to include a variety of ethnic groups and former leaders in policy discussion. Local elections allow a more open expression of popular desires. The government depends on French troops to protect it against internal enemies. Subnationalities: The southern Ewe are culturally dominant and the largest group (twenty percent), but militant northerners now rule.

Civil Liberties. No criticism of the government is allowed in the government or church media, and foreign publications may be confiscated. There are prisoners of conscience, and torture occurs. Jehovah's Witnesses are banned. Foreign travel may be restricted. Union organization is closely regulated. It is yet to be seen whether the establishment of a government-sponsored human rights organization will have a positive effect. In this largely subsistence economy the government is heavily involved in trade, production, and the provision of services. All wage earners must contribute to the ruling party.

Comparatively: Togo is as free as Gabon, freer than Ethiopia, less free than Sudan.

TONGA

Economy: noninclusive capitalist
Polity: traditional nonparty
Population: 110,000

Political Rights: 5
Civil Liberties: 3
Freedom Rating: 8

A relatively homogeneous population

Political Rights. Tonga is a constitutional monarchy in which the king and nobles retain power. Only a minority of the members of the legislative assembly are elected directly by the people; but the veto power of the assembly can be effectively expressed. Corruption of political leaders has been alleged. Regional administration is centralized; there are some elected local officials.

Civil Liberties. The main paper is a government weekly; radio is under government control. Other foreign and local media are available, and recently, a critical monthly has gained an attentive readership. There is a rule of law, but the king's decision is still a very important part of the system. Private rights within the traditional Tonga context seem guaranteed.

Comparatively: Tonga is as free as China (Taiwan), freer than Fiji, less free than Western Samoa.

TRANSKEI

Economy: noninclusive capitalist
Polity: military nonparty
Population: 2,660,000 (est.)

Political Rights: 7
Civil Liberties: 6
Freedom Rating: 13

A relatively homogeneous population

Political Rights. Following a coup, Transkei is under direct military rule. South Africa has de facto power over the state, both because of its massive budgetary support and the large number of nationals that work in South Africa. However, Transkei is at least as independent as several Soviet satellites; it has had continuing public disputes with South Africa.

Civil Liberties. The press is private, but under strong government pressure. Broadcasting is government controlled. Freedom of organization is very limited. Private rights are respected within the limits of South African and Transkei custom. Capitalist and traditional economic rights are diminished by the necessity of a large portion of the labor force to work in South Africa.

Comparatively: Transkei is as free as Chad, freer than Somalia, less free than Sierra Leone.

TRINIDAD AND TOBAGO

Economy: capitalist–statist
Polity: decentralized multiparty
Population: 1,300,000

Political Rights: 1
Civil Liberties: 1
Freedom Rating: 2

An ethnically complex state

Political Rights. Trinidad and Tobago is a parliamentary democracy in which the ruling party was replaced in a landslide election in December, 1986. Power has been decentralized; elections are vigorously contested by a variety of parties. Local government is elected. Tobago has an elected regional government with significant independent power.

Civil Liberties. The private or party press is generally free of restriction; broadcasting is under both government and private control. Opposition is regularly and effectively voiced. There is a full spectrum of private rights. Violence and communal feeling reduce the effectiveness of such rights for some, as does police violence. Many sectors of the economy are government owned. Human rights organizations are active. Labor is powerful and strikes frequent.

Comparatively: Trinidad and Tobago is as free as Barbados, freer than Grenada.

TUNISIA

Economy: mixed capitalist
Polity: dominant party
Population: 7,700,000

Political Rights: 6
Civil Liberties: 4
Freedom Rating: 10

A relatively homogeneous population

Political Rights. Optimistically, Tunisia appears to be in transition from a dominant party system to multiparty democracy. Its increasingly senile and erratic ruler was replaced in 1987 through a palace coup. The step was generally approved by opposition and government elites. In spite of good signs, the new leader continued to rule with few constitutional restraints in 1988. Regional government is centrally directed; there is elected local government.

Civil Liberties. The private, party, and government press is no longer directly censored. Broadcasting is government controlled. Private conversation is relatively free; rights of assembly and organization are respected. Organizational activity is restricted. The courts demonstrate a limited independence; it is possible to win against the government. Many exiles have recently returned. Unions have been relatively independent despite periods of repression. There are few if any long-term prisoners of conscience, and arrests for unauthorized political activity or expression have been largely eliminated over the last year. At least until recently, unemployed young have been drafted for government work, and overseas travel has occasionally been blocked for political reasons. Most other private rights have been respected, including economic freedoms since doctrinaire socialism was abandoned and much of agriculture returned to private hands.

Comparatively: Tunisia is as free as Bahrain, freer than Algeria, less free than Egypt.

TURKEY

Economy: capitalist-statist
Polity: centralized multiparty
Population: 52,900,000

Political Rights: 2
Civil Liberties: 4
Freedom Rating: 6

An ethnic state with a major territorial subnationality

Political Rights. Power is divided between a military president and a civilian prime minister. The current president was confirmed in power on a questionable adjunct to a constitutional referendum in late 1982. Opposition campaigning was restricted and the vote not entirely secret. However, most power is now in the hands of a freely elected parliamentary government. A referendum in 1987 and a subsequent legislative election further strengthened democracy. Military power to influence government has been reduced but not eliminated. Power is centralized, but local and provincial elections are significant. Subnationalities: Denied the least self-determination or cultural existence, several million Kurds support a violent, leftist movement in eastern Turkey.

Civil Liberties. The press is private; the government controls the broadcasting system directly or indirectly. In spite of suspensions and arrests, the press is generally free. Kurds and Armenians remain prohibited topics, even in books. Religious expression is free only if religion is not related to politics, law, or "way of life". Arrests continue for demonstration or expression favoring communists, Kurds, or Islamic society. Torture has been common, but the government has made arrests of some accused torturers. The courts exhibit some independence in political decisions. Human rights organizations are active. Independent union activity has been curtailed; but strikes are now permitted. Nearly fifty percent of the people are subsistence agriculturists. State enterprises make up more than half of Turkey's industry.

Comparatively: Turkey is as free as Thailand, freer than Yugoslavia, less free than Greece.

TUVALU

Economy: noninclusive capitalist
Polity: traditional nonparty
Population: 8,400

Political Rights: 1
Civil Liberties: 1
Freedom Rating: 2

A relatively homogeneous state

Political Rights. Tuvalu is a parliamentary democracy under the British monarch. Each island is represented; seats are contested individually. Opposition blocs have been formed in the assembly and have been able to achieve power. There are local councils for each island. Continued dependence on the United Kingdom is self-chosen and economically unavoidable.

Civil Liberties. Media are government owned but little developed. The rule of law is maintained in the British manner, alongside traditional ideals of justice. The economy is largely subsistence farming; much of the labor force is employed overseas.

Comparatively: Tuvalu is as free as New Zealand, freer than Mauritius.

UGANDA

Economy: noninclusive
    capitalist–statist
Polity: transitional military
Population: 16,400,000 (est.)

Political Rights: 5

Civil Liberties: 5

Freedom Rating: 10

A transethnic heterogeneous state with major subnationalities

Political Rights. A rebel movement representing ethnically the majority of the population attained power by military victory in 1986. The announced goal is to build a democratic society; the inclusion of a variety of former political leaders in government reinforces this presumption. Subnationalities: The population is divided among a wide variety of peoples, some of which are subnationalities based on kingdoms that preceded the present state. The most important of these was Buganda.

Civil Liberties. Newspapers are private, party, or government; radio and television are government owned. Papers have been banned for criticism of the government. Free discussion has again emerged. Assembly and travel are restricted within the country. Unions are weak and government influenced. The murder of opposition politicians has declined, and over 1,000 political prisoners have been released. The courts have some independence. A human rights organization is active, but its leaders are in and out of prison. Religious freedom has been partially reestablished, and the churches play a balancing role to a limited extent. The economy has suffered severe dislocation: property is not secure, the black market flourishes.

Comparatively: Uganda is as free as Madagascar, freer than Kenya, less free than Sudan.

UNION OF
SOVIET SOCIALIST REPUBLICS

Economy: socialist
Polity: communist one-party
Population: 286,000,000

Political Rights: 6
Civil Liberties: 5
Freedom Rating: 11

A complex ethnic state with major territorial subnationalities

Political Rights. The Soviet Union is ruled by parallel party and governmental systems: the party system is dominant. Elections are held for both systems, but until recently ordinary citizens have had little impact. Experiments have now begun with democracy at local party and communal levels. In 1988 discussion in both Party and governmental congresses has been remarkably open and contentious––votes are no longer automatically unanimous. The Soviet Union is in theory elaborately divided into subnational units, but the all-embracing party structure has rendered local power minimal, at least until recently.

Subnationalities. Russians account for half the Soviet population. The rest belong to a variety of subnational groupings ranging down in size from the forty million Ukrainians. Most groups are territorial, with a developed sense of subnational identity. The political rights of all of these to self-determination, either within the USSR or through secession, is effectively denied. In many cases Russians or other non-native peoples have been settled in subnational territories in such numbers as to make the native people a minority in their own land (for example, Kazakhstan). In the past, expression of opinion in favor of increased self-determination has been repressed at least as much as anticommunist opinion; in 1988 repression of both was relaxed. Most of these peoples have had independence movements, or movements for enhanced self-determination, since the founding of the USSR. In 1988, movements in the Baltic republics, Armenia, Azerbaijan, and elsewhere, involving the regional communist leadership, were remarkably free in expression——if not accomplishment.

Civil Liberties. The media are totally owned by the government or party and are, in addition, regularly censored. However, in 1988 in well-known publications a wide range of opinion was available from right to left——although unofficial or underground publication continued. Particularly striking is the opening up of the historical record ——and thus what is taught in the schools——to fundamental reevaluation. Social and economic problems that were formerly ignored are now being freely discussed. With all this, detentions for expression continue and publications are closed. Nearly all imprisonment and mistreatment of prisoners in the Soviet Union have been carried out in accordance with Soviet security laws——even though these laws conflict with other Soviet laws written to accord with international standards. Acquittals in major political trials are still unheard of. Insofar as private rights, such as those to religion, education, or choice of occupation, exist, they are de facto rights that may be denied at any time. Restrictions on unofficial travel within and outside of the country have been eased. Some private entrepreneurial activity has been legalized; there have always been rights to nonproductive personal property. Private organizational activity has increased. Other rights, such as those to organize independent labor unions, are strictly denied. Literacy is high, few starve, and private oppression is no more.

Comparatively: The USSR is as free as Iran, freer than China (Mainland), less free than Hungary.

U N I T E D   A R A B   E M I R A T E S

Economy: capitalist-statist
Polity: decentralized nonparty
Population: 1,500,000

Political Rights: 5
Civil Liberties: 5
Freedom Rating: 10

A relatively homogeneous citizenry

Political Rights. The UAE is a confederation of seven shaikhdoms in which the larger are given the greater power both in the appointed assembly and the administrative hierarchy. There is a great deal of consultation in the traditional pattern. Below the confederation level there are no electoral procedures or parties. Each shaikhdom is relatively autonomous in its internal affairs. The majority of the people are recent immigrants and noncitizens. Most officers and enlisted men in the army are foreign.

Civil Liberties. The press is private or governmental. Although relatively free by regional standards, self-censorship is practiced, and overt criticism may lead to detention. Broadcasting is under federal or shaikhdom control. There are no political assemblies, but there are also few prisoners of conscience. The courts dispense a combination of British, tribal, and Islamic law. Labor unions are prohibited, but illegal strikes have occurred. Private rights are generally respected; there is freedom of travel. As in most Muslim countries there is freedom of worship for established religions, but only the favored Muslims may proselytize. Many persons may still accept the feudal privileges and restraints of their tribal position. The rights of the alien majority are less secure: "troublemakers" are deported. Private economic activity exists alongside the dominance of government petroleum and petroleum-related activities.

Comparatively: United Arab Emirates are as free as Bahrain, freer than Saudi Arabia, less free than Sudan.

UNITED KINGDOM

Economy: mixed capitalist
Polity: centralized multiparty
Population: 57,100,000

Political Rights: 1
Civil Liberties: 1
Freedom Rating: 2

An ethnic state with major subnationalities

Political Rights. The United Kingdom is a parliamentary democracy with a symbolic monarch. Plurality elections from single-member districts on the basis of party affiliation rather than personal record lead to strong parties and political stability. Fair elections are open to all parties, including those advocating secession. Unchecked by a written constitution or judicial review, parliament is restrained only by tradition. Between elections this means potentially great powers for the prime minister. Local and regional governments are elected; their limited powers are gradually being increased. Subnationalities: Scots, Welsh, Ulster Scots, and Ulster Irish are significant and highly self-conscious territorial minorities. In 1978 parliament approved home rule for Scotland and Wales, but the Welsh and (more ambiguously) the Scots voters rejected this opportunity in 1979. Still, in law, education, and other areas, Scotland continues to have separate systems. Northern Ireland's home rule has been in abeyance because of an ethnic impasse. Ulster Scot and Irish live in intermixed territories in Northern Ireland. Both want more self-determination——the majority Ulster Scots as an autonomous part of the United Kingdom, the minority Ulster Irish as an area within Ireland.

Civil Liberties. The press is private and powerful; broadcasting has statutory independence although it is indirectly under government control. British media are comparatively restrained because of strict libel and national security laws, and a tradition of accepting government suggestions for the handling of sensitive news. In Northern Ireland a severe security situation has led to the curtailment of private rights, to imprisonment, and on occasion to torture and brutality. However, these conditions have been relatively limited, thoroughly investigated by the government, and improved as a result. Elsewhere the rule of law is entrenched, and private rights generally respected. Unions are independent and powerful. In certain areas, such as medicine, housing, inheritance, and general disposability of income, socialist government policies have limited choice for some while improving opportunities for others.

Comparatively: The United Kingdom is as free as the United States, freer than West Germany.

UNITED STATES OF AMERICA

Economy: capitalist
Polity: decentralized multiparty
Population: 246,100,000

Political Rights: 1
Civil Liberties: 1
Freedom Rating: 2

An ethnically complex state with minor territorial subnationalities

Political Rights. The United States is a constitutional democracy with three strong but separate centers of power: president, congress, and judiciary. Elections are fair and competitive, but voter participation is frequently less than fifty percent. Parties are remarkably weak: in some areas they are little more than temporary means of organizing primary elections. States, and to a less extent cities, have powers in their own rights; they often successfully oppose the desires of national administrations. Each state has equal representation in the upper house, which in the USA is the more powerful half of parliament.

Subnationalities. There are many significant ethnic groups, but the only clearly territorial subnationalities are the native peoples. The largest Indian tribes, the Navaho and Sioux, number 100,000 or more each. About 150,000 Hawaiians still reside on their native islands, intermingled with a much larger white and oriental population. Spanish-speaking Americans number in the millions; except for a few thousand residing in an area of northern New Mexico, they are mostly twentieth-century immigrants living among English-speaking Americans, particularly in the large cities. Black Americans make up over one-tenth of the U.S. population; residing primarily in large cities, they have no major territorial base. In spite of this, black and Hispanic political power has been steadily growing in recent years. Black and Spanish-speaking Americans are of special concern because of their relative poverty; their ethnic status is comparable to that of many other groups in America, including Chinese, Japanese, Filipinos, Italians, or Jews.

Civil Liberties. The press is private and free; both private and public radio and television are government regulated. There are virtually no government controls on the content of the printed media (except in nonpolitical areas such as pornography) and few on broadcasting. There are no prisoners of conscience or sanctioned uses of torture; some regional miscarriages of justice and police brutality have political and social overtones. Widespread use of surveillance techniques and clandestine interference with radical groups, or groups thought to be radical, have occurred sporadically; as a reduction of liberties the threat has remained largely potential. A new threat is control over the expression of former government employees. Wherever and whenever publicity penetrates, the rule of law is generally secure, even against the most powerful. The government often loses in the courts. Private rights in most spheres are respected, but rights to travel to particular places, such as Cuba, are circumscribed. Unions are independent and politically influential. Although a relatively capitalistic country, the combination of tax loads and the decisive government role in agriculture, energy, defense, and other industries restricts individual choice as it increases majority power.

Comparatively: The United States is as free as Australia, freer than Spain.

U R U G U A Y

Economy: mixed capitalist
Polity: centralized multiparty
Population: 3,000,000

Political Rights: 2
Civil Liberties: 2
Freedom Rating: 4

A relatively homogeneous population

Political Rights. Uruguay has a democratically elected president and parliament. All parties have been legalized; the former guerrilla movement has joined the political process. Since the military is not completely under civilian control, trials of military officers implicated in human rights offenses have been delayed.

Civil Liberties. The press is private, and broadcasting private and public. Both are free, as are books and journals. Foreign media are widely available. Rights of assembly and organization, including free union activity, as well as the independence of the judiciary and the civil service have been reestablished. All prisoners of conscience have been released. Private rights are generally respected. The tax load of an overbuilt bureaucracy and emphasis on private and government monopolies in major sectors still restrict choice in this now impoverished welfare state.

Comparatively: Uruguay is as free as Ecuador, freer than Brazil, less free than Argentina.

V A N U A T U

Economy: noninclusive
        capitalist-statist
Polity: decentralized multiparty
Population: 150,000 (est.)

Political Rights: 2

Civil Liberties: 4
Freedom Rating: 6

A relatively homogeneous society with geographical subnationalities

Political Rights. Vanuatu has a parliamentary system with an indirectly elected president. Elections have been freely contested by multiple parties. Opposition exists between islands and between the French- and English-educated. Local government is elected; a decentralized federal system of regional government is being developed.

Civil Liberties. Government controls both print and broadcast media; criticism is not welcomed; access to the media by the opposition is restricted. Rights to political, economic, and union organization are observed, but unions have been under pressure. The judiciary is independent. Other civil liberties are generally respected.

Comparatively: Vanuatu is as free as Turkey, freer than Tonga, less free than Solomon Islands.

VENEZUELA

Economy: capitalist-statist
Polity: centralized multiparty
Population: 18,800,000

Political Rights: 1
Civil Liberties: 2
Freedom Rating: 3

A relatively homogeneous population

Political Rights. Venezuela is a constitutional democracy in which power has alternated between major parties in recent years. As in most of Latin America, presidential power is dominant. Campaigns and voting are fair and open; turnout is very low. Regional and local assemblies are relatively powerful, but governors are centrally appointed. Each state has equal representation in the upper house.

Civil Liberties. The press is private and generally free; most broadcasting is also in private hands. Censorship occurs only in emergencies, but television scripts on certain subjects must be approved in advance; journalists have been warned or arrested, and programs suspended, for normal reportage. The rule of law is generally secure, but police brutality is commonly reported in poorer areas. However, there are no prisoners of conscience, and the government has taken steps to prevent torture. The courts can rule against the government, and charges are brought against the security forces. Most private rights are respected; government involvement in the petroleum industry has given it a predominant economic role. Human rights organizations are very active. Unions are well organized and powerful.

Comparatively: Venezuela is as free as France, freer than Ecuador, less free than Costa Rica.

V I E T N A M

Economy: socialist
Polity: communist one–party
Population: 65,200,000

Political Rights: 6
Civil Liberties: 7
Freedom Rating: 13

An ethnic state with subnationalities

Political Rights. Vietnam is a traditional communist dictatorship with the forms of parliamentary democracy. Actual power is in the hands of the communist party; this is, in turn, dominated by a small group at the top. Officially there is a ruling national front, as in several other communist states, but the noncommunist parties are facades. However, recent elections have allowed a semblance of choice and campaigning. Government has become more open. Administration is highly centralized, with provincial boundaries arbitrarily determined by the central government. The flow of refugees and other evidence suggest that the present regime is very unpopular, especially in the South which is treated as an occupied country. Subnationalities: Continued fighting has been reported in the Montagnard areas in the South. Combined with new resettlement schemes, non-Vietnamese peoples are under pressure in both North and South Vietnam. Many Chinese have been driven out of the country.

Civil Liberties. The media are under direct government, party, or army control; only the approved line is presented. While the people have essentially no rights against the state, there is occasional public criticism and passive resistance, especially in the South. Newspaper letter columns have begun to offer an outlet for alternative opinion. Arbitrary arrest is frequent. Repression of religious groups has eased, at least in the South. Perhaps one-half million persons have been put through reeducation camps, hundreds of thousands have been forced to move into new areas, or to change occupations; thousands are prisoners of conscience or in internal exile. Former anticommunist and other groups are regularly discriminated against in employment, health care, and travel. There are no independent labor union rights, rights to travel, or choice of education; many have been forced into collectives.

Comparatively: Vietnam is as free as East Germany, freer than Mongolia, less free than China (Mainland).

W E S T E R N   S A M O A

Economy: noninclusive capitalist
Polity: centralized multiparty
Population: 170,000 (est.)

Political Rights: 4
Civil Liberties: 3
Freedom Rating: 7

A relatively homogeneous population

Political Rights. Western Samoa is a constitutional monarchy in which the assembly is elected by 16,000 "family heads." There have been important shifts of power among parties in the assembly as the result of elections, or the shift of allegiance of factions without elections. A recent election was voided in the courts on a corruption issue. Campaigning by lavish distribution of gifts is common. Village government has preserved traditional forms and considerable autonomy; it is also based on rule by "family heads."

Civil Liberties. The press is private and government; radio is government owned; television is received only from outside. Government media have limited independence. There is general freedom of expression, organization, and assembly. The judiciary is independent and the rule of law and private rights are respected within the limits set by the traditional system. Most arable land is held by customary tenure. Health and literacy standards are very high for a poor country.

Comparatively: Western Samoa is as free as Senegal, freer than Indonesia, less free than Nauru.

YEMEN, NORTH

Economy: noninclusive capitalist
Polity: military nonparty
Population: 6,700,000 (est.)

Political Rights: 5
Civil Liberties: 5
Freedom Rating: 10

A complex but relatively homogeneous population

Political Rights. North Yemen is a military dictatorship supplemented by an appointive and elected assembly. The tribal and religious structures still retain considerable authority, and the government must rely on a wide variety of different groups in an essentially nonideological consensual regime. Local elections allow meaningful competition. Political parties are forbidden, but de facto play a part in elections. The country is divided between city and country, a variety of tribes, and two major religious groupings, and faces a major revolutionary challenge.

Civil Liberties. The weak media are largely government owned; the papers have occasional criticisms—the broadcast media have none. Foreign publications are routinely censored. Yet proponents of both royalist and far left persuasions are openly accepted in a society with few known prisoners of conscience. There is no right of assembly. Politically active opponents may be encouraged to go into exile. The traditional Islamic courts give some protection; many private rights are respected. There is no right to strike or to engage in religious proselytizing. Unions and professional associations are government sponsored. Economically the government has concentrated on improving the infrastructure of Yemen's still overwhelmingly traditional economy. Most farmers are tenants; half the labor force is employed abroad.

Comparatively: North Yemen is as free as Bhutan, freer than Ethiopia, less free than Egypt.

YEMEN, SOUTH

Economy: noninclusive socialist
Polity: socialist one-party
     (military influenced)
Population: 2,400,000

Political Rights: 7
Civil Liberties: 7

Freedom Rating: 14

A relatively homogeneous population

Political Rights. South Yemen is formally organized according to the Marxist-Leninist one-party model. In practice, it is government of tribal factions by coup and violence. Soviet influence in internal and external affairs is powerful.

Civil Liberties. The media are government owned or controlled, and employed actively as means of indoctrination. Even conversation with foreigners is highly restricted. In the political and security areas the rule of law hardly applies. Political imprisonments, torture, and "disappearances" have instilled a pervasive fear in those who would speak up. Death sentences against protesting farmers have been handed down by people's courts. Independent private rights are few, although some traditional law and institutions remain. Unions are under government control. Industry and commerce have been nationalized, some of the land collectivized.

Comparatively: South Yemen is as free as Albania, less free than Oman.

YUGOSLAVIA

Economy: mixed socialist
Polity: communist one-party
Population: 23,600,000

Political Rights: 5
Civil Liberties: 5
Freedom Rating: 10

A multinational state

Political Rights. Yugoslavia is governed on the model of the USSR, but with the addition of unique elements. These include: the greater role given the governments of the constituent republics; and the greater power given the managers and workers of the self-managed communities and industrial enterprises. The Federal Assembly is elected indirectly by those successful in lower-level elections. The country has been directed by a small elite of the communist party; no opposition member is elected to state or national position. However, public discussion and opposition within and without assemblies on all levels has been growing. The increasing tendency of mass demonstrations and strikes to influence policy, and the rise and fall of governments at least at regional levels has produced a rough form of "mass democracy".

Subnationalities. The several peoples of Yugoslavia live largely in their historical homelands. The population consists of forty percent Serbs, twenty-two percent Croats, eight percent Slovenes, eight percent Bosnian Muslims, six percent Macedonians, six percent Albanians, two percent Montenegrins, and many others. The Croats have an especially active independence movement; Albanians have agitated for more self-determination. Republics and autonomous areas are accumulating more and more power. For example, both politically and economically Slovenia is developing western rather than eastern-bloc traditions——while remaining within the official limits of the system. In 1988 the country was rocked by the continuing struggle between Serbia and its autonomous Albanian region, Kosovo.

Civil Liberties. The media in Yugoslavia are controlled directly or indirectly by the government, although there is ostensible worker control. The range of ideas and criticism of government policy in domestic and available foreign publications is greater than in most communist states: there is no prepublication censorship. Although the right of assembly is not accepted, assemblies and demonstrations outside government control are increasing in frequency and size. Over the last few years, hundreds have been imprisoned for ideas expressed verbally or in print that deviated from the official line (primarily through subnationalist enthusiasm, anticommunism, or communist deviationism). Torture and brutality occur; psychiatric hospitals are also used to confine prisoners of conscience. As long as the issue is not political, however, the courts have some independence; there is a realm of de facto individual freedom that includes the right to seek employment outside the country. Travel outside Yugoslavia is often denied to dissidents; religious proselytizing is forbidden, but sanctioned religious activity is increasing. Labor is not independent, but has rights through the working of the "self-management" system; local strikes are common, but illegal. Although the economy is socialist or communalist in most respects, agriculture in this most agricultural of European countries remains overwhelmingly private.

Comparatively: Yugoslavia is as free as Poland, freer than Zambia, less free than Hungary.

Z A I R E

Economy: noninclusive
    capitalist-statist
Polity: nationalist one-party
    (military dominated)
Population: 34,700,000

Political Rights: 6

Civil Liberties: 7

Freedom Rating: 13

A transethnic heterogeneous state with subnationalities

Political Rights. Zaire is under one-man military rule, with the ruling party essentially an extension of the ruler's personality. Presidential elections are farces. Elections at both local and parliamentary levels are restricted to one party, but allow for extensive choice among individuals. Members of the opposition are brought into the government. Elections in 1987 evidenced an intention to improve electoral procedures. Parliament has little if any power. Regions are deliberately organized to avoid ethnic identity: regional administrative and party officials are appointed from the center, generally from outside the region. The president's personal exploitation of the system delegitimizes it for many.

Subnationalities. There are such a variety of tribes or linguistic groups in Zaire that no one group has as much as twenty percent of the population. The fact that French remains the dominant language reflects the degree of this dispersion. Until recently most Zaire citizens have seen themselves only in local terms without broader ethnic identification. The revolts and wars of the early 1960s saw continually shifting patterns of affiliation, with the European provincial, but not ethnic, realities of Katanga and South Kasai being most important. The most self-conscious ethnic groups are the Kongo people living in the west (and Congo and Angola) and the Luba in the center of the country. In both cases ethnicity goes back to important ancient kingdoms. There is continuing disaffection among the Lunda and other ethnic groups.

Civil Liberties. Private newspaper ownership remains only in name. Broadcasting is government owned and directed. Censorship and self-censorship are pervasive. There is no right of assembly, and union organization is controlled. Government has been arbitrary and capricious. The judiciary is not independent; prisoners of conscience are numerous, and execution and torture common. Ethnic organizations are closely restricted. Arrested conspirators have been forbidden their own lawyers. There is relative religious freedom; the Catholic church retains some power. Through the misuse of government power, the extravagance and business dealings of those in high places reduces economic freedom. Nationalization of land has often been a prelude to private development by powerful bureaucrats. Pervasive corruption and anarchy significantly reduce human rights. There is also considerable government enterprise.

Comparatively: Zaire is as free as Vietnam, freer than Angola, less free than Rwanda.

ZAMBIA

Economy: noninclusive
      mixed socialist
Polity: socialist one-party
Population: 7,500,000

Political Rights: 6

Civil Liberties: 5
Freedom Rating: 11

A transethnic heterogeneous state

Political Rights. Zambia is ruled as a one-party dictatorship. The elements of freedom within the party have been largely eliminated. Government and party strive for ethnic balance. Party organs are constitutionally more important than governmental ministries. Although elections have some meaning within this framework, the government no longer allows those who disagree to compete. Expression of dissent is possible through abstention or negative votes. There are some town councils with elected members.

Civil Liberties. All media are government controlled. A considerable variety of opinion is expressed, but it is a crime to criticize the president, the parliament, or the ideology. Foreign publications are censored. There is a rule of law and the courts have some independence; political cases are won against the government. Political opponents are often detained, and occasionally tortured, yet most people talk without fear. Traditional life continues. The government does not fully accept private or traditional rights in property or religion; important parts of the economy, especially copper mining, have been nationalized. Union, business, and professional organizations are under government pressure but retain significant independence.

Comparatively: Zambia is as free as Maldives, freer than Kenya, less free than Morocco.

Z I M B A B W E

Economy: noninclusive   Political Rights: 6
           capitalist-statist
Polity: socialist one-party   Civil Liberties: 5
Population: 9,700,000   Freedom Rating: 11

An ethnically complex state with a territorial subnationality

Political Rights. Zimbabwe is now a one-party state with the trappings of a parliamentary system. The ruling party has achieved power through elections marked by coercion of the electorate both before and after the actual process. Opposition parties have been banned. Subnationalities: The formerly dominant white, Indian, and colored populations (five percent altogether) are largely urban. The emerging dominant people are the majority Shona-speaking groups (seventy-four percent). The Ndebele (eighteen percent) are territorially distinct and politically self-conscious. Their political party has been absorbed into the single party.

Civil Liberties. The major papers are indirectly government owned and follow the government line, except occasionally in the letters columns. The government-owned broadcast media are active organs of government propaganda. However, minor regional and scholarly publications occasionally present critical viewpoints. The rule of law is threatened; opposition politicians have seen their rallies banned, and been personally forced into exile or imprisoned. Acquittals in political cases are often followed by rearrests. Racial discrimination is officially outlawed, especially in residence, occupation, and conscription. At least until recently, many citizens have lived in fear of the nationalist parties and their former guerrilla forces. Many have been killed or beaten in an attempt to force change of party allegiance. Unions and private associations retain some independence, but are increasingly being unified under government direction. The economy has capitalist, socialist, and statist aspects. The white population still wields disproportionate economic power.

Comparatively: Zimbabwe is as free as Zambia, freer than Mozambique, less free than Sudan.

PART IV

Related Territory Summaries

RELATED TERRITORY SUMMARIES

Using the same format as the Country Summaries, the dependent territories of each superordinate country are discussed below as a group. Exceptions to the general pattern are pointed out. It is often unclear whether a political unit should be regarded as a territory or an integral unit of its ruling state. For example, only the history of the Survey explains why the "independent" homelands of South Africa are considered dependent territories while the Republics of the USSR are not. Depending on the historical background, geographical separation—as by water and distance—often leads to the political unit being defined as a related territory. Many additional separated islands, such as those belonging to India or Indonesia, could well be defined as dependent territories rather than as integral parts of the states to which they are attached. In general, if a unit is considered a full equal of the units of the superordinate state, it is not a territory.

AUSTRALIA

CHRISTMAS ISLAND

Economy: capitalist-statist
Polity: agent
Population: 3,300

Political Rights: 4
Civil Liberties: 2
Freedom Rating: 6

An ethnically complex territory

Comparative Survey

COCOS ISLANDS

Economy: capitalist–statist   Political Rights: 4
Polity: agent and council   Civil Liberties: 2
Population: 600   Freedom Rating: 6

A relatively homogeneous population (nonwhite)

NORFOLK ISLAND

Economy: capitalist   Political Rights: 4
Polity: council and administrator   Civil Liberties: 2
Population: 2,200   Freedom Rating: 6

A relatively homogeneous population

Australia apparently follows democratic practices in so far as possible. Christmas Island is economically based on a state-run phosphate mine, which is soon to be depleted. The population is Chinese and Malay. Formerly a personal fiefdom, Cocos Islands has been placed under Australian administration, with the assistance of a local council. In 1984 the people voted in a UN supervised referendum to be integrated with Australia. Yet distance, the Malay population, and the plantation economy may make this difficult in more than theory. There appears to be free expression and a rule of law, but in neither are communications media developed.

Norfolk Island has a freely elected legislative assembly. It is in large measure self-governing; the wish of some residents for more independence is currently under consideration. An Australian "administrator" remains appointed. At least one lively free newspaper is published——in spite of threats and arson against the editor. Other rights of organization and law appear to be guaranteed.

C H I L E

RAPANUI (EASTER ISLAND)

Economy: capitalist–statist
Polity: appointed governor
Population: 2,000

Political Rights: 5
Civil Liberties: 4
Freedom Rating: 9

A relatively homogeneous population (nonwhite)

The Island is granted limited autonomy within the generally repressive Chilean context. In 1984 the appointed governor was for the first time a native of the island. Discussion of local problems is quite open, and local elective institutions function. However, ninety-five percent of the land is controlled by the Chilean government.

D E N M A R K

FAROE ISLANDS

Economy: mixed capitalist
Polity: multiparty
Population: 44,000

Political Rights: 1
Civil Liberties: 1
Freedom Rating: 2

A relatively homogeneous population

GREENLAND

Economy: mixed capitalist
Polity: multiparty
Population: 51,000

Political Rights: 1
Civil Liberties: 1
Freedom Rating: 2

An ethnically complex population (nonwhite majority)

Both territories have elected parliamentary governments responsible for internal administration, and are free to discuss their relationship to Denmark. In addition they elect representatives to the Danish parliament. They also have considerable freedom in international affairs—by their own choice neither is a member of the European Economic Community of which Denmark is a member. On major issues referendums are also held. Full freedoms of expression and organization are recognized. The local languages are dominant in both territories. The majority Inuit population is now politically in charge of Greenland.

F R A N C E

FRENCH GUIANA

Economy: noninclusive   Political Rights: 3
      capitalist–statist
Polity: dependent multiparty   Civil Liberties: 2
      (limited)
Population: 73,000   Freedom Rating: 5

An ethnically complex state (nonwhite majority)

FRENCH POLYNESIA

Economy: capitalist–statist   Political Rights: 3
Polity: dependent multiparty   Civil Liberties: 2
Population: 170,000   Freedom Rating: 5

A relatively homogeneous population (few French)

GUADELOUPE

Economy: capitalist–statist   Political Rights: 3
Polity: dependent multiparty   Civil Liberties: 2
      (limited)
Population: 324,000   Freedom Rating: 5

Relatively homogeneous with a small, dominant French minority

MAHORE (formerly MAYOTTE)

Economy: noninclusive capitalist
Polity: dependent multiparty
    (limited)
Population: 47,000

Political Rights: 2
Civil Liberties: 2

Freedom Rating: 4

A relatively homogeneous population (non-French)

MARTINIQUE

Economy: capitalist-statist
Polity: dependent multiparty
    (limited)
Population: 342,000

Political Rights: 3
Civil Liberties: 2

Freedom Rating: 5

Relatively homogeneous with a small, dominant French minority

MONACO

Economy: capitalist-statist
Polity: dependent constitutional
    monarchy (limited)
Population: 26,000

Political Rights: 4
Civil Liberties: 2

Freedom Rating: 6

An ethnically heterogeneous population

NEW CALEDONIA

Economy: capitalist-statist
Polity: dependent multiparty
Population: 150,000

Political Rights: 2
Civil Liberties: 2
Freedom Rating: 4

An ethnically complex territory (large French component)

Comparative Survey

REUNION

Economy: capitalist-statist   Political Rights: 3
Polity: dependent multiparty   Civil Liberties: 2
    (limited)
Population: 495,000   Freedom Rating: 5

An ethnically complex territory (few French)

ST. PIERRE AND MIQUELON

Economy: capitalist   Political Rights: 2
Polity: dependent multiparty   Civil Liberties: 2
    (limited)
Population: 6,260   Freedom Rating: 4

A relatively homogeneous territory (French)

WALLIS AND FUTUNA

Economy: capitalist-statist   Political Rights: 4
Polity: dependent assembly   Civil Liberties: 3
Population: 12,300   Freedom Rating: 7

A relatively homogeneous population (non-French)

The territories of French Guiana, Guadeloupe, Martinique, and Reunion are considered overseas departments of France. They have elected representatives in the French parliament (who need not be from the territory) and local councils. However, French law applies; a French administrator is the chief executive; both French subsidies and numbers of French bureaucrats, and sometimes troops or police are substantial. Open advocacy of independence in such integral parts of France is often repressed. Nevertheless, small independence movements exist in at least Guadeloupe and Martinique. Local elected governments have little power. The governance of the "collectivities" of Mahore (Mayotte) and St. Pierre and Miquelon is similar. In the latter, mainland French bureaucrats are numerous

496

and dominant, and French rule may be increasingly resented. Two recent referendums in Mahore have confirmed the desire of the people for their island to remain a part of France (because the Christian population would otherwise be ruled by the Muslim Comoros). Women are especially active in the anti-Comoros movement. Beyond the special colonial position, French law and its civil guarantees are maintained in the group.

The overseas territories of French Polynesia, New Caledonia, and Wallis and Futuna in the South Pacific are more traditional colonies in theory. In practice, the administrative structure is similar to that of the overseas departments. Assemblies have limited powers, although in the large territories perhaps as great as those in the overseas departments since the automatic application of French law does not apply to the territories. Independence is a lively and accepted issue, especially in New Caledonia. A 1987 referendum confirmed the desire of the majority of the inhabitants of New Caledonia to stay with France. The native people, the Kanaks (about forty percent), are highly organized and pro-independence—if the post-independence system could guarantee their control. A successful referendum in mainland France on the issue promises new arrangements favorable to the Kanaks in the future. Wallis and Futuna chose territorial status by referendum in 1959.

Monaco is not normally considered a dependent territory. However, by treaty with France, Monacan policy must conform to French security, political, and economic interests; the head minister must be chosen from a list submitted by the French government, and France controls foreign relations. The hereditary ruler appoints the government, but shares legislative power with a one-party elected council. There is also elected local government. Foreign publications are freely available. Civil freedoms approximate those in France. The government owns the casino and major hotels.

Of the traditional colonial powers only France retains a grip on its colonies that seems to be resented by important segments of their populations. In particular, independence movements in Guadeloupe and Martinique have not had the opportunity for fair electoral tests of their desires that those in American and British colonies have had. France does not allow such electoral tests of independence sentiment in its overseas departments, and seldom elsewhere.

ISRAEL

OCCUPIED AREAS

Economy: capitalist
Polity: external administration;
    local government
Population: 1,150,000

Political Rights: 5
Civil Liberties: 5

Freedom Rating: 10

A complex population with a dominant minority

The Gaza Strip and the West Bank have had some elected local government; the decisive power is in the hands of the occupying force. Opposition to the occupation is expressed through demonstrations, local elections, and the media, but heavy pressure against any organized opposition is applied in an atmosphere of violence on both sides. In 1988 this violence escalated in cycles of violence and counter-violence. There is censorship as well as other controls on the media and on movement. Settlement by the occupying people has steadily infringed upon the rights of the Arab majority.

ITALY

SAN MARINO

Economy: capitalist
Polity: dependent multiparty
Population: 19,380

Political Rights: 1
Civil Liberties: 1
Freedom Rating: 2

A relatively homogeneous state

VATICAN

Economy: statist
Polity: elected monarchy
Population: 860

Political Rights: 6
Civil Liberties: 4
Freedom Rating: 10

A relatively homogeneous population

San Marino is ruled by a multiparty parliamentary government with active elected local governments. The media are independent; in addition, Italian media are available. Although often considered independent, the influence of Italy is overwhelming. Defense and many foreign-relations areas are handled by the Italian government; major court cases are tried in Italian courts; the political parties are essentially branches of the respective Italian parties. Citizenship was recently extended to long-term residents for the first time.

The political situation of the Vatican is anomalous. On the one hand, the Vatican is ostensibly an independent state under absolutist rule, with the ruler chosen for life by a small international elite, which also has advisory functions. On the other hand, the international relations of the state are actually based on its ruler's status as head of a church rather than as head of a state. The people of the Vatican live more as Italian citizens than as citizens of the Vatican, regardless of their formal status. Vatican media represent the views of the church, yet Italian media and avenues of expression are fully available, and the dissatisfied can leave the context of the Vatican with minimal effort.

NETHERLANDS

ARUBA

Economy: mixed capitalist
Polity: multiparty internal
Population: 65,000

Political Rights: 1
Civil Liberties: 1
Freedom Rating: 2

An ethnically complex territory (few Dutch)

NETHERLANDS ANTILLES

Economy: mixed capitalist
Polity: multiparty internal
Population: 190,000

Political Rights: 1
Civil Liberties: 1
Freedom Rating: 2

Comparative Survey

An ethnically complex territory (few Dutch)

The Netherlands Antilles consist of two groups of islands in the Caribbean. Although the governor is appointed, the islands are largely self-governing at both the territory and island levels. The parliament is freely elected. The Netherlands has been urging the islands to accept independence, but the smaller islands have resisted independence in federation with the dominant island, Curacao. Full freedom of party organization, expression, and abstention are fully recognized. The press, radio, and television are private, free, and highly varied.

Aruba achieved autonomy in 1986 and is expected to attain full independence in 1996. The pattern of government is similar to that of the Netherlands Antilles.

N E W   Z E A L A N D

COOK ISLANDS

Economy: capitalist-statist
Polity: multiparty internal
Population: 18,000

Political Rights: 2
Civil Liberties: 2˙
Freedom Rating: 4

A relatively homogeneous population (nonwhite)

NIUE

Economy: capitalist-statist
Polity: internal parliamentary
Population: 3,000

Political Rights: 2
Civil Liberties: 2
Freedom Rating: 4

A relatively homogeneous population (nonwhite)

TOKELAU ISLANDS

Economy: capitalist–statist
Polity: limited assembly
Population: 1,600

Political Rights: 4
Civil Liberties: 2
Freedom Rating: 6

A relatively homogeneous population (nonwhite)

The Cook Islands and Niue are largely self–governing territories with elected parliaments. There is continuing oversight by New Zealand, particularly in defense, foreign affairs, and justice. Niue has been unable to arrest a steady decline in population. Tokelau is administered by appointed officials with the help of the assembly. The assembly's powers have been growing, and it is becoming less aristocratic. Tokelau's assembly has informed the United Nations of satisfaction with its current relationship with New Zealand. Elsewhere, political life, particularly in the Cook Islands, has been vigorous and free. The economies of all three territories are heavily subsidized.

PORTUGAL

AZORES

Economy: capitalist–statist
Polity: internal multiparty
Population: 292,000

Political Rights: 2
Civil Liberties: 2
Freedom Rating: 4

A relatively homogeneous population

MACAO

Economy: capitalist–statist
Polity: limited internal assembly
Population: 400,000

Political Rights: 3
Civil Liberties: 4
Freedom Rating: 7

An ethnically complex population (majority Chinese)

Comparative Survey

MADEIRA

Economy: capitalist–statist
Polity: internal multiparty
Population: 266,000

Political Rights: 2
Civil Liberties: 2
Freedom Rating: 4

An ethnically complex but relatively homogeneous population

    The Azores and Madeira are considered "autonomous regions," whose multiparty governments have a large degree of internal self-rule, including the right to issue their own stamps. The islands also have elected representatives in the Portuguese parliament. They have the same civil freedoms as on the mainland. Both regions have independence movements. Land holding has traditionally been very concentrated on Madeira. With populations made up largely of Portuguese settlers of past centuries, neither island group has been seen as a colony. Macao is administered by a Lisbon-appointed governor with the help of an elected local assembly. Peking and its supporters affect all levels of government and constrain the news media, as well as rights of assembly and organization. However, democratic institutions are more developed here than in Hong Kong.

SOUTH AFRICA

BOPHUTHATSWANA

Economy: capitalist–statist
Polity: dependent dominant party
Population: 1,400,000

Political Rights: 6
Civil Liberties: 5
Freedom Rating: 11

An ethnically complex population

CISKEI

Economy: capitalist–statist
Polity: dependent dominant party
Population: 740,000

Political Rights: 6
Civil Liberties: 6
Freedom Rating: 12

An ethnically homogeneous territory

SOUTH WEST AFRICA (NAMIBIA)

Economy: capitalist-traditional
Polity: appointed multiparty-
    traditional
Population: 1,100,000

Political Rights: 6
Civil Liberties: 5

Freedom Rating: 11

An ethnically heterogeneous territory

VENDA

Economy: capitalist–statist
Polity: dependent multiparty
Population: 550,000

Political Rights: 6
Civil Liberties: 6
Freedom Rating: 12

A relatively homogeneous territory

South West Africa, or Namibia, is ruled as a colony of South Africa, with the help of a multiparty government appointed in 1985. There is considerable freedom of the press, of discussion, and organization—although with occasional interventions. The judiciary is relatively independent and quite authoritative. Native chiefs and councils play political and judicial roles in their home areas. The northern or Ovambo half of the country is under police rule in a guerrilla war setting.

The other territories are homelands that have accepted formal independence—except for Transkei, which the Survey accepts as independent. Characteristically, most wage earners ascribed to these states work in South Africa proper; the states receive extensive South African aid, and they are not viable units geographically. South Africa exerts considerable control over their foreign affairs and security, although there are often disputes. Formally governed by parliamentary systems, the control of political organization and expression, the large number of appointed parliamentarians, and the violent atmosphere makes them more dictatorial than democratic.

Expression of opinion in regard to the existence of the state is especially perilous. There are arrests for reasons of conscience and reports of torture. Nevertheless, these territories protect their peoples from many of the worst insults of apartheid, and, in Bophuthatswana, a much closer approximation to justice exists for blacks than in South Africa itself.

S P A I N

CANARY ISLANDS

Economy: capitalist
Polity: centralized multiparty
Population: 1,500,000

Political Rights: 1
Civil Liberties: 2
Freedom Rating: 3

A complex but relatively homogeneous population

CEUTA

Economy: capitalist–statist
Polity: dependent, unrecognized
Population: 78,000 (12,000 military)

Political Rights: 2
Civil Liberties: 3
Freedom Rating: 5

An ethnically homogeneous population

MELILLA

Economy: capitalist–statist
Polity: dependent, unrecognized
Population: 63,000

Political Rights: 2
Civil Liberties: 3
Freedom Rating: 5

An ethnically complex population

Spain has no official colonies. Its outposts in North Africa, Ceuta and Melilla, ruled as parts of the Spanish provinces across from them, remain anomalies. Both have been Spanish for centuries.

Only after demonstrations in Melilla in 1986 did the government move to give most Muslims citizenship—but the process will evidently be very slow.

The Canary Islands are governed as two provinces. Although the people are of diverse origins and preserve many pre-Spanish customs, the culture today is largely Hispanic. There is an independence movement, but the development of internal self-determination on a regional basis may help to reduce the desire for separation. Spanish law guarantees rights as in Spain itself.

SWITZERLAND

LIECHTENSTEIN

Economy: capitalist-statist
Polity: constitutional monarchy
Population: 124,000

Political Rights: 3
Civil Liberties: 1
Freedom Rating: 4

A relatively homogeneous population

Foreign affairs, defense, and some economic regulations are controlled by Switzerland. Swiss money is used, as is the Swiss postal service. The government is responsible both to the hereditary monarch and an elected parliament. Referendums supplement parliamentary rule. There is local government. Women have recently attained the right to vote and have entered parliament. The media are mostly Swiss, although there are local papers.

UNITED KINGDOM

ANGUILLA

Economy: mixed capitalist
Polity: dependent limited
assembly
Population: 6,500

Political Rights: 2
Civil Liberties: 2

Freedom Rating: 4

Comparative Survey

A relatively homogeneous population (nonwhite)

BERMUDA

Economy: mixed capitalist   Political Rights: 2
Polity: multiparty   Civil Liberties: 1
Population: 55,000   Freedom Rating: 3

An ethnically complex state (largely nonwhite)

BRITISH VIRGIN ISLANDS

Economy: mixed socialist   Political Rights: 2
Polity: limited internal   Civil Liberties: 1
       assembly
Population: 11,000   Freedom Rating: 3

A relatively homogeneous population (nonwhite)

CAYMAN ISLANDS

Economy: capitalist   Political Rights: 2
Polity: limited internal   Civil Liberties: 2
       assembly
Population: 17,000   Freedom Rating: 4

An ethnically mixed population (largely white)

CHANNEL ISLANDS

Economy: capitalist   Political Rights: 2
Polity: traditional   Civil Liberties: 2
       parliamentary
Population: 132,000   Freedom Rating: 4

An ethnically mixed population (white)

FALKLAND ISLANDS

Economy: capitalist–statist
Polity: limited representative
Population: 1,800

Political Rights: 2
Civil Liberties: 2
Freedom Rating: 4

A relatively homogeneous population (white)

GIBRALTAR

Economy: capitalist–statist
Polity: internal parliamentary
Population: 30,000

Political Rights: 1
Civil Liberties: 2
Freedom Rating: 3

An ethnically complex population

HONG KONG

Economy: capitalist
Polity: colonial
Population: 5,700,000

Political Rights: 4
Civil Liberties: 3
Freedom Rating: 7

A relatively homogeneous population (Chinese)

ISLE OF MAN

Economy: capitalist
Polity: parliamentary
Population: 65,000

Political Rights: 1
Civil Liberties: 1
Freedom Rating: 2

A relatively homogeneous population (white)

Comparative Survey

MONTSERRAT

Economy: capitalist
Polity: colonial legislative
Population: 12,000

Political Rights: 2
Civil Liberties: 2
Freedom Rating: 4

A relatively homogeneous population (nonwhite)

ST. HELENA

Economy: capitalist-statist
Polity: colonial legislative
Population: 5,200

Political Rights: 2
Civil Liberties: 2
Freedom Rating: 4

A relatively homogeneous population (white)

TURKS AND CAICOS

Economy: capitalist
Polity: colonial legislative
Population: 7,400

Political Rights: 2
Civil Liberties: 2
Freedom Rating: 4

A relatively homogeneous population (nonwhite)

The dependencies of the United Kingdom all have the civil rights common to the homeland. Nearly all have expressed, through elections, elected representatives, or simply lack of controversy in a free atmosphere, a desire to stay a dependency of the United Kingdom under present arrangements. For example, the party winning decisively in 1984 in Turks and Caicos ran on an anti-independence stand. The people of Gibraltar have often affirmed their desire to remain a colony. For the other colonies, there is little evidence of a significant denial of political or civil liberties. An exception may be the Channel Island of Guernsey, with a not fully representative parliament, exceptional lack of separation of powers, and an uncritical local media.

Constitutionally, the dependencies may be divided into three groups. The first consists of those units with essentially full internal autonomy, expressed through freely elected parliaments. The second group is administered by a strong appointed governor and a largely elected assembly or council. The third group consists of colonies with little if any power in elected assemblies or officials. The first group includes the Channel Islands, the Isle of Man, and possibly Bermuda. Midway between the first and second groups are the British Virgin Islands, Cayman Islands, Gibraltar, and possibly Montserrat. In the second group are Anguilla, Falkland Islands, St. Helena, and Turks and Caicos. The last group consists only of Hong Kong, whose political development, and to some extent even civil liberties have been arrested by the presence of communist China. In preparation for the turning back of sovereignty to China in 1997, legislative institutions are being developed, and political conscious-ness is growing. To date the suffrage is very limited. At the same time the self-censorship of the press is increasing.

UNITED STATES OF AMERICA

AMERICAN SAMOA

Economy: capitalist-communal
Polity: parliamentary self-
    governing
Population: 32,000

Political Rights: 2
Civil Liberties: 2

Freedom Rating: 4

A relatively homogeneous population (nonwhite)

BELAU

Economy: capitalist-communal
Polity: parliamentary self-
    governing
Population: 12,000

Political Rights: 2
Civil Liberties: 2

Freedom Rating: 4

A relatively homogeneous population (nonwhite)

Comparative Survey

GUAM

Economy: capitalist–statist   Political Rights: 2
Polity: parliamentary self–   Civil Liberties: 2
    governing
Population: 106,000   Freedom Rating: 4

An ethnically complex population (mostly nonwhite)

MARSHALL ISLANDS

Economy: capitalist–statist   Political Rights: 2
Polity: parliamentary self–   Civil Liberties: 2
    governing
Population: 31,000   Freedom Rating: 4

A relatively homogeneous population (nonwhite)

MICRONESIA, FEDERATED STATES OF

Economy: capitalist–communal   Political Rights: 2
Polity: parliamentary self–   Civil Liberties: 2
    governing
Population: 74,000   Freedom Rating: 4

A relatively homogeneous population (nonwhite)

NORTHERN MARIANAS

Economy: capitalist   Political Rights: 1
Polity: parliamentary self–   Civil Liberties: 2
    governing
Population: 17,000   Freedom Rating: 3

A relatively homogeneous population (nonwhite)

PUERTO RICO

Economy: capitalist
Polity: self governing quasi-state
Population: 3,300,000

Political Rights: 2
Civil Liberties: 1
Freedom Rating: 3

A relatively homogeneous population (Spanish speaking)

VIRGIN ISLANDS

Economy: capitalist
Polity: appointed governorship
Population: 97,000

Political Rights: 2
Civil Liberties: 2
Freedom Rating: 4

A complex population (mostly nonwhite)

Puerto Rico is an internally self-governing commonwealth with a political system modeled on that of the states of the United States. Control alternates between the major regional parties. Both directly and indirectly the Puerto Ricans have voted to remain related to the United States. (Independence parties have never received more than a small fraction of the vote.) There is full freedom of discussion and organization. The press and broadcast media are highly varied and critical. There are political prisoners, and instances of brutality and unnecessary killings, but no good evidence of imprisonment or killing simply for expression of opinion.

The rest of America's dependent territories are now either internally self-governing or have accepted in free referenda their present status. The territories have elective institutions including in most cases an elected governor or chief administrator. There have been a number of recent referendums approving free association with the United States in the Micronesian territories. However, except for the commonwealth of Northern Marianas, the agreements are not yet fully approved by the American Congress. Full independence was not discussed extensively by either the United States or the islanders. In Belau, dispute over the compact with the U.S. has led to violent deaths, doubtful judicial verdicts, and fear among some who disagree. Political activity on Guam is increasingly mature and independent. Guamanians also may soon wish to achieve commonwealth status similar to that of the Northern Marianas. Traditional chiefs have special powers in most other Pacific territories. Island groupings, such as the Marshalls or Micronesia (Federated States), are loose federations with strong local governments on the separate islands. Overdependence on American largesse is arguably the greatest hindrance to complete freedom in the Pacific territories. Freedom of expression, assembly, and organization are recognized in all territories.

FRANCE-SPAIN CONDOMINIUM

ANDORRA

Economy: capitalist
Polity: limited multiparty
Population: 31,000

Political Rights: 3
Civil Liberties: 2
Freedom Rating: 5

A relatively homogeneous population (Catalan)

Andorra has a parliamentary government overseen by the representatives of the French President and the Bishop of Urgel. Formal parties are not permitted, but "groupings" contest the elections in their stead. There has been agitation for more self-determination. External relations are handled primarily by France, a responsibility France has insisted on in recent discussions with the EEC. An independent weekly is supplemented by French and Spanish publications. Only recently has the Andorra Council been able to regulate its own radio stations. There is, however, a free flow of information into, and out of, the territory. Internally, the full range of opinions is aired.

INDEX

See also tables 3-10, listed on page vii.

Index

Index